D1538904

MORAL CONFLICT
AND POLITICS

Moral Conflict
and Politics

Steven Lukes

CLARENDON PRESS · OXFORD
1991

Oxford University Press, Walton Street, Oxford OX2 6DP
Oxford New York Toronto
Delhi Bombay Calcutta Madras Karachi
Petaling Jaya Singapore Hong Kong Tokyo
Nairobi Dar es Salaam Cape Town
Melbourne Auckland
and associated companies in
Berlin Ibadan

Oxford is a trade mark of Oxford University Press

Published in the United States
by Oxford University Press, New York

British Library Cataloguing in Publication Data
Lukes, Steven
Moral conflict and politics.
1. Politics. Moral values
I. Title
172
ISBN 0–19–827536–6

Library of Congress Cataloging in Publication Data
Lukes, Steven.
Moral conflict and politics/Steven Lukes.
p. cm.
Includes bibliographical references and index.
1. Political ethics. 2. Ethical relativism. 3. Social values.
I. Title.
JA79.L83 1991 172—dc20 90-21227
ISBN 0–19–827536–6

Typeset by Rowland Phototypesetting Ltd,
Bury St Edmunds, Suffolk
Printed in Great Britain by
Bookcraft (Bath) Ltd,
Midsomer Norton, Avon

For
DANIEL
MICHAEL
and
ALEXANDRA

PREFACE AND ACKNOWLEDGEMENTS

The various essays gathered here, written over the last decade or so, are rather diverse in form and style. I have tried to arrange them in order of increasing informality and decreasing abstraction from current political issues and events. Those in Parts I and II are the most academic, conceptual, and abstract in character, though none is written without a pretty concrete and usually political target or set of targets, in mind. Part III is directly angled at the structure of Marxist thought and at the non-obvious role of morality within it. The essays in Part IV are all about the writings of various contemporary social and political thinkers, one of whom has, in the last exhilarating months, become a major actor (or should I say director?) on both his country's and indeed the world's stages. The three essays of the final part are 'occasional' pieces, doubtless reflecting the more particular circumstances on which they, in turn, reflect; but, for all that, I hope it was not a mistake to disinter and preserve them. Like all the others, they are reprinted here without substantial alteration.

As to their substance, it appears to me—perhaps the least capable of judging the matter—that they exhibit a singular unity of theme, which I have sought to capture by the title of this book. Making sense of moral conflict, and of value pluralism generally, and reflecting on their political implications, is at the heart of some of the most interesting writing among contemporary moral philosophers and political theorists, both Anglo-Saxon and European. It has also been at the centre of the sociological tradition ever since Durkheim, Simmel, and Weber (who is cited rather often in these pages) —though, oddly, as an area for sociological research it has, until recently, been rather neglected. The practical and political, as well as abstract and conceptual, dilemmas generated by the value pluralism and moral conflicts of our ever more polyglot and culturally heterogeneous societies show no signs of imminent decline. Both 'communitarian' visions of one or another kind of moral unity and Enlightenment-inspired hopes of progressive moral convergence seem equally Utopian in the kind of world in which more and more of us are coming to live. It therefore seems unlikely that the cluster of issues discussed here will become less urgent with the passing of time.

The chapters of this book first appeared in the following places:

Chapter 1 in Nancy L. Rosenblum (ed.), *Liberalism and the Moral Life* (Cambridge, Mass.: Harvard Univ. Press, 1989).

Chapter 2 in T. Honderich (ed.), *Morality and Objectivity: A Tribute to J. L. Mackie* (London: Routledge and Kegan Paul, 1985).

Chapter 3 (in Italian), in *Iride: Filosofia e discusione pubblica*, 3 (1990).

Chapter 4 in D. Held (ed.), *Modern Political Theory* (Cambridge: Polity, 1990).

Chapter 5 (in French), in *Singularités: Les Voies d'émergence individuelle. Textes pour E. de Dampierre* (Paris: Plon, 1989).

Chapter 6 in T. Bottomore and R. Nisbet (eds.), *A History of Sociological Analysis* (London: Heinemann, 1979).

Chapter 7 in J. R. Pennock and J. W. Chapman (eds.), *Authority Revisited. Nomos XXIX* (New York: New York Univ. Press, 1987).

Chapter 8 in D. Miller and L. Siedentop (eds.), *The Nature of Political Theory* (Oxford: Clarendon Press, 1983).

Chapter 9 in *Praxis International*, 1/4 (1982).

Chapter 10 in E. F. Paul, J. Paul, F. D. Miller, Jr., and J. Ahrens (eds.), *Marxism and Liberalism* (Oxford: Blackwell, 1986).

Chapter 11 in J. R. Thompson and D. Held (eds.), *Jürgen Habermas: Critical Debates* (London: Macmillan, 1982).

Chapter 12 in A. Kontos (ed.), *Powers, Possessions and Freedoms: Essays in Honour of C. B. Macpherson* (Toronto: Univ. of Toronto Press, 1979).

Chapter 13 in *New Statesman* (4 Sept. 1981) and *New Statesman and Society* (19 Aug. 1988).

Chapter 14 as the Introduction to V. Havel, *et al.*, *The Power of the Powerless: Citizens against the State in Central Eastern Europe* (London: Hutchinson, 1985).

Chapter 15 in *Times Literary Supplement* (31 Mar.–6 Apr. 1989).

Chapter 16 in B. Pimlott (ed.), *Fabian Essays in Socialist Thought* (London: Heinemann, 1984).

Chapter 17 in *The Philosophical Forum*, 18/2–3 (Winter–Spring 1986–7).
Chapter 18 in *Ethics and International Affairs*, 4 (1990).

S.L.

Florence
February 1990

CONTENTS

PART I

1

Making Sense of Moral Conflict

The title of this chapter might suggest that there is a phenomenon, or set of phenomena, that can be recognized as moral conflict and a separate question, namely: How is one to make sense of it? That would be misleading. For the recognition of moral conflict cannot be separated from making sense of it. What sense, if any, one makes of it, will determine the range of recognizable instances. Indeed, there are several well-known ways of making no sense of it at all.

In such cases what we have are at most instances of merely apparent moral conflict—of ignorance or error, or of individual or social pathology. In either case, it is an affliction to be overcome. Thus, Aristotle saw conflicting moral beliefs as a mark of ignorance, never as a recognition of conflicting moral requirements, while Aquinas further thought that the moral virtues formed a harmonious unity and could not exclude one another.[1] Plato followed early Greek thought in contrasting the valid norm of *nomos* with its deformation, *anomia*, which he identified variously with injustice, godlessness, impiety and iniquity, the less beneficial, terrible and fierce desires, cruelty, anarchy, and disorder.[2] In modern times utilitarianism and Kantianism have advanced comprehensive moral theories, each of which proposes an overarching principle that purports to accommodate or else force us to revise our existing moral intuitions, providing us with a practical decision procedure for all moral situations. As Charles Larmore writes:

when moral theories of this monistic sort have run up against recalcitrant moral intuitions that conflict with their favored higher-order principle, they

This chapter first published in 1989. It was written with Leszek Kolakowski and Allan Bloom in mind. I am grateful to G. A. Cohen for his incisive criticisms.

[1] See discussion in Charles Larmore, *Patterns of Moral Complexity* (Cambridge: Cambridge Univ. Press, 1987), pp. 10, 37–8, 159–60.

[2] See Marco Orru, *Anomie: History and Meanings* (Boston: Allen & Unwin, 1987), p. 28. See also Martin Ostwald, *Nomos and the Beginnings of the Athenian Democracy* (Oxford: Clarendon Press, 1969).

have too often resorted to the tactic of denying those intuitions their very status as 'moral' ones. (Recall the charges of squeamishness and rule-worship that many utilitarians have leveled against those who morally reject an action knowingly injuring another, even though it happens to maximize the general happiness; recall also the censure of principlelessness that Kantians have often directed toward those that have held that sometimes a great good should be obtained at the price of doing evil).[3]

Ethical relativism is another way of depriving moral conflict of any sense, for the point of relativism is to explain it *away* by proposing a structure in which apparently conflicting claims are each acceptable in their own place. The trouble is that this raises the puzzle, which relativism finds hard to solve, of explaining why the claims appeared to conflict in the first place. Worse, it fails to take such claims seriously by denying their applicability beyond cultural boundaries (assuming these are not in dispute). Nor is it clear how ethical relativism can handle conflicts *within* such boundaries. Finally, subjectivist ethical theories of various sorts constitute a further way of depriving moral conflict of sense, by removing the notion of conflicting *claims* based on reasons. For instance, emotivism, in its various forms, sees morality as just a way of expressing or inducing states of mind and feeling. But, as Bernard Williams compellingly argues, if anything attests to the objectivity of ethics, it is the experience of moral conflict: 'That there is nothing that one decently, honourably or adequately *can* do seems a kind of truth as firmly independent of the will and inclination as anything in morality.'[4]

In short, none of these attempts to make nonsense of moral conflict seems to succeed. None is adequate to our moral experience, to what has been called 'the fragmentation of value' or the 'heterogeneity of morality' as we know it in our personal and public lives. Accordingly, I shall ask three questions: What kinds of moral conflict could there be? What kinds of important or significant moral conflicts are there and why should we believe they are important? What bearing does making sense of such conflicts have upon the defence of liberty and of a liberal political order?

Is moral conflict possible and what forms could it take? In addressing these questions, I am concerned with the possibility of conflicting moral claims or requirements that face agents, individual or collect-

---

[3] Larmore, *Patterns*, p. 10.
[4] Bernard Williams, 'Conflicts of Values', *Moral Luck* (Cambridge: Cambridge Univ. Press, 1981), p. 75.

ive, not with how to reconcile or regulate interpersonal or social conflicts between individuals, between individuals and groups and communities, or between groups and communities. Moral conflicts are conflicts between moral claims that may face persons or groups or communities or governments representing them, when individually or collectively they deliberate about what to do. Sometimes these are experienced as one-person conflicts, when individuals experience the pull of conflicting demands, as in the case of tragic dilemmas of choice or where people—the children of immigrants, for instance —have internalized the requirements of mutually incompatible cultural traditions. Accordingly, I shall now ask: What are such conflicts between? In what exactly does the conflict consist?

The Sources of Conflict

The form of conflict to which moral philosophers have paid most attention is that of conflicting obligations. Here the conflict consists, not in an incompatibility between duties abstractly defined, but between the actions they require in a given situation. Sartre's pupil could not both go to England to fight with the Free French Forces *and* stay with his mother, deeply affected by the semi-treason of his father and by the death of her eldest son, and thereby help her to survive. The state of the world generated the conflict, and no ethical standpoint, certainly neither the Kantian nor the Christian (this was Sartre's point), can remove it without *mauvaise foi*—partly (as Sartre says) because values are too 'vague', too 'general for such a precise and concrete case',[5] but also because each action involves the violation of an obligation. Here, as in other such cases, there is no way of avoiding moral loss, of not committing an uncancelled wrong.

Secondly, there are conflicts between purposes, ends, goals, or (more vaguely still) 'values'. These too are best thought of, not as instances of inconsistency, but as yielding incompatible directives for action or policy, given the way the world is. This is what Sir Isaiah Berlin had in mind when he wrote that 'ends may clash irreconcilably':

Should democracy in a given situation be promoted at the expense of individual freedom; or equality at the expense of artistic achievement; or

[5] J.-P. Sartre, *L'Existentialisme est un humanisme* (Paris: Nagel, 1959), pp. 39–43.

mercy at the expense of justice; or spontaneity at the expense of efficiency; or happiness, loyalty, innocence, at the expense of knowledge and truth? The simple point which I am concerned to make is that where ultimate values are irreconcilable, clear-cut solutions cannot, in principle, be found.[6]

And it is what Leszek Kolakowski doubtless meant when he wrote:

If socialism is to be anything more than a totalitarian prison, it can only be a system of compromises between different values that limit one another. All-embracing economic planning, even if it were possible to achieve—and there is almost universal agreement that it is not—is incompatible with the autonomy of small producers and regional units, and this autonomy is a traditional value of socialism, though not of Marxist socialism. Technical progress cannot co-exist with absolute security of living conditions for everyone. Conflicts inevitably arise between freedom and equality, planning and the autonomy of small groups, economic democracy and efficient management, and these conflicts can always be mitigated by compromise and partial solutions.

There are also, Kolakowski argues, 'internally inconsistent' values such as 'the ideal of perfect equality', but this is not, as he says, 'contradictory in itself'. Rather, it involves conflict because, given the way the world is, it yields incompatible policies. It implies 'more equality and less government', but 'in real life, more equality means more government, and absolute equality means absolute government'.[7]

Thirdly, there are even more holistic and less well-defined entities between which moral conflicts may be thought to hold: moral codes or systems or world views or, in Rawls's phrase, 'conceptions of the good.' These are what Pascal may have had in mind when he observed that what is truth on one side of the Pyrenees is error on the other.[8] (What he meant was perhaps that what is seen as truth on one side is seen as error on the other.) Conflicts of this sort are marked by incompatibilities of perception and belief, in particular over 'how good and evil are to be recognized and distinguished from each other'. Such cultural differences of moral perception can certainly seem real enough. As Kolakowski remarks, they cannot be removed

---

[6] Isaiah Berlin, *Four Essays on Liberty* (Oxford: Oxford Univ. Press, 1969), pp. xlix–1.

[7] Leszek Kolakowski, *Main Currents of Marxism*, 3 vols. (Oxford: Clarendon Press, 1978), iii. 528.

[8] Blaise Pascal, *Pensées*, xxv ed. Victor Girand (Paris: Les Éditions G. Grès, 1928), p. 117.

by retreating to some common ground which the adversaries share or by appealing, as in science, to some 'higher tribunal' capable of an intersubjective adjudication of controversies.[9] But, as Pascal and Voltaire in his *Essai sur les mœurs* assumed, and as Allan Bloom and Kolakowski both rightly insist, real confrontations between culturally defined moral perceptions in no way imply relativism of moral judgement.[10] As Kolakowski rather dramatically puts it,

I may perceive, say, the evil of killing malformed babies, but I have to admit that this kind of perception is not universal and that people in other civilisations—which I am perfectly entitled to describe in pejorative terms and call barbarous—see things differently.[11]

The example is extreme and does not capture a real confrontation that many face. Inhabitants of multi-ethnic or religiously divided societies or societies caught between secularism and religiosity can think of many more familiar and mundane instances—as when communities disagree over what constitutes respect for women or parents, or the centrality of religious instruction to education, or the right to free choice in marriage.

Finally, and most interestingly, there are conflicts between different kinds of moral claim. A number of writers have pointed to the irreconcilability of the conflict between consequentialism and deontology, and I have already referred to the way in which utilitarians (who embody the dominant form of consequentialism in Anglo-Saxon cultures) and Kantians seek to deny its very existence. Consequentialism requires that the agent maximize the overall good (on some interpretation of that good), by so acting as to produce the best outcome, all things considered, for all those affected by this action. Deontology, by contrast, proposes a set of (sometimes absolute) side-constraints on action done to others, set by the requirements of the Moral Law or by divine prohibitions or by their moral rights, whatever the consequences to them or to others may be.

The irresolvability of this conflict was perhaps foreshadowed in Machiavelli's dictum that 'While the act accuses, the result excuses', if we interpret it to mean that, while the act is (consequentially) justified in retrospect, the accusation *stands*.[12] And indeed, the

---

[9] Kolakowski, *Religion* (London: Fontana, 1982), pp. 187, 189.

[10] Allan Bloom, *The Closing of the American Mind* (New York: Simon and Schuster, 1987), p. 39.   [11] Kolakowski, *Religion*, p. 187.

[12] See Michael Walzer, 'Political Action: The Problem of Dirty Hands', *Philosophy and Public Affairs* 2 (Winter 1973), p. 175.

problem of dirty hands in politics is the *locus classicus* of this kind of clash of moral claims—a clash inadequately captured by the so-called problem of 'means and ends'. It is perhaps rather the problem of bringing together Lenin's question 'What is to be done?' with another that Lenin certainly never asked, namely, 'What is not to be done?'—or, as Machiavelli put it, of the Prince learning, 'among so many who are not good', how to enter evil when necessity commands for the good of the Republic.[13] Politics, as Max Weber saw, is the arena in which such dilemmas can take their most dramatic form, though they reappear in all areas of life, wherever doing what is best overall requires the committing of a wrong, or the violation of a right.

For utilitarians and some other consequentialists (among whom I include Marxists, for reasons mentioned later and spelt out in Chapter 10) such dilemmas cannot exist, if the appropriate calculations for measuring the best overall outcome, all things considered, have been correctly made. (Of course consequentialists could deny value monism, if they were to recognize types of outcome as ineliminably pluralistic. Generally, however, they do not.) If the consequentially right answer to the question 'What is it right to do?' requires one to override the constraints of ordinary morality, then in that case to do so could not be wrong, and neither guilt nor regret would be appropriate. Apparently dirty hands are clean. For Kantian and other deontologists—exponents of what Trotsky called 'Kantian-priestly and vegetarian-Quaker prattle'[14]—following the appropriate maxim is all that is required in cases of moral choice, thereby relieving the moral agent of the need to take responsibility for consequences that, in any case, flow in part from the choices and actions of others. The moral agent takes responsibility only for what he alone does. On this view, one's hands must always be clean, whatever the consequences.

All this is familiar, if contested, ground, but in *Patterns of Moral Complexity* Charles Larmore advances the discussion by suggesting that we are caught up in conflicts between three equally objective practical demands or principles of practical reasoning which urge independent claims upon us (we cannot plausibly see one as a means for promoting another) and so can draw us in irreconcilable ways.

---

[13] Niccolò Machiavelli, *Il Principe*, chap. 15.
[14] Leon Trotsky, *Terrorism and Communism* (Ann Arbor, Mich.: Univ. of Michigan Press, 1951), p. 82.

These are the principles of deontology, consequentialism, and partiality. The principle of partiality underlies 'particularistic duties'. For example,

Partiality requires that we show an overriding concern for the interests of those who stand to us in some particular relation of affection. There are, for example, the duties of friendship and the demands that stem from our participation in some concrete way of life or institution, to protect and foster it. There are also the obligations that arise from more abstract commitments, as when we speak of an artists's duty to his art.

The duties encompassed by this principle 'arise from the commitment to some substantial ideal of the good life. The other two principles are universalistic and support categorical obligations.'[15]

I cannot here pursue Larmore's interesting exploration of the ways in which the claims of partiality—our commitments to particularistic projects—can conflict, on the one hand, with consequentialism ('If we were only consequentialists, we constantly would have to set aside our own projects and friendships, since each of us has countless opportunities for increasing preference-satisfaction within a wider sphere') and, on the other, with deontology (against Kant, not every categorical duty, say keeping a promise, overrides every particularistic commitment).[16] Nor can I discuss his interesting, but I suspect mistaken, suggestion that in a liberal political order neutrally justifiable principles of justice, whether consequentialist or deontological, must always rank higher than the principle of partiality (how else could the foreign-aid budget be limited?). Larmore succeeds admirably in developing the arguments of others for the view that the basic sources of morality are plural and against the belief that human beings could inhabit a world without moral loss and unsettleable conflict.

The Nature of Conflict

In what do such conflicts consist? I suggest that various senses of 'conflict' can be ranged along a scale of increasing intractability. Conflict may signify diversity, incompatibility, or incommensurability.

---

[15] Larmore, *Patterns*, p. 132.
[16] Ibid. 141, 143.

Diversity. First, there is what used to be called 'the diversity of morals', a topic of profound interest to early anthropologists and sociologists, much discussed in the late nineteenth and early twentieth centuries by Wilhelm Wundt, Lucien Lévy-Bruhl, W. G. Summer, L. T. Hobhouse, Edward Westermarck, and Morris Ginsberg and still intermittently addressed by social anthropologists and some sociologists,[17] but somehow lost as a central topic for systematic social inquiry. I shall allude later to the interpretation of the data and the inherent difficulties of discerning the actual range of such diversity. Here I simply observe that mere diversity becomes a form of conflict when notional confrontations become real, that is, where in a confrontation between two outlooks, 'there is a group of people for whom each of the outlooks is a real option'. An outlook is a real option for a group 'either if it is already in their outlook or if they could go over to it; and they could go over to it if they could live inside it in their actual historical circumstances and retain their hold on reality, not engage in extensive self-deception, etc.'[18]

In such cases—as opposed, say, to our contemplation of Athenian democracy or life among the Incas—conflict involves a more or less deep but relevant difference of life-world and life-style, that may be responded to in various ways. Among these ways are rejection, conversion, and various kinds of syncretistic adaptation. Not all moral diversity, in short, is conflictual. Nor does all conflictual diversity issue in incompatible ways of living.

Incompatibility. Some moral conflicts are instances of incompatibility. I have already alluded to some of them. Antigone cannot both obey the dictates of family loyalty by burying Polynices and those of the law decreed by Creon. Agamemnon at Aulis cannot save both his fleet and his daughter. Sartre's pupil cannot both join the Free French and console his mother. Likewise, there are what are significantly called trade-offs between policies designed to promote democracy, equality, liberty, and so on, and other trade-offs internal to the pursuit of any one of them (see Chapter 4). Alternative conceptions of the good can turn out to dictate incompatible ways of treating

17 Notably by the Polish sociologist Maria Ossowska. The following books by her are available in English: *Social Determinants of Moral Ideas* (London: Routledge & Kegan Paul, 1971); *Bourgeois Morality*, trans. G. L. Campbell (London: Routledge & Kegan Paul, 1986); and *Moral Norms: A Tentative Systematisation*, trans. Irena Gulowska (Warsaw and Amsterdam: PWN, 1980).

18 Williams, *Ethics and the Limits of Philosophy* (London: Fontana, 1985), p. 160.

persons in particular situations. Should the immigrant's daughter attend college? Should the sick Amish child go to hospital? Should abortion be permitted?

These undoubted incompatibilities are not yet incommensurable. All moralists and most moral philosophers will assume that they are not, that there is always a point of view from which they are amenable to the discovery of the 'right answer'. (The law of course is one such point of view, by the very reason of its social role.[19]) Indeed, it is generally assumed that to assert the contrary is a form of irrationalism. Buried very deep in our philosophical consciousness and implicit in our social scientific practice is the nearly universal presumption that consistency of preference and of ethical beliefs is a mark of our rationality. But is it?

Incommensurability. Incompatible moral claims become incommensurable when the trade-offs become unavailable because there is no common currency. In recent times several writers have appealed to this difficult notion (examined in Chapter 3). Berlin writes:

If the claims of two (or more than two) types of liberty prove incompatible in a particular case, and if this is an instance of the clash of values at once absolute and incommensurable, it is better to face this intellectually uncomfortable fact than to ignore it, or automatically attribute it to some deficiency on our part which could be eliminated by an increase in skill or knowledge; or, what is worse still, suppress one of the competing values altogether by pretending that it is identical with its rival—and so end by distorting both.[20]

Williams, citing Berlin, writes that 'values, or at least the most basic values, are not only plural but in a real sense incommensurable', adding that this claim says 'something true and important'.[21] For Rawls, a 'workable conception of political justice' must allow for 'a diversity of doctrines and the plurality of conflicting, and indeed incommensurable, conceptions of the good affirmed by the members of existing democratic societies.[22] For Thomas Nagel, 'values come from a number of viewpoints, some more personal than others, which cannot be reduced to a common denominator', and when 'faced with conflicting and incommensurable claims, we still have to

---

[19] Cf. Ronald Dworkin, 'Is There Really No Right Answer in Hard Cases', *A Matter of Principle* (Cambridge, Mass.: Harvard Univ. Press, 1985).

[20] Berlin, *Four Essays*, p. 1.

[21] Williams, 'Conflicts of Values', pp. 76, 77.

[22] John Rawls, 'Justice as Fairness: Political not Metaphysical', *Philosophy and Public Affairs* (Summer 1985), 225.

do something—even if it is only to do nothing'. For Nagel, the 'fragmentation of value' encompasses conflicts *between* 'moral and other motivational claims of very different kinds' coming from 'many perspectives—individual, relational, impersonal, ideal, etc.'[23] This is to deepen and broaden the issue we are seeking to confront. And Larmore advocates that we 'suspend the monistic assumption underlying so much of moral theory' and 'acknowledge that not everything is good or right to the extent that it is commensurable with respect to any single standard'.[24]

The key idea, then, is that there is no single currency or scale on which conflicting values can be measured, and that where a conflict occurs no rationally compelling appeal can be made to some value that will resolve it. Neither is superior to the other, nor are they equal in value. To believe in incommensurability is not to hold that all or even most value conflicts or even moral conflicts are of this sort; only that some are and that they are non-trivial. Conflicts could be trivially incommensurable where preference rankings are indeterminate because incomplete or discontinuous, as where I just don't know how much more I value Mozart than Bach or how much the weather must improve before I prefer a walk in the park to staying at home with a book.[25] But they could also be non-trivially so if and when I cannot appeal to some single value standard to determine whether, say, E. M. Forster was right to place the value of friendship above patriotism, or how far local autonomy should be protected against policies of equalization, or how things stand between your belief in the foetus's right to life and mine in the mother's right to choose. The fact that one must decide in such cases, in favour of one or the other or by appeal to some value independent of both (such as maximizing utility or well-being), does not show which is worth more. That question does not admit of a 'right answer', refusal to accept which is a sure sign of irrationality. However one decides, it will be *from* and not just *for*, one of the viewpoints in contention, or from a further viewpoint that is no less contentious.

[23] Thomas Nagel, 'The Fragmentation of Value', *Mortal Questions* (Cambridge: Cambridge Univ. Press, 1979), pp. 134, 138, 134.

[24] Larmore, *Patterns*, p. 10. Larmore clearly uses a broader (and vaguer?) sense of 'moral' than does Nagel. His 'projects and friendships' would not, it seems, fall within Nagel's definition.

[25] See Joseph Raz, *The Morality of Freedom* (Oxford: Oxford Univ. Press, 1986), chap. 13.

So far I have sought to suggest the *possibility* of moral conflict, in all the senses I have distinguished. I have done this in two ways: by seeking to discredit various attempts (by Aristotelians, Platonists, Kantians, utilitarians, relativists, and subjectivists) to make nonsense of such conflicts; and by suggesting that our moral experience bears witness to their presence and to their importance. In doing this, I have enlisted, by citing them, various recent allies in this argument against the prevailing view in both philosophy and social science. I now wish further to motivate the thought that the possibility is actualized and that it is central to our personal and public lives.

Consider first the diversity of morals. Those who have sought to deny, or minimize, this have, appealing to Hume's thought that 'mankind is much the same in all times and places',[26] interpreted differences of belief and practice as best explained by differences in the circumstances human beings face. There is a deep interpretive problem here. Any study of the moral thought and action of others is inexorably caught up in a hermeneutic circle: Is there any way into, say, Navaho or Hopi ethics that does not already presuppose our moral categories and distinctions? Is there, in other words, any way that such a study could avoid John Ladd's criticism of Richard Brandt's study of Hopi ethics, that it 'consists in a cross-cultural investigation of the extent to which the Hopi accept principles like our own'?[27] Or, more deeply and worryingly, that they should emerge as reflecting some recognizable fragment of our own moral world? The problem is only deepened by the plausible suggestion that it is a condition of successful translation that 'the imputed pattern of relations between beliefs, desires and the world be as similar to our own as possible'.[28] If all this is so, perhaps it is no accident that Brandt's Hopi end up as impartial and disinterested and Ladd's Navaho as egoistic prudentialists.

These are deep waters into which I propose to go no further (but

---

[26] David Hume, *Essays Moral and Political*, ed. T. H. Green and T. H. Grose, 4 vols. (London, 1875), ii. 68.

[27] John Ladd, *The Structure of a Moral Code: A Philosophical Analysis of Ethical Discourse Applied to the Ethics of the Navaho Indians* (Cambridge, Mass.: Harvard Univ. Press, 1957), p. 316. Cf. Richard Brandt, *Hopi Ethics* (Chicago: Chicago Univ. Press, 1954).

[28] R. Grandy, 'Reference, Meaning and Truth', *Journal of Philosophy* 70 (1973), 445. See 'Relativism in its Place', my concluding chapter to Martin Hollis and Steven Lukes (eds.), *Rationality and Relativism* (Oxford: Blackwell, 1982).

see Chapter 5) except to suggest that the diversity of morals reveals itself clearly in what, following Bernard Williams, I have called 'real confrontations', as in intercultural conflicts within and between contemporary societies. It is possible but not easy to deny the diversity of morals when contemplating cultural conflicts in South Africa or Northern Ireland or the Middle East and the clash between secularism and the various forms of religious fundamentalism.

As for moral conflict as incompatibility, that too is surely a pervasive feature of the modern world. There are two ways of taking the sting out of this, neither of which looks very plausible in the late twentieth century. One is to deny its reality via theodicy: by believing, as Bishop Butler did, that God has so arranged the world and our natures that, though in acting morally we may appear to follow divergent moral principles that exclude general benevolence, nevertheless, *sub specie aeternitatis*, the general happiness is secured.[29] Leszek Kolakowski has well said, 'in an apologist's eyes God's inscrutable ways can always be plausibly defended'.[30]

The other implausible way of removing the sting from moral conflict as incompatibility is to deny, not its reality, but its necessity via the secular inheritance of theodicy: moral Utopianism. A moral Utopian believes that there is in prospect a perfect world in which all actual moral incompatibilities will be overcome because the subjective and objective conditions of life will render them impossible, even inconceivable. Like Kolakowski, I think that Marxism is committed to such a belief: for the present to a kind of long-term consequentialism in which pursuing the perfectionist goal of human emancipation is the overriding practical guide to action; and for the future to the undefended and indefensible hope that under 'truly human' conditions there will be (1) a maximization of overall good (welfare and perfectionist achievement); (2) a transcendence of the conditions that have made the lawlike ethics of obligations, justice, and rights necessary; and (3) an overcoming of the conditions that render partial obligations and commitments to particular communities and groups incompatible with universal ones.[31] Neither the conceivability nor the feasibility nor indeed the desirability of such a reconciliatory future can any longer be plausibly defended (see Chapter 18).

[29] See Larmore, *Patterns*, chap. 6.
[30] Kolakowski, *Religion*, p. 192.
[31] See Steven Lukes, *Marxism and Morality* (Oxford: Oxford Univ. Press, 1985).

I turn finally to the difficult issue of incommensurability. Why should we believe that significant incommensurabilities exist between the apparently conflicting moral claims we face? I suggest that there are two main reasons for believing this. First, as Max Weber and Kolakowski have powerfully argued, in a disenchanted world, there is no longer any reason to believe in the commensurability of basic values.[32] As Weber, 'speaking directly', memorably put it 'the ultimately possible attitudes towards life are irreconcilable, and hence their struggle can never be brought to a final conclusion. Thus it is necessary to make a decisive choice'. What man, he asks,

will take upon himself the attempt to 'refute scientifically' the ethic of the Sermon on the Mount? For instance, the sentence 'resist no evil,' or the image of turning the other cheek? And yet it is clear, in mundane perspective, that this is an ethic of undignified conduct: one has to choose between the religious dignity which this ethic confers and the dignity of manly conduct which preaches something quite different: 'resist evil—lest you be co-responsible for an overpowering evil.' According to our ultimate standpoint, the one is the devil and the other the God, and the individual has to decide which is God for him and which is the devil. And so it goes throughout all the orders of life.[33]

Some believe that this position amounts to a denial that moral judgement can be rationally based and others believe further that it leads somehow inexorably to moral anarchy or fascism or at least to the inability to resist them. (By contrast, I believe it to be essential to a properly defended liberalism.) Bloom, rightly seeing Nietzsche behind Weber, objects that, on that kind of view, 'it is our *decision* to esteem that makes something estimable', that 'the objects of men's reverence' become 'projections of what is most powerful in man and serve to satisfy his strongest needs or desires', that 'values are not discovered by reason, and it is fruitless to seek them, to find the truth or the good life', that 'producing values and believing in them are acts of the will' and that we have thereby abandoned 'the distinction between true and false in political and moral matters', that the choice lies between Plato and Nietzsche and that by choosing against the former, we have thereby sacrified 'reason'.[34] Alasdair MacIntyre

[32] Max Weber, *Politik als Beruf*, trans. in H. H. Gerth and C. W. Mills (eds.), *From Max Weber* (London: Routledge & Kegan Paul, 1948). Kolakowski, 'Ethics without a Moral Code', *Triquarterly* 22 (1971), esp. 72–4.

[33] Weber, *Wissenschaft als Beruf* ('Science as Vocation'), in Gerth and Mills, *From Max Weber*, p. 148.

[34] Bloom, *Closing of the American Mind*, pp. 143, 197, 201, 207, 219.

argues, in a not dissimilar way, that, by choosing Nietzsche and Weber, in his case against Aristotle, we have abandoned the possibility of a rational foundation for ethics. He seeks to vindicate Aristotle's 'pre-modern view of morals and politics' against the central thesis that he takes to underpin Nietzsche's position—

that all rational vindications of morality manifestly fail and that *therefore* belief in the tenets of morality need to be explained in terms of a set of rationalisations which conceal the fundamentally non-rational phenomena of the will.[35]

Jürgen Habermas, from a very different standpoint, nevertheless holds to a 'cognitivist position . . . that there is a universal core of moral intuition in all times and in all societies' and thus rejects 'the Weberian pluralism of value systems, gods and demons' and the 'empiricist and/or decisionist barriers, which immunize the so-called pluralism of values against the efforts of practical reason.'[36] (Here, I believe, he wrongly identifies Weber's position with that of Carl Schmitt.) He proposes, through the Utopianism of a counterfactually posited 'ideal speech situation', to 'vindicate the power of discursively attained rational consensus' and show that 'practical questions admit of truth'.[37]

But Weber, for what it is worth, did not derive values from decisions and the will. Quite the contrary, decisions, based on moral judgement, are needed just because conflicting values, some objective, some not, are incommensurable. Neither going back (in Bloom's words) to 'great wise men in other places and times who can reveal the truth about life'[38] nor looking forward to the imagined consensus of ideal speech serves to gainsay this uncomfortably objective truth.

A second reason for holding that incommensurability is both real and important to our contemporary lives is suggested by Joseph Raz in *The Morality of Freedom*. It applies more particularly to that which holds between partiality, on the one hand, and deontology or consequentialism, on the other. Many of the commitments, loyalties, and obligations that we have to relationships and activities that

[35] Alasdair MacIntyre, *After Virtue* (London: Duckworth, 1981), p. 111. See Chap. 13.

[36] Jürgen Habermas, *Autonomy and Solidarity: Interviews*, ed. P. Dews (London: Verso, 1986), p. 206.

[37] Id., *Legitimation Crisis* (London: Heinemann, 1973), pp. 107, 111. See Chap. 11.

[38] Bloom, *Closing of the American Mind*, p. 34.

matter to us consist in part in a refusal to engage in the very kind of trade-off that full commensurability would require (but see qualification below, p. 46). If I were prepared even to consider how much the obligations of friendship are worth in relation to some greater future good to persons unknown, or whether my parental duties can be traded for some greater overall benefit, or against, say, some promise I have made, that might only show that I am not a true friend or parent. Such refusals to compare suggest that constitutive attachments are what they are in part by virtue of their very incommensurability with more universalistic moral claims. To engage in such forms of thinking is itself an expression of the weakening or absence of those very relationships or else a degraded simulacrum of them. The very assumption of commensurability would subvert certain values, which are what they are in part just because they deny it. If all this is right, then we can only conclude that modernity—in which the separation between the partial and the universal, like that between fact and value, has become a prevalent cultural fact—renders incommensurability inescapable. There is no route back from modernity.

Moral Conflict and Liberalism

What, finally, does the recognition of moral conflict have to do with the defence of liberalism? Liberalism was born out of religious conflict and the attempt to tame it by accommodating it within the framework of the nation-state. The case for religious toleration was central to its development; and out of that there developed the crucial but complex thought that civil society is an arena of conflicts, which should be co-ordinated and regulated by the constitutional state. In part that conflict is, as Hume saw, a result of scarcity and conflicting claims that arise out of selfishness and competing interests. But, more deeply, it also arises out of conflicting moral claims, which raises the problem of how to treat these justly within a framework of social unity and mutually acceptable laws and principles of distribution. Given all this, the prospects for a morally based defence of liberalism—a defence that derives from a comprehensive or all-embracing moral view—look dim, even self-contradictory.

This has led critics of liberalism to condemn it for being anaemic, pale, morally half-hearted, sceptical, even indifferent. Others, notably Kant and the utilitarians, and in some moods John Stuart

Mill, defend it by appealing to just such a comprehensive moral theory. But it leads others to argue that its proper defence requires that such a defence be unavailable. Thus, Isaiah Berlin attacks those he calls 'single-minded monists', arguing that

The notion that there must exist final objective answers to normative questions, truths that can be demonstrated or directly intuited, that it is in principle possible to discover a harmonious pattern in which all values are reconciled, and that it is toward this unique goal that we must make; that we can uncover some single central principle that shapes this vision, a principle which, once found, will govern our lives—this ancient and almost universal belief, on which so much traditional thought and action and philosophical doctrine rests, seems to me invalid, and at times to have led (and still to lead) to absurdities in theory and barbarous consequences in practice.[39]

Rawls too distinguishes between

those that allow for a plurality of opposing and even incommensurable conceptions of the good and those that hold that there is but one conception of the good and which is to be recognized by all persons, so far as they are fully rational.

He sees the latter as the 'dominant tradition', which includes Plato, Aristotle, the Christian tradition as represented by Augustine and Aquinas, and classical utilitarianism. He contrasts that tradition with liberalism as a political doctrine, which holds that 'there are many conflicting and incommensurable conceptions of the good, each compatible with the full rationality of human persons' and that 'the question the dominant tradition has tried to answer has no practicable answer . . . for a political conception of justice for a democratic society'.[40]

---

[39] Berlin, *Four Essays*, pp. lv–lvi. Berlin is rather tough on 'single-minded monists', calling them 'ruthless fanatics, men possessed by an all-embracing coherent vision', who 'do not know the doubts and agonies of those who cannot wholly blind themselves to reality'. I tend to agree with James Griffin, who, in a discussion of incommensurability, observes that computation on a single scale does not need a substantive 'single central principle'. He suggests plausibly that: 'if we assembled all the deplorable fanatics that history has ever seen and asked them to divide into two lobbies, labelled "monists" and "pluralists", my money would be on the pluralists' winning hands down.' It is hard to think that a happy, productive life counts for nothing, but unfortunately it seems terribly easy to think that it counts for nothing up against what is seen as the 'incommensurably higher'! (James Griffin, *Well-Being* (Oxford: Clarendon Press, 1987), p. 91). Liberalism is about fairness between conflicting moral and religious positions, but it is also about filtering out those that are incompatible with a liberal order and taming those that remain.

[40] Rawls, 'Justice as Fairness', pp. 248–9.

Allan Bloom, by contrast, while defending 'liberal education', is plainly a monist and a full subscriber to the 'dominant tradition'. I doubt that there could be a more devout form of adherence to that tradition than the Straussianism he has so successfully popularized. For him, the Rawlsian defence of liberalism is nothing short of a plea for moral indifference and scepticism, even 'value-relativism'. Rawls's *A Theory of Justice*, he writes, argues that

the physicist or the poet should not look down on the man who spends his life counting blades of grass or performing any other frivolous or corrupt activity. Indeed, he should be esteemed, since esteem from others, as opposed to self-esteem, is a basic need of all men. So indiscriminateness is a moral imperative because its opposite is discrimination. This folly means that men are not permitted to seek for the natural human good and admire it when found, for such discovery is coeval with the discovery of the bad and contempt for it.[41]

This is certainly an imaginative Straussian reading of the inner meaning of Rawls's text, which explicitly and repeatedly states the contrary. More important, it misses the point and the force of Rawls's defence of liberalism altogether. Fortunately, in anticipation of such a charge, Rawls has fully answered it and I will quote him doing so. He has forthrightly denied advocating

either scepticism or indifference about religious, philosophical, or moral doctrines. We do not say that they are all doubtful or false, or address questions to which truth and falsehood do not apply. Instead, long historical experience suggests, and many philosophical reflections confirm, that on such doctrines reasoned and uncoerced agreement is not to be expected. Religious and philosophical views express outlooks toward the world and our life with one another, severally and collectively, as a whole. Our individual and associative points of view, intellectual affinities and affective attachments are too diverse, especially in a free democratic society, to allow of lasting and reasoned agreement. Many conceptions of the world can plausibly be constructed from different standpoints. Diversity naturally arises from our limited powers and distinct perspectives; it is unrealistic to suppose that all our differences are rooted solely in ignorance and perversity, or else in the rivalries that result from scarcity. Justice as fairness tries to construct a conception of justice that takes deep and unresolvable differences on matters of fundamental significance as a permanent condition of human life. Indeed, this condition may have its good side, if only we can delineate the character of social arrangements that enable us to appreciate its possible benefits.[42]

41 Bloom, *Closing of the American Mind*, p. 30.
42 Rawls, 'Kantian Constructivism in Moral Theory'. The John Dewey Lectures, *Journal of Philosophy* 77 (Sept. 1980), p. 542.

This raises the deep and difficult issue of specifying just what sense liberalism is to make of moral, and more generally value, conflicts. Some, most obviously some religious conflicts, cannot be resolved, because their justification seems to be internal all the way down: what is to count as good or overriding reasons remains to the end internal to the opposed parties and not susceptible to common or public argument.[43] Others—and these are what Rawls has in mind in the passage quoted—are so susceptible but are nevertheless irresolvable because there is no prospect of publicly available evidence and argument yielding uniquely determinate solutions rationally compelling upon all.[44] For the state to impose any single solution on some of its citizens is thus (not only from their standpoint) unreasonable. Hence the liberal's commitment to impartiality, at the level of social and political institutions, among such conflicting conceptions of the good—and the right—as are compatible with the survival of a liberal order. The question of how far that commitment is a merely strategic one (as a means to securing a *modus vivendi*) and how far, and in what ways, itself a substantive moral one (appealing, for instance, to an interpretation of the Kantian categorical imperative) is one I cannot explore further here.

This, then, is how moral conflict bears on the proper defence of liberalism. That defence cannot, for the reasons I have sought to develop, rely on the gleaning of ineffable truths from ancient texts or on the elaboration of comprehensive moral theories. It cannot be based on either a return to or a contemporary restatement of Plato or Aristotle or Natural Law or Kantianism or utilitarianism; or on a resort to relativism or subjectivism or an appeal to theodicy or moral utopianism. It can rest only on taking moral conflict seriously and making sense of it.

---

[43] For a sophisticated argument that these exhaust the field, see MacIntyre, *Whose Justice? Which Rationality?* (Notre Dame, Ind.: Univ. of Notre Dame Press, 1988), for example: 'There is no standing ground, no place for enquiry, no way to engage in the practice of advancing, evaluating, accepting, and rejecting reasoned argument apart from that which is provided by some particular tradition or other' (p. 350), and 'Progress in rationality is achieved only from a point of view' (p. 144). See Chap. 13, Sect. II, below.

[44] See Nagel, 'Moral Conflict and Political Legitimacy', *Philosophy and Public Affairs* 16 (1987), pp. 215–40.

2
Taking Morality Seriously

'Protagoras, Hobbes, Hume and Warnock', writes John Mackie,

are all at least broadly in agreement about the problem that morality is needed to solve: limited resources and limited sympathies together generate both competition leading to conflict and an absence of what would be mutually beneficial cooperation.[1]

Mackie endorses this view, meaning by 'morality' what he calls morality 'in the narrow sense', namely, 'a system of a particular sort of constraints on conduct—ones whose central task is to protect the interests of persons other than the agent and which present themselves to an agent as checks on his natural inclinations or spontaneous tendencies to act'.[2] In this chapter, I shall seek to establish three conclusions: first, that Mackie's account of morality 'in the narrow sense' is useful and important, and denotes a central domain within morality more widely construed; second, that his account of the problem to which morality, thus conceived, is a solution is inadequate and misleading; and third, that is importantly so.

Morality in the Narrow Sense

The broad sense of morality with which the narrow sense contrasts is 'a general, all-inclusive theory of conduct: the morality to which someone subscribed would be whatever body of principles he allowed ultimately to guide or determine his choices of action'.[3] So, in the narrow sense, 'moral considerations would be considerations

This chapter was first published in 1985. I am grateful to Ted Honderich and Jo Raz for comments that have helped improve it.

[1] J. L. Mackie, *Ethics: Inventing Right and Wrong* (Harmondsworth: Penguin, 1977), p. 111.

[2] Ibid. 106.   [3] Ibid.

from some limited range, and would not necessarily include everything that a man allowed to determine what he did'.[4]

This contrast between senses of 'morality' is already useful, given the cacophony of senses in which the term is used, ranging from the 'moral majority' to the 'moral sciences'. But it does not, in itself, enable us to denote a specific object of reference as 'morality in the narrow sense'. What *is* the limited range of considerations that present themselves as constraints on conduct and protect interests in the manner indicated?

Mackie gives hints as to how to answer this question[5] by focusing attention on rights and obligations, rules and prohibitions, and, following Hume, on the notion of justice. We can consolidate these hints by drawing on some observations of H. L. A. Hart, John Stuart Mill, and R. M. Hare. According to Hart, the German '*Recht*', like the French '*droit*' and the Italian '*diritto*', is a term used by continental jurists for which there is no direct English translation: these expressions

seem to English jurists to hover uncertainly between law and morals, but they do in fact mark off an area of morality (the morality of law) which has special characteristics. It is occupied by the concepts of justice, fairness, rights and obligation (if the last is not used as it is by many moral philosophers as an obscuring general label to cover every action that morally we ought to do or forbear from doing).[6]

Hart adds that there are four factors that distinguish morality from law itself; namely, importance, immunity from deliberate change, the voluntary character of moral offences, and the distinctive form of moral pressure.[7]

It is doubtless this area of morality that Mill had in mind when he observed that justice is 'the chief part, and incomparably the most sacred and binding part, of all morality',[8] meaning by 'justice' 'certain classes of moral rules' which protect rights that 'reside in persons' and which

[4] Mackie, *Ethics*.

[5] Mackie, *Ethics: Inventing Right and Wrong*, and 'Can there be a Right-based Moral Theory?' *Midwest Studies in Philosophy*, iii. *Studies in Ethical Theory*, 1978 (Univ. of Minnesota Press, Minneapolis, Minn., 1980).

[6] H. L. A. Hart, 'Are There any Natural Rights?' *Philosophical Review* 64 (1955), 177–8.

[7] Id., *The Concept of Law* (Oxford: Clarendon Press, 1961).

[8] J. S. Mill, *Utilitarianism* (1861) (London: Fontana Library, Collins, 1962), p. 315.

concern the essentials of human well-being more nearly, and are therefore of more absolute obligation, than any other rules for the guidance of life . . . The moral rules which forbid mankind to hurt one another (in which we must never forget to include wrongful interference with each other's freedom) are more vital to human well-being than any other maxims, however important, which only point out the best mode of managing some department of human affairs.[9]

And consider finally R. M. Hare's suggestion that

within the general area of morality marked out by the use of 'ought' and 'must' (which is not the whole of morality, because the word 'good' and the virtues have been left out of this picture), there is a smaller field of obligation and rights, distinguished by being person-related and by being, unlike 'must', overridable, but not so easily as 'ought'.[10]

And Hare, significantly, goes on to discuss, within the same chapter, 'the parallel problem of justice',[11] which he divides into judicial and quasi-judicial justice on the one hand and distributive or social and economic justice on the other—that is, 'justice in the distribution of the various benefits and harms which arise from membership in a society and its economy, including small societies such as families and partnerships and groups of friends'.[12]

From these various suggestions we may conclude that the narrow sense of morality serves to demarcate a distinct and central *domain* of morality which has a certain distinctive form and function. It is the domain of the Right rather than the Good, or at least it bears on the Good only indirectly, by setting limits (which may be more or less narrow) to what actions conceptions of the good may legitimately advocate or encourage. It does not directly address the pursuit of virtue or happiness or perfection, but purports to protect individuals' pursuit of these, as they severally conceive them. It is the domain of principles of justice, and of rights and obligations; these present themselves as constraints on conduct, that are powerful but over-ridable, and serve to protect vital interests of persons, touching on 'the essentials of their well-being', including their freedom; and they have, taken together, a distinctive function or purpose in human life. It is to Mackie's account of that function that we now turn.

---

[9] Ibid. 316.
[10] Hare, *Moral Thinking: Its Levels, Methods and Point* (Oxford: Oxford Univ. Press, 1981), p. 153.
[11] Ibid. 156.
[12] Ibid. 161.

The Object of Morality

What, Mackie asks, gives morality in the narrow sense its point? His answer, nor surprisingly, is Humean. He cites with approval Hume's statement that it is 'only from the selfishness and confin'd generosity of men, along with the scanty provision nature has made for his wants, that justice derives its origin',[13] and comments, interpreting Hume, that 'If men had been overwhelmingly benevolent, if each had aimed only at the happiness of all, if everyone had loved his neighbour as himself, there would have been no need for the rules that constitute justice.'[14] In this section, I shall seek to show that this view is radically mistaken, both with regard to justice in particular, and, in general, to the area of morality we have identified as morality in the narrow sense.

Mackie's developed Humean view is that morality in the narrow sense (which we shall henceforth call morality$_n$) is a device for solving a problem that he identifies as follows:

We must think of a 'game' in which most, perhaps all, of the 'players' are largely selfish, or have limited sympathies, in a situation where scarce resources and the like tend to produce conflicts of interest; further, it is important for most of the 'players' that certain roughly specifiable evils (which, other things being equal, would result from the basic situation) should be prevented or reduced.[15]

Morality$_n$ provides

acceptable principles of constraint on action the general encouragement of and widespread respect for which will do most to counter these evils, subject to the assumption that these constraints will not be respected by all the 'players' all the time.[16]

The point of morality$_n$ is 'that it is necessary for the well-being of people in general that they should act to some extent in ways that they cannot see to be (egoistically) prudential and also in ways that in fact are not prudential.' The function of morality$_n$ is of 'checking what would be the natural result of prudence alone'.[17]

In criticizing this thesis of Mackie's, I shall argue (1) that it is unsatisfactory in itself, and (2) that it is an inadequate response to the

[13] Hume, *A Treatise of Human Nature* (1739), ed. L. A. Selby-Bigge, (Oxford: Clarendon Press, 1951), p. 495.
[14] Mackie, *Ethics: Inventing Right and Wrong*, p. 110.
[15] Ibid. 165.　　[16] Ibid.　　[17] Ibid. 190.

question asked: that it takes far too narrow a view of the problem to which morality in the narrow sense is a solution.

(1) Consider the two key elements of the Hume–Mackie account of the conditions calling forth morality$_n$: scarcity and limited sympathies.

What, in the first place, is scarcity? Hume and Mackie present it as a matter of nature's 'scanty provision' for man's wants and of 'limited resources'. But scarcity is a more complex notion than either of these formulations suggest. Consider the following four forms of scarcity: (i) insufficiency of production inputs (e.g. raw materials) relative to production requirements; (ii) insufficiency of produced goods relative to consumption requirements; (iii) limits upon the possibility of the joint realization of individual goals, resulting from external conditions (e.g. limitations of space or time); and (iv) limits upon the possibility of the joint realization of individual goals resulting from the nature of those goals (e.g. 'positional goods': we cannot all enjoy high status, or the quiet solitude of our neighbourhood park). Plainly these possibilities bring into view a range of determinants of scarcity, of which the niggardliness of nature and men's wants are only two (and these are themselves dependent variables, in turn determined by a range of social, cultural, scientific, and technological factors). Scarcity (ii) can exist without scarcity (i): it may result entirely from the existing system of production and distribution. Scarcity (ii) can be absent despite 'limited resources'. And scarcity (iii) and (iv) may result from social, organizational and cultural factors and exist without scarcity (i) or (ii). All these forms of scarcity can generate interest conflicts. Furthermore, overcoming them all would involve an immense growth in the productive forces of society, changes in social organization and appropriate preference changes, eliminating all non-compatible desires. I shall call this (unrealizable) state of affairs 'co-operative abundance'. The point being made here is that both the nature and the sources of scarcity are more complex and diverse than Hume and Mackie indicate.

Consider next what Hume calls 'selfishness and confin'd generosity' and Mackie 'egoism and self-referential altruism'[18] or 'limited sympathies'. Are these notions, as they say, perspicuous? I doubt it. For what counts, in any particular case, as 'egoism' or 'selfishness' depends on context and, in particular, on how the 'self' and its

[18] Ibid. 170.

'interests' are understood. Assume a world in which, over certain ranges of human interaction, a so-called zero-sum relation holds, such that if A gains B loses, and the self is seen as typically having interests which conflict with those of others, and with the public or common interest. Then, of course, 'egoism' and 'selfishness', or the pursuit of self-interest, will result in conflicts of interest. But imagine a world in which the Golden Rule always applied or the Buddhist notion of the self was widely shared. Then 'egoism' or 'selfishness' or 'self-interest' would result in, or at least be compatible with, social harmony, even under conditions of scarcity. In short, 'egoism' and 'selfishness', as we ordinarily understand them, presuppose, and are not themselves the source of, conflicting interests.

The same argument applies, *pari passu*, to 'confin'd generosity' and 'self-referential altruism'. *Whether* the limits upon and self-referential character of altruistic sentiments result in conflicts of interest will depend on the social relations that prevail and on what pursuing the happiness or interests of those for whom one cares is taken to involve. From the mere fact that sympathies are limited nothing follows: only if specific ways of acting on them means acting against those beyond the limits do conflicts of interest result.

Mackie himself sees this when he asks: 'what action will be the most prudent or the most egoistically rational?' and answers that 'that depends partly on what sort of a person you are, and consequentially on what sort of a person you want to be'.[19] If someone, he writes,

from whatever causes, has at least fairly strong moral tendencies, the prudential course, for him, will almost certainly coincide with what he sees as the moral one, simply because he will have to live with his conscience. What *is* prudent is then not the same as what would be prudent if he did not have moral feelings.[20]

But Mackie's account of what is moral$_n$ relies on a contrast between constraints on an agent's conduct and 'his natural inclinations and spontaneous tendencies to act'.[21] Yet what these are will depend on what sort of a person he is and whether they harm the interests of others will depend on this and on the sort of society in which he and they live. From all of which I conclude that the second element of the Hume–Mackie account—egoism and limited sympathies—

---

[19] Mackie, *Ethics*, 192.　　　[20] Ibid.　　　[21] Ibid. 106.

presupposes rather than explains the conflicting interests it adduces morality to resolve.

(2) That the Hume–Mackie account of the conditions that call forth morality$_n$ is too narrow can be seen clearly if we ask whether the conditions so far (albeit unsatisfactorily) specified exhaustively explain the bases of interest conflicts in social life. Plainly, scarcity, in its several forms, combined with various familiar forms of egoism and limited sympathies among competing individuals and groups —such as 'possessive individualism', acquisitiveness, status striving, wage-bargaining, etc.—will generate conflicting claims and thus the need to adjudicate upon which claims are valid and of these which have priority.

There are, however, roots of interest conflict that lie deeper than this—that are less tied to a particular type of society and its social relations. Rawls gives a clue to what these might be in his account of the 'circumstances of justice': these are 'the normal conditions under which human co-operation is both possible and necessary' and they 'obtain whenever mutually disinterested persons put forward conflicting claims to the division of social advantages under conditions of moderate scarcity'.[22] Rawls's point here is (I take it) that the conflicting claims result not, or not only, from the attitudes and activities mentioned above but from the diversity of human ends: as he writes, 'the plurality of distinct persons with distinct systems of ends is an essential feature of human societies'.[23] In other words, it is the conflict of interests resulting from different individuals' and groups' different and conflicting conceptions of the good, that in turn define those interests, that render adjudication and interest-protecting constraints necessary.

Notice that this condition is independent of the Hume–Mackie conditions (though of course it may coexist with them). Hume mistakenly thought that if you increase 'to a sufficient degree the benevolence of men or the bounty of nature . . . you render justice useless by supplying its place with much nobler virtues, and more favourable blessings'.[24] But even under conditions of co-operative abundance and altruism, there will, if conceptions of the good conflict, be a need for the fair allocation of benefits and burdens, for the assigning of obligations and the protection of rights; but we should then need them in the face of the benevolence rather than the

---

[22] J. Rawls, *A Theory of Justice* (Oxford: Clarendon Press, 1972), p. 128.
[23] Ibid. 28–9.   [24] Hume, *A Treatise of Human Nature*, pp. 494–5.

selfishness of others. Altruists, sincerely and conscientiously pursuing their respective conceptions of the good, can certainly cause injustice and violate rights. For every conception of the good will favour certain social relationships and ways of defining individuals' interests—or, more precisely, certain ways of conceiving and ranking the various interests that individuals have. It will also disfavour others, and in a world in which no such conception is fully realized, and universally accepted, even—perhaps especially—the non-egoistic practitioners of one threaten the adherents of others: hence the need for justice, rights, and obligations.

But what if divergent conceptions of the good, and of basic or vital interests, were to converge within a single moral and political consensus? Here a fourth set of conditions for morality$_n$ come into view: lack of perfect rationality, information, and understanding. Even under co-operative abundance, altruism, and the unification of interests within a common conception of the good, people may, after all, get it wrong: they may fail to act as they should toward others, because they do not know how to or make mistakes, with resulting misallocations of burdens and benefits, and damage to individuals' interests.

In seeking to supplement and deepen Mackie's account of the conditions of morality$_n$, I have so far been arguing very much in the spirit of his account, seeking to explain the point, function, or object of morality$_n$ in terms of 'certain contingent features of the human condition'.[25] I shall now depart from that spirit and turn to fantasy, by asking whether *any* human society could dispense with morality$_n$: is its dispensability *conceivable*?

Joseph Raz has suggested that the co-ordinating, dispute-resolving and damage-remedying functions of law would be needed even in 'a society of angels'.[26] Presumably by the same argument morality$_n$ would also be needed in such a society. On what grounds might one reject such a suggestion? Only on the ground that it takes too low a view of angels: that they would, in Hume's words, be endowed with 'much nobler virtues, and more favourable blessings', and in particular that the communal relations between them would be such as to render morality$_n$ unnecessary. But what could such communal relations be like?

---

[25] Mackie, *Ethics: Inventing Right and Wrong*, p. 121.
[26] Raz, *Practical Reason and Norms* (London: Hutchinson, 1975), p. 159.

Here there seem to be only two alternatives. On the one hand, such angels (or rather perhaps saints?) could agree upon and live by shared moral principles, in a kind of communal *Sittlichkeit*. Such principles would guide what would otherwise be conflictual into harmonious and mutually advantageous behaviour, by mediating and reconciling claims on common resources, enforcing respect for others' interests and views, settling disagreements of interpretation and fact, and so on. But what could such principles be but principles of morality$_n$?

The other alternative is that angels would be free of conflicting self-interests. The relations between them would be relations between individuals without any sense of a self-interest conflicting with that of others, or with the public or collective interest. There is good reason to think that this was indeed Marx's conception of communism. For he always tended to see self-interest as tied to civil society and private property, and characteristic of 'egoistic man, of man separated from other men and from the community'[27] and he envisaged communism, not as the 'love-imbued opposite of selfishness'[28] but as the end of 'a cleavage between the particular and the common interest', as a state in which 'the contradiction between the interest of the separate individual or the individual family and the common interest of all individuals who have intercourse with one another' has been abolished.[29]

It is difficult to get this image into clear focus, but it may help to imagine a range of possibilities from what we might call the minimum to the maximum picture. On the minimum picture, the diverse interests that individuals severally pursue are always overridden, when the need for choice arises, by the principle of preserving communal relations with others. The maintaining of the latter always takes priority over individuals' other desires and needs, wherever the two conflict. On the maximum picture, communal relations undercut rather than override individuals' conflicting interests: they enter into or help to constitute one's very conception of one's interests and one's self, and thus one's self-interest. The projects I value, the life-plans I pursue, the fulfilments I seek, and

[27] Marx, 'On the Jewish Question' (1843), in K. Marx and F. Engels, *Collected Works* (London: Lawrence and Wishart, 1975–), iii. p. 162.

[28] Marx and Engels, 'Circular against Kriege' (1846), *Collected Works*, vi. p. 41.

[29] Marx and Engels, *The German Ideology* (1845–6), *Collected Works*, v. p. 46–7.

indeed my view of myself are what they are only because of the relations in which I stand to others; indeed, they cannot be conceived apart from such relations. My 'natural inclinations and spontaneous tendencies to act' and also my considered and reflective purposes and projects are always such as to maintain and enhance the communal relations in which I stand. My inclinations are 'naturally' communal, in this sense, but should they 'unnaturally' deviate, for whatever reason, reflection will make them so. I suppose that on the maximal maximum picture there just would be no such deviation. (There seems little doubt that Marx inclined towards some version of the maximum picture.)

Supposing such a community of angels or saints to exist, we must ask: what *are* its distinctive social relations? Are they face-to-face relations or do they hold between strangers, are they intimate or anonymous, are they relations of love, friendship, comradeship, neighbourliness or kinship, or of class, ethnicity, nationality, citizenship, or common humanity, do they hold between producers, or between producers and consumers, or between citizens, are they relations of commitment and loyalty binding members to sub-communities or to the community as a whole? If the society in question is of any complexity, if indeed it is a *society*, then the only possible answer is: at least all of these. But then how are these various relations themselves related? Will not the interests dictated by these various social relations be likely to conflict with one another? If so, which should have priority and when? When, for example, should patriotism override friendship, or meeting the needs of one's family outweigh impersonal charity? How are we to balance the require-ments of consumers and producers, of locality, citizenship, and internationalism, and of all the diverse groupings—ethnic, cultural, occupational, regional, and so on—into which our social or com-munal attachments inevitably divide us? Which of these sometimes conflicting requirements are more, and which less, fundamental to what J. S. Mill called 'the essentials of human well-being'? How can the individual, on whom all these relations bear, and who must interpret their import, avoid hard choices between their various requirements? And how could such choices be avoided in any community in which policy priorities have to be decided, public choices made and resources allocated? And how could such conflicts at the individual and at the collective level be resolved other than by appeal to agreed principles of justice and to rights and obligations? In short, do not even high-level, communally related angels stand in need of morality$_n$?

From all of which I draw three conclusions. First, that Mackie's account of the object of morality$_n$ is, with respect to scarcity, too simple, and, with respect to egoism and limited sympathies, question-begging. Second, that it is far too narrow, ignoring, in particular, the significance of conflicting conceptions of the good and limited rationality, information, and understanding. And third, that the conditions of morality$_n$ are nothing like as 'contingent' as Mackie suggests but appear to characterize all conceivable societies.

Taking Morality Seriously

Why should the arguments just advanced matter? The reason is, I think, practical and, indeed, moral. It concerns the practical consequences of taking the Hume–Mackie view (though I hasten to add that the arguments stand or fall independently of such consequences; the consequences are not here intended as an argument against the view).

If morality$_n$—the domain of justice, rights, and obligations—is seen as a 'device' for solving the problem of limited resources and limited sympathies, the question immediately arises: what impact does seeing it in this way have upon how one sees the constraints it imposes? What difference would taking the Hume–Mackie view make to our moral beliefs and attitudes?

In answering this, we should note that an interesting parallel exists, in the form of indirect utilitarianism. This is the view that there are two levels of moral thinking: ordinary everyday thinking guided by ordinary morality (including rights, obligations, virtues, etc.) and higher-level critical thinking, which is utilitarian, reflecting on, guiding, and testing judgements at the first level. Of this doctrine Mackie writes that the problem is

the practical difficulty, for someone who is for part of the time a critical moral philosopher in this utilitarian style, to keep this from infecting his everyday moral thought and conduct. It cannot be easy for him to retain practical dispositions of honesty, justice and loyalty if in his heart of hearts he feels that these don't really matter, and sees them merely as devices to compensate for the inability of everyone, himself included, to calculate reliably and without bias in terms of aggregate utility.[30]

[30] Mackie, 'Can There be a Right-based Moral Theory?' p. 353.

I suggest that there is an analogous infection at work in the Hume–Mackie view (though, as with indirect utilitarianism, one far from its authors' intentions). For an adherent of that view must be aware that the domain of morality$_n$ is only needed to counteract certain unfortunate and contingent features of social life, which it might, after all, be better to attack directly, in the hope of eliminating them, or at least reducing their significance. Increase 'to a sufficient degree the benevolence of men or the bounty of nature' and you can 'render justice useless'. (This thought, of course, can only be strengthened by the arguments advanced in part (1) of the previous section: scarcity can be attacked at a number of points, and 'egoism' will seem more contingent than ever.)

Hence the inclination to see justice as a merely 'remedial virtue'[31] and the tendency among both liberal-minded jurists and Marxist critics, to see 'rights' as linked to the 'individualism' of capitalist societies.[32] Hence the altogether disastrous tendency of Marxism, and certain other forms of socialist and communitarian thinking, to take a hostile view of 'justice', 'rights', and the morality of duty and to look forward to a withering away of this kind of morality —morality$_n$—in a more communitarian society which has overcome, or greatly diminished, scarcity and egoism, and in which 'nobler virtues, and more favourable blessings' will prevail—a community beyond justice and rights.

If the arguments of this chapter are cogent, all of this is a deep and dangerous mistake (not that John Mackie made it; but his view encourages it). If they hold, then morality, in the narrow sense, is a fundamentally important part of morality as a whole, deeply rooted in every possible form of social life and inseparable therefore from every attainable social ideal. To think otherwise is not to take morality seriously.

---

[31] M. Sandel, *Liberalism and the Limits of Justice* (Cambridge: Cambridge Univ. Press, 1982), pp. 31–2.

[32] See T. Campbell, *The Left and Rights: A Conceptual Analysis of the Socialist Idea of Rights* (London: Routledge & Kegan Paul, 1983).

3
Incommensurability in Science and Ethics

L'Addition

LE CLIENT. Garçon, l'addition!

LE GARÇON. Voila. [*Il sort son crayon et note.*] Vous avez . . . deux œufs durs, un veau, un petit pois, une asperge, un fromage avec beurre, une amande verte, un café filtre, un téléphone.

LE CLIENT. . . . Et puis des cigarettes!

LE GARÇON. [*Il commence à composer.*] C'est ça même . . . des cigarettes . . . Alors ça fait . . .

LE CLIENT. N'insistez pas, mon ami, c'est inutile, vous ne réussirez jamais.

LE GARÇON. !!!

LE CLIENT. On ne vous a donc pas appris à l'école que c'est ma-thé-ma-ti-que-ment impossible d'additioner les choses d'espèce différente!

LE GARÇON. !!!

LE CLIENT. Enfin, tout de même, de qui se moque-t-on? . . . Il faut réellement être insensé pour oser essayer de tenter d'additionner' un veau avec des cigarettes, des cigarettes avec un café filtre, un café filtre avec une amande verte et des œufs durs avec des petits pois, des petits pois avec un téléphone. Pourquoi pas un petit pois avec un grand officier de la Légion d'Honneur, pendant que vous y êtes! [*Il se lève.*] Non, mon ami, croyez-moi, n'insistez pas, et vous fatiguez pas, ça ne donnerait rien, vous entendez, rien . . . pas même le pourboire.

[*Et il sort en emportant le rond de serviette à titre gracieux.*]

Jacques Prévert,
Histoires et d'autres Histoires
(Paris: Galimard, 1963).

Incommensurability is not, in itself, a particularly exciting idea. At its simplest, it is the thought that, in some respect, certain things cannot

This chapter was first published (in Italian) in 1990. I am grateful to Daniela Gobetti, Giandomenico Majone, Giovanni Mari, and Michael Otsuka for their comments on an earlier draft.

be ranked. Of course, everything can be compared with anything in *some* respect, so, secondly, an assertion of incommensurability could be the claim that, in some significant or relevant respect, things are not rankable. Or, thirdly, if two things are said to be incommensurable *overall*, it could simply be that they are rankable in too many different ways that cannot in turn be combined into a single way. Whichever of these is meant, to rank is to make some kind of a mistake. More formally, we can say that two items I_1 and I_2 are incommensurable if and only if, in respect of a given variable F, I_1 is neither superior nor inferior to I_2, nor are they equal in value (call this *specific incommensurability*); or they are incommensurable if and only if this is so in some significant or relevant respect or respects $F_{r...n}$ (call this *relevant incommensurability*); or, finally, if and only if the various ways of ordering them, $F_{1...n}$, are non-congruent (call this *overall incommensurability*).

The first sense is illustrated by the diversity of pleasures. It makes no sense (for those who appreciate both and are not utilitarians) to weigh the joy of listening to Mozart against the satisfaction of a good meal, in respect of pleasure or utility. Jacques Prévert's client illustrates the second by subverting our conventional acceptance of Pigou's 'measuring rod of money' as significant and relevant to restaurant life. (Other areas of life are, fortunately, as yet still immune to its rule and to the pretensions of cost-benefit and utilitarian styles of thinking.) We exhibit the third when we refuse to make an overall ranking of, say, the music of Bach and that of Beethoven.

Yet the idea of incommensurability has become a source of excitement in two areas of contemporary thought: the philosophy and history of science, on the one hand, and moral and political philosophy, on the other. Some have suggested that there is at least an analogy between the two areas, and thus perhaps the idea plays a similar role in both. Thus Kuhn makes much of the analogy between scientific and political revolutions, and Feyerabend says both that he is an anarchist and a follower of John Stuart Mill's liberalism; while W. Newton Smith can entitle his chapter on Kuhn 'From Revolutionary to Social Democrat' and that on Feyerabend 'The Passionate Liberal'.[1] In this chapter I shall argue that the idea of incommensur-

---

[1] Newton Smith, *The Rationality of Science* (London: Routledge & Kegan Paul, 1981), chaps. 5 and 6. I am much indebted to Newton Smith's arguments in the first part of this essay.

ability, in both domains, is exciting because of the reasons for which
it has been held to obtain, and that these differ across the two
domains of science and ethics. I shall also argue that in the former
they are poor reasons; but that in the latter they are compelling and
important.

I

The two philosophers of science who have made most of this notion
and have made the greatest impact with it are, of course, Thomas
Kuhn and Paul Feyerabend. Feyerabend observes that, for Kuhn,
paradigms between which incommensurability may hold incorporate (A) *concepts* which, when it does hold, cannot be brought into
the usual logical relations of inclusion, exclusion, and overlap; (B)
perceptions, which 'make us see things differently'; and (C) *methods*
(intellectual, as well as physical instruments of research) for setting
up research and evaluating its results.[2] And it is true that the early
Kuhn penned sentences like this: 'Practising in different worlds, the
two groups of scientists see different things when they look from the
same point in the same direction.'[3] By contrast, Feyerabend reports,
his 'own research started from certain problems in area A and
concerned theories only'—though he later resumed 'the more general approach',[4] whose results are to be found in *Against Method*,
where he defines incommensurability as holding when 'a discovery, a
statement, or an attitude' suspends some of the principles which
constitute and impose 'something like a "closure"' upon 'a point of
view (theory, framework, cosmos, mode of representation) . . .
whose elements (concepts, "facts", pictures) are built up in accordance with' such principles.[5]

Where Kuhn and Feyerabend may have continued to differ is over
the question of the interrelations between A and B. For Feyerabend,
'not all conceptual changes lead to changes in perception' for 'there
exist conceptual changes that never leave a trace in the
appearances':[6] thus one cannot automatically infer from 'popular
theories in science, such as the theory of relativity, or the idea of the

[2] Feyerabend, *Science in a Free Society* (London: NLB, 1978), p. 66.

[3] T. S. Kuhn, *The Structure of Scientific Revolutions* (Chicago, Ill.: Univ. of
Chicago Press, 2nd edn., 1970), p. 150.

[4] Feyerabend, *Science in a Free Society*, p. 67 and n.

[5] Id., *Against Method* (London: NLB, 1975), p. 269.   [6] Ibid.

motion of the earth, to cosmology and modes of perception'.[7] And indeed, in his 'Second Thoughts on Paradigms', Kuhn continues to stress what he sees as the intimate connections between community-relative conceptual structures and perception: 'shared examples can serve cognitive functions', he claims, namely to induce 'a learned perception of similarity'. Indeed, this idea of 'shared examples' was the originally intended meaning of 'paradigm', which he then 'unfortunately' allowed to expand.[8]

In short, we may conclude that, unlike Kuhn, Feyerabend for a while confined the scope of incommensurability to concepts and theories; and that Kuhn tends to assume, as Feyerabend does not, that the various elements—concepts, perceptions, and methods —between which they both claim it to hold, are tightly inter-dependent and mutually reinforcing.

We have thus far considered the scope of incommensurability, but the question of the alleged basis or reasons for it is of greater interest. Here it is unquestionably Feyerabend who is the bolder, or more reckless, of the two thinkers. For him, it arises when 'the conditions of concept formation in one theory forbids the formation of the basic concepts of the other',[9] or again when

the conditions of meaningfulness for the descriptive terms of one language (theory, point of view) do not permit the use of the descriptive terms of another language (theory, point of view); mere difference of meanings does not yet lead to incommensurability in my sense.[10]

Thus 'A-facts and B-facts cannot be put side by side, not even in memory', nor is it 'possible to *translate* language A into language B':[11] they both 'never make sense together'.[12] With incommensurability, in short, the differences between A and B go as deep as can be, for they result from 'a change of the very conditions that permit us to speak of objects, situations, events'. What we *mean* in so speaking is radically, that is incommensurably, transformed. In this way, when theories are incommensurable, 'they deal with different worlds . . . the change [from one world to another] has been brought about by a switch from one theory to another'.[13]

[7] Feyerabend, *Science in a Free Society*, p. 238.
[8] Kuhn, *The Essential Tension* (Chicago, Ill.: Univ. of Chicago Press, 1977), pp. 309 n., 318–19.   [9] Feyerabend, *Science in a Free Society*, p. 68 n.
[10] Id., *Farewell to Reason* (London: Verso, 1987), p. 272.
[11] Id., *Against Method*, p. 270.
[12] Id., *Science in a Free Society*, p. 70.   [13] Ibid.

This is heady stuff, and indeed the early Kuhn was inclined to write in similar ways (e.g. 'the proponents of competing paradigms practise their trades in different worlds'.[14]) But his later pronouncements are significantly more restrained. For Kuhn, unlike Feyerabend (whose irrationalism he finds 'vaguely obscene'),[15] the question of how, if theories are to be incommensurable, they could be incompatible was real, as was the need to make sense of scientific progress. Accordingly, the later Kuhn speaks, as Feyerabend does not, of the proponents of different incommensurable theories being like 'native speakers of different languages' between whom 'communication . . . goes on by translation'. That communication can be 'partial' and break down; indeed, Kuhn now asserts, there are 'significant limits to what the proponents of different theories can communicate to one another'.[16] Moreover, there are shared 'canons that make science scientific', which are '*the* shared basis for theory choice', though 'individually the criteria are imprecise' and 'when deployed together, they repeatedly prove to conflict with one another'.[17] These, in fact, constitute Kuhn's surviving reasons for sticking with incommensurability (continuing, as he does, to refer to 'duck-rabbits', Gestalt-switches, conversion, etc.): namely, that theory choice is influenced, but not uniquely determined, by values, that are in turn ambiguously interpretable and mutually conflicting, and are themselves without further justification; and that, in consequence, there is no paradigm-neutral standard for what counts as a good explanation.

It may help, at this point, if we try to list the reasons, or alleged reasons, for claiming that theories, or their components, can be incommensurable, in order of increasing boldness (or recklessness). First, there is (1) the claim, just alluded to, that scientists appeal to *values* in theory choice. As examples Kuhn cites five: accuracy, consistency, broad scope, simplicity, and fruitfulness. To these Newton Smith has added others: the preservation of past observational successes, track-record, inter-theory support, smoothness in coping with failures, and compatibility with well-grounded metaphysical beliefs.[18] Why should such values, or good-making features of theories, suggest incommensurability?

[14] Kuhn, *The Structure of Scientific Revolutions*, p. 150.
[15] I. Lakatos and A. Musgrave (eds.), *Criticism and the Growth of Knowledge* (Cambridge: Cambridge Univ. Press. 1970), p. 264.
[16] Kuhn, *The Essential Tension*, p. 338.   [17] Ibid. 324–5, 322.
[18] Newton Smith, *The Rationality of Science*, pp. 226–32.

I suggest that there are three such reasons, but they do not, even together, add up to a good reason. The first is that values are not uniquely interpretable: 'individuals may legitimately differ about their application to concrete cases'—indeed this 'individual variability in the application of shared values may serve functions essential to science'.[19] The second is that they conflict: scientists will differ about the 'relative weights to be accorded to these and to other criteria when several are deployed together'.[20] The third is that they are held to be without justification: in Kuhn's words, 'the experience of scientists provides no philosophical justification for the values they deploy (such justification would solve the problem of induction)'.[21] But the first two reasons together only serve to make Kuhn's familiar, if important, point that for practising scientists there is no '*shared* algorithm of choice'.[22] At most, the second implies that, for them, theories may manifest 'overall incommensurability', since *ex ante* they are rankable in too many ways that cannot be combined into a single way. *Ex post*, however, the problem dissolves: subsequent developments sooner or later select out which criterion or criteria turn out to have been the best indicator(s) of progress.

These first two reasons certainly do not, as Kuhn seems to think, show that theory-choice cannot be rationally grounded, which is the third (alleged) reason for incommensurability, namely, that all we can say is that theory-choice goes according to 'different sets of shared values'[23] and 'the decision of the scientific group'.[24] To say this is to deny that these values have a rational basis as reliable, if fallible, inductive indicators of increasing verisimilitude and of scientific progress, as measured by observational success. Neither Kuhn nor Feyerabend, nor anyone else, has given any good reason for denying this. At best, Kuhn has pointed to the crucial role of *judgement* in interpreting, applying, and weighing these values and, importantly, to the role of the scientific community's traditions and practices of training, debate, and mutual monitoring in developing, testing, and combining individual scientists' powers of judgement. But, once again, Kuhn has not shown that what makes for good judgement is just a matter of community decision.

The second alleged reason for incommensurability of theories is what is claimed to be variation in the standards which specify what

19 Kuhn, *The Essential Tension*, p. 322.
20 Ibid. 324.   21 Ibid. 335.   22 Ibid. 331.   23 Ibid.
24 Kuhn, *The Structure of Scientific Revolutions*, p. 170.

counts as a good explanation. This may be thought to be a consequence of variance of values, which we have already considered, or it may go beyond this to cover the 'method, problem-field and standards of solution accepted by any mature scientific community at any given time'.[25] So, Kuhn writes,

as the problems change, so, often, does the standard that distinguishes a real scientific solution from a mere metaphysical speculation, word game or mathematical play. The normal scientific tradition that emerges from a scientific revolution is not only incompatible but often actually incommensurable with that which has gone before.[26]

But this is a poor argument. For, first, the examples Kuhn cites appear to show, rather, shifts in assumptions about what is to be explained. And second, and more deeply, the argument trades on an ambiguity, or worse an equation, between 'explanation' as a psychological or 'subjective' category (whatever is considered to solve puzzle X by scientist Y) and explanation as an evaluative notion (distinguishing between success and failure, about which Y may be mistaken). In short, successful revolutionaries (Galileo, Newton, Faraday, etc.) have generated results that bear on the observation, prediction, and control of nature, to which their Old Regime forebears, whatever their views about the scope and nature of explanation, could not but attend. Doubtless they had different views about what constitutes explanation and doubtless they drew the boundary between science and metaphysics in a different place, but they shared with their successors the cognitive interests and goals in terms of which those successors eventually come to win the argument. As Richard Rorty admits, 'Galileo, so to speak, won the argument' with Cardinal Bellarmine, but this is not, as he suggests, because Galileo *created* 'the notion of "scientific values"',[27] except in the sense that he detached them from others with which they were previously indistinguishably fused. What was new was the focus on observational success, predictive accuracy, and so on, irrespective of theological and cosmological warrant. Of course, who 'wins the argument' may only emerge in time, long after the revolution is over, but the reasons for declaring the winners are not themselves just another product of the Revolution itself.

25 Ibid. 103.   26 Ibid.
27 R. Rorty, *Philosophy and the Mirror of Nature* (Oxford: Blackwell, 1980), p. 331.

I turn, finally, to the third, and boldest, alleged reason for incommensurability, namely (3) the thesis of *meaning variance*. This is a thesis abandoned in any radical form by Kuhn but one to which Feyerabend appears ever more closely wedded. It is a position which, however often it is refuted, continues to have a remarkably seductive power, even over philosophers.

At its weakest, (3*a*), it is only theoretical terms that are affected. On this account the meaning of observational terms remains constant while that of theoretical terms may change, if there is a corresponding change in what Carnap calls the 'meaning postulates' that fix their meaning. Under a radical or dramatic theory change, as from Newton to Einstein, this would occur, so that 'mass' would have a different meaning in the two theories, and Einstein would no longer be disagreeing with Newton in respect of its invariance.

A stronger version, (3*b*), still allows that the meaning of observational terms can remain constant, but, appealing to a holistic theory of meaning, holds that the meaning of all theoretical terms necessarily changes with every theory change. On this account, the whole of Newton's and Einstein's theories are incommensurable, and therefore non-conflicting, at the theoretical level, though they could be incompatible at the observational level.

The strongest version, Feyerabend's, (3*c*), abandons the distinction between theoretical and observational levels and the assumption of a theory-neutral observation language. On this account, again assuming a holistic theory of meaning, every theory change entails meaning change in all terms, and hence neither theories nor their components can be compared, judged compatible or incompatible, superior or inferior or equal to one another.

None of (3*a*), (3*b*), and (3*c*) has yet been coherently defended. (3*a*) relies on the separate identification of 'meaning postulates' in a theory, and both (3*a*) and (3*b*) on the satisfactory drawing of an observation/theory distinction—neither of which can be done. It is, in any case, (3*c*) that constitutes the full-blown case for incommensurability, and that case is in poor shape. To assert incommensurability thus understood is, as Feyerabend admits, to deny translatability across putatively incommensurable theories. But, if this denial is meant seriously, what grounds do we have for regarding a putatively incommensurable theory as a theory at all? Is it not incoherent to 'tell us that Galileo had "incommensurable" notions *and then go on to* *describe them at length*'?[28] To do the latter, one must be able to make sense of others' (e.g. Galileo's) utterances, beliefs, and desires so that they come out as intelligible (that is, as either true or explicable). For this to be possible, there must be a bridgehead across theories of common reference, of a concept of truth and related notions, and indeed of a vast fund of shared assumptions about what it is reasonable to believe.[29]

It might seem that the above requirements are too strong. Might a scientist (Galileo, say) not be able to recognize as a theory another that was so *advanced* (Einstein's, say) that he could not understand it (e.g. because it employed a branch of mathematics higher than any he could grasp)? But this would, so to speak, be *one-way* incommensurability, for Einstein, in this case, could, *ex hypothesi*, both understand and rank the two theories. Incommensurability, to do the work its advocates expect of it, must be a reflexive, two-way relation: incommensurable theories must be mutually unintelligible. Notice, moreover, that the supposition of one-way incommensurability here entertained itself presupposes the idea of scientific progress, which the advocates of two-way incommensurability are precisely concerned to debunk.

So (3c)—the full version of incommensurability as radical meaning variance—fails too. The trouble with it is its dependence on a holistic theory of meaning that has been cut adrift from reference and truth, and makes meaning dependent on a particular stock of beliefs. Were it coherently stateable, its effect would be to render unintelligible 'what makes science scientific', the convergence of theories and the possibility of scientific progress. None of this would be an objection, however—indeed for some it would be an advantage—if this version of incommensurability could be coherently stated in the first place.

From all of which I conclude that the notion of incommensurability, in any form, in science has not yet been advanced for any good reasons. Theories are not specifically incommensurable, with respect to explanatory power, or any of the other science-relative values we have considered. They do not display relevant incommensurability: no one, from within science, can claim that such rankings of theories

[28] H. Putnam, *Reason, Truth and History* (Cambridge: Cambridge Univ. Press, 1981), p. 114.
[29] See M. Hollis and S. Lukes (eds.), *Rationality and Relativism* (Oxford: Blackwell, 1982), esp. the essays by Hollis, Lukes, and Newton Smith.

are irrelevant from some standpoint from which they appear unrankable. And, as we have seen, *ex ante* conflicts between multiple value-rankings are dissolved *ex post*. Therefore, the idea of incommensurability has nothing to contribute to the explication of theory choice or to the solution of other issues in the philosophy of science. There is, in short, no good reason for doubting that scientific theories can in principle be judged to be better or worse or equivalent to each other.

II

Among certain Anglo-Saxon anti-utilitarian and liberal moral and political philosophers the idea of incommensurability of 'values' has, in recent years also been a persistent theme. In his *Two Concepts of Liberty*, Sir Isaiah Berlin wrote:

> If the claims of two (or more than two) types of liberty prove incompatible in a particular case, and if this is an instance of the clash of values at once absolute and incommensurable, it is better to face this intellectually uncomfortable fact than to ignore it, or automatically attribute it to some deficiency on our part which could be eliminated by an increase in skill or knowledge; or, what is worse still, suppress one of the competing values altogether by pretending that it is identical with its rival—and so end by distorting both.[30]

Bernard Williams endorses Berlin's view that there is no 'common currency' in which certain 'gains and losses of value can be computed, that values, or at least the most basic values, are not only plural but in a real sense incommensurable' and argues that 'the claim that values are incommensurable does say something true and important'.[31] For John Rawls, liberalism as a political doctrine supposes that 'there are many conflicting and incommensurable conceptions of the good, each compatible with the full rationality of human persons': indeed, this plurality of incommensurable conceptions of the good' is a 'fact of modern democratic culture' and 'must be taken as given'.[32] Charles Larmore writes that 'we have an

---

[30] Introduction to Berlin's *Four Essays on Liberty* (Oxford: Oxford Univ. Press, 1969), p. 1.

[31] Williams, 'Conflicts of Values', in his *Moral Luck* (Cambridge: Cambridge Univ. Press, 1981), pp. 76–7.

[32] Rawls, 'Justice as Fairness: Political not Metaphysical', *Philosophical and Public Affairs* 14 (1985), pp. 248, 249.

allegiance to several different moral principles that urge independent claims upon us (we cannot plausibly see the one as a means for promoting the other)' and that 'the ultimate sources of moral value are not one, but many'. He therefore advocates that we 'suspend the monistic assumption underlying so much of moral theory' and acknowledge that 'not everything is good and right to the extent that it is commensurable with respect to any single standard'.[33]

According to Charles Taylor, 'Integrity, charity, liberation, and the like stand out as worthy of pursuit in a special way, incommensurable with other goals we might have, such as the pursuit of wealth, or comfort, or the approval of those who surround us'; 'admiration and contempt are bound up with our sense of the qualitative contrasts in our lives, of their being modes of life, activities, feelings, qualities, which are incommensurably higher'.[34] (This last phrase is either self-contradictory or paradoxical. If the latter, perhaps the paradox can be resolved by the thought that from *within* certain modes of life, etc., certain others appear not fit to be compared.) Amartya Sen allows the possibility of an approach to value conflict which, 'faced with an irreducible conflict of compelling principles . . . may admit both the superiority of one alternative over the other and the converse'.[35] For Joseph Raz, incommensurability obtains where, when an agent is faced with only two options, 'one cannot compare the value of the options, one can only judge their value each one on its own'. He also writes of 'constitutive incommensurabilities' which

play their part in conventions of fidelity to relationships and pursuits. Being engaged in a pursuit or a relationship includes belief that certain options are not comparable in value . . . Regarding a particular relationship as a proper subject for an exchange damages or even destroys it.

Thus it is 'impoverishing to compare the value of a marriage with an increase in salary. It diminishes one's potentiality as a human being to put a value on one's friendship in terms of improved living conditions.'[36] Finally, Thomas Nagel, who has explored this issue

[33] Larmore, *Patterns of Moral Complexity* (Cambridge: Cambridge Univ. Press, 1987), pp. 138, 10.
[34] Taylor, 'The Diversity of Goods', in his *Philosophical Papers*, ii. *Philosophy and the Human Sciences* (Cambridge: Cambridge Univ. Press, 1985), pp. 236–7, 240.
[35] Sen, *Ethics and Economics* (Oxford: Blackwell, 1987), p. 66.
[36] Raz, *The Morality of Freedom* (Oxford: Clarendon Press, 1986), pp. 364, 355–6, 353.

most deeply, argues that, when 'faced with conflicting and incommensurable claims we still have to do something—even if it is only to do nothing', but the fact that action must be unitary does not imply that justification must be, and that, unless it is, 'nothing can be either right or wrong and all decisions under conflict are arbitrary'. For Nagel, 'values come from a number of viewpoints, some more personal than others, which cannot be reduced to a single denominator'.[37]

What does this battery of assertions amount to? Notice, first, that several different items are here said to be incommensurable, and that some of these exemplify the bases or criteria by which we judge what is of value, and others what we take to *have* value: thus they refer variously to alternative 'values', 'conceptions of the good', 'goals', and 'claims' upon moral agents, but also to 'alternatives' or 'options' facing them, to 'relationships and pursuits, and to 'modes of life, activities, feelings, qualities'. Notice, too, that here—as opposed to the idea of scientific incommensurability—what is incommensurable is assumed to be in conflict. Moreover, some of these writers appear to be denying cardinal commensurability only (with respect to a 'common currency' or 'any single standard' or a 'single denominator'); others seem to be denying both cardinal and ordinal commensurability—the very possibility, in certain cases, of consistently ordering moral and political alternatives.

As in the case of alleged incommensurability in science, there are several different ideas in play here that, likewise, range from the cautious to the bold, or reckless. Let us begin with the simple idea of incomplete ordering. In this sense, life is full of insignificant or marginal incommensurabilities,[38] cases where we just don't know which of two options we value more. I may just not know whether I value going for a walk more or less highly than reading a book or that I value them equally (and that I do either or neither does not show that I do).[39] As Raz observes, marginal incommensurability creates 'pockets of breakdown of comparability' which, however, pose no threat, say, to a consequentialist who believes, among other things, that all reasons are rankable in strength or weight or importance.[40] But, the consequentialist will argue, once the choice becomes signi-

---

[37] Nagel, 'The Fragmentation of Value', in his *Mortal Questions* (Cambridge: Cambridge Univ. Press, 1979), pp. 134, 138.

[38] Raz, *The Morality of Freedom*, p. 328.

[39] Ibid.   [40] Ibid. 268–9.

ficant, that is, where the reasons for them are weighty and different, that the options must be rankable. But why? The only reason for holding that non-trivial choices must be between rankable options is that one's reductionist meta-ethical assumptions, or prejudices, dictate that it must be so, that diverse kinds of good must be reducible to a homogeneous descriptive magnitude (such as utility) and subject to a complete and transitive ordering.

There are several reasons for holding that it is not so. Consider, first, the case of moral dilemmas. Sartre's young man caught between the claims of consoling his mother and joining the Free French, Antigone between those of family loyalty and Creon's law, Agamemnon between saving his fleet and his daughter, Weber's heroic politician between the Sermon on the Mount and the 'dignity of manly conduct'—and most of us at some time or another in less exalted and tragic circumstances—face the pull of conflicting demands where it looks as if neither choice is unambiguously right and either involves the committing of an uncancelled wrong. It is always possible, of course, to treat such cases as opportunities for consequentialist calculation, on the assumption that the question 'what is the best thing to do, all things considered?' has a right answer that is in principle ascertainable. It is also possible to treat them as subject to universalizable categorical principles or maxims of action of a formal kind that would clearly specify what is right. The trouble is that each of these modes of treatment eliminates the essential feature of the cases in question that requires articulation: namely, the conflict of obligations, that clash of right with right where whatever one does cannot but cause a wrong.

Consider, next, the cases, raised by Raz, of what he calls 'constitutive incommensurabilities'. The idea here is that the commitments, loyalties, and obligations we have to certain relationships and activities that matter to us precisely involve 'the belief that certain options are not comparable in value':

My claim . . . is that belief in incommensurability is itself a qualification for having certain relations. The attitude of mind which constitutes such a belief is analogous to attitudes such as respect for the other person, which are commonly accepted as prerequisites for a capacity for these relations.

Thus, for example, 'only those who hold the view that friendship is neither better nor worse than money or other commodities are *capable* of having friends'.[41] To assume commensurability between certain options is itself evidence of the weakening or absence of those very relationships, or else a degraded simulacrum of them. Unfortunately, Raz distracts us from the point of this very interesting argument by confusing non-rankability with non-exchangeability. Ranking friends and money does not imply exchanging money for friendship, or being prepared to do so. Doing the second may mean doing the first, but the argument in question concerns the first, not the second. And indeed, there does seem to be something in the idea that the very thought of comparing the value of certain activities and relationships with certain alternatives is evidence of a failure of those who think it to live up to them.

Thirdly, consider alternatives that are yet broader in scope: modes of life, ways of interpreting and responding to the world and acting within it. Taylor invites us to consider a life devoted to the pursuit of personal integrity, or Mother Teresa as exemplifying 'a Christian model of *agape*', or what is involved in a movement for colonial liberation. One could add other examples: the Hindu world-renouncer,[42] the Evangelical soldier of God, the Muslim fundamentalist, the militant nationalist, the epicurean, the ecologist. Each of these is expressed in 'languages of qualitative contrast' which embody the sense that 'some ways of living and acting have a special status' and 'stand out above others' while others are 'debased'.[43] There is no way of ranking such modes of life and the virtues they encourage other than from within one or another of them, or from some standpoint, such as utilitarianism or Kantianism, that makes a special claim to objectivity or impartiality. But these also express particular modes of life and their special claims are precisely what the modes of life they would evaluate put in question.

I have here presented various kinds of alternative that are held to have value, between which a choice is indubitably significant, and I have offered reasons why they can be unrankable in respect of their value. What is the source of this incommensurability? The answer to this lies, I suggest, in what Thomas Nagel calls the 'fragmentation of

[41] Raz, *The Morality of Freedom*, pp. 356, 351, 352.

[42] See L. Dumont, *Homo Hierarchicus: Essai sur le système des castes* (Paris: Gallimard, 1966) (trans as: *Homo Hierarchicus: The Caste System and its Implications*) (London: Paladin, Granada, 1972).

[43] Taylor, 'The Diversity of Goods', p. 236.

value', John Rawls the 'fact of pluralism',[44] and Charles Larmore the 'heterogeneity of morality'—though the trouble with this last phrase is its suggestion that 'morality' is a domain whose boundaries are uncontested: better to say that the heterogeneity or pluralism or fragmentation characterize evaluation in general. They identify what monism denies: that our judgments about what has value are not located within a single scheme of values but are made from various irreducibly diverse standpoints.

This is what Max Weber saw when he wrote that 'the various value spheres of the world stand in irreconcilable conflict with one another'. What is sacred may not be beautiful; indeed, it may be sacred because it is not. Since Nietzsche, Weber wrote, we know that

> something can be beautiful, not only in spite of the aspect in which it is not good, but rather in that very aspect. You will find this expressed earlier in the *Fleurs du Mal*, as Baudelaire named his volume of poems. It is commonplace to observe that something may be true although it is not beautiful and not holy and not good. Indeed it may be true in precisely those aspects. But all these are only the most elementary cases of the struggle that the gods of the various orders and values are engaged in.[45]

And within the ethical sphere itself, contested though its boundaries are, we can be drawn in irreconcilable ways. On the one hand, there are compelling moral demands of an impersonal or impartial kind that are couched in thin ethical concepts that abstract from context, such as maximizing of happiness or welfare or well-being, or the maxims of the categorical imperative or the protection of rights. Such demands may themselves pull us in opposing ways. But, on the other hand, there are also demands of a more personal or partial kind, couched in the thicker, more contextual concepts that express our commitments to particular relationships, or communities or activities.[46] And these, in turn may conflict both with one another and with the demands of more impersonal moralities.

---

[44] Rawls, 'The Idea of an Overlapping Consensus', *Oxford Journal of Legal Studies* 7/1 (1987), 4. Rawls characterizes the 'fact of pluralism' as the diversity of general and comprehensive doctrines, and . . . the plurality of conflicting, and indeed incommensurable, conceptions of the meaning, value and purpose of human life (or what I shall call for short 'conceptions of the good') affirmed by the citizens of democratic societies (p. 4).

[45] Weber, 'Science as a Vocation', in H. H. Gerth and C. W. Mills (eds.), *From Max Weber* (London: Routledge & Kegan Paul, 1948), pp. 147–8.

[46] See the writings of Alasdair MacIntyre and Bernard Williams for reflections on this contrast between types of morality and moral language.

This diversity of standpoints from which moral demands come has two consequences. The first is that what is valuable about what we value cannot be identified in terms of a single category: the idea that there is a 'descriptive homogeneity of goods' is, as Sen puts it, an 'arbitrary requirement'.[47] The second is that the diversity of standpoints explains the possibility that not all of these diverse goods can be ranked. They may be *specifically* commensurable, that is, from one specific value standpoint—as when E. M. Forster ranked the obligations of friendship above those of patriotism, or when one judges the claims of one's own children to outweigh a larger donation to relief of poverty in the Third World, or vice versa, or when the achievement of a measure of well-being outranks, say, the fulfilment of a person's or collectivity's goals or commitments, or the promotion of their freedom, or when rights 'trump' utility. But a wider, or truer, view of the moral complexity of the choice between such alternatives suggests that these rankings are, in one sense, *irrelevant*, since the *relevant* standpoint is one which incorporates the two, or several, standpoints from which the alternatives in conflict are seen to have value. From that reflexive and inclusive standpoint they may exhibit *relevant incommensurability*.

Of course, the fact that alternatives may be rankable multi-dimensionally—that is, along independent scales—does not itself entail incommensurability. One might solve the problem by constructing social welfare or social choice functions that are consistent and complete, ranging over sets of alternatives whose ranking *vis à vis* one another is a matter of 'balancing': one such combination is taken to be 'on balance' superior, inferior, or equal to another. But, as Sen has justly remarked, although the case for such 'balanced complete ordering' is strong in the case of institutional public policy-making, which 'must at some stage, require unambiguous instruction' (since something must be done even if it is nothing), it does not follow that 'there must be *adequate reason* for choosing one course rather than another'. The mere need for a decision does not resolve the conflict or show that the alternatives thus ordered are commensurable—that is that there are adequate reasons for judging them superior, inferior, or equal to one another.

Another possibility is that an overall ranking across the independent scales can yield a determinate solution by 'dominance reasoning'

[47] Sen, *Ethics and Economics*, p. 67.

where one alternative is better than another in all respects. But such orderings are partial and depend on the congruence of parallel evaluations from the different value standpoints. In the absence of such special conditions, evaluations from diverse standpoints will exhibit *overall incommensurability* where those standpoints cannot be combined to form a single, coherent picture. Pluralists assert, and monists deny, that morality is heterogeneous and that valuation in general is fragmented in just this way.

III

In the first part of this chapter I argued that in science, theory choice is guided by values whose interpretation is contested and which sometimes conflict with one another. Why, in that case, should the pluralism just endorsed for valuation in general not apply to science in particular, thereby implying that scientific theories can be incommensurable?

The reason is that the values that guide theory choice are just that—guides. They serve as uncertain and fallible clues to scientific success. And *that* is not generally subject to disputes from diverse value standpoints; it is, on the contrary, what justifies scientists in judging and comparing theories according to these various, not always congruent values. For they furnish criteria for particular theory choices that, inductively, can generally be relied on to satisfy what Mary Hesse has called the general 'pragmatic criterion' for the long-term acceptability of theory complexes taken as wholes, and if they fail to satisfy it, it is because the latter overrides them. This general criterion is 'the ability to use science to learn the environment, and to make predictions whose results we can rely on not to surprise us'.[48] It is over this underlying and overriding value of predictive success and hence control of the external world that scientists unite (though of course it does not capture all that they do *qua* scientists), and it is by means of it that their various value-guided theory choices are eventually judged. What can make alternatives incommensurable is the ineliminable plurality of standpoints from which their value can be described and compared. What makes science scientific is the common evaluative standpoint that scientists share over time, whatever values may at any given time divide them.

[48] M. Hesse, *Revolutions and Reconstructions in the Philosophy of Science* (Brighton: Harvester, 1980), pp. 190, xviii–xix.

4
Equality and Liberty: Must they Conflict?

It is often said that equality and liberty conflict and sometimes that they conflict irreconcilably. Such claims can be understood sociologically: as generalisations about the dangers posed by the advance or pursuit of the one for the survival or the prospects of the other.

This is how Tocqueville memorably presented the issue in his *Democracy in America*. He thought of the advance of equality as irresistible and cumulative:

It is impossible to believe that equality will not eventually find its way into the political world as it does everywhere else. To conceive of men remaining forever unequal upon a single point, yet equal on all others, is impossible; they must come in the end to be equal upon all.[1]

Tocqueville saw equality—and more particularly equality of political resources and power, or democracy—as posing several likely dangers to the survival of liberty: mass conformity, majority tyranny, where a majority of citizens oppresses individuals or minorities or even subverts or abandons democracy itself, and a kind of mass-based despotism in which we see

an innumerable multitude of men all equal and alike, necessarily endeavouring to procure the petty and paltry pleasures with which they glut their lives. Each of them, living apart, is as a stranger to the fate of all the rest,—his children and his private friends constitute to him the whole of mankind; as for the rest of his fellow-citizens, he is close to them, but he sees them not, he touches them, but he feels them not; he exists but in himself and for himself alone; and if his kindred still remain to him, he may be said at any rate to have lost his country.

This chapter was first published in 1990. I must thank David Held for encouraging me to improve it.

   [1] A. de Tocqueville, *Democracy in America*, 2 vols. (New York: Schocken Books, 1961), i. pp. 46–7.

Above such men there stands 'an immense and tutelary power, which takes upon itself alone to secure their gratifications, and to watch over their fate' and which 'renders the exercise of the free agency of man less useful and less frequent, it circumscribes the will within a narrower range, and gradually robs a man of all the uses of himself'.[2] This striking and complex sociological analysis had a deep impact on nineteenth-century liberalism (through John Stuart Mill) and (especially in this last aspect) on twentieth-century theories of mass democracy, from Ortega y Gasset to William Kornhauser —alongside Tocqueville's suggestive ideas about how these supposed egalitarian threats of liberty could be counteracted, by the happy existence of favouring economic, political, constitutional, and cultural conditions.

Liberty can also threaten equality. It is a commonplace of Marxist historiography to stress the ways in which the practice of bourgeois freedoms and the formal framework of rights that protect them, both generate and conceal class inequalities. Thus Georges Lefebvre interpreted the *Déclaration des droits de l'homme* as proclaiming a formal equality of rights, centering on property, the better to prevent the according of real, social equality to the poor and disinherited. As Albert Soboul eloquently put it,

If, in the Declaration, equality was associated with freedom, this was more a statement of principle, legitimizing the downfall of the aristocracy and the abolition of noble privilege, than an authorization of popular aspirations. By placing the right of property among the indefeasible natural rights, the members of the Constituent Assembly introduced a contradiction into their proposals which they could not surmount: the retention of slavery and of property qualifications made this manifest. Voting rights were granted in accordance with a predetermined financial contribution, in other words, according to affluence and wealth. Thus the rights which the constitutional bourgeoisie had recognized as belonging to man in general and citizens in particular were really only valid for the bourgeoisie; for the mass of 'passive' citizens they remained theoretical abstractions.[3]

For such analyses of the inegalitarian consequences of 'formal' bourgeois rights and freedoms, there was of course ample warrant in the classical marxist canon, from *The Jewish Question* onwards: as Marx and Engels wrote in the *Communist Manifesto*, 'By freedom is meant, under the present bourgeois conditions of production, free

---

[2] Ibid. ii. 380–1.
[3] A. Soboul, *The French Revolution 1787–1799*, trans. A. Forrest, 2 vols. (London: NLB, 1974), i. p. 15.

trade, free selling and buying.'[4] Not that the general idea was either original or unique to Marxism. It has long been known that freedom for the pike spells death for the minnows; as Clermont-Tonnerre remarked to the Constituent Assembly,

To say that the equality of rights amounts to possessing an equal right to a very unequal portion of liberty and property belonging to everyone, is to utter an abstraction of such thinness and such silliness as to be absolutely useless.[5]

It is, moreover, a truth not lost on contemporary liberal democratic theorists, such as Charles Lindblom and Robert Dahl.[6] Dahl, after examining Tocqueville's analysis of equality's threats to liberty, comments that we must also 'strive to reduce the adverse effects on democracy and political equality that result when economic liberty produces great inequality in the distribution of resources and thus, directly and indirectly, of power'.[7]

These sociological questions, however, intriguing and important as they are, are not directly the subject of this chapter. They embody hypotheses about complex causal connections between specific social processes and practices, the test of which is, of course, empirical and requires a comparative assessment of the evidence from different societies. Nor will I address the weighty matter of this century's experience of socialism and its bearing on the momentous question of what limits basic political liberties, on the one hand, and economic freedoms, on the other, may set to the realizability of social equality. Neither will I here examine the Marxist tradition's fateful tendency to treat basic political liberties as merely 'formal' (see Chapters 9 and 10). This is a congenital defect of Marxism in particular, not of egalitarianism in general. Here I am concerned rather with the claim, often made these days, that there is something about the very 'values' of equality and liberty that renders them incompatible, even 'incommensurable'—that, in short, equality and liberty *must* conflict and that they *cannot* coexist.

Those who make this claim sometimes do so in order to illustrate a general point about the plurality of values and the dangerous illusion

[4] Marx and Engels, *The Communist Manifesto, Selected Works*, 2 vols. (Moscow: Foreign Languages Publishing House, 1962), i. p. 48.

[5] Quoted in M. Ozouf, 'Egalité', in F. Furet and M. Ozouf (eds.), *Dictionnaire critique de la Révolution Française* (Paris: Flammarion, 1988), p. 704.

[6] See C. E. Lindblom, *Politics and Markets* (New York: Basic Books, 1977), chap. 13 and R. A. Dahl, *A Preface to Economic Democracy* (Cambridge: Polity, 1985).

[7] Dahl, *A Preface to Economic Democracy*, p. 51.

of supposing that it can feasibly be overcome. 'Conflicts of value', Sir Isaiah Berlin suggests, are 'an intrinsic, irremovable element in human life': we are

faced with choices between ends equally ultimate, and claims equally absolute, the realisation of some of which must inevitably involve the sacrifice of others . . . The ends of men are many and not all of them are in principle compatible with each other.

Thus,

The extent of a man's, or a people's liberty to choose to live as they desire must be weighed against the claims of many other values, of which equality, or justice, or security, or public order are perhaps the most obvious examples.[8]

'Marxism,' according to Leszek Kolakowski, 'was a dream offering the prospect of a society of perfect unity, in which all human aspirations would be fulfilled, and all values reconciled' but '[c]onflicts inevitably arise between freedom and equality' and such conflicts can 'only be mitigated by compromises and partial solutions'.[9]

On the other hand, the point of saying this may be a point about *these* values. Interestingly, it seems to be only libertarian anti-egalitarians who have this point in mind, rather than liberals or egalitarians. Thus, for Milton and Rose Friedman, 'equality of outcome is in clear conflict with liberty'; there is 'a fundamental conflict between the *ideal* of "fair shares" or of its precursor, "to each according to his needs" and the *ideal* of personal liberty'.[10] More generally, for Robert Nozick, 'no end-state principle or distributional patterned principle of justice can be continuously realized without continuous interference with people's lives'.[11] More generally still, for Friedrich Hayek, the very term ' "social justice" is wholly devoid of meaning or content' in 'a society of free men whose members are allowed to use their own knowledge for their own purposes' because 'the ubiquitous dependence on other people's power, which the enforcement of any image of "social justice"

---

[8] Berlin, 'Two Concepts of Liberty', in his *Four Essays on Liberty* (Oxford: Oxford Univ. Press, 1969), pp. 167, 168–9, 170.

[9] Kolakowski, *Main Currents of Marxism*, 3 vols. (Oxford: Clarendon Press, 1978), iii. p. 508.

[10] Friedman and Friedman, *Free to Choose* London: Secker and Warburg, 1980), pp. 128, 135.

[11] Nozick, *Anarchy, State and Utopia* (Oxford: Blackwell, 1974), p. 163.

creates, inevitably destroys that freedom of personal decisions on which all morals must rest'.[12]

Conversely, those who deny that equality and liberty conflict, or that the conflict is irreconcilable, may either be relying on a general point about the possibility of reconciling values or restricting themselves to a specific one about the congruence of equality and liberty. In the former vein, Condorcet thought of nature as linking together 'by an unbreakable chain, truth, happiness and virtue' and as uniting 'the progress of enlightenment and that of liberty, virtue and respect for the natural rights of man': these,

the only real goods, so often separated from each other that they are even believed to be incompatible, should, on the contrary, become inseparable, as soon as enlightenment has reached a certain level simultaneously among a large number of nations and has penetrated throughout the whole mass of a great people, whose language is universally known and whose commercial relations embrace the whole globe.[13]

In the same vein, and making specific reference to the Enlightenment in this connection, Jürgen Habermas, in our own time, attacks what he calls 'decisionism' and the assumption that there is 'an impenetrable pluralism of apparently ultimate value orientations' and defends the view that 'there is a universal core of moral intuition in all times and in all societies' that stems 'from the conditions of symmetry and reciprocal recognition which are unavoidable presuppositions of communicative action' (see Chapter 11). Indeed, '[i]nsofar as we master the means for the construction of the ideal speech situation, we can conceive the ideas of truth, freedom and justice, which interpenetrate each other—although only of course as ideas'.[14]

In the latter vein, many contemporary liberal thinkers, notably John Rawls, propose 'a reconciliation of liberty and equality'.[15] For Rawls, liberty and equality are conflicting values that can be 'lexically ordered', furnishing, as Amy Gutmann has put it, 'an integration

---

[12] Hayek, *Law, Legislation and Liberty*, 3 vols. (Chicago, Ill. and London: Univ. of Chicago Press, 1976), ii. *The Mirage of Social Justice*, pp. 96, 99.

[13] A.-N. de Condorcet, *Esquisse d'un tableau historique des progrès de l'esprit humain* (Paris: Vrin, 1970), pp. 228, 9.

[14] Habermas, *Autonomy and Solidarity: Interviews*, ed. and introd. by Peter Dews (London: Verso, 1986), pp. 206–7.

[15] Rawls, *A Theory of Justice* (Oxford: Clarendon Press, 1972), p. 204.

of liberal and socialist principle' that appeals to left liberals.[16] 'Freedom as equal liberty' (the 'complete system of the liberties of equal citizenship') is basic; given that, the Difference Principle maximizing benefits to the least advantaged, and the equalizing of life chances are required for justice to be done. Whatever remaining inequalities the latter conditions permit or generate will constitute no restriction or diminution of liberty overall, for the equal liberties of the less fortunate or successful are, on this account, simply of less value to them but equal liberties none the less.[17] Others go further and argue for the view that 'freedom and equality, far from being opposed ideals, actually coincide'.[18] R. H. Tawney, Harold Laski, and John Dewey argued in this way. But to such arguments, libertarians typically respond, as Hayek did to Dewey, with accusations of conceptual 'jugglery'.[19] I shall, in this chapter, offer an argument of a somewhat similar sort; and, as will soon be evident, I shall roundly claim that, as far as conceptual jugglery goes, it is the accusers who stand accused.

With the general proposition that values may conflict irreconcilably I have no quarrel, at least on one interpretation of that claim.[20] I do, however, doubt that it can ever be illuminating or perspicuous to speak of 'liberty' and 'equality' as instances of such irreconcilably conflicting values.

What I shall seek to show here is that there are various senses in which it can be claimed that equality and liberty are values in conflict, but that in none of these senses does this formulation adequately express what is meant. In each case the simplistic formula 'equality *versus* liberty' demands to be interpreted and, upon interpretation, turns out to obscure what can, and therefore should, be more accurately expressed. The first case is an instance of ideological sophistry which, while trading on our ordinary understanding of these notions, seeks to persuade us by artful redefinition of their meanings. The second deploys the economists' idea of a 'trade-off' as

[16] Gutmann, 'The Central Role of Rawls's Theory', *Dissent* (Summer 1989), p. 339. According to Gutmann, and I agree, Rawls offers 'a liberalism for the least advantaged, a liberalism that pays moral tribute to the socialist critique' (ibid.).

[17] Rawls, *A Theory of Justice*, pp. 204–5.

[18] R. Norman, *Free and Equal: A Philosophical Examination of Political Values* (Oxford: Oxford Univ. Press, 1987), p. 133.

[19] Hayek, *The Constitution of Liberty* (London: Routledge & Kegan Paul, 1960), p. 424.   [20] See Chaps. 1 and 3, above.

applied to equality and liberty but rests upon a misreading of the internal complexity of each and of the relations between them. The third purports to characterize two contending value-standpoints in the contemporary world and prevalent in both East and West[21] —namely, egalitarianism and libertarianism[22]—but fails to capture what is essentially at issue between them. I shall conclude by suggesting at least part of what this might be, and why it is an egalitarian standpoint that can plausibly claim to take both equality and liberty seriously.

(1) The first case concerns the polemical libertarian claim, already alluded to, that these concepts are by their very nature inconsistent: that, once we understand the meaning of the one, we will see its incompatibility with the pursuit of the other, that liberty overall is, as a matter of conceptual necessity, always reduced by the very pursuit of equality. As I shall now show, this result is obtained, in polemical vein, by juxtaposing definitions of each that generate the desired incompatibility.

The Friedmans call the equality that conflicts with liberty 'equality of outcome' and by this they say they mean the idea that 'everyone should have the same level of living or of income, should finish the race at the same time'. It is not explained why just these 'outcomes' should be the ones to be equalized, nor why they should be valued, nor indeed who (apart from Babeuf) has ever attached value to such a state of affairs. They then make a second move, identifying 'equality of outcome' with the very idea of 'fair shares for all'. But since, they say, this is not an 'objective' matter, it must be arbitrary, and cannot be rationally defended, and, so, if 'all are to have "fair shares", someone or some group of people must decide which shares are fair—and they must be able to impose their decisions on others, taking from those that have more than their "fair" share and giving to those who have less'.[23] But, of course, first, if liberty is the 'freedom to choose', and its basic form, 'economic freedom' means essentially the 'freedom to choose how to use our income', then any redistributive policy limits freedom since it will restrict some choices;

[21] See A. Walicki, 'Liberalism in Poland', *Critical Review*, 2/1 (1988), pp. 8–38.

[22] The very label of 'libertarianism' has been captured from the left by free-market liberalism. For a good general account of the latter in its contemporary forms, see A. H. Shand, *Free Market Morality: The Political Economy of the Austrian School* (London and New York: Routledge, 1990).

[23] Friedman and Friedman, *Free to Choose*, pp. 128, 134, 135.

second, if equality of outcome denotes the levelling policy indicated, it will drastically restrict many such choices; and, third, if 'fairness' just means 'what some arbitrarily believe to be fair', then others, with other equally 'arbitrary' beliefs, can only be manipulated or forced to be fair.

For Robert Nozick, by definition, 'an end-state principle or distributional patterned principle of justice' and notably 'any distributional pattern with any egalitarian component' will be 'overturnable by the voluntary actions of individual persons over time'—such as 'exchanging goods and services with other people, or giving things to other people, things that the transferrers are entitled to under the favoured distributional pattern'. If freedom just means non-interference with voluntary actions of this sort, then it certainly follows that, under realistic assumptions, in Nozick's happy phrase, 'liberty upsets patterns', including egalitarian patterns. But Nozick goes further. For he also claims that what makes an action non-voluntary (and thus presumably unfree) depends on whether other people's actions that limit one's available opportunities are actions they had the right to perform.[24] But since, on Nozick's theory, they have no right to implement an egalitarian distribution since this would be unjust, then it follows that an egalitarian policy must, by definition, violate liberty. QED.

For Hayek, the 'most common attempts to give meaning to the concept of "social justice" resort to egalitarian considerations' but the very notion of 'justice' is, by definitional fiat, individualistic: 'only human conduct can be called just or unjust . . . To apply the term "just" to circumstances other than human actions or the rules governing them is a category mistake'. 'Social justice' is a 'mirage' because it is regarded as an 'attribute which the "actions" of society, or the "treatment" of individuals and groups by society ought to possess'. Hayek's claim is that 'in a society of free men (as distinct from any compulsory organisation) the concept of social justice is strictly empty and meaningless'. A society of free men is one in which 'each is allowed to use his knowledge for his own purposes' and implementing what is misleadingly called 'social justice' would require imposing 'some pattern of remuneration based on the assessment of the preferences or the needs of different individuals or groups by an authority possessing the power to enforce it'. (And, as

[24] Nozick, *Anarchy, State and Utopia*, pp. 160–4.

Hayek famously argues, '[s]o long as the belief in "social justice" governs political action, this process must progressively approach nearer and nearer to a totalitarian system').[25] So the argument is essentially threefold: (i) any scheme of 'social justice' is by definition wrongly so-called; (ii) and (wrongly) so-called scheme of social justice must in practice, by definition, really be a coercively imposed pattern of remuneration based on centrally acquired and interpreted knowledge; therefore (iii) any attempt to realize social justice, and thus equality, must impinge on the unrestricted freedom of men to use their knowledge for their own purposes. So, by definition, social justice cannot be realized, and every attempt to do so must limit (and eventually destroy) freedom.

To these and similar arguments, three comments seem at this stage to be required. First, a common thread runs through these definitional victories: the contrast between a view of equality as simply the redistribution of 'things' (income, remuneration, goods and services, etc.) and a view of liberty as the availability of choice and voluntary action. But this contrast conceals what is valued by those who value equality, and why they favour redistribution, if their objective is to equalize the availability of choice and voluntary action. Second, while in their anti-egalitarian polemics, libertarians thus define equality as a wholly arbitrary, groundless, and valueless ideal that must exclude liberty, they are in fact, as we shall see, committed to the value of equality as well as liberty, both of which they interpret in a particular way. And third, these arguments *appear* to confront what non-libertarians believe about 'equality', 'liberty', and 'justice', but they do not. For whatever strengths such arguments have derives entirely from the definitions they propose of the concepts in which they are couched, in such a way as to foreclose political argument with their adversaries. Interpret those concepts otherwise—as we shall see non-libertarians do—and this part of the libertarian case loses all its force. The issue then becomes that of *how* these concepts *should* be interpreted. To this question I shall turn in the last section of this chapter.

(2) The second sense in which equality and liberty are said to be in conflict has two variants both of which are versions of the economist's idea of a 'trade-off'. The paradigm of that idea is, of course, individuals making consumption decisions: there 'trade-off' refers to

---

[25] Hayek, *The Mirage of Social Justice*, pp. 80, 31, 62, 68–9.

where they are indifferent between various combinations of goods. By extension this has suggested the idea of value-substitutability. 'The fundamental idea', according to Brian Barry,

is that although two principles need not be reducible to a single one, they may normally be expected to be to some extent substitutable for one another. The problem of someone making an evaluation can thus be regarded as the problem of deciding what mixture of principles more or less implemented out of all the mixtures which are available would be, in his own opinion, best.[26]

Thus, from the evaluator's point of view, the 'extent' to which, say, liberty is attained can be traded off, or substituted for, the 'extent' to which equality is attained.

A second and distinct application of the 'trade-off' idea concerns not 'value-substitutability' but what, following Le Grand, we may call 'production-substitutability', that is, 'the ability of a welfare programme or of other aspects of the economic and social system to *deliver* different combinations of objectives'.[27] Here what is at issue is not how evaluators mix principles or substitute values but rather the feasibility of meeting alternative objectives. What are the various combinations of 'extents' of liberty and equality that are feasible? How much of one must be sacrificed to achieve a given level of the other? Obviously, the determinants of a system's productive capacity, in this sense, will be determined partly by material and physical factors, and partly by prevalent beliefs and attitudes and, indeed, evaluations.

These two ways in which there may be said to be a trade-off between equality and liberty share a common feature. They both imply the following picture: that there are discrete, free-standing, and independently characterizable 'values'—in this case 'equality' and 'liberty'—the extent of whose realization can in each case be measured according to some scale that enables people to express a preference between such 'extents', or indifference between them; or, alternatively, economic and social policies or institutions or systems can be seen as capable of producing different combinations of such 'extents'. How plausible is this picture?

The first difficulty is that each of these values is internally complex

[26] B. Barry, *Political Argument* (London: Routledge & Kegan Paul, 1965), p. 6.
[27] J. Le Grand, *Equality versus Efficiency: The Elusive Trade-Off*, Discussion Paper: Welfare State Programme, 36, Suntory International Centre for Economics and Related Disciplines (London: 1988), p. 3.

in more than one way. Thus liberty or freedom is not only, first, freedom to act on one's present desires and beliefs but also, second, freedom to act otherwise, and, third, freedom to examine and, if one's judgement so requires, revise one's desires and beliefs. Of course, the third freedom requires the first or second, if it is to be effective, and thus to be worthwhile, but you can have any without the others and still be to that extent free.

Moreover—and this is a deeper complexity that spells trouble for any scale on which liberty is to be measured—the range of options that constitutes the extent of one's freedom is not, so to speak, a brute fact of the matter on which all rational persons must agree. For individuating 'options' is a matter of contestable judgement and, worse still, assessing the *range* of available options inevitably 're-quires no less contestable judgements about which options are significant' and how wide the differences between them are.[28] Some choices or actions we may be free to make or perform 'count' more than others in the assessment of how much overall freedom we have. That some of these—such as Rawls's 'basic liberties'[29]—may be uncontentiously freedom-enhancing does not alter the general point: that the counting cannot be done without judging what counts. And similarly, in comparing degrees or extents of freedom, what counts is the difference that different options make. In short, assessments of the extent or degrees of the realization of freedom are unavoidably contaminated by judgements about what matters.

The idea of equality is not less complex. Consider various recent attempts to specify a yardstick for equality: that is, to specify in a perspicuous way what it is that justice requires all to have equally if the value of equality is to be realized. The simplest—and most naïve—answer is welfare or utility, whether conceived as happiness or as the fulfilment of desire, but this answer fails, as Rawls and others have shown, above all in the face of the objection that it would unjustly compensate those with expensive tastes (or, more precisely, those with expensive tastes for which they could be held responsible).[30] All the other, more plausible current attempts to

[28] C. Taylor, 'What's Wrong with Negative Liberty?' in A. Ryan (ed.), *The Idea of Freedom: Essays in Honour of Sir Isaiah Berlin* (Oxford: Oxford Univ. Press, 1979).

[29] Rawls, *A Theory of Justice*, p. 61.

[30] See G. A. Cohen, 'On the Currency of Egalitarian Justice', *Ethics*, 99 (July 1989), pp. 906–44.

specify what is fundamental to equality—to answer Sen's question 'Equality of What?'[31]—clearly exhibit what is to be equalized as irreducibly heterogeneous.

Rawls takes *primary goods* as the yardstick for equality. Equality of primary goods is the baseline to which the Difference Principle is applied. He characterizes primary goods as 'liberty and opportunity, income and wealth, and the bases of self-respect' and elsewhere as 'rights and liberties, opportunities and powers, income and wealth'.[32] For Dworkin, it is *resources*, including within these material resources, and mental and physical capacities—'those features of body or mind or personality that provide means or impediments to a successful life'.[33] Sen concentrates on basic *capabilities* which are the 'real opportunities faced by the person' to achieve a range of 'functionings' that are part of a normal life, the deprivation of which may fail to register on a scale of utilities because of adaptive preferences (as examples Sen cites those involving longevity, nourishment, basic health, avoiding epidemics, being literate, etc., and, within the richer countries, the ability to entertain friends, be close to people one would like to see, take part in the life of the community, live a life without being ashamed of one's clothing, and those involving cultural and intellectual pursuits, vacationing and travelling, etc.).[34] Arneson proposes *opportunity for welfare*[35] and, most recently, Cohen has proposed *access to advantage*, which is intended to capture what Sen intends by capabilities but takes 'advantage' to include also states of persons that are not capabilities —such as being well-nourished and housed or free, say, from malaria—and are reducible neither to their goods or resources (e.g. their food supply) nor to their welfare level.[36]

What all these answers, separately and together, show is that the aspects or features of individual persons' conditions which plausibly

---

[31] See Sen, 'Equality of What?' in S. M. McMurrin (ed.), *The Tanner Lectures on Human Values*, (Salt Lake City, Utah: Univ. of Utah Press, and Cambridge: Cambridge Univ. Press, 1980), vol. i.

[32] Rawls, *A Theory of Justice*, pp. 62, 92.

[33] Ronald Dworkin, 'Equality of Resources', *Philosophy and Public Affairs* 10 (1981), p. 303.

[34] Sen, *Commodities and Capabilities* (Amsterdam, New York, and London, North-Holland, 1985), pp. 5, 21, 16.

[35] R. Arneson, 'Equality and Equality of Opportunity for Welfare', *Philosophical Studies*, 55 (1989), pp. 77–93.

[36] Cohen, 'On the Currency of Egalitarian Justice'.

attract the requirement that they be rendered equal are inherently diverse: they have different causes and require compensation in different ways. To measure the 'extent' to which equality overall is realized is, then, to aggregate different features of people's circumstances and it is not easy to see how to decide which of these 'count' more or less in any such assessment. Moreover, liberties are, on all these accounts except the first, a crucial part of what is to be equalized, and therefore the contamination alluded to in the case of liberty extends also to the measurement of equality.

This leads me to the second, and more serious, objection to seeing liberty and equality in a trade-off relation: namely, that they are not discrete, independently characterizable values. Of course, one is an attribute of the condition of individuals or groups; while the other characterizes the relation between their conditions. The point, however, is that, to some very large degree, the *same aspects* of their condition are at issue in both cases. For as the analyses of what is to be equalized reviewed in the last paragraph show, liberty is, under one or another guise, in all cases but the first, a constitutive part of the *equalisandum*. All the plausible answers to Sen's question include as a central component those aspects of the circumstances of persons that maintain or expand their range of significant choices, and almost all explicitly focus on opportunity. Indeed Sen goes so far as to describe his favoured notion of a person's 'capabilities'—'the various alternative functioning bundles he or she can achieve through choice'—as 'the natural candidate for reflecting the idea of freedom to do'. His central concern is with those human interests he calls 'advantage' (as opposed to 'well-being'). 'Advantage' is a notion which 'deals with a person's real opportunities compared with others' and is 'a "freedom" type notion'.[37] All, though with differing emphases, see freedom—in the sense of the availability of significant choices between options of desire, belief, and action—as integral to equality.

I have shown that equality and liberty are internally complex and interdependent values. How do these features bear upon the proposition that the one must be traded off against the other, that in this sense equality and liberty must conflict? Let us examine that proposition more closely. As it stands, it is radically incomplete, for it leaves

---

[37] Sen, *Commodities and Capabilities*, pp. 27, 5, 6. Also id., 'Rights and Capabilities', in his *Resources, Values and Development* (Oxford: Blackwell, 1984), p. 316.

open whose equality, whose liberty, what is equalized and which liberties are in question. Assuming some population, for example the citizens of a state, as the community of reference, the idea of equality suggests that all its members, or citizens, are, in some respect, equal. So the proposition can be made more precise: to say that equality must conflict with liberty is to say that equalizing some aspects of the conditions of all must reduce the liberty or liberties of some, or all. Or, more precisely still, that to render all members more equal in respect of some set of diverse goods, including some set of liberties, is to reduce the extent of some set of liberties of some or all.

But from internal complexity it follows that both the equalization and the reduction can only be identified, in the first place, on the basis of judgements about which goods and which liberties 'count', and which count more than others. And from interdependence—that is, the centrality of liberty among the conditions to be equalized—it follows that what is at issue here is, largely, a change from one distribution of (some set of) liberties to another. To equalize liberties is not, of course, always plausibly to reduce them. Indeed, there are plainly liberties—such as freedom of speech—that can be seen as public goods, that is, goods used by all in such a way that use by one does not detract from use by another. Let us, however, suppose that the postulated relation holds, for whatever reason.

There are then six possibilities. As (some set of) liberties for all become more equal, there will be a reduction in (i) the same liberties of some, (ii) other liberties of some, (iii) the overall liberty of some, (iv) the same liberties of all, (v) other liberties of all, and (vi) the overall liberty of all. Possibility (i) describes the case of effective property rights, or use rights; and (vi) the extreme Hayekian thesis of the 'road to serfdom'. But the important point is this: that in all cases, except for the extreme case of (vi), the verdict on the prospects for liberty after equalization remains open. This is so *even if*, as here assumed, equalization reduces the liberties asserted in (i) to (v), since these at most show the existence of a trade-off between the liberties indicated. The verdict on liberty awaits an assessment of the worth of all those liberties that survive or are unaffected by the postulated trade-offs. If these are basic or urgent, then equality need not have reduced liberty overall. And this result will hold for two reasons: that measuring liberty cannot, as we have seen, be conducted independently of assessing the worth or significance of what one is free to do or be; and that the trade-offs, when they hold, affect only the liberties concerned, leaving others unaffected. And, of course, egalitarians argue, further, that the equalizing of conditions, including liberties, enhances the scope of and thus gives reality to other liberties that would otherwise be worth little.

Thus, in general, what some misleadingly characterize as a trade-off between liberty and equality typically turns out to be a conflict between claims whose specificity this formula fails to capture. Moreover, the demand for liberty relates to the provision of what is of value; the demand for equality to the distribution of that provision. These demands exhibit different concerns: that of making a life or lives go better, and that of fairness across lives. But in political conflicts, the claims that are in conflict usually each embody *both* concerns: the claims conflict because they spring from different views about what would meet both. The notion of 'rights' neatly expresses this double concern: we claim as our 'rights' what will fairly protect our interests. Perhaps, indeed, part of what makes conflicting claims 'political' is that they are not simply conflicting demands expressing naked interests but conflicting *claims* that, as public justification, invoke some notion of fairness. So it is no surprise that the natural way to express political conflicts is often as a clash between rights to various liberties: welfare rights versus taxpayers' rights, tenants' rights versus the right to market freedom of landlords, parents' right to choose versus the educational rights of deprived children, the right to health insurance versus the right to opt out, and so on. Consider the case of the right of bequest. During the French Revolution, this right was debated in the Constituent Assembly. It was denounced by Pétion, in the name not of equality but of rights: to leave fathers and mothers the freedom to favour one or another of the children was to give them the power to produce active or inactive citizens, those who were eligible and those who were not: it was 'to deprive numberless citizens of their political rights'.[38]

I conclude that the 'trade-off' interpretation of how equality and liberty may be said to conflict is, in the first place, an inaccurate account of how we evaluate alternative systems or institutions or policies. We do not 'weigh' alternative amounts of the value of equality against amounts of the value of freedom and decide which mixtures we prefer. Rather we judge the impact of a particular programme or policy, say, as a particular distribution of various

[38] Cited in Ozouf, 'Égalité', p. 705.

goods, including various liberties. We do so in the light of our political morality, which will embody a particular interpretation of both liberty and equality and a basis for deciding which liberties and which claims to liberty have priority. And, in the second place, when assessing the productive capabilities of social and economic institutions, the idea of production-substitutability of equality and liberty makes little sense. For institutions do not produce 'quanta' of equality and liberty, but rather feasible sets of valued outcomes that, among other things, distribute different liberties in different ways. These will have different values depending upon different construals of both these internally complex and interdependent values.

(3) Perhaps finally then, we should interpret the claim that equality and liberty conflict as a claim about contending interpretations of both, from the most egalitarian to the most libertarian? Perhaps, in particular, it is a claim about the conflict between what egalitarians favour and what libertarians favour? Note that both proclaim their allegiance to liberty, while only libertarians tend to say that they are 'against equality'.[39] In the last section of this chapter, I shall argue that what libertarians are really against is non-libertarian equality, while egalitarians are unsatisfied with merely libertarian liberty.

Values conflict but they also unite. According to Max Weber,

the ultimately possible attitudes towards life are irreconcilable, and hence their struggle can never be brought to a final conclusion . . . According to our ultimate standpoint, the one is the Devil and the other the God, and the individual has to decide which is God for him and which is the Devil[40]

yet from Durkheim we learn that a society's unity is made by 'collective sentiments and collective ideas' and that under modern, post-Enlightenment conditions it is the morality of individualism, 'the religion of the individual', centering on liberty and equality, which is 'the sole link which binds us one to another' and has 'penetrated our institutions and our customs'.[41] The paradox is resolved when we see that Weberian value pluralism can manifest itself through divergent interpretations of abstract Durkheimian

[39] See W. Letwin (ed.), *Against Equality* (London: Macmillan, 1983).

[40] Weber, 'Science as a Vocation', in H. H. Gerth and C. W. Mills (eds.), *From Max Weber* (London: Routledge & Kegan Paul, 1948, p. 148.

[41] E. Durkheim, 'Individualism and the Intellectuals', trans. in *Political Studies*, 17 (1969), pp. 27, 22. Cf. the Durkheimian Louis Dumont's remark that 'Our two cardinal ideals are called equality and liberty' (*Homo Hierarchicus: The Caste System and its Implications* (London: Paladin, Granada, 1972), p. 38).

values. Thus 'liberty' and 'equality' unite us at a very high level of abstraction; what divides us is the interpretation of what they mean. Ask the questions 'what must be equal for opportunity to be equal?' 'where do the sources of unfreedom lie?' and so on, and apparent consensus dissolves into politically real dissensus. (This is, I think, where Michael Walzer's notion of 'shared understandings' and common meanings goes wrong:[42] it postulates value consensus at the wrong level). To which we may add that the abstract unity often serves to conceal, and thus tame, real disagreements. So Christopher Jencks, after distinguishing between five meanings of 'equality of opportunity', observes that it is 'an ideal consistent with almost every vision of a good society' and suggests that

without common ideals of this sort, societies disintegrate; with them, conflict becomes a bit more muted. But the constant reiteration of such rhetoric also numbs the senses and rots the mind. This may be a price we have to pay for gluing together a complex society.[43]

I assume, then, that 'we' agree in valuing both equality and liberty—where 'we' means at least all those contemporary citizens within the political spectrum that ranges from libertarians to egalitarians (for the rest of this chapter I shall use 'we' and 'our' in this technical sense). What, then, can be said at the most abstract level about our shared *concepts* of equality and liberty, alternative interpretations, or *conceptions*,[44] of which divide us politically? In valuing liberty and equality, what is it that we value? In the case of liberty, it is, I suggest, being in control of one's life, or as much of one's life as possible. That means leading one's life, so to speak, from the inside[45]—according to one's own beliefs, desires, and purposes; but it also means being able, and in a position, to examine and, if appropriate, revise these. And thirdly, it means being able, and in a position, to pursue, over some significant range, alternative paths, real options, substantial or genuine choices, so that one is not forced into living a particular life. Freedom, in short, is what makes an *autonomous* life possible, and autonomy is what gives freedom its value. Freedom is the name for the various conditions of autonomy,

---

42 Walzer, *Spheres of Justice* (Oxford: Martin Robertson, 1983).

43 Jencks, 'What Must be Equal for Opportunity to be Equal?' in N. E. Bowie (ed.), *Equal Opportunity* (Boulder and London: Westview Press, 1988).

44 See Rawls, *A Theory of Justice*, pp. 5–6.

45 See W. Kymlicka, *Liberalism, Community and Culture* (Oxford: Clarendon Press, 1989), p. 12.

which, we will agree, must at least include the absence of manipulation and coercion, the availability of adequate information and alternative ideas and conceptions of the good, and the absence of removable impediments to or constraints upon a significant range of feasible actions.

As for equality, what we value is, I think, the root idea that each person's essential interests be given equal weight or consideration, that there be no *discrimination* between individuals or groups in respect of those interests (I use 'discrimination' here in a sense that does not necessarily imply that for it to occur there must be an agent or agents intending to discriminate. Whether it does or not—whether there can be 'structural' or institutional discrimination—is another of the questions that divide 'us'). Everything, of course, hinges on how these 'essential interests' are to be interpreted. As Thomas Nagel has shown,[46] there is a range of such interpretations. A utilitarian counts all a person's interests (understood as his enjoyments or his preferences) as essential, giving them equal weight in his calculus; rights theorists count only those basic interests that rights protect (though they may differ about what these are); and the 'egalitarian' gives priority to those that constitute an urgent claim on resources. To these we might add the communitarian, for whom certain kinds of social relations and prevailing attitudes are public goods in which all can be said to have an essential interest. Equality, in short, is the condition of *non-discrimination* and it is of value because our essential interests matter equally. We further agree, I think, that such non-discrimination requires the elimination of those disadvantages that harm essential interests and for which those who suffer them are not responsible.

If these—the conditions of autonomy and non-discrimination —are indeed 'values' that unite us what then divides us, and, more particularly, libertarians from egalitarians? Not, of course, a commitment to liberty as opposed to a commitment to equality, for both are committed to both, but, rather, differences about what the conditions for autonomy are and what it is not to discriminate.

For a libertarian, liberty is conceived as the absence of certain, narrowly defined constraints, and so a free life is compatible with extremely narrow options, provided that these are not constrained in

---

[46] Nagel, 'Equality', in his *Mortal Questions* (Cambridge: Cambridge Univ. Press, 1979).

inappropriate ways. Thus for Hayek freedom is 'the state in which a man is not subject to coercion by the arbitrary will of another or others'.[47] In similar vein, Joseph and Sumption argue that

> Freedom consists in the absence of external coercion, and no man is unfree unless other people intentionally use coercion to prevent him from doing something which he is able and willing to do and which could be done without encroaching on the freedom of others.

Thus '[a] person who cannot afford to buy food may well have a justifiable grievance which ought to be rectified politically, but it would be misleading [*sic*] to describe his grievance as lack of freedom'.[48] And for Nozick, a worker 'Z', 'faced with working or starving', nevertheless 'does choose voluntarily' if 'what limits his alternatives', namely, the actions of other individuals from A to Y, are done 'voluntarily and within their rights'. For, according to Nozick,

> A person's choice among different degrees of unpalatable alternatives is not rendered unvoluntary by the fact that others voluntarily chose and acted within their rights in a way that did not provide him with a more palatable alternative.[49]

For libertarians like these the conception of liberty diminishing constraints is maximally narrow: they must be external, coercive, arbitrary, intentionally imposed by particular persons or sets of persons, who (according to Nozick) are acting outside their rights. All else that restricts our options, according to such views, it is 'misleading' to call lack of freedom and is, presumably, therefore compatible with leading an autonomous life.

Libertarians have a similarly constricted view of what constitutes non-discrimination, or the equal consideration of essential interests. For, in the first place, they hold a view of those interests that limits them to only those interests that are protected by certain rights —more particularly property rights and, as Cohen makes clear in respect of Nozick, above all the right to self-ownership.[50] And secondly, they have a very restricted notion of disadvantage for which its sufferers are not responsible, or 'involuntary

47 Hayek, *The Constitution of Liberty*, p. 11.
48 K. Joseph and J. Sumption, *Equality* (London: John Murray, 1979), p. 49.
49 Nozick, *Anarchy, State and Utopia*, pp. 263–4.
50 Cohen, 'Nozick on Appropriation', *New Left Review* 150 (1984), pp. 89–107.

disadvantage'[51] that calls for compensation or rectification. So, for example, in respect of educational opportunity, they will stop with the mere removal of 'formal' barriers to entry and will reject what Jencks calls the 'humanist' idea that people may suffer disadvantage from their environment or from their genes and that compensation in the form of additional resources is therefore in order; least of all will they accept that 'disadvantage' and 'opportunity' could be interpreted to include the lack and possession of the appropriate attitudes and beliefs that would render individuals 'internally' able to seize 'external' possibilities. More generally, libertarians see inequalities of resources in general as an assumed 'normal' or 'natural' background against which rights and opportunities are deemed equal provided that certain minimal conditions of access and competition are in operation.

Egalitarians can respond to these various conceptual restrictions by asking various questions. Why, they will ask, should liberty-diminishing constraints be confined to those that are deliberately imposed by particular persons or sets of persons, and, moreover, arbitrarily, coercively and unjustly? Are lives not also rendered less autonomous by unintended actions, by social relationships and by impersonal and anonymous processes that may radically restrict people's alternatives of thought and of action, and may even shape their beliefs and preferences; and also by the *absence* of facilitating conditions, by the lack of resources, including skills and even motivations? Why, they will further ask, should we conceive of their 'essential interests' as what narrowly conceived rights protect and narrowly conceived opportunities promote? Why should they not include basic needs, or the conditions of normal 'functioning', and their access to wider opportunities and a fuller life, and why should these not have a more urgent claim on a society's resources to the extent that they remain unmet? And why, finally, should the domain of disadvantage that is beyond their control—comprising luck, on the one hand, and exploitation, on the other[52]—be thought of as the 'natural' background to the practice of non-discrimination, or equal consideration, rather than as the field within which it should be practised? Libertarians do not ask such questions but rather appeal

---

[51] Id., 'On the Currency of Egalitarian Justice,' p. 916.
[52] Ibid. 908.

to various doctrines[53] whose combined effect is to close off the
political debate where it should begin: over the manifold and
complex conditions under which both autonomy and non-
discrimination can be enhanced in contemporary societies. They
seek, rather, to win the argument by blocking further argument, by
capturing the meanings of words—notably 'liberty' and 'equality'
—in such a way that these questions no longer arise. Egalitarians, by
contrast, make ambitious, and doubtless contestable, claims about
what such conditions are. But they at least address the questions and,
for that reason alone, they can plausibly claim to take both liberty
and equality seriously.

[53] I have in mind, in particular, the methodological doctrine—methodological
individualism—which proscribes all explanations not couched wholly in terms of
facts about individuals; a doctrine of property rights which derives from individuals'
ownership of their personal powers the right to indefinitely unequal resources as a
result of their use; and a doctrine about the nature of society as a 'spontaneous order'
(Hayek), of which the market is allegedly the archetype, unamenable to unified
direction or indeed rational planning of any kind.

5

The Use of Ethnocentricity

'The emergence of the individual' is a grand theme that has preoccupied a wide range of thinkers in the West for the last two centuries, ever since Joseph de Maistre spoke in 1820 of 'this deep and frightening division of minds, this infinite fragmentation of all doctrines, political protestantism carried to the most absolute individualism'[1] and Tocqueville, noting that 'individualism' was 'a recent expression to which a new idea has given birth', observed that it was 'of democratic origin and threatens to develop in so far as conditions are equalized' —a 'deliberate and peaceful sentiment which disposes each citizen to isolate himself from the mass of his fellows and to draw apart with his family and friends', abandoning 'the wider society to itself'.[2]

The semantic history of the very term 'individualism' reveals a rich variety of accumulated meanings, following initially divergent national paths[3] but all these usages display a common concern with identifying some distinctive set of traits, principles, or ideas that are, it is usually supposed, constitutive of modernity. These constitutive features of modernity were, of course, variously conceived: by Maistre as the thought of the Enlightenment and revolutionary politics, by Tocqueville as the egalitarian spirit of democracy, by Weber as rational capitalism, by Durkheim as organic solidarity, by Meinecke as Romanticism ('this deepening individualism of uniqueness . . . a new and more living image of the State, and also a new picture of the world'),[4] by Dicey as utilitarian liberalism, by Walt Whitman as the progressive force of modern history, reconciling

This chapter was first published in 1989.

[1] J. de Maistre, 'Extrait d'une conversation', in Œuvres complètes, 14 vols. and Index (Lyon and Paris, 1884–7), xiv. p. 286.

[2] A. de Tocqueville De la démocratie en Amérique (1835), bk. II, pt. ii, chap. 2, in Œuvres complètes, ed. J.-P. Mayer (Paris: Gallimard, 1951), i. pp. 104–6.

[3] See my Individualism (Oxford: Blackwell, and New York: Harper & Row, 1973), pt. I.

[4] F. Meinecke, Die Idee der Staatsräson (1924), in Werke. (Munich 1957–62), i. p. 425.

liberty and social justice.[5] 'Individualism', across all this rich diversity of interpretations, distinguished the moderns from the ancients, 'us' from 'them'.

From very early on, of course, historians and social scientists have sought to date 'its' emergence. The dramatic diversity of their accounts reveals all too clearly their disaccord over what it is they have sought to date. For Tocqueville, as we have seen, individualism's origins stem from modern democracy; for Burckhardt it was the Italians of the Renaissance who 'have emerged from the half-conscious life of the race and become themselves individuals';[6] Troeltsch, and following him Louis Dumont, detected its origins in Primitive Christianity; Weber and Tawney in Calvinism; Gierke in Natural Law Theory; von Mises and von Hayek in classical economics; and Michel Foucault in the development since the nineteenth century of 'a closely linked grid of disciplinary coercions' through which 'certain bodies, certain gestures, certain discourses, certain desires, come to be identified and constituted as individuals'.[7] Others (I pick virtually at random) pin its origins on Protagoras and the doctrine of *homo mensura*,[8] on the Epicureans,[9] on Christianity's fusion of the legal and dramatic concepts of a person, making 'every being with a will, qualify as a person, in order to make them all equally qualified to receive divine judgment',[10] on an alleged turning-point between the third and fourth centuries of our era which gave 'to the history of the individual in the west its original traits, its distinctive features', with the rise of the holy man, the man of God, the ascetic, the anchorite, lending a 'ferocious importance' to introspection and self-examination.[11] For yet others the modern 'atomis-

[5] See Whitman, *Democratic Vistas* (1871), in *Complete Prose Works*, (Philadelphia: 1891), ii. p. 67.

[6] J. Burckhardt, *The Civilisation of the Renaissance in Italy* (1860), trans. S. G. C. Middlemore (London: Phaidon, 1955), p. 279.

[7] M. Foucault, *Power/Knowledge: Selected Interviews and other Writings*, ed. C. Gordon (Brighton: Harvester, 1980), pp. 106, 98.

[8] See Arthur Danto, Postscript: 'Philosophical Individualism in Chinese and Western Thought', in D. Munro (ed.), *Individualism and Holism: Studies in Confucian and Taoist Values* (Ann Arbor, Mich.: Michigan Univ. Press, 1985), pp. 385–90.

[9] A. D. Lindsay, 'Individualism', *Encyclopedia of the Social Sciences*, 15 vols. (New York, 1930–5), vii. p. 676.

[10] Amélie Oksenberg Rorty, 'A Literary Postscript: Characters, Persons, Selves, Individuals', *The Identities of Persons* (Berkeley, Calif.: Univ. of California Press, 1976), pp. 309–10.

[11] J.-P. Vernant, 'L'Individu dans la cité', in *Sur l'individu* (contributions by Paul Veyne, *et al.*) (Paris: Éditions de Seuil, 1987).

tic' conception of the individual is found in 'those philosophical traditions which come to us from the seventeenth century and which started with the postulation of an extensionless subject, epistemologically a *tabula rasa* and politically a presuppositionless bearer of rights'[12] or in the seventeenth-century roots of 'possessive individualism'.[13] Indeed, I am prepared to bet that there is no historical period on which, or significant thinker on whom, the accolade or accusation of inaugurating the 'modern individual' has not been placed by somebody.

All these suggestions are, of course, 'presentist' and 'ethnocentric': the question is always 'where do *we* come from?' They seek the 'origins' of our present constitutive characteristics in alien contexts, and thereby court several dangers, or supposed dangers: that in seeking pre-reflections of ourselves we misinterpret the world from within of those we study, asking anachronistic questions, seeing illusory continuities between ourselves and our supposed forebears, and illusory contrasts between both 'us' and '*them*'—the supposed embodiments of 'the Other' the 'world we have lost', societies of 'the holistic type'. Furthermore, these suggestions all stem, of course, from what Weber called 'value-relevant' perspectives: every conception of 'us' in pursuit of 'our' origins is itself a partisan view among us of what makes 'us' distinctive and worthy of scientific investigation. Does this not further distort the investigation of where 'we' come from?

Here, perhaps, modern, comparative ethnology can help. Modern ethnology has 'sought to discern the notion of a person as a category that is culturally defined and therefore of a varying constitution by reason of the "ethnies" it encompasses'.[14] The suggestion here is that there is, indeed, a (constant) 'category' whose (variable) cultural forms can be studied comparatively, while the dangers cited above can be avoided. But is there, and can they?

It is indeed true that social anthropology and ethnology have taken warmly to this theme, ever since Marcel Mauss's remarkable essay on 'The Category of the Person', first delivered at a largely unnoticed

[12] C. Taylor, 'Atomism', in his *Philosophical Papers*, ii. *Philosophy and the Human Sciences* (Cambridge: Cambridge Univ. Press, 1985), p. 210.

[13] See C. B. Macpherson, *The Political Theory of Possessive Individualism: Hobbes to Locke* (Oxford: Clarendon Press, 1962).

[14] *Singularités: Les Voies d'émergence individuelle, Textes pour Eric de Dampierre* (Paris: Plon, 1989).

lecture in 1938,[15] which in turn inspired Dumont's *Homo Hierarchicus* and his subsequent studies of the development of Western individualism.[16] Mauss's essay and Dumont's work reveal, rather interestingly, a certain continuity with the earlier pre-ethnological discussions, while taking a step or two beyond them. A consideration of their work raises the question: how much further should, or can, the ethnologist go?

Mauss's theme was 'the way in which one of the categories of the human mind,

the notion of the person, the notion of the self, originated and slowly developed over many centuries and through numerous vicissitudes, so that even today it is still an imprecise, delicate and fragile one requiring further elaboration.

In other words, he treated 'the person' (1) as a 'fundamental category' in the Durkheimian manner—one of those 'notions distinguished from all other knowledge by their universality and necessity'; (2) as like an 'anatomical structure' which takes different 'forms in various times and places', taking on 'flesh and blood, substance and form' in modern times; and (3) as a historical product, the end of an evolutionary story, when the notion becomes 'clear and precise', becoming identified with 'self-knowledge and the psychological consciousness', formulated 'only for us, among us', involving

[15] Mauss, 'Une catégorie de l'esprit humain: La Notion de Personne, celle de "moi"', first pub. in *The Journal of the Royal Anthropological Institute*, 68 (1938) and repr. in id., *Sociologie et anthropologie* (Paris: 1950) Sir Edmund Leach, who was present at the lecture, has remarked to me that at the time it was paid little attention. It has been translated into English by W. D. Halls, in M. Carrithers, S. Collins, and S. Lukes (eds., *The Category of the Person: Anthropology, Philosophy, History* (Cambridge: Cambridge Univ. Press, 1985), together with various essays that discuss and develop its theme and arguments.
[16] L. Dumont, *Homo Hierarchicus* (Paris: 1966); *Homo Aequalis* Paris: Gallimard, 1977); and *Essais sur l'individualisme: Une perspective anthropologique sur l'idéologie moderne* (Paris: Editions du Seuil, 1983), published in a later version in English as *Essays on Individualism: Modern Ideology in Anthropological Perspective* (Chicago, Ill.: Chicago Univ. Press, 1986). Among many anthropological/ethnological works on this theme, one may cite K. Burridge, *Someone No One: An Essay on Individualists* (Princeton, NJ: Princeton Univ. Press, 1979); S. Collins, *Selfless Persons: Imagery and Thought in Theravada Buddhism* (Cambridge: Cambridge Univ. Press, 1982); M. Dieterlen (ed.), *Le Notion de personne en Afrique Noire* (Paris: Univ. de Nanterre, 1973); M. Leenhardt, *Do Kano: Person and Myth in the Melanesian World* Chicago, Ill.: Chicago Univ. Press, 1979); I. Meyerson (ed.), *Problèmes de la personne* (Paris: 1973); and A. Ostor, L. Frazzetti, and S. Barnett, *Concepts of a Person: Kinship, Casts and Marriage in India* (Cambridge, Mass.: Harvard Univ. Press, 1982).

'the sacred character of the human person'. Recall his masterly summing up of his argument:

From a simple masquerade to the mask, from a 'role' (*personnage*) to a 'person' (*personne*), to a name, to an individual; from the latter to a being possessing metaphysical and moral value; from a moral consciousness to a sacred being; from the latter to a fundamental form of thought and action—the course is accomplished.

Dumont, by contrast, sees 'the idea of the individual as a value' as being 'as idiosyncratic as it is fundamental' and argues that 'modern individualism, when seen against the background of the other great civilizations that the world has known, is an exceptional phenomenon'.[17] Employing 'the comparative anthropological view of modernity', placing 'individualistic ideology into a hierarchical perspective', he uses Indian holism and hierarchy as the baseline from which to interpret 'this unique development that we call "modern"'.[18] In the former,

society imposes upon every person a tight interdependence which substitutes constraining relationships for the individual as we know him, but, on the other hand, there is the institution of world-renunciation which allows for the full independence of the man who chooses it.[19]

Generalizing from the Indian case, Dumont argues that Western individualism first appeared in the form of 'the individual outside the world' opposed to society. The Hellenistic world was, it seems, 'permeated' with this 'outworldly' conception (among the educated) and the early Christians ('nearer to the Indian renouncer than ourselves') built on it through their relation to the other world and their devaluation of this.[20] The this-worldly individuals of modern individualism are the ultimate culmination of the progressive contamination and penetration of the entire social world by Christianity's other-worldly values.

Both Mauss and Dumont take the idea of the 'cultural definition' of the person or self or individual seriously. They both pursue the Durkheimian thought that even so fundamental a 'category' is socially or culturally determined. As ethnologists they are also sensitive to the stress on difference and the role of comparison to

---

[17] Dumont, *Essays on Individualism*, p. 23.
[18] Id., *Homo Aequalis*, p. 16.
[19] Id., *Essays on Individualism*, p. 25.
[20] Ibid. chap. 1.

make the self-evident puzzling, and vice versa. Each confronts modern views of the individual or person with apparently dramatic contrast-cases. On the other hand, each does so within a grand evolutionary story (however 'idiosyncratic' and exceptional) that culminates in 'our' conception of the individual. And each assumes this last to be a 'fundamental' unitary whole to which earlier stages of development teleologically tend, and with which other, holistic conceptions contrast. Just like the earlier, pre-ethnological discussions of 'individualism', we are still in search of 'our' pre-reflections, and a contrasting 'holistic' mirror-image of ourselves in earlier times or other cultures.

Dumont suggests that Mauss's claims in his 1938 lecture, when read closely, were 'after all modest', but he maintains nevertheless that

in a broad sense, 'the social history of the categories of the human mind' is still the order of the day for us, only it seems infinitely more complex, more multiplex and arduous to us than it did to the Durkheimian enthusiasts at the beginning of the century.[21]

But why *the* social history? Perhaps, as Michael Carrithers has argued, we should abandon the idea of a 'grand procession through history'. At least, as he suggests, we should start to discriminate between *different* histories with 'their own development, their own logic and their own relative autonomy'—for example between what he calls the *personne* tradition, centring on social and legal history and on the person as the locus of relations of kinship, clan membership, citizenship, and so on; and the *moi* tradition, concerned, rather, with the individual's relation to the natural and spiritual cosmos and his face to face relations with other moral agents. From the vantage-point of this distinction, for instance, Roman law is a crucial stage of the former, and Buddhism a decisive step in the latter. Perhaps, as Carrithers suggests, we should forsake the search for overall stories and look rather for 'distinct episodes moving toward no very clear conclusion'.[22]

But at this point a deeper question arises. How far can this topic be relativized? How far can the ethnological approach go beyond Mauss and Dumont in rejecting presentism and ethnocentricity

---

[21] Dumont, *Essays on Individualism*, p. 4.
[22] Carrithers, 'An Alternative Social History of the Self', in Carrithers, Collins, and Lukes, *The Category of the Person*, pp. 190–216.

without abandoning the coherence of the *explanandum*? Are we, in exploring this theme, condemned to one or another kind of narcissism—to seeking and finding prereflections or reverse mirror-images of ourselves?

We can, of course, divide the topic up. We can explore particular manifestations of, say, the valuing of exemplary or unique individuals, such as heroes, or the cultivation of a sphere of privacy, or the importance accorded to individual moral autonomy, or the concern with subjectivity, and the inner life, with what Foucault calls *le souci de soi*, or the individualization of responsibility or punishment, or the expression of role distance in, say, humour and drama, and through the 'perception of individual eccentricities, the deliberate or accidental flouting of convention, slips of the tongue should reveal private reservations, clever calculations of private advantage, as selfish obsessions',[23] or the emancipation of individuals from an inferior or marginal status, or the development of lyric poetry or of autobiography or of biography or of confessions, and so on. But what licenses us to see all these as parts or elements of a single topic—'the emergence of the individual'—if not some underlying presumption of a unitary *ensemble* from which they appear united?

We could, as Jean-Pierre Vernant does in his argument against Dumont's thesis with respect to archaic and classical Greece,[24] distinguish between the 'individual' (*l'individu*), the 'subject' (*le sujet*), and the 'self' (*le moi*). Vernant's argument is that in the highly this-worldly and egalitarian religions and social world of the Greeks, several developments can be discerned. The *individual*, seen as distinct from his role and social attachments, was valued in the archaic period in the form of a hero, exemplifying ordinary socially valued virtues to an extraordinary degree, and in the form of the magician, acting in periods of crisis to regulate public affairs. The development of the individual's private sphere can be seen in Athens in relationships between relatives and friends, notably in the *symposion*, widespread since the sixth century, where friends and courtesans would celebrate Dionysos, Aphrodite, and Eros, and in the appearance, from the last quarter of the fifth century of more familiar family tombs, on which the epitaphs for the first time celebrate 'personal sentiments of affection, of regret, of esteem between

---

[23] G. Lienhardt, 'Self: Public, Private. Some African Representations', ibid., p. 144.
[24] Vernant, 'L'Individu dans la cité'.

husband and wife, parents and children'. The individual's emergence in social institutions is shown, Vernant argues, in the appearance of the individual testament in the third century, formulated in writing and respecting the individual's wishes in respect of the disposal of all he possesses. The *subject*—marked by the expression of the first-person singular in discourse—Vernant finds in the growth of Greek lyric poetry where the author publicly expresses his own sensibility and the sense of 'time lived subjectively by the individual'. As for the *self*, Vernant's case is that this barely existed for ancient and classical Greece as a delimited and unified field for introspection: such a concern for the inner life had to await the early centuries of the Christian era.

But here too there seems to be some implicit teleology. What, after all, unites all these various developments if it is not their assumed interconnection within our own world view?

The problem becomes even more acute when we study cultures that are more remote from and less historically connected with our own, and in particular to the extent that our individualistic assumptions about morality and moral psychology, and many other matters, fail to mesh with indigenous conceptual structures. Does 'the emergence of the individual' offer a promising means of access to these? Only, I suggest, if it functions as a theoretical starting-point, rather than an interpretive category. In other words, while our questions may, perhaps must, be presentist and ethnocentric, we should allow maximum scope for indigenous concepts to structure our answers.

Consider the interpretation of the Confucius of the *Analects*. According to Herbert Fingarette, Confucius

does not elaborate the language of choice and responsibility as these are intimately intertwined with the idea of the ontologically ultimate power of the individual to select from genuine alternatives to create his own spiritual destiny, and with the related ideas of spiritual guilt, and repentance and retribution for such guilt.

The absence of this complex of concepts, Fingarette suggests,

warrants the inference in connection with such an insightful philosopher of human nature and morality, that the concepts in question and their related imagery, were not rejected by Confucius but rather were simply not present in his thinking at all.

Fingarette's conclusion is that for Confucius,

Man is not an ultimately autonomous being who has an inner and decisive power, intrinsic to him, a power to select among real alternatives and thereby to shape a life for himself. Instead he is born as 'raw material' who must be civilised by education and thus become a truly human man.[25]

To this Irene Bloom responds, not by doubting the cogency of Fingarette's observations concerning the absence of a developed imagery of choice in the *Analects*, but rather by suggesting that 'choice is not only and necessarily to be viewed as part of the complex of ideas which involves moral responsibility, guilt, retributive punishment and repentance', as it was, for instance, in Augustine. Obviously, she writes,

all human beings make choices of varying degrees of moral and practical significance all the time, with some degree of self-consciousness. What is variable among individuals, living in the presence of a variety of religious and philosphical traditions and in the context of different cultures, is the way choices are perceived: which situations are viewed as morally problematic, which options present themselves for serious consideration, what immediate or ultimate criteria are adduced—or simply felt—as applicable to any given instance, what degree of emotional intensity or anguish is invested in the choice.

Her suggestion is that, because of other differences of a metaphysical and philosophical character, individual choice has a significantly different meaning in Confucian thought:

With the example of Augustine in mind, one is prompted to speculate that the greater the degree of conflict perceived within the individual—for example, as between mind and body, reason and desires, a purer a baser self—or the greater the distance between the individual and infinite, the greater the drama that is likely to attend the problem of choice.

Perhaps, in the Confucian setting, 'these conflicts are minimal and the distances less than formidable'. In short, where Fingarette *uses* the Western structure of thought about the autonomous individual to interpret Confucian thought, Bloom *starts* from that structure but goes on to develop a hypothesis about an alternative conceptual configuration that is otherwise structured. If she is right, Confucian thinking about individual choice is revealed as neither a prefiguration nor a mirror-image of our own.[26]

[25] H. Fingarette, *Confucius: The Secular and Sacred* (New York: 1972), pp. 18, 34–5.
[26] Bloom, 'On the Matter of Mind: The Methaphysical Basis of the Expanded Self', in Munro, *Individualism and Holism* pp. 293–330.

I cite this last example to make a general point: that an ethnocentric question—'Under what conditions did the individual emerge'—can yield a rich variety of compelling and rigorous indigenous answers.

PART II

6
Power and Authority*

Tracing the history of power and authority poses peculiar problems. The history of political theory and of sociology is in part a history of unending disagreement as to how power and authority are to be conceptualized and how they relate to one another. Moreover, that disagreement is endemic, and it is so for deep reasons. These concepts are not labels for discrete phenomena: they have distinct roles in social and political theorizing and in social and political life. Different and contending theories and world views yield different ways of conceiving power and authority and the relations between them. Thus an adequate history of power and authority would have to include an account of those theories and world views and their basis in social and political life.

Consider the following questions. Is power a property or a relationship? Is it potential or actual, a capacity or the exercise of a capacity? By whom, or what, is it possessed or exercised: by agents (individual or collective?) or by structures or systems? Over whom or upon what is it exercised: agents (individual or collective?) or structures or systems? Is it, by definition, intentional, or can its exercise be partly intended or unintended? Must it be (wholly or partly) effective? What *kinds* of outcomes does it produce: does it modify interests, options, preferences, policies, or behaviour? Is it a relation which is reflexive or irreflexive, transitive or intransitive, complete or incomplete? Is it asymmetrical? Does exercising power by some reduce the power of others? (Is it a zero-sum concept?) Or can its exercise maintain or increase the total of power? Is it demonic or benign? Must it rest on or employ force or coercion, or the threat of sanctions or deprivations? (And, if so, what balance of costs and rewards must there be between the parties for power to exist?) Does the concept only apply where there is conflict of some kind, or resistance? If so, must the conflict be manifest, or may it be latent:

* This chapter was first published in 1979.

must it be between revealed preferences or can it involve real interests (however defined)? Is it a behavioural concept, and, if so, in what sense? Is it a causal concept?

Parallel questions arise in relation to authority, along with others such as these: Is authority by definition legitimate? Is it by definition consensual? (And are these two questions the same question?) Can it (or must it) be coercive? Is it exercised over belief or over conduct or both? Is it a concept whose use is 'normative' or 'empirical'; is it 'quasi-performative' or 'neutral'? Is it *de jure* or *de facto* or both? Does it indicate a causal or an 'internal' relation? Does it presuppose a normative relationship? Can it be accounted for in individualist and behavioural or influence terms? Does it presuppose inequality? Is submission to authority compatible with the exercise of reason? Is it a denial, or sometimes a condition, of freedom and autonomy?

And what of the relationship between power and authority? Is authority a form of power? Or are only some forms of authority forms of power? Or does power (always or sometimes?) underlie authority? Or is there a radical opposition between power and authority? Or perhaps 'power is essentially tied to the personality of individuals' whereas 'authority is always associated with social positions or roles'?[1]

The alternative answers offered to questions such as these have wider theoretical and often philosophical import and they cannot be systematically treated here. What I propose to do instead is to offer a formal and abstract account of the *concepts* of power and authority respectively which inhere within the many *conceptions* of power and authority that have been used by particular thinkers within specific contexts, in development from and in reaction to one another. Any given conception of power and of authority (and of the relation between them) can be seen as an interpretation and application of its concept. The various conceptions of power and authority are, as John Rawls writes of conceptions of justice, 'the outgrowth of different notions of society against the background of opposing views of the natural necessities and opportunities of human life'. To understand any such conception fully, 'we must make explicit the conception of social co-operation from which it derives.'[2] I shall classify and indicate something of the range of alternative concep-

---

[1] R. Dahrendorf, *Class and Class Conflict in an Industrial Society* (London: Routledge & Kegan Paul, 1959), p. 166.

[2] Rawls, *A Theory of Justice* (Oxford: Clarendon Press, 1972), pp. 9–10.

tions. I shall then sketch the outlines of a number of traditions of conceptualizing power and authority, and the relations between them, within political and social theory. I shall conclude by indicating a number of contemporary controversies in which alternative conceptions are at issue.

I

First, the concept of power. The absolutely basic common core to all conceptions of power is the notion of the capacity to bring about consequences, with no restriction on what the consequences might be or what brings them about. When used in relation to human beings in social relations with one another, it is attributed to persons or collectivities or, sometimes, to systems or structures within which they act. It is, therefore, no surprise that any given conception of power will necessarily incorporate a theory of that to which it is attributed: to identify the power of an individual, or a class, or a social system, one must, consciously or unconsciously, have a theory of the nature—that is, the causal powers—of individuals, classes, or social systems. In applying this basic notion to the understanding of social and political life, however, something further is required than the mere idea that persons, groups, or systems generate causal consequences: namely, the idea that such consequences are non-trivial or significant in some way. Clearly, we all affect the world and one another in countless ways all the time; any given use of the concept of power—and related concepts such as authority, influence, coercion, force, violence, manipulation, and so on—picks out ranges of such consequences that are held to be significant in specific (and related) ways. A conception of power useful for understanding social relationships must incorporate a criterion of significance—that is, it must imply an answer to the question: What makes the consequences that can be brought about by A significant in such a way as to count as power?

A wide range of answers is to be found—answers which dictate specific responses to some or all of the questions raised in the second paragraph of this chapter. For some, what is essential to power is the realization of a will or desire. This will yield an intentional conception of power, which may be *potential*, as in Hobbes's view that 'the POWER *of a man*' is 'his present means to obtain some future apparent good',[3] or *actual*, as in Voltaire's view that 'power consists in making others act as I choose',[4] or, even more simply, Bertrand Russell's 'the production of intended effects'.[5] In intentional conceptions, the focus is on individual agents, and on collective agents only in so far as intentions can be attributed to them (hence, in this view, groups such as élites will not have or exercise power unless they are united and consciously pursue their goals). Other conceptions do not take intention, or the realization of will, to be essential to power; such conceptions broaden the application of the concept to cover the actions, and perhaps inaction, of (individual or collective) agents which further their interests (which may or may not coincide with their intentions, if such they have).

Such an approach allows in not just unintended effects but various forms of individual and collective power (class power, state power) which the former conceptions do not. Some writers go so far as to see power as a variant of systemic or structural determinism (whether this be in the context of structural functionalism, systems theory, or structuralist Marxism). However, there is, it seems to me, much to be said for the view that this is an overextended and confusing use of the concept: power (and its cognate concepts) would seem to be an 'agency' notion (though, of course, views differ about what constitutes an 'agent'). Thus it is held and exercised by agents (individual or collective) within systems and structural determinants.[6] There are, however, as we shall see, conceptions of power that deny this (or appear to).

It seems that conceptions of power may be divided into two very broad categories. On the one hand, there are those which are asymmetrical and tend to involve (actual or potential) conflict and resistance.[7] Such conceptions appear to presuppose a view of social or political relations as competitive and inherently conflictual; as

---

[3] T. Hobbes, *Leviathan*, pt. I, chap. 10.

[4] Cited in H. Arendt, *On Violence* (Harmonsworth: Penguin, 1970), p. 36.

[5] Russell, *Power: A New Social Analysis* (London: Allen & Unwin, 1938), p. 35.

[6] See S. Lukes, 'Power and Structure', in *Essays in Social Theory* (London: Macmillan and New York: Columbia Univ. Press, 1977).

[7] This is sometimes described, as by Talcott Parsons, as a zero-sum notion of power. This is, however, confusing, since 'zero-sum' is a term from the theory of games, where its use presupposes a closed system confined to the players and the measurability of power on a single scale. It is, moreover, unclear *what* is supposed to sum to zero—the pay-offs to the players or their power. By 'asymmetrical' I mean simply that, in virtue of his power, *A* can or does affect *B*, in some given respect, more than *B* affects *A*.

Hobbes remarked, 'because the power of a man resisteth and
hindereth the effects of the power of another: power simply is no
more, but the excess of the power of one above that of another'.[8] On
the other hand, there are those conceptions which do not imply that
some gain at others' expense but rather that all may gain: power is a
collective capacity or achievement. Such conceptions appear to rest
on a view of social or political relations as at least potentially
harmonious and communal. As Montesquieu observed, quoting the
seventeenth-century Italian jurist Gravina, 'the combining of all
power held by individuals . . . constitutes what is called the political
state'; the 'power of individuals', he maintained, 'cannot be united
without the conjunctions of all their wills.'[9]

The first category may, in turn, be seen as composed of three
closely related but analytically distinct ways of conceiving power.
First are those conceptions which focus on the *securing of compliance*, on the (attempted or successful) *control* by some of others.[10]
Among these, some take the prevailing of some men's wills over
others, and thus overt conflict and resistance, as essential to power.
From Hobbes to those behaviourist political scientists in the contemporary community-power debate who identify power by discovering
'who prevails in decision-making', this is the most clear-cut and also
the narrowest of all conceptions of power. Some writers analyse
power in terms of the concept of force (Cartwright),[11] others follow
Georg Simmel in stressing the aspect of voluntary compliance in all
superordinate–subordinate relations, the 'spontaneity and coef-
ficiency of the subordinate subject'[12] (force, unlike power, being a
non-social relation which destroys the subordinate's freedom). Some
see the securing of compliance as achieved by the manipulation of
utility functions or incentive systems (Karlsson;[13] others (Riker,

[8] Hobbes, *Elements of Law, Natural and Politic*, pt. i, chap. 8, sects. 3 and 4.

[9] Montesquieu, *L'Esprit des lois*, bk. i, chap. 3.

[10] Cf. A. Etzioni's definition of compliance as 'a relationship consisting of the
power employed by superiors to control subordinates and the orientation of subordinates to this power', in his *A Comparative Analysis of Complex Organizations* (New
York: Free Press, 1961), p. xv. This work advances a comprehensive typology of
compliance relations.

[11] D. Cartwright, 'A Field Theoretical Conception of Power', in id. (ed.), *Studies in
Social Power* (Ann Arbor, Mich.: Univ. of Michigan Press, 1959).

[12] G. Simmel, *The Sociology of Georg Simmel*, ed. K. H. Wolff, (Glencoe, Ill.: Free
Press, 1950), p. 183.

[13] G. Karlsson, 'Some Aspects of Power in Small Groups', in J. H. Criswell, H.
Salomon, and P. Suppes (eds.), *Mathematical Methods in Small Group Process*
(Stanford, Calif. Stanford Univ. Press, 1962), pp. 193–202.

Shapley, and Shubik)[14] locate power by identifying the last-added member of a minimum winning coalition. Within systems theory, power as control can be conceptualized (as by Niklas Luhmann)[15] as a medium of communication by means of which one party makes more probable selections of action alternatives by another party than would otherwise be less probable. Among those who stress the conflict of wills, it is commonly assumed that power must involve the use or threat of deprivations. Thus for Lasswell and Kaplan, power is 'the process of affecting the policies of others with the help of (actual or threatened) deprivations for nonconformity with the policies intended.'[16] Blau is even more specific, defining power as

the ability of persons or groups to impose their will on others despite resistance through deterrence either in the form of withholding regularly supplied rewards or in the form of punishment inasmuch as the former, as well as the latter, constitute, in effect, a negative sanction.[17]

Others follow Machiavelli, seeing power as social control that is made the more effective by the averting of conflict and the economizing of the use and the threat of sanctions. For such writers, power is asymmetrical but need not involve manifest conflict and resistance.

Distinct from the notion of securing compliance by exercising power is the closely related idea of power as *a relation of dependence*, in which B conforms to A's will or interests not by virtue of any discernible actions or threats of A, but by reason of the very relationship between A and B. This way of conceiving power could be seen as a variant of the first, on the argument that it is simply a matter of A securing B's compliance *indirectly* and at low cost to himself. But it seems more perspicuous to see it as constituting a distinct range of conceptions, since there are many cases where B may be dependent on A, irrespective of A's actions, purposes, or even knowledge. James Mill had this idea in mind when he defined power as 'security for the conformity between the will of one man and the

---

[14] W. Riker, 'Some Ambiguities in the Notion of Power', *American Political Science Review*, 58 (1964), pp. 341–9; L. S. Shapley and M. Shubik, 'A Method for Evaluating the Distribution of Power in a Committee System', *American Political Science Review* 48 (1954), pp. 787–92.

[15] Luhmann, *Macht* (Stuttgart: Enke, 1975).

[16] H. Lasswell and A. Kaplan, *Power and Society* (New Haven, Conn.: Yale Univ. Press, 1950), p. 76.

[17] P. M. Blau, *Exchange and Power in Social Life* (New York: John Wiley & Sons, 1967), p. 117.

acts of other men.'[18] Such security is typically a function of social and economic relations and institutional arrangements rather than, or as well as, the action, and inaction, of individuals and groups. Perhaps the most clearly articulated and worked-out version of this idea is to be found in the literature on dependency theory, which pictures development and underdevelopment as interdependent within a single global system. Thus, Dos Santos writes:

dependence is a *conditioning situation* in which the economies of one group of countries are conditioned by the development and expansion of others. A relationship of interdependence between two or more economies or between such economies and the world trading system becomes a dependent relationship when some countries can expand through self-impulsion while others, being in a dependent position, can only expand as a reflection of the expansion of the dominant countries, which may have positive or negative effects on their immediate development.[19]

A third way of conceiving asymmetric power is again very closely related to the second, but distinct from it; this is the notion of power as *inequality*—that is, a distributive notion which focuses on the differential capacities of actors within a system to secure valued but scarce advantages and resources. Power as control and as dependence are measured by determining A's net advantage and B's net loss from B's compliance; power as inequality is measured by determining who gains and who loses—that is, A's ability to gain at B's expense.[20] Power in this sense may be held or exercised without A securing B's compliance and with B being dependent on A: consider the power of organized *vis à vis* unorganized workers (though, of course, inequality, dependence, and control are very often likely to

[18] James Mill, *An Essay on Government*, ed. E. Barker, sect. IX (Cambridge: Cambridge Univ. Press, 1937), p. 17.

[19] T. Dos Santos, 'The Crisis of Development Theory and the Problem of Dependence in Latin America', in H. Bernstein (ed.), *Underdevelopment and Development* (Harmondsworth: Penguin, 1973), p. 76. 'In either case', writes Dos Santos, 'the basic situation of dependence causes these countries to be both backward and exploited. Dominant countries are endowed with technological, commercial, capital and socio-political predominance over dependent countries—the form of this predominance varying according to the particular historical moment—and can therefore exploit them, and extract part of the locally produced surplus. Dependence, then, is based upon an international division of labour which allows industrial development to take place in some countries while restricting it in others, whose growth is conditioned by and subjected to the power centres of the world' (pp. 76–7).

[20] See B. Barry, 'Power: An Economic Analysis', in id. (ed.), *Power and Political Theory: Some European Perspectives* (London: John Wiley, 1976), pp. 67–101.

coexist empirically). It is in this sense that power is often used by stratification theorists. Max Weber evidently had this conception of power in mind when he observed that '"classes", "status groups" and "parties" *are phenomena of the distribution of power within a community.*'[21] Lenski argues that

if we can establish the pattern of [the distribution of power] in a given society, we have largely established the pattern for the distribution of privilege, and if we can discover the causes of a given distribution of power we have also discovered the causes of the distribution of privilege linked with it.[22]

Frank Parkin has articulated this conception of power as inequality with the greatest clarity:

to speak of the distribution of power could be understood as another way of describing the flow of rewards; the very fact that the dominant class can successfully claim a disproportionate share of rewards vis-à-vis the subordinate class, is in a sense a *measure* of the former's power over the latter. In other words, power need not be thought of as something which exists over and above the system of material and social rewards; rather it can be thought of as a concept or metaphor which is used to depict the flow of resources which constitutes the system. And as such it is not a separate dimension of stratification at all.[23]

In sum, control, dependence, and inequality represent three major ways of conceptualizing power, understood as an asymmetric relation. It is, perhaps, worth noting that Max Weber's celebrated definition of power as 'the probability that one actor within a social relationship will be in a position to carry out his own will despite resistance, regardless of the basis on which this probability rests'[24] is compatible with all three.

Conceptions of power as a collective capacity or achievement tend to stress the benign and communal rather than the demonic and competitive aspect of power: power is exercised with rather than over others. Benjamin Constant remarked that the ancient, as opposed to the modern, citizen engaged in 'the active and constant participation in collective power.'[25] For Plato and Aristotle, accord-

---

[21] Weber, *Economy and Society*, ed. G. Roth and C. Wittich, 2 vols. (New York: Bedminster, 1968), ii. p. 927.

[22] G. Lenski, *Power and Privilege* (New York: McGraw-Hill, 1966), p. 45.

[23] Parkin, *Class, Inequality and Political Order* (London: MacGibbon & Kee, 1971), p. 46.   [24] Weber, *Economy and Society*, i. p. 53.

[25] B. Constant, *De la liberté des anciens comparée á celle des modernes*, in his *Œuvres Politiques*, ed. C. Louandre (Paris: 1874), p. 260.

ing to Franz Neumann, 'political power is the total power of the community'.[26] Cicero said that 'in no other city except in one where the people has the supreme power, can liberty find its abode', and he distinguished between '*potestas in populo*' and '*auctoritas in senatu*'.[27] Similarly, the *Digest* of Justinian's code of Roman Law (*Corpus Iuris Civilis*) derives the legal force of the prince's decision from the fact that 'the people has conferred to him and upon him the whole of its government and power'.[28] These republican and imperial conceptions of collective power were succeeded in the Middle Ages by more hierarchical conceptions; for Aquinas 'order principally denotes power' and 'power properly denotes active potentiality, together with some kind of pre-eminence.'[29] There is Burke's Whiggish conception that 'liberty, when men act in bodies, is *power*'[30] and the distinctive liberal conception of collective power according to which reciprocal and complementary activities promote the individual good as part of the common good. Thus, for Humboldt, human powers are to be cultivated and developed through 'the mutual freedom of activity among all the members of a nation' (an idea taken up by Rawls),[31] while T. H. Green defined 'freedom in the positive sense' as 'the liberation of powers of all men equally for contributions to a common good' and 'a power which each man exercises through the help or security given him by his fellow-men.'[32] Marxism also contains a collective conception in application to the task of building socialism: Soviet power, wrote Lenin,

paves the way to socialism. It gives those who were formerly oppressed the chance to straighten their backs and to an ever-increasing degree to take the whole government of the country, the whole administration of the economy, the whole management of production, into their own hands.[33]

---

[26] Neumann, 'Approaches to the Study of Political Power', in *The Democratic and Authoritarian State* (New York: Free Press, 1964), p. 5.

[27] Cicero, *De Re Publica*, bk. I, art. 31.

[28] *Digesta Justiniani Augusti*, vk. I, chap. 4, sect. 1.

[29] Aquinas, *Summa Theologica*, pt. III (suppl.), q. 34, art. I.

[30] E. Burke, *Reflections on the Revolution in France*, Everyman edn. (London: Dent, 1910), p. 7.

[31] W. von Humboldt, *The Sphere and Duties of Government*, trans. J. Coulthard (London: Trubner, 1854), pp. 189–90. Rawls refers to Humboldt on pp. 523–4 of his *Theory of Justice*.

[32] Green, 'Lecture on Liberal Legislation and Freedom of Contract', in *Works*, 6th imp. (London: Longmans Green, 1911), iii. pp. 370–3.

[33] V. I. Lenin, 'What is Soviet Power?' in *Selected Works* (in 1 vol.) (London: Lawrence & Wishart, 1969), pp. 476–7.

Among contemporary theorists, as we shall see, Hannah Arendt and Talcott Parsons advance collective conceptions, the former by reference to a classical, republican conception of politics in which the essence of power does 'not rely on the command-obedience relationship' but corresponds rather to 'the human ability to . . . act in concert';[34] while for the latter power is a system resource, being the 'capacity to mobilize the resources of the society for the attainment of goals for which a general "public" commitment has been made, or may be made.'[35] Conceptions such as these are, it will be clear, at the other end of the spectrum from the Hobbesian and the Weberian.

Of course, asymmetric and collective conceptions of power are not, in any simple way, exclusive of one another. What some may see as an asymmetric relation, others may see merely as a collective capacity, simply by confining their analytic focus to a given collectivity abstracted from its relations with others. Conversely, a system (such as capitalism) may be seen as having certain collective capacities (for instance, productive power) in virtue, at least in part, of its internal and conflictual power relations.

The concept of authority, as the common core of all the various conceptions of authority, has a more complex structure than the concept of power. That structure is basically two-tiered.[36] On the one hand, authority involves the non-exercise of private judgement. He who accepts authority accepts as a sufficient reason for acting or believing something the fact that he has been so instructed by someone whose claim to do so he acknowledges. To accept authority is precisely to refrain from examining what one is being told to do or believe. It is to act or believe not on the balance of reasons, but rather on the basis of a second-order reason that precisely requires that one disregard the balance of reasons as one sees it. Likewise, to exercise authority is precisely not to have to offer reasons, but to be obeyed or believed because one has a recognized claim to be. Aquinas made the

[34] Arendt, *On Violence*, pp. 40, 44.

[35] T. Parsons, *Structure and Process in Modern Societies* (New York: Free Press, 1960), p. 221.

[36] I owe much in the following analysis to the very fine paper by R. B. Friedman, 'On the Concept of Authority in Political Philosophy', in R. Flathman (ed.), *Concepts in Social and Political Philosophy*, (New York: Macmillan, 1973), pp. 121–46, and to my colleague Joseph Raz, who let me see his paper, 'On Legitimate Authority', since incorporated into his book *The Authority of Law* (Oxford: Clarendon Press, 1979), discussed in the next chapter, and from which I derived much profit.

point in relation to authority over belief as follows: the 'decisive factor is who it is whose statement is assented to; by comparison the subject matter which is assented to is in a certain sense secondary.'[37] And Hobbes made the point in relation to authority over conduct by drawing the following distinction between advice (counsel) and authority (command):

counsel is a precept, in which the reason of my obeying it is taken from the thing itself which is advised; but command is a precept, in which the cause of my obedience depends on the will of commander. For it is not properly said . . . I command, except the will stands for reason. Now when obedience is yielded to the laws, not for the thing itself, but by reason of the advisor's will, the law is not a counsel but a command . . .[38]

The first component of the concept of authority, then, is the giving and acceptance of a reason which is both a first-order reason for action and/or belief and a second-order reason for disregarding conflicting reasons. A number of points are worth noting here. First, the giving of such a reason (i.e., the exercise of authority) need not be intentional: I may accept as authoritative what you intend, say, as advice. Second, whether a given case counts as an instance of authority will depend on the point of view from which it is being identified. I may be using the term in a 'normative' or non-relativized way: in such a case I am judging whether an authoritative reason has been given (against standards which, however, I may claim to be objective). Alternatively, I may (as a sociologist, say) be using the term in a 'descriptive' or relativized way (see next chapter). Here there are at least two possibilities. I may identify which reasons are authoritative by reference to the beliefs and attitudes of those subject to authority (this being what is called *de facto* authority), or I may do so by reference to a set of rules prevalent in a given society, whatever the parties to a particular relationship might believe (this being *de jure* authority).[39] This is the standpoint of legal theorists—and also that of Max Weber. 'In a concrete case', Weber writes,

the performance of the command may have been motivated by the ruled's own conviction of its propriety, or by his sense of duty, or by fear, or by 'dull'

---

[37] Aquinas, *Summa Theologica*, 2nd pt. of the 2nd pt. II. i, cited in Friedman, 'On the Concept of Authority in Political Philosophy'.

[38] Hobbes, *De Cive*, chap. 14, pt. 1, cited Friedman, 'On the Concept of Authority in Political Philosophy'.

[39] See R. S. Peters, 'Authority', *Proceedings of the Aristotelian Society*, supp. vol. 32 (1958).

custom, or by a desire to obtain some benefit for himself. Sociologically these differences are not necessarily relevant.

The sociologist

will normally start from the observation that 'factual' powers of command usually claim to exist 'by virtue of law'. It is exactly for this reason that the sociologist cannot help operating with the conceptual apparatus of the law.[40]

The third point worth noting is that a considerable range of variation is possible with respect to the *range* of conflicting reasons which the authoritative reason excludes. If subject to authority, I might be permitted to act on my conscience or on certain of my interests (e.g. survival, as in Hobbes, or self-regarding actions, as in John Stuart Mill) or indeed on the basis of another authority, as for instance that of the king should he be present within a feudal lord's jurisdiction. Authority, in this analysis, is not a matter of one reason *overriding* other, conflicting reasons because it is weightier; rather, it excludes them by kind not weight.[41] Some very weighty reasons might be excluded: the point is that authority excludes action or belief on the balance of reasons. Of course, those who accept authority assume that authoritative utterances contain, as Friedrich puts it, 'the potentiality of reasoned elaboration'.[42] Authority, like intuition, is thus seen as a short cut to where reason is presumed to lead. The point is that authority dispenses with the elaboration of the reasons; the short cut is taken (sometimes on entirely rational grounds, as when one accepts the authority of an expert). With every attribution of authority there goes an assumption about the circumstances under which it applies and the kinds of reasons which it excludes. (Accordingly, authority can be absolute in two ways: applying to all circumstances and excluding all conflicting reasons). This first component of authority is sometimes described as the

---

[40] Weber, *Economy and Society*, iii. pp. 946–7, 948.

[41] This is Raz's formulation.

[42] C. J. Friedrich, 'Authority, Reason and Discretion', in id. (ed.), *Authority. Nomos I*. The American Society of Political and Legal Philosophy (Cambridge, Mass.: Harvard Univ. Press, 1958), p. 35. Diderot's *Encyclopédie* gives a more graphic picture of authority as a useful human contrivance for leading us to rational ends: reason is 'a torch lit by nature, and destined to enlighten us'; authority is 'no more than a walking-stick made by human hands, which has the virtue of helping us, when weak, along the road shown us by reason' (art. on '*Autorité*').

'surrender of private judgement.' This, however, supposes that a distinction already exists between the 'individual's private judgement' and the dictates of authority. But in some traditional authority relationships, such a distinction, which presupposes that the individual is able to stand outside custom and tradition in order to apply critical standards to them, may not, or may not yet, exist. Authority may be accepted unconditionally and uncritically because the culture may not provide the individual with alternatives to the established mode of thought: the preconditions for moral autonomy and independent 'private' judgement may not have appeared. Moreover, one could say that what counts as 'private judgement' does not relate to a distinction between 'private' and 'public' drawn elsewhere but is itself determined by the scope of authority—private judgement being precisely that judgement which is non-authoritative—that is, based on reasons that are excluded when authority prevails. When authority goes unquestioned, private judgement does not exist.[43]

The second component of the concept of authority is the identification of the possessor or exerciser of authority as having a claim to do so. Any use of the concept must presuppose some criterion for identifying the source (as opposed to the content) of authoritative utterances. Since accepting authority excludes evaluation of the *content* of an utterance as the method of identifying whether it is authoritative, there (logically) must be some means of identifying its source as authoritative—a criterion which picks out, in Hobbes's words, not 'the saying of a man' but 'his virtue'. Thus Hobbes wrote of 'marks whereby a man may discern in what men, or assembly of men, the sovereign power is placed and resideth',[44] and Bentham, of 'a common signal . . . notorious and visible to all'.[45] It is instructive to consider the wide range of such marks or signals there have been in different historical periods and kinds of community. These may be age; gender; status, whether of kinship, occupation, caste, or race;

---

[43] See Friedman, 'On the Concept of Authority in Political Philosophy, and Robin Horton, 'African Traditional Thought and Western Science', *Africa*, 37 (1967), pp. 50–71 and 155–87, repr. (in abridged from) in B. R. Wilson (ed.), *Rationality*, (Oxford: Blackwell, 1970).

[44] Hobbes, *Leviathan*, ed. Oakeshott (Oxford: Oxford Univ. Press, n.d.), chap. 7, pp. 41–2; chap. 18, p. 118; Cf. chap. 26, p. 178. Cited in Friedman, 'On the Concept of Authority in Political Philosophy'.

[45] J. Bentham, *A Fragment on Government*, ed. W. Harrison (Oxford: Oxford Univ. Press, 1948) p. 99. Cited in Friedman, 'On the Concept of Authority in Political Philosophy'.

wealth; property; military prowess; religious claims, whether traditional or charismatic; honour or esteem of all kinds; credentials;
functional role; office—and, not least, power itself. Such an identifying criterion for designating the source of authoritative utterances
requires that there must be some mutually recognized norms or 'rules
of recognition' (in H. L. A. Hart's phrase)[46] which enable the parties
to distinguish who is authoritative from who is not. Such accepted
rules of recognition need not be formalized; they may indeed
amount to unarticulated norms that are subject to highly personal
interpretation. So in *King Lear* there is this exchange:

KENT. . . . you have that in your countenance which I would fain call master.
LEAR. What's that?
KENT. Authority.[47]

And sometimes the interpretation may be innovative, even revolutionary, as in Weber's case of charismatic authority.

The ways in which alternative conceptions of authority derive
from alternative 'notions of society' and 'conceptions of social
co-operation' and indeed philosophical presuppositions may be
briefly illustrated. We may distinguish three broad ways of
conceptualizing authority.

In the first place, authority may be seen as exercised *over belief*, as
opposed to conduct (a distinction often indicated by contrasting
being 'an authority' and 'in authority'). To accept authority understood this way is to assent to propositions as true or valid because
their source is recognized as an authority. This covers a continuum of
cases from that blind faith (as in priests or prophets) to rationally
grounded acceptance (as of expert opinion).

Originally, *auctoritas* for the Romans and throughout the Middle
Ages signified the possession by some of some special status or
quality or claim that added a compelling ground for trust or obedience, and this could derive from some special relation to some
founding act or past beginning or to a sacred being, or some special
access to or knowledge of some set of truths. The Roman senate had
authority in this sense, as did Augustus.[48] In Matthew it says that
Jesus taught the people 'as one having authority and not as the
scribes'.[49] Augustine distinguished God's 'divine authority',

---

[46] Hart, *The Concept of Law* (Oxford: Clarendon Press, 1961), chap. 6.
[47] I. IV.
[48] See L. Krieger, 'Authority', in P. P. Wiener (ed.), *Dictionary of the History of
Ideas* (New York: Scribners, 1973), i. pp. 141–62.   [49] Matt. 7:29.

'Christ's authority', 'scriptural authority', 'patristic authority', and 'church authority', observing in relation to the last that 'I would not believe the Gospel if the authority of the Catholic Church did not impel me to it.'[50] And Hooker wrote that by 'a man's authority we here understand the force which his word hath for the assurance of another's mind that buildeth upon it'.[51]

In all these cases, authority is claimed over belief on the grounds of some special wisdom, revelation, skill, insight, or knowledge. This, of course, requires the epistemological assumption that such knowledge is to be had. Pre-Reformation Christians and, say, nineteenth-century positivists and twentieth-century technocrats have supposed that such knowledge is available but that access to it is restricted —for medieval Christians, to the papacy or the Church; for August Comte and his followers, to the spiritual leaders of society; for modern technocrats, to the scientific and administrative élites. It is evident that such conceptions are inherently inegalitarian, since those who have restricted access to such knowledge are, by virtue of that very fact, superior to others and entitled to their deference and submission. On the other hand, where there is no assumption of restricted access to religious or scientific truths (whether on grounds of revelation or status or office or natural ability) authority may be accepted as a pragmatic matter of convenience or economy of effort, as in the intellectual division of labour. The notion of 'moral authority' perhaps only makes sense in a community which shares values and principles about which some persons are assumed to be capable of greater knowledge than others; such a notion loses its sense where such values and principles come to be seen not as objects of knowledge but as subject to individual choice.[52]

One may contrast with authority as a compelling ground for belief, based on special and accepted claims, two further broad ways of conceiving authority.

The first of these is authority *by convention*. Here authority is seen as a matter of binding decisions compelling obedience, the source of which is assumed to be voluntarily accepted as authoritative by those

---

[50] St Augustine, *Contra epistolam quam vocat fundamenti*, cited in Krieger, 'Authority'.

[51] Hooker, *Laws of Ecclesiastical Polity*, vol. II, chap. VII, bk. 2, cited in Friedman, 'On the Concept of Authority in Political Philosophy'.

[52] See A. MacIntyre, *Secularisation and Moral Change* (London: Oxford Univ. Press for the Univ. of Newcastle upon Tyne, 1967).

subject to it. Here authority is the solution to a predicament: a collectivity of individuals wish to engage in some common activity or activities but cannot agree on what is to be done. Co-ordinated action is necessary but unachievable if everyone follows his own judgement. As James Fitzjames Stephen put it: 'No case can be specified in which people unite for a common object from making a pair of shoes up to governing an empire in which the power to decide does not rest somewhere; and what is this but command and obedience?'[53] The claim to obedience by a person or persons *in authority* does not rest of any claim to connection with traditional origins or sacred beings or special knowledge, but rather on their having been put in authority by some agreed procedure. Those subject to such authority are obliged by individual decisions (within given limits), whatever their merits in any given case, because the pursuit of their common activity requires this sacrifice of their individual private judgements. Note, however, that unlike authority over belief, which necessarily compels the assent of those subject to it (i.e., if I believe an opinion on authority, I cannot at the same time dissent from it), this kind of authority simply requires that the subject refrains from *acting* on his own judgement: he remains free to dissent privately from the particular command whose authority he accepts.

Conceptions of voluntarily accepted authority by convention are, of course, extremely widespread in the post-medieval world. For Hobbes and Spinoza, the very existence of society was held to require the acceptance of such authority in order to provide the requisite security for social life to be possible, while the liberal tradition from Locke onward has taken the requirements of co-ordination to be more specific, imposing a more limited sacrifice of individuals' right to follow their own judgement. Sometimes, as in social-contract and state-of-nature theories, the predicament and its solution are hypothetical (people are to be regarded 'as if' they had accepted authority); alternatively, people are assumed to have registered their voluntary acceptance by, for instance, voting, possessing property, etc. For others—radical democrats since Rousseau, anarchists, Marxists, and socialists of many kinds—authority by convention, at least in society as a whole and in particular the political sphere, has yet to be achieved.

[53] Stephen, *Liberty, Equality, Fraternity* (London: Smith, Elder & Co., 1874), p. 234.

The third way of conceiving authority is as authority *by imposition*—and that is how these last thinkers tend to see authority in the past and present though not in possible future societies. In this view, the acceptance of both authoritative reasons and the rules of recognition is imposed by means of power. Notions such as 'hegemony', 'legitimation', and indeed 'ideology' as used by neo-Marxist writers and 'the mobilization of bias' and 'false consensus' as used by radical critics of liberal democracy all signify the idea that in contemporary societies authority is (at least in part) imposed by power, either directly by control, or indirectly, through dependence relations.

More generally, 'realist' thinkers from Thrasymachus to Machiavelli to the neo-Machiavellian élite theorists and beyond have argued as though authority over belief and the voluntary acceptance of authority by convention are *always* largely illusory, and that behind the authoritative reasons and rules of recognition ('derivations', 'political formulas') there always lies the *force majeure* of the ruler or rulers.[54] Hobbes is a key figure here too, since his view ingeniously straddles the views of authority by convention and authority by imposition. (Compare Hobbes's own distinction between sovereignty by institution and sovereignty by acquisition.[55]) For he assumed that the sovereign, once voluntarily established as the solution to the predicament of the war of all against all, would thereafter be the continuing source of all authority relations through the exercise of will: hence his theory of law as command (taken up by Bentham and Austin) and his view of the sovereign as the Great Definer, whose power extends to assigning the very meanings of words and the enforcement of their definitions.[56] Combining a voluntarist and a power analysis of authority, he thus stands both in the liberal and the 'realist' traditions.

II

I now turn to a sketch of various broad traditions within political theory and sociology. Such categorization is not, of course, intended

---

[54] See Dahrendorf, 'In Praise of Thrasymachus', in *Essays in the Theory of Society* (London: Routledge & Kegan Paul, 1968).

[55] Hobbes, *Leviathan*, pt. II, chap. 17.

[56] See S. S. Wolin, *Politics and Vision* (London: Allen & Unwin, 1961), pp. 265–72.

to capture the total positions of the thinkers referred to, only the background and the thrust of their ways of conceiving power and authority and the relations between them.

First are all those who take it for granted that social order is constituted, largely or wholly, by shared beliefs, held for the most part on authority—whether divinely inspired, as for the French counter-revolutionary theocrats; or traditional, 'as if in the presence of canonized forefathers', as for Burke;[57] or anchored in science, as for Saint-Simon and Comte; or in a central value system, as for normative functionalists. In such conceptions, authority over belief is central to the explanation both of social cohesion and political order; power is conceptualized in relation to this central role of authority—partly as functional, even integral to it, and partly as threatening, in so far as it is abused or diffused in such a way as to jeopardize its continuance.

In medieval thought, authority and power (seen as institutionalized social control involving coercion) became ever more closely linked. Aquinas used the term 'the authorities' to refer both to 'the principle of origins ... in divine matters' and to the agency of 'coercive force' in public affairs: 'all those who govern' follow a plan derived from 'the eternal law' and are part of the order 'Divine Providence' imposes 'on all things'.[58] Within the Church, *auctoritas* and *potestas* came to be used interchangeably, conflating the right to evoke assent and the right to compel obedience. And from the thirteenth century onward, authority, both within and without the Church, came to be seen as the basis for coercive power; thus, for both the papalists and the conciliarists, 'the idea of authority in Church–State relations ... became inseparable from coercive dominion.'[59] Similarly, the main Protestant reformers (as opposed to the radical sects) preached individual submission to the authority of the churches and, unless they grossly violated God's word, to the temporal authorities, who facilitated the operation of the true Church.

Perhaps the most pronounced linkage of divinely inspired authority over belief and power in the modern era is to be found among the Catholic counter-revolutionaries of the early nineteenth century. For

57 Burke, *Reflections on the Revolution in France* (London: Dent, 1910, p. 32.
58 Aquinas, *Summa Theologica*, pt. III (suppl.) q. 34, art. 2, ad. 2.
59 Krieger, 'Authority', p. 149.

de Maistre, 'religion and patriotism' are 'the great and solid bases of all possible institutions' and a 'powerful binding force . . . in the state'; they know 'only two words, *submission and belief*; with these two levers they raise the world.' What is more, in politics, 'we *know* that it is necessary to respect those powers established we know not how or by whom'; indeed, the most extreme form of coercive power becomes integral to political authority and social cohesion: 'all grandeur, all power, all subordination rests on the executioner: he is the horror and bond of human association. Remove this incomprehensible agent from the world, and at that very moment order gives way to chaos, thrones topple, and society disappears'.[60]

For Bonald, bitter opponent of 'atheism and anarchy' and of 'that doctrine which substituted the reason of each for the religion of all, and the calculations of personal interest for the love of the Supreme Being and of one's fellows', there was 'a religion for social man, just as there is a political constitution for society': the 'power and force of religion' achieving 'the repression of [man's] depraved desires' and 'the power and force of political society' achieving the 'repression of the external acts arising from those same desires.' Authority, in the form of the 'power of God' and power in the form of the 'power of man' formed an 'intimate, indissoluble union'.[61] Thomas Carlyle, similarly, proclaimed that, man being 'necessitated to obey superiors',

Aristocracy and Priesthood, a Governing Class and a Teaching Class: these two, sometimes separate, and endeavouring to harmonise themselves, sometimes conjoined as one, and the King a Pontiff-King:—there did no Society exist without these two vital elements, there will none exist.[62]

Other conservatives, reacting to the ideas, practice, and consequences of the French Revolution, identified authority over belief at least as much in terms of submission to precedent and tradition as to divinely revealed truths. For Burke, 'we procure reverence to our civil institutions . . . on account of their age, and on account of those from whom they are descended'; the bond which 'holds all physical

---

[60] J. de Maistre, *Essai sur le principe générateur des constitutions politiques et des autres institutions humaines*, bk. I, chaps. 10, 12, trans. in J. Lively (ed.), *The Works of Joseph de Maistre* (London: Allen & Unwin, 1965), pp. 108–11; and *Les Soirées de Saint-Petersbourg, Ier. entretien*, trans. ibid., p. 192.

[61] L. de Bonald, *Théorie du pouvoir politique et religieux, Œuvres* (Paris, 1854), i. pp. 122, 494–5, 157, 159.

[62] Carlyle, *Past and Present* (London: Chapman & Hall, 1888), p. 207.

and moral natures, each in their appointed place' and prevents
society dissolving into 'an unsocial, uncivil, unconnected chaos of
elementary principles' is 'a necessity to which men must be obedient
by consent or force.' Accordingly, 'We fear God; we look up with
awe to Kings: with affection to Parliaments; with duty to magis-
trates; with reverence to priests; and with respect to nobility.' Such
social authority, inculcating 'this mixed system of opinion and
sentiment', all these 'pleasing illusions' made 'power gentle and
obedience liberal'. This was a much less harsh doctrine than de
Maistre's. Authority restrained the use of power: 'All persons possessing any portion of power ought to be strongly and awfully
impressed with an idea that they act in trust' on behalf of 'the one
great Master, Author and Founder of Society'. On the other hand,
when 'ancient opinions and rules of life are taken away', power will
'find other and worse means of its support'; the 'present French
power is the very first body of citizens, who, having obtained full
authority to do with their country what they pleased, have chosen to
dissever it', acting 'as conquerors' of the French and destroying 'the
bonds of their union'. Power thus escapes from the gentling constraints of traditional authority.[63]

These conservative and traditionalist ideas lend support to R. A.
Nisbet's claim that the French Revolution's impact upon traditional
society generated a 'seminal distinction between authority and
power': 'the image of *social authority* is cast from materials drawn
from the old regime; the image of *political power*—rational, centralized and popular—from the legislative pattern of the Revolution.[64]
Thus, as Carlyle said, 'we worship and follow after Power', and
Burckhardt attributed to the diffusion of the doctrine of human
perfectibility 'the complete disintegration of the idea of authority in
the hands of mortal men, whereupon, of course, we periodically fall
victims to sheer power.'[65]

---

[63] Burke, *Reflections on the Revolution in France*, pp. 32, 93–4, 83, 73, 74,
89–90, 75, 179. According to Burke, 'society requires not only that the passions of
individuals should be subjected, but that even in the mass and body, as well as in the
individuals, the inclinations of men shall frequently be thwarted, their will controlled,
and their passions brought into subjection. This can only be done by *a power out of
themselves*; and not, in the exercise of its function, subject to that will and to those
passions which it is its office to bridle and subdue. In this sense the restraints on men,
as well as their liberties, are to be reckoned among their rights' (ibid. 57–8).
[64] Nisbet, *The Sociological Tradition* (New York: Basic Books, 1966), p. 112.
[65] Cited ibid. 109, 108.

On the other hand, nineteenth- and twentieth-century thinkers developed a very wide range of conceptions of authority over belief which were not, as Nisbet seems to suppose, exclusively, or even primarily, tied to traditional conceptions. Nisbet writes:

Social authority *versus* political power is precisely the way in which the issue was drawn, first by the conservatives and then all the way through the century to Durkheim's reflections on centralization and social groups and Weber's on rationalization and tradition. The vast and continuing interest in social constraint, social control and normative authority that the history of sociology reveals, as well as its own special distinction between authority and power, has its roots in the same soil that produced its interest in community.

Although Nisbet acknowledges that it 'would be false to think of this distinction between social authority and political power as one resting solely in conservative thought', his account of nineteenth-century sociological theories of authority focuses entirely on 'the rediscovery of custom and tradition, of patriarchal and corporate authority, all of which, it is argued, are the fundamental (and continuing) sources of social and political order.'[66]

Here, on the contrary, it is argued that a range of alternative conceptions to traditional authority over belief form a central part of the history of nineteenth- and twentieth-century sociology. Montesquieu had already treated the 'Spirit of the Laws' under republican, monarchical, and despotic governments as distinct. Republican governments and monarchies were 'moderate' forms, but only the latter involved 'preeminence and ranks'; despotism, by contrast, put 'mankind . . . all upon a level', so that 'all are slaves'. As these types of government differed, so also did 'the manner of obeying'.[67]

In the nineteenth and twentieth centuries, authority over belief came to be seen in a number of non-traditionalist ways and in ways that combined the traditional and the modern in a number of different mixtures, relating both the nature of authoritative utterances and the rules of recognition to specifically modern conditions of life. For Saint-Simon, the new political system suitable for an industrial society would be based on 'positive knowledge', on

a state of enlightenment with the consequence that Society, aware of the means it must employ to improve its lot, can be guided by principles, and no longer has any need to give arbitrary powers to those whom it entrusts with the tasks of administering its affairs.

---

[66] Ibid. 112, 114, 116.   [67] Montesquieu, *L'Esprit des lois*, bk. III.

No longer need society find its leaders among the 'nobility and the clergy'; the new system would be 'conceived and organized according to principles derived from a healthy morality and a true philosophy.' This would consist in 'scientific opinions clothed in forms which make them sacred.' It would be recognized that 'all government will be arbitrary so long as its leaders are taken from military men and metaphysicians'; by contrast, 'scientists, artists and industrialists and the heads of industrial concerns are the men who possess the most eminent, varied and most positively useful ability for the guidance of men's minds at the present time.' These would henceforth exercise authority over men's minds, administration would replace 'the governmental machine' and the functions of government would be 'limited to maintaining public order'. A wholly new principle of authority and type of social integration, a quite new social structure, based on the functional requirements of industrial production, would replace the old system of hierarchy and subòrdination. The government of men would give way to the administration of things, and power, in the form of political action, would be 'reduced to what is necessary for establishing a hierarchy of functions in the general action of men on nature'. Thus 'the desire to dominate' would be 'harnessed to the collective good'.[68]

Auguste Comte saw the new 'positive philosophy' as justifying a new form of 'social subordination', a 'positive hierarchy' to replace the old order. The new 'spiritual power' would 'set up morality' to guide society: its role would be 'the government of opinion, that is the establishment and maintenance of the principles that must govern the various social relations.' It would exercise an authority which would be effective 'on account both of its educational function and of its regular intervention in social conflicts'. 'Moral' would prevail over 'political solutions'. Comte clearly believed that this would be a *new* principle of authority, a 'modern spiritual power'. T. H. Huxley was to call this 'Catholicism without Christianity', but Comte wrote that 'the allegiance of the people to their new scientific leaders would be of quite a different character from the unreasoning obedience to priests in the theological phase'. Comte's motto was, after all, 'order and progress'; we need, he argued, 'equally the inheritance of de Maistre and Condorcet . . . a doctrine equally

[68] Saint-Simon, *Œuvres de Saint-Simon et d'enfantin* (Paris: Dentu, 1865–78), xx. pp. 38–43; i. 219; vol. xxxix. pp.125–32.

progressive and hierarchic.' The *savants* 'alone as regards theory exercise an uncontested authority'; they are 'exclusively invested with the moral force essential to secure [the new organic doctrine's] recognition'. The '*savants* in our day possess, to the exclusion of all other classes, the two fundamental elements of spiritual government, capacity and authority in matters of theory.'[69]

Tocqueville likewise contrasted traditional and modern forms of social authority, though for him the latter was democratic and based on equality. All societies needed 'common belief'—'opinions that men receive on trust and without discussion'. In aristocratic periods, men are 'naturally inclined to shape their opinions by the superior standard of a person or class of persons'; in 'ages of equality', the individual's 'readiness to believe the multitude increases' and 'common opinion' becomes 'the only guide which private judgment retains among a democratic people.' Tocqueville's contrast was not, as Nisbet claims, between traditional authority and political power, but between traditional and democratic authority. The former imposed all kinds of obligations, responsibilities, and constraints upon superiors in their relations to inferiors, thus limiting their power and directing it to the national interest. In a democracy, the links of the chain binding all 'from the peasant to the King' were broken, the individual turned in on himself and was threatened by the tyranny of public opinion ('acting on the will as much as on the actions of men and preventing both opposition and the desire to oppose') and by the political coercion of a centralizing state—a new kind of despotism or 'democratic dictatorship', which 'cramps, represses, enervates, deadens, dulls and finally reduces every nation to a flock of timid and industrious animals, whose shepherd is the government.' For Tocqueville, this form of authority, backed by centralized power and ramifying administration, was a real danger. It could be contained by institutional safeguards, regional diversity, and, above all, by 'the gradual development of democratic institutions and attitudes', by freedom of association and 'democratic liberty'. One of Tocqueville's aims was precisely to show traditionalists that 'society was advancing and sweeping them each day toward the equalization of

---

[69] *The Positive Philosophy of Auguste Comte*, trans. H. Martineau (London: Trubner, n.d.), ii. pp. 480–3, 485–7; Saint-Simon, *Œuvres*, xx. p. 156; Wolin, *Politics and Vision*, p. 397; G. Lenzer (ed.), *Auguste Comte and Positivism; The Essential Writings* (New York: Harper Torchbooks, 1975), pp. 26–7.

conditions: the task was to find ways to achieve 'a democratic society advancing . . . with order and morality'.[70]

Durkheim similarly came to see all societies as integrated, indeed partially constituted by shared beliefs authoritatively communicated —*représentations collectives* whose content and manner of transmission varied with different types of social order. The components of authority—authoritative reasons for belief and action and rules of recognition—in modern societies were distinctive. Modern society required a 'religion' in the sense of a 'system of collective beliefs and practices that have a special authority'. Its priests were to be the schoolteachers of the nation and, more generally, the intellectuals, who would themselves be brought by instruction to an understanding of the morality determined and required by society. Its content was, in a word 'individualism'—a 'social product, like all moralities and all religions'. Individualism, Durkheim maintained, against the anti-Dreyfusards, was 'henceforth the only system of beliefs which ensure the moral unity of the country.' It was a religion of which man is 'both believer and God', in which the 'rights of the person are placed above the State', glorifying 'not the self' but 'the individual in general', committed to 'sympathy for all that is human' and to economic and social justice. Interestingly, Durkheim claimed that his 'religion', 'faith', or 'cult' whose social authority was necessary to modern society's cohesion was entirely compatible with reason and autonomy. Indeed, it had 'for its first rite freedom of thought'. Liberty of thought, he argued, was entirely compatible with respect for authority when that authority was rationally grounded. Conversely, and in a neat circle, he saw liberty as 'the fruit of regulation', defining it as self-mastery—'the ability to act rationally and do one's duty'; while he defined autonomy as having 'as clear and complete an awareness as possible of the reasons for our conduct' when 'deferring to a rule or devoting ourselves to a collective ideal'. As for power, Durkheim (in contrast to Weber) had nothing to say about power as an asymmetric relation between individuals and groups. Like Saint-Simon, he saw not class conflict, but an emerging functional hier-

---

[70] A. de Tocqueville, *De la Démocratie en Amérique* (1835), bk. II, pt. I, chap. II; bk. II, pt. II, chap. II; bk. II, pt. III, chap. XXI; bk. I, pt. I, chap. III; bk. II, pt. IV, chap. VI; 'Lettre à Eugene Stoffels', in *Œuvres et correspondance inédite*, ed. G. de Beaumont (Paris, 1861), i. pp. 427–49.

archy, and, like Comte, he foresaw the prevalance of 'moral' over 'political' solutions.[71]

These various visions of authority over belief under modern conditions—technocratic, democratic, individualist—could be supplemented by many others advanced in the nineteenth and twentieth centuries. There are, for instance, those forms of nationalist doctrine which identified authority with the expression of the national culture, or the *Volksgeist*, or the 'spirit of the people'. From Herder onward, the idealist background of such theories provided the assumption that there was something to be known and authoritatively transmitted by those able to discern and interpret it; as Savigny, the leader of the German historical school of law, observed, 'the common consciousness of the people is the peculiar seat of law'.[72] Various forms of socialist doctrine have likewise implied the dependence of social order and progress upon the authoritative transmission of certain beliefs taken to be true. Thus, for example, Fabian socialists supposed the 'nascent science of and art of democratic institutions', offering 'greater knowledge of the successful working of social institutions', gave authority to the public-spirited leaders of the socialist commonwealth.[73] And the state socialist societies of Eastern Europe since Lenin were ruled on the officially unquestionable assumption that the Party is the authoritative interpreter and inculcator of the truths that Marxist–Leninist theory has discovered.

Again, technocratic theorists of all kinds see authority as deriving from newly indispensable knowledge and skills. Thus, for Daniel Bell, the 'axial principle' of 'postindustrial society' is 'the centrality of and codification of theoretical knowledge'. 'Engineering and economics become central to the technical decisions of the society', and we see 'a new social order based, in principle, on the priority of educated talent'. Bell defines authority as

a competence based upon skill, learning, talent, artistry, or some similar attribute. Inevitably it leads to distinctions between those who are superior and those who are not. A meritocracy is made up of those who have earned

---

[71] E. Durkheim, 'L'Individualism et les Intellectuels', *Revue bleue*, 4th ser., (1898), pp. 7–13; *L'Education morale* (Paris, 1925), pp. 62, 136–7.

[72] F. C. von Savigny, *Vom Beruf unserer Zeit für Gesetzgebung*, ed. J. Sern (Berlin: Thibaut & Savigny, 1914), p. 78.

[73] Sidney Webb and Beatrice Webb, *A Constitution for the Socialist Commonwealth of Great Britain* (London: Longmans, Green & Co., 1920), pp. 350–6.

their authority. An unjust meritocracy is one which makes these distinctions invidious and demeans those below.

Power, by contrast, is 'the ability to command, which is backed up, either implicitly or explicitly, by force'; it 'allows some men to exercise domination over others'; but, says Bell, 'in the polity at large, and in most institutions, such unilateral power is increasingly checked'.[74]

The functionalist consensus theories of recent American sociology and political science are simply the generalized and relativized form of all these conceptions of authority over belief. Here what counts as authoritative or 'legitimate' is simply what any given society's value system is taken (or imputed) to be. Thus Parsons writes: 'Without the attachment to the constitutive common values the collectivity tends to dissolve'; these values are 'the commitments of individual persons to pursue and support certain *directions* or types of action for the collectivity as a system and hence derivatively for their own roles in the collectivity.'[75] (Lipset similarly defines legitimacy as 'the capacity of the system to engender and maintain the belief that the existing political institutions are the most appropriate ones for the society'.[76]) For Parsons, the shared values and norms specify what and who is authoritative: authority amounts to 'the complex of institutionalized rights to control the actions of members of the society with reference to their bearing on the attainment of collective goals'—the rights being those of 'leaders to expect support from the members of the collectivity'. Given Parsons's view of power as the *generalized capacity of a social system to get things done in the interest of collective goals*,[77] it will be clear how for him power derives from authority.

In general, it may be said of all these conceptions of authority over belief that they take the authority relation as primary. Power is seen as integral to or derivative from it but also as a threat when abused so as to weaken or destroy consensual beliefs and thus social and political order. Under consensual conditions, power tends to assume a non-asymmetric, non-conflictual form, at least internally to the

[74] Bell, *The Coming of Post-Industrial Society* (New York: Basic Books, 1973), pp. 118, 426, 453, 455.

[75] Parsons, *The Social System* (London: Routledge & Kegan Paul, 1951), p. 41; 'Authority, Legitimation and Political Action', in Friedrich, *Authority, Nomos I*, p. 199.

[76] S. M. Lipset, *Political Man* (Garden City, NY: Doubleday, 1960), p. 77.

[77] Parsons, 'Authority, Legitimation and Political Action', pp. 210, 206.

society in question, and the notion of 'leadership' is emphasized. Individuals are seen as moulded, even constituted, by the authority relation. Their role identifications, their self-perceptions, indeed their very identity is seen as dependent on it. Conflicts of interest between individuals and groups, at least in a well-functioning society, are understressed—partly because the very existence of authority is taken to create and promote an identity of interests between those exercising it and those subject to it.

A quite different tradition of conceptualizing authority developed in reaction to the early forms of the first tradition, the later form of which in turn reacted against it. This tradition sees authority as conventional and power as asymmetric, indeed coercive. It assumes a natural conflict of interests between individuals, whose identities are unaffected and whose freedom is limited by authority, which is, in turn, seen as exercised over conduct, even in the absence of shared beliefs and values. Their ends are private and conflicting, and the task of authority is to co-ordinate their actions so that common enterprises are possible. This view tends to focus on the authority of the state *vis-à-vis* individuals, who are taken to be given, with (conflicting) private ends, values, and opinions; rules of conduct are needed to enable such individuals to pursue their respective ends. Authority does not produce shared beliefs but rather a common framework within which individuals pursue their interests—and neither the identity of the individuals nor that of their interests is modified by the exercise of authority.[78] Authority in this sense produces co-ordinated action rather than common belief. Indeed, it allows for a gap to open up between private belief and public action. The individual may submit to authority while privately dissenting. As Hobbes saw it, though men obey the sovereign, 'belief and unbelief never follow men's commands',[79] and as Spinoza said, 'No man's mind can possibly lie wholly at the disposition of another, for no man can willingly transfer his natural right of free reason and judgment, or be compelled to do so.'[80]

'What manner of life would there be', asked Hobbes, 'where there were no common power to fear?' The Hobbesian predicament, the

---

[78] See Wolin, *Politics and Vision*, chap. 9, and S. Lukes, *Individualism* (Oxford: Blackwell, and New York: Harper & Row, 1973).

[79] Hobbes, *Leviathan*, chap. XLII.

[80] Spinoza, *Tractatus Theologico-Politicus*, chap. XX.

state of nature, consists in the equal powers of individuals with irreducibly conflicting interests: 'equal powers opposed, destroy one another; and such this opposition is called contention.' The price of peace is to erect a 'common power', for men 'to confer all their strength and power upon one man, or upon one assembly of men that may reduce all their wills, by plurality of voices, unto one will.' Thus a 'multitude of men, are made *one* person, when they are by one man, or one person represented; so that it be done with the consent of every one of that multitude in particular.' Here lies Hobbes's innovatory theory of authority. The covenant is an agreement of 'every one with every one' to obey the commands of the sovereign as if they were his own; the sovereign is 'authorized' to command them as he wills, since they have, given their irreducibly conflicting interests, agreed to 'own and be reputed author' of all the sovereign's decisions. Authority is 'a right of doing any act; and *done by authority*, done by commission, or licence from him whose right it is.' Thus: 'Every particular man is author of all the sovereign doth.'[81]

Two points are to be noted here. First, though the sovereign's authorized power is (almost) absolute, in the sense of excluding all conflicting reasons for action (save self-preservation), it is only applicable in a selected range of human activities: 'In all kinds of actions by the laws praetermitted, men have the liberty of doing what their own reasons shall suggest, for the most profitable to themselves', such as 'the liberty to buy and sell, and otherwise contract with one another'. Second, and relatedly, in contrast with the claims of tradition and divine right, and indeed all the views of authority so far considered, Hobbes did not require any sense of public involvement or active support by the citizen for the sovereign, nor did the latter's authority confer any communal or collective benefits upon the citizens—their nature and purposes were unaffected by it. The 'body politic' was simply a 'multitude of men, united as one person by a common power, for their common peace, defence and benefit'. Fear and insecurity held them together and authority was exercised simply to secure a framework within which they could pursue their unending search for 'felicity':

The use of laws, which are but rules authorised, is not to bind the people from all voluntary actions; but to direct and keep them in such a motion, as

[81] Hobbes, *Leviathan*, chap. XIII; *The Elements of Law*, I, VIII, 4; pt. I, chap. 19, sect. 8; *Leviathan*, chaps. XVII, XVI.

not to hurt themselves by their own impetuous desires, rashness or indiscretion; as hedges are set, not to stop travellers, but to keep them in their way.[82]

This conception of authority by convention, as derived from the consent of individuals with conflicting interests who agree to obey a public power whose role is to guarantee their continued pursuit of private interests, runs like a thread through the whole history of liberalism. It is Locke's theory of contract, however, which pointed the direction in which liberal theories developed, by drawing tighter bounds around the scope of authority. The Lockean predicament to which authority is the solution was less drastic than the Hobbesian: it was a matter of 'inconveniences', the 'fears and continual dangers' caused by 'the corruption and viciousness of degenerate men'. The 'remedy' of 'civil government' had as its 'chief and great end' the 'preservation of property'. As with Hobbes, the new authority had no communal or integrative function; on the contrary, 'the commonwealth' was 'a society of men constituted only for the procuring, preserving and advancing their own civil interests'. Political authority was bounded by the terms of the original compact: 'there remains still in the people a supreme power to remove or alter the legislative, when they find the legislative act contrary to the trust reposed in them'.

This should, however, not be misunderstood. Men are described as agreeing in the contract to resign their natural powers to the community which in turn puts the legislative power into the hands of those it trusts; moreover, each agrees to submit to 'the determination of the majority'. Furthermore, the language of 'express consent' shifts to that of 'tacit consent', and this comes to be seen as registered by the mere possession of property.[83] Authority based on consent thus becomes inverted into the imposition of authority over the holders of property. There was no recurrent renewal of consent, but rather the establishment of a way of thinking about government and authority which suggested a basis of consent, setting indeterminate

---

[82] Id., *Leviathan*, chap. XXI; *Elements of Law*, pt. I, chap. 19, sect. 8; *Leviathan*, XXX. Spinoza took this authority conferred by consent to be more absolute (with regard to its circumstances of application) than did Hobbes: the individual 'has determined to obey' the sovereign 'in everything without exception'. Authority, in his view, yields 'supreme power to coerce all', though with the ultimate aim of freeing men from fear, thereby enabling them 'to develop their minds and bodies in security, and to employ their reason unshackled' (*Tractatus Theologico-Politicus*, chap. XVI).

[83] J. Locke, *Two Treatises of Government: Second Treatise*.

and flexible limits to the power of governments. Society came to be seen as 'civil society'—the 'natural' arena in which individuals pursued their 'civil interests', which it was the function of authority to secure. And power was seen by Locke, as by Hobbes, as personal and coercive control. Hence the liberal project of both restraining the coercive power of government while claiming its authority to be based on consent and to promote the general interest.

The history of liberalism has been the history, among other things, of this combination of ideas. Authority is granted by individuals whose conflicting interests have free play in the economic sphere (society) but which require co-ordination and control (whose extent varies with different thinkers and periods) from the political. Government maintains the conditions for an effectively competitive order, maintaining 'law and order'. Authority is based on voluntary consent to this necessary co-ordination and control; the resulting coercions are seen as 'interferences' to be minimized. As Locke put it, 'the community comes to be umpire by setting standing rules, indifferent and the same to all parties'.[84] though Adam Smith was nearer the bone when he observed that 'Civil government, so far as it is instituted for the security of property, is in reality instituted for the defence of the rich against the poor, or of those who have some property against those who have none at all.'[85] Scottish classical economists, French Liberals, English radicals and utilitarians, and American constitutional democrats all reasoned in this way. In Paine's words, 'Society is produced by our wants and government by our wickedness . . . Society, in every state, is a blessing, Government, even in its best state is but a necessary evil.'[86] While for Bastiat the choice lay between '*société libre, gouvernement simple*' and '*société constrainte, gouvernement compliqué*',[87] Smith advocated leaving 'nature'—that is, the economic life of society (whose constraints were, unlike the government's, impersonal)—alone, as did Jefferson and liberals of all kinds down to Herbert Spencer and beyond to von Mises, Hayek, and Milton Friedman.

All these views offer a contrast between authority and power

---

[84] Locke, *Two Treatises of Government: Second Treatise*.

[85] Smith, *Wealth of Nations*, Everyman edn. (London: Dent, 1961), ii. p. 203.

[86] T. Paine, *Common Sense*, in *The Political and Miscellaneous Works of Thomas Paine in Two Volumes*, (London: R. Carlile, 1819), i. p. 5.

[87] F. Bastiat, *Œuvres complètes* (Paris, 1862–78), i. p. 427, cited in Wolin, *Politics and Vision*, q.v. for an excellent discussion of this mode of thinking.

different from those previously considered. Authority is here restricted to the 'standing rules' of Locke's umpire and rests on consent; power is coercive and personal and threatens the 'natural' order of society. As Diderot's *Encyclopédie* put it, '*authority* is communicated by the laws; power by those in whose hands they are placed'. Thus:

> The prince derives from his subjects the authority he holds over them; and this authority is limited by the laws of nature and of the state. The laws of nature and of the state are the conditions under which they have or are supposed to have submitted themselves to his rule. One of these conditions is that, having no power or authority over them except by their choice and their consent, he can never use this authority to break the act or contract by which it has been conferred on him . . .

His 'authority can only subsist by the entitlement that established it', and he 'cannot therefore dispose of his power or his subjects without the consent of the nation and independently of the choices indicated in the contract of submission'.[88]

This did not, however, mean that authority set any determinate limits to power's exercise. The story of how consent, seen as self-assumed obligation, was actually registered was always sufficiently mysterious for the limits it set upon the exercise of power to be very flexible.[89] We have already noticed Locke's shift from express to tacit consent. Adam Ferguson offered an even less constraining account of how consent was registered:

> The consent, upon which the right to command is founded may not be prior to the establishment of government; but may be obtained under the reasonable exercise of an actual power, to which every person within the community, by accepting of a customary protection, becomes bound to pay the customary allegiance and submission. Here is a compact ratified by the least ambiguous of all signs, the whole practice, or continued observance of an ordinary life.[90]

All liberal-democratic thinkers assume that authority is, in one way or another, a form of voluntary, self-assumed obligation. But *who* assumed it and how is it assumed? The social-contract tradition

---

[88] Diderot, *Encyclopédie, ou dictionnaire raisonné des sciences, des arts et des métiers* (Paris, 1752–72), i.

[89] I have been much helped on this topic by Carole Pateman, *The Problem of Political Obligation* (Chicester: Wiley, 1979).

[90] A. Ferguson, *Principles of Moral and Political Science* (London, 1792), ii. pp. 245–6.

offered an account of the *creation* of such obligations by voluntary agreement, and the various forms of consent theory an account of how individuals' action, or inaction, might be taken to signify continuing consent to them. Thus for Madison, the 'people' are the sole legitimate source of political power, its authority grounded through the 'elective mode' (and its power limited through checks and balances, federalism, and the 'vigilant and manly spirit' of the American people).[91] Bentham likewise sought to prevent the abuse of power by government, the 'exercise of its powers' consisting in 'the giving of directions or commands, positive and prohibitive, and incidentally in securing compliance through the application of rewards and punishments', and the basis of its authority lying in the expression of 'the will of the governed' manifested at periodic elections.[92] James Mill took a similar view.[93]

John Stuart Mill's views, however, were more complex. He had learnt much from Comte, Tocqueville, and Coleridge. A 'permanent political society' required 'the feeling of allegiance or loyalty', '*something* which is settled, something permanent, and not to be called in question'. There was not, and had never been 'any state of society in which collisions did not occur between immediate interests and passions of powerful sections of the people'.

What, then, enables society to weather these storms . . . that however important the interests about which men fall out, the conflict did not affect the fundamental principles of the system of social union which happened to exist; nor threaten large portions of the community with the subversion of that on which they had built their calculations, and with which their hopes and aims had become identified.

Mill, like other liberals, naturally saw power as coercive and associated it with the deprivation of liberty, but he also, like Tocqueville, saw the individual as needing protection against 'the tyranny of the prevailing opinion and feeling'. As for the basis of political authority, his views were similarly complex. Democratic authority was based on consent but, ideally, consent in the form of

[91] A. Hamilton, J. Madison, and J. Jay, *The Federalist Papers*, ed. I. Kramnick (Harmondsworth: Penguin, 1987).

[92] Bentham, 'The Constitutional Code', in *The Works of Jeremy Bentham*, ed. J. Bowring (Edinburgh, 1843), ix.

[93] See James Mill, *Essay on Government*. In fact, it is most plausible to date Bentham's conversion to democracy from about 1809, when he came under the influence of James Mill.

universal participation, in other words, 'the whole people partici-pate'. Moreover, as with Hobbes, Locke, Madison, and Bentham, government must not merely provide the framework for the pursuit of individual interests; the government must seek to 'promote the general mental advancement of the community' and 'organise the moral, intellectual and active worth already existing'. Mill himself recognized that he was thus led toward a 'qualified socialism', as were his successors in the Anglo-Saxon tradition, such as Green and Hobhouse.[94]

The entire liberal-democratic tradition gave a voluntarist account of authority by convention and a coercive account of asymmetric power. Liberal democracy, as Rawls has put it, comes 'as close as society can to being a voluntary scheme . . . its members are auto-nomous and the obligations they recognise self-imposed'.[95] The 'selves' who impose such obligations upon themselves are mutually disinterested and conflicting, and the authority over their conduct to which they are said to consent sets them free to pursue their otherwise mutually incompatible and unrealizable interests.

An alternative tradition begins exactly at this point, similarly aiming at a reconciliation of autonomy and authority, but rejecting the picture of conflicting, mutually disinterested selves as given. Thus Rousseau transformed the notion of the social contract and the idea of authority as based upon consent into a wholly new perspective. Ancient and medieval thinkers had often derived political authority from the consent of subjects, alongside traditional and divine sources. With the rise of individualistic theories of contract and consent and opposition to divine-right theories of absolutism in the sixteenth and seventeenth centuries, authority came to be seen as based on an agreement to protect the rights and pursuit of the conflicting interests of autonomous individuals.

Rousseau's view of authority was a new departure, aiming to retain the gains of individualism—the autonomous individual—while uniting him in community with others to achieve a collective will, as among the ancients. The basic problem to which the social contract provides the solution is to find 'a form of association' as a result of which 'the whole strength of the community will be enlisted

[94] See *Mill on Bentham and Coleridge*, ed. F. R. Leavis (London: Chatto & Windus, 1959), p. 123; J. Mill, *On Liberty: Principles of Political Economy*, 3rd edn.
[95] Rawls, *A Theory of Justice*, p. 13.

for the protection of the person and property of each constituent member, in such a way that each, when united to his fellows, renders obedience to his own will, and remains as free as he was before.' Citizenship confers 'moral freedom', which 'alone makes a man his own master': 'to obey the laws laid down by society is to be free'. The key to Rousseau's notion of community-with-autonomy is the idea of freedom from the *power* of others: 'dependence on men, being out of order, gives rise to every kind of vice, and through this master and slave become mutually depraved.' The *impersonal authority* of a community of individuals, whose identity and interests have become moralized and harmonized, derives from the expression of those individuals' general will. 'Each in giving himself to all gives himself to none'; in conditions of social equality and direct democracy, everyone becomes both ruler and subject. Asymmetric power, as control, dependence, and inequality, is abolished, and authority, being self-prescribed, is compatible with equality, autonomy, and reason.[96].

Hegel took this explosive combination of ideas further. Like Rousseau's, Hegel's idea of the state implies that its laws

are not something alien to the subject. On the contrary, his spirit bears witness to them as to its own essence, the essence in which he has a feeling of own self-hood, and in which he lives on in his own element which is not distinguished from himself. The subject is thus directly linked to the ethical order by a relation which is more like an identity than even the relation of faith or trust.

The state unites subjective consciousness and objective order, and in such conditions, 'to say that men allow themselves to be ruled counter to their own interests, ends and intentions is preposterous'. In a manner strongly recalling Rousseau, Hegel observed that 'in the state, as something ethical, as the interpenetration of the substantive and the particular, my obligation to what is substantive is at the same time the embodiment of my particular freedom'. The 'essence of the modern state is that the universal is bound up with the complete freedom of its particular members and with private well-being'. Hegel rejected the restoration thinkers (Haller, Müller, Savigny) who had sought to rest the authority of the state on tradition and on power. He also disagreed with the liberal view of the state as

---

[96] J. J. Rousseau, *Le Contrat social, passim*; *Émile*, trans. B. Foxley (London and New York: Dutton, 1911), p. 149.

inherently coercive and at best providing a framework for the pursuit of self-interest. On the contrary, he saw the state as the positive embodiment of man's self-consciousness—the 'actuality of the substantial will'—the basis of the state's authority being the rational wills of individuals who are precisely not mutually disinterested in that they will each others' goals—that is, the common good. For Hegel, the 'individual finds his liberation' in the differentiated spheres of 'ethical life'—the family, civil society (the interdependent sphere of economic self-interest) and the state. Civil society, left to itself, leads to 'physical and ethical degeneration'. However, the state can only fulfil its role as the concrete rational manifestation of human will by containing within itself a differentiated civil society.[97]

Rousseau envisaged the self-annihilating authority of consensual rational wills in an ideal community, fit, as he remarked, only for gods. For Hegel, such authority was to be exercised in the public domain in the post-Napoleonic constitutional state.[98] Others—from Fichte onward—saw such authority, arising from united, rational wills, in the context of the nation. Most varieties of nationalism have made use of this idea in some form.[99] Power is seen as derivative from such authority—a collective capacity harnessed to transcendent ends. Fascist doctrine carried this idea further. Elaborating 'the fascist theory of authority'. Mussolini proclaimed the fascist state to be 'a will to power and to government'. It has 'a consciousness of its own, a will of its own'; on this account it is called an 'ethical state' and it is 'strong, organic and at the same time founded on a wide popular basis'.[100]

Ideas of authority and power (deriving from interpretations and misinterpretations of Rousseau and Hegel) basing the former on united rational wills and the latter on the former had a very wide impact in the nineteenth century. Apart from the history of nationalism, they entered into liberalism at various points (notably with Green in England and Croce in Italy) and into both conservative and socialist thought. The anarchist tradition too sought to transcend

[97] G. W. F. Hegel, *Philosophy of Right* § 147, Addition to § 281, §261, § 260 and Addition.

[98] See *Hegel's Political Writings*, ed. Z. A. Pelczynski (Oxford: Oxford Univ. Press, 1964).

[99] See E. Kedourie, *Nationalism* (London: Hutchinson, 1960).

[100] B. Mussolini, 'The Doctrine of Fascism' trans. in *The Social and Political Doctrines of Contemporary Europe*, ed. M. Oakeshott (London: Cambridge Univ. Press, 1940), pp. 175–9.

both the tradition of authoritative belief and the liberal tradition of conventional authority guaranteeing a market society by postulating an ideal community of consensual wills. But the anarchists saw this not as the realization of authority but rather as its removal.

Proudhon's project was 'to live without government, to abolish all authority, absolutely and unreservedly'; 'industrial organization' would be substituted for government, contracts for laws, 'economic forces' for 'political powers', and 'identity of interests' for police.[101] Bakunin, aiming at 'the most complete liberty of individuals and associations', rejected 'the establishment of regulative authority of whatever kind';[102] and Kropotkin similarly saw progress as *the abolition of all the authority of government, as a development of free agreement* for all that was formerly a function of church and state, and *as a development of free initiative* in every individual and every group.'[103] It is distinctive of the anarchist tradition to denounce both authority over belief ('the old system', said Proudhon, stood on 'authority and Faith')[104] and *political* authority over conduct. Anarchist society would be free of politics, though it would still require co-ordination and thus the performance of administrative functions. Also, anarchists have tended to respect the authority of science. They see power in all hitherto existing societies as asymmetrical and inherently coercive, and as having its natural home in the state; as Rudolph Rocker said, 'the modern state' was 'the organ of political power for the forcible subjugation and aggression of the nonpossessing classes'.[105] However, power was also potentially collective and benign: as Bakunin put it, in the people 'there is a great deal of elemental power, more power indeed than in the government, taken together with all the ruling classes; but an elemental force lacking organisation is not a real power.'[106]

The Marxist tradition also sees the authority and power typical of class societies as destined to be historically surpassed, though it

[101] P. J. Proudhon, *General Idea of the Revolution in the Nineteenth Century*, trans. J. B. Robinson (London: Freedom Press, 1923), pp. 245–77.

[102] M. Bakunin, *Œuvres* (Paris: P. V. Stock, 1895), pp. 54–9.

[103] P. Kropotkin, *Modern Science and Anarchism* (London: Freedom Press, 1912), repr. in I. L. Horowitz (ed.), *The Anarchists* (New York: Dell, 1964), p. 163.

[104] Proudhon, *General Idea of the Revolution*, pp. 245–7.

[105] Rocker, 'Anarchism and Anarcho-Syndicalism', repr. in Horowitz, *The Anarchists*, p. 190.

[106] Bakunin, 'Science and the Urgent Revolutionary Task', repr. in Horowitz, *The Anarchists*, p. 132.

offers a much more complex account of their nature and interrelation. In the first place, power is class power (political power Marx and Engels defined as 'merely the organised power of one class for oppressing another'), and authority is a form of it. Both are exercised within, and in turn reinforce, the economic constraints set by the mode of production. These are imposed by economic relations whose 'dull compulsion . . . completes the subjection of the labourer to the capitalist'. The nature of these exploitative relations of production is concealed from the agents of production by ideology —a whole web of 'conceptions which arise about the laws of production in the minds of agents of capitalist production and circulation' which 'will diverge drastically from the real laws'.[107] In general, the dynamics and possibilities of transformation of class society are concealed from subordinate classes by the ruling ideas of any age, these being 'the ideas of the ruling class'. In this way, authority over belief—whether it be religion or political economy or social science—is successfully imposed by class power. Moreover, the illusion of authority by convention, voluntarily granted to the government by free and equal citizens, is similarly imposed as the ideology of bourgeois democracy. To this must be added a whole arsenal of instruments of rule—though it must be said that Marxism in general lacks a properly worked out theory of domination. The most one has is a series of historically located aperçus in Marx and Engels, a few rudimentary generalizations in Engels and Lenin, and the only (flawed) attempt at a more developed theory in Gramsci.

For Marx and Engels, class power (of its very nature asymmetric) is exercised by superordinate over subordinate classes in a variety of ways, ranging from ideological mystification through all the various forms of inducement, persuasion, influence, and control—through the family, in the educational and legal system, in the labour market and the labour process—to outright coercion and force, typically exercised by the state. There are of course considerable variations among capitalist states, with respect both to the extent of the state's control of civil society and to the state's relative autonomy from class control. This has posed a crux for Marxist thinkers. Were these just different forms of class domination, or were certain forms—namely, bourgeois parliamentary democracy—based on the (genuine rather

---

[107] K. Marx and F. Engels, *The Communist Manifesto*; Marx, *Capital* (Moscow: Foreign Languages Publishing House, 1962), i. p. 737; iii. p. 307.

than imposed) consent of the working class to advanced capitalism? If so, clearly the 'parliamentary road to socialism' was on the cards. In other words, was bourgeois democracy merely a way of keeping people in subjection by deception and concession, as Lenin thought ('concessions of the unessential, while retaining the essential')[108] or was it, as Engels and at times Marx came to suspect, a framework within which class power could be peacefully transferred to the working class?

Central to this discussion has been the work of Gramsci, whose theorizing about power and authority is encapsulated in his much-discussed concept of 'hegemony', the suggestive complexities of which can only be hinted at here. Beginning from a traditional, if rather simple, dichotomy between 'force and consent' characteristic of Italian thought (found in Machiavelli, in the élitist Machiavellians, and in Gentile), Gramsci added the parallel contrasts 'domination and hegemony', 'violence and civilization', and he spoke of hegemony as 'intellectual and moral direction', and also as 'the moment of consent, of cultural direction' as opposed to 'the moment of force, of constraint, or of state-legislative or police intervention'. When speaking thus, he was thinking of class power as cultural and ideological and exercised within civil society ('through so-called private organisations, like the church, trade unions, schools, and so on'). Elsewhere, he spoke of hegemony as 'a combination of force and consent which form variable equilibria, without force ever prevailing too much over consent'. In this sense, hegemony was exercised both within the state and civil society; this allowed him to take account of the ideological functions of the state and corrected the earlier exclusive focus on cultural hegemony. In a third version, hegemony is again seen as a mixture of force and consent, but exercised within the state, which is now seen as incorporating both political and civil society—'not merely the governmental apparatus, but also the "private" apparatus of hegemony or civil society.'[109] This last, expanded notion of the state was taken over by Louis

[108] Lenin, *Collected Works* (London: Lawrence & Wishart, 1960–70), xxiv. pp. 63–4.

[109] A. Gramsci, *Selections from the Prison Notebooks*, ed. Q. Hoare and G. Nowell-Smith (London: New Left Books, 1971), pp. 169–70, 57; *Lettere del Carcere* (Turin: Einardi, 1965), pp. 616, 481; *Selections from the Prison Notebooks*, pp. 80 n., 242. These quotations are cited by Perry Anderson in his extremely valuable essay, 'The Antinomies of Antonio Gramsci', *New Left Review*, 100 (1976–7), pp. 5–78.

Althusser, who speaks of the state's 'repressive' and 'ideological' apparatuses.[110] Gramsci's original insight into the consensual dimension of class power operating *outside* the state, and indeed the crucial differences between cases where it lies outside and inside the state, is lost. At all events, Gramsci's inconclusive and shifting treatment of hegemony raised the discussion of the relations between power and authority to a new level within the Marxist tradition. In particular, he raised (though he did not answer) the closely related questions of the relation between the legitimacy of parliamentary institutions in the West and the state's monopoly of force and of the role of consensual direction and coercion in the struggle of the working class, in alliance with others, for power.

The Marxist tradition, like the anarchist, is committed to the proposition that power, as control, dependency and inequality, and authority—in so far as it conflicts with equality, freedom, and reason—are to be eliminated. (This, doubtless, must occur within communist rather than socialist society, though Marx never faced the issue of what power and authority would be like in the latter). In their futuristic projections, there are interesting differences between the Marxist founding fathers.

Marx (especially the early Marx) often spoke as though all forms of superordination and subordination would be abolished. Communism would deprive men of 'the power to subjugate the labour of others by means of . . . appropriation'; and when 'class distinctions have disappeared, and all production has been concentrated in the hands of a vast association of the whole nation, the public power will lose its political character.'[111] Engels echoed this, claiming that

the political state, and with it political authority, will disappear as the result of the coming social revolution, that is . . . public functions will lose their political character and be transformed into the simple administrative functions of watching over the true interests of society.[112]

Here Engels and Lenin, who followed up these thoughts in *State and Revolution*, rejoin Saint-Simon. As Lenin wrote:

From the moment all members of society, or at least the vast majority, have learned to administer the state *themselves*, have taken this work into their

---

[110] See Althusser, *Lenin and Philosophy, and Other Essays* (London: New Left Books, 1971).   [111] Marx and Engels, *The Communist Manifesto*, sect. II.
[112] F. Engels, 'On Authority', in Marx and Engels, *Selected Works*, 2 vols. (Moscow: Foreign Languages Publishing House, 1962), i. p. 639.

own hands, have organised control over the insignificant capitalist minority, over the gentry who wish to preserve their capitalist habits and over the workers who have been thoroughly corrupted by capitalism—from this moment the need for government of any kind begins to disappear altogether. The more complete the democracy, the nearer the moment when it becomes unnecessary.[113]

But Marx's image of the dissolution of power and authority extended (at times) even to the labour process itself. Under capitalism 'the mass of direct producers is confronted by the social character of their production in the form of strictly regulating authority and a social mechanism of the labour process organised as a complete hierarchy.' Though 'physical necessity'—that is, nature—set constraints, Marx's image of freedom was of 'socialised man, the associated producers, rationally regulating their interchange with Nature, bringing it under their control, instead of being ruled by it as by the blind forces of Nature.' The need to 'coordinate and unify the labor process' in the workshops of the future would be met as if by 'an orchestra conductor'. Eventually,

the human being comes to relate more as a watchman and regulator to the production process itself . . . He steps to the side of the production process, instead of being its chief actor. In this transformation, it is neither the direct human labour he himself performs, not the time during which he works, but rather the appropriation of his own general productive power, his understanding of nature and his mastery over it by virtue of his presence as a social body—it is, in a word, the development of the social individual which appears as the great foundation-stone of production and of wealth.[114]

Engels, however, struck a more 'realistic' note, arguing in opposition to the anarchists that it was not possible to have organization without authority (by 'authority' he meant 'the imposition of the will of another upon ours') and claimed that it 'presupposes subordination'. The forces of nature, he argued, require the organization of labour to be settled 'in an authoritarian way'. Thus, 'a certain authority, no matter how delegated, and . . . a certain subordination, are things which, independently of all social organization, are imposed upon us, together with the material conditions under which we produce and make products circulate.' Hence:

113 Lenin, *State and Revolution, Selected Works*, p. 337.
114 Marx, *Capital*, iii. 859, 800, 376; *Grundrisse*, trans. Martin Nicholaus (Harmondsworth: Penguin Books in assoc. with *New Left Review*, 1973), p. 705.

it is absurd to speak of the principle of authority as being absolutely evil, and of the principle of autonomy as being absolutely good. Authority and autonomy are relative things whose spheres vary with the various phases of the development of society. If the autonomists confined themselves to saying that the social organisation of the future would restrict authority solely to the limits within which the conditions of production render it inevitable, we would understand each other . . .[115]

Thus Engels rejected the anarcho-syndicalist dream (of which there are more than hints in Marx) of the abolition of power (as control) and authority (by imposition) within the sphere of production itself. However, he shared with Marx and all other classical Marxists the belief that elsewhere, especially in the political sphere, such power and authority would disappear—however authoritarian and co-ercive might be the means necessary to achieve that happy end state.

In contrast with all those—radical democrats, anarchists, Marxists, and others—who contemplate the possibility of such an end state of benign collective power and consensual authority, we may identify what might be called a 'realist' tradition of viewing power and authority, whose prime modern exponents are the neo-Machiavellian élite theorists, notably Pareto, Mosca, and Michels. However, this tradition stands no less in opposition to liberal democracy, lacking its distrust of power and debunking its justifica-tion of authority. Again, its attitude to doctrines of authoritative belief, whether traditionalist, religious, or secular, is reductionist: 'ruling classes', Mosca observed, 'do not justify their power solely by de facto possession of it, but try to find a moral and legal basis for it, representing it as the logical and necessary consequence of doctrines and beliefs that are generally recognised and accepted'—though for Mosca such political formulas are not 'mere quackeries aptly in-vented to trick the masses into obedience'; they answer 'a real need in man's social nature . . . of governing and knowing that one is governed not on the basis of mere material or intellectual force, but on the basis of a moral principle.' 'Every governing class', he remarked, 'tends to justify its actual exercise of power by resting it on some universal moral principle' which 'has come forward in our time in scientific trappings'. Indeed, Mosca asked whether 'a society can

[115] Engels, 'On Authority', pp. 635–9. 'Wanting to abolish authority in large-scale industry', wrote Engels, 'is tantamount to wanting to abolish industry itself, to destroy the power loom in order to return to the spinning wheel' (p. 637).

hold together without one of these "great superstitions"'—whether a universal illusion is not a social force that contributes powerfully to consolidating political organization and unifying peoples or even whole civilizations.[116]

Likewise, Pareto has some splendid debunking paragraphs on authority as a tool of proof and a tool of persuasion. It is 'an instrument for logicalizing nonlogical actions and the sentiments in which they originate'; it is appealed to by the Protestant, the Catholic, 'the humanitarian who swoons over a passage of Rousseau', the 'socialist who swears by the Word of Marx and Engels', and 'the devout democrat who bows reverent head and submits judgment and will to the oracles of suffrage, universal or limited, or what is worse to the pronouncements of parliaments and legislatures.' It holds 'in our present-day societies, not only for the ignorant, and not only touching matters of religion and morality, but even in the sciences, especially in those branches with which a person is not directly familiar.'[117]

Such realist writers agree with Marxists and anarchists in uncovering the asymmetric power dimension behind authority over belief and by convention, and in debunking liberal illusions, but they generalize the attack, seeing control, dependence, and inequality, and authority by imposition as inevitable and ineradicable features of all societies, not least those which purport to be socialist and democratic. Hence Michels's claim that 'the formation of oligarchies within the various forms of democracy is the outcome of organic necessity, and consequently affects every organization, be it socialist or even anarchist'. The government or state 'cannot be anything other than the organization of a minority'. As for the majority, it is 'permanently incapable of self-government':

Even when the discontent of the masses culminates in a successful attempt to deprive the bourgeoisie of power, this is after all, so Mosca contends, effected only in appearance; always and necessarily there springs from the masses a new organized minority which raises itself to the rank of a governing class. Thus the majority of human beings, in a condition of eternal tutelage, are predestined by tragic necessity to submit to the dominion of a

---

[116] G. Mosca, *The Ruling Class (Elementi de Scienza Politica)*, trans. H. D. Kahn; ed. A. Livingston (New York: McGraw-Hill, 1939), pp. 70, 71, 62, 71.
[117] V. Pareto, *The Mind and Society: A Treatise on General Sociology* (New York: Dover, 1963), §§ 583, 585, 590.

small minority, and must be content to constitute the pedestal of an oligarchy.[118]

Pareto is harsher still:

All governments use force and all assert that they are founded on reason. In the fact, whether universal suffrage prevails or not, it is always an oligarchy that governs, finding ways to give to 'the will of the people' the expression which the few desire . . .

He argued that

one finds everywhere a governing class of relatively few individuals that keeps itself in power partly by force and partly by the consent of the subject class, which is much more populous. The difference lies principally, as regards substance, in the relative proportions of force and consent; and as regards forms, in the manners in which the force is used and the consent obtained.

But Pareto had a most cynical, 'realistic' view of the nature of consent: consent is always manipulated, authority always imposed by means of power. Both consent and force were for Pareto 'instruments of governing'—consent being achieved by the skilful manipulation of 'sentiments and interests'.[119]

Others can be included within the 'realist' tradition who, no less wary of what Michels called 'excessive optimism', offered a more rounded, less reductionist account of power and authority. Thus Simmel sensitively explored the forms of superordination and subordination (under an individual, under a plurality, under a principle), commenting on the 'sociological error of socialism and anarchism'.[120] Freud, too, can be seen as exploring, at the level of the individual, the many forms that social control may take of coercion and dependence and the acceptance of authority, in the face of 'the human instinct of aggression and self-destruction'.[121]

It was, however, unquestionably Max Weber who was the 'realist' who offered the subtlest and richest account of power and authority in the whole history of social and political theorizing. We have already seen that Weber's view of power as asymmetrical covers

---

[118] R. Michels, *Political Parties*, trans. E. Paul and C. Paul (New York: Dover, 1959), pp. 402, 390.
[119] Pareto, *Mind and Society*, §§ 2183, 2244, 2251, 2252.
[120] Simmel, 'Superordination and Subordination', *The Sociology of Georg Simmel*, pp. 282–3.
[121] See S. Freud, *Civilisation and its Discontents* (London: Hogarth Press, 1961).

control, dependence, and inequality—power being 'the probability that one actor within a social relationship will be in a position to carry out his own will despite resistance, regardless of the basis on which this probability rests'. Weber stressed that there was an extremely wide variety of such bases: 'All conceivable qualities of a person and all conceivable combinations of circumstances may put him in a position to impose his will in a given situation.' For this reason, Weber regarded the concept of power as 'sociologically amorphous' and proposed the 'more precise' concept of *Herrschaft*, or domination, which he saw as a 'special case of power'. What, then, did he mean by *Herrschaft*?[122]

He distinguished between 'the most general' and a 'narrower sense'. The former simply designated all structures of power relations: on such a broad definition, dominant positions could

emerge from the social relations in a drawing room as well as in the market, from the rostrum of a lecture hall as well as from the command post of a regiment, from an erotic or charitable relationship as well as from scholarly discussion of athletics.[123]

Weber therefore drew a distinction between 'domination by virtue of a constellation of interests (in particular: by virtue of a position of monopoly)' and 'domination by virtue of authority, i.e., power to command and duty to obey'. Domination in the narrower sense excluded the former—that is 'domination which originates in the market or other interest constellations' (even though this may 'because of the very absence of rules . . . be felt to be much more oppressive') and was equated with '*authoritarian power of command*'. More specifically, he wrote:

domination will thus mean the situation in which the manifested will (*command*) of the *ruler* or rulers is meant to influence the conduct of one or more others (the *ruled*) and actually does influence it in such a way that their conduct to a socially relevant degree occurs as if the ruled had made the content of the command the maxim of their conduct for its very own sake.[124]

These are, of course, Weberian 'types', and in reality the border-line between them is fluid: 'the transitions are gradual', since 'sharp differentiation in concrete fact is often impossible' (this making 'clarity in the analytical distinctions all the more important'). Hence,

---

[122] Weber, *Economy and Society*, pp. 53, 941.
[123] Ibid. 941, 946, 943.
[124] Ibid. 943, 946.

'Any type of domination by virtue of constellation of interests may . . . be transformed into domination by authority', as when economic, market-based dependencies are formalized into norm-governed authority relations; thus a vassal freely enters into the relation of fealty with a feudal lord, who thenceforth acquires authority over him; or contracts 'concluded in the labor market by formally "equal" parties through the "voluntary" acceptance of the terms offered by the employer' become transformed into formalized positions in (public or private) corporate hierarchies. Moreover, 'a certain minimum interest of the subordinate in his own obeying will normally constitute one of the indispensable motives of obedience even in the completely authoritarian duty-relationship.'[125]

There has been much scholarly debate about how *Herrschaft* is to be understood. Parsons (typically interpreting Weber as a pre-Parsonian) translates it (in the narrower sense) as 'authority' rather than 'domination' on the grounds that the latter term suggests the fact that 'a leader has power over his followers . . . rather than the integration of the collectivity in the interest of effective function-ing . . . is the critical factor from Weber's point of view.'[126] By contrast, Bendix, who rightly prefers 'domination', argues that 'as a realist in the analysis of power, [Weber] would have been critical of any translation that tended to obscure the "threat of force" present in all relations between superiors and subordinates.'[127]

It is clear that by *Herrschaft* (in the narrower sense) Weber meant to identify such structured relations between superiors and subordin-ates in which compliance could be based on a wide variety of motives ('all the way from simple habituation to the most purely rational calculation of advantage') and achieved by a wide variety of means. The primary virtue of his whole approach is its sensitivity to this variety, and the resultant questions it opens up about how such relations are established and maintained. His general hypothesis was that:

in no instance does domination voluntarily limit itself to the appeal to material or affectual or ideal motives as a basis for its continuance. In addition every such system attempts to establish and to cultivate the belief in

---

[125] Ibid. 944, 214, 943, 944–5.
[126] Parsons, review art. of R. Bendix's *Max Weber: An Intellectual Portrait, American Sociological Review* 25 (1960), p. 752.
[127] R. Bendix, *Max Weber: An Intellectual Portrait* (Garden City, NY: Anchor Books, Doubleday, 1962), p. 482.

its legitimacy. But according to the kind of legitimacy which is claimed, the type of obedience, the kind of administrative staff developed to guarantee it, and the mode of exercising authority will all differ fundamentally.

Hence Weber's decision to classify the types of domination according to the kind of claim to legitimacy typically made by each, since the differences between kinds of claims were held to be basic to, to vary with, and to be explanatory of power relations and forms of administration. In other words, 'the sociological character of domination will differ according to the basic differences in the major modes of legitimation'.[128]

Parsons is therefore quite mistaken in translating *Herrschaft* as 'authority'. Rather, the celebrated 'three pure types of authority' single out prevailing rationales for obedience to authority *within* structures of domination.[129] They do not, moreover, refer to motives of obedience or to structures of power. People, according to Weber, may obey hypocritically, opportunistically, out of material self-interest, or 'from individual weakness or helplessness, because there is no acceptable alternative'. What is important is

the fact that in a given case the particular claim to legitimacy is to a significant degree and according to its type treated as 'valid': that this fact confirms the position of the person claiming authority and that it helps to determine the choice of means of its exercise.[130]

The types of authority invoke types of norms which specify who and what is to count as authoritative. Thus traditional, rational or legal, and charismatic authority signify publicly advanced types of reasons or 'grounds' for obeying, each of which, according to Weber, tends to prevail under certain conditions and is in turn associated with and explanatory of power relations and forms of administration. Weber postulated that one or another type tends to predominate in any given political association or institutional order: rational-legal authority in the modern state and in bureaucratic forms of organization, private and public; traditional authority in patriarchal, patrimoninial, and feudal societies and in the medieval manor; while charismatic authority erupts (only to be subsequently routinized) in all communities up to the modern world in periods of transition. However, although one type of authority will pre-

---

[128] Weber, *Economy and Society*, pp. 212, 213, 947.
[129] See Denis Wrong, introd. to *Max Weber* ed. D. Wrong (Englewood Cliffs, NJ Prentice-Hall, 1976), p. 50.   [130] Weber, *Economy and Society*, p. 214.

dominate in any given structure of domination, 'the forms of domination occurring in historical reality constitute combinations, mixtures, adaptations or modifications of these "pure" types'.[131]

What, then, was Weber's ultimate view of the relations between power and authority? No simple answer can be given, but four remarks may serve to indicate the essence of his way of seeing the issues.

First, he saw power as extending much further than authority, and, in particular, as covering all cases of domination excluded by the more narrow sense—that is, 'forms of power . . . based upon constellations of interests', of which the 'purest type' is 'monopolistic domination in the market', but which include 'all relationships of exchange, including those of intangibles'. Thus Weber listed, apart from market relations, those produced by 'society'—as, for instance, the position of a *salon*—and those between political entities—as in the role of Prussia within the German Customs Union or New York within the United States. (He might well have included all patron–client relations.) Certainly, Weber was keenly sensitive to the exertion of economic power within 'civil society', through the dictation of the terms of exchange to contractual partners: 'influence derived exclusively from the possessions of goods or marketable skills guaranteed in some way and acting upon the conduct of those dominated, who remain, however, formally free and are motivated simply by the pursuit of their own interests.' His theory of classes was based on this idea.[132]

Second, he did not, as did the neo-Machiavellians, see all consent to authority as imposed by rulers. Thus, for example:

As a rule . . . the political patrimonial ruler is linked with the ruled through a consensual community which also exists apart from his independent military force and which is rooted in the belief that the ruler's powers are legitimate insofar as they are traditional.

On the other hand, he naturally inclined to a 'realistic' power analysis, especially of 'democratic' forms of authority. 'Direct democratic administration' he saw as a 'marginal type case', 'unstable', and manifesting a tendency 'to turn into rule by notables', and, like Michels and the other élite theorists, he accepted 'the law of the small number'—namely, the principle that (because of complexity, the

---

[131] Ibid. 954.   [132] Ibid. 946, 943, 947, 943.

need for specialized skills and organizational dynamics) ruling minorities, whether collegial or monocratic, are indispensable to the very existence of organization. Thus he was systematically doubtful about the claims of democracy, direct or indirect:

> the fact that the chief and his administrative staff often appear formally as servants or agents of those they rule does nothing whatever to disprove the quality of dominance ... a certain minimum of assured power to issue commands, thus of domination, must be provided for in nearly every conceivable case.

And, more generally, he spoke of the acceptance of the 'myth' of the natural superiority of the highly privileged by negatively privileged strata 'under conditions of stable distribution of power and, consequently [*sic*], of status order.' Indeed, 'the continued exercise of every domination ... always has the strongest need of self-justification through appealing to the principles of its legitimation.'[133]

   Third, as we have seen, he assumed that the type of authority ('the ultimate grounds of the validity of a domination') is, in any particular case of domination, basic to, and to a significant extent explanatory of, 'the kind of relationship between the master or masters and the apparatus, the kind of relationship of both to the ruled, and ... its specific *organizational* structure, i.e. its specific way of distributing the powers of command.'[134]

   Finally, Weber stressed the ultimate role of power, in the form of coercion, or the threat of force, as an indispensable underpinning for the exercise of authority: for

> the political community, even more than other institutionally organized communities, is so constituted that it imposes obligations on the individual which many of them fulfil only because they are aware of the probability of physical coercion backing up such obligations.[135]

III

There is little in modern debates about the concepts of power and authority that is not implicit in their history. I shall here refer to four such debates, the first of which is between a collective and an asymmetric conception of power; the second and third, between

[133] Weber, *Economy and Society*, pp. 1020, 949, 950, 952, 215, 953, 954.
[134] Ibid. 953.   [135] Ibid. 903.

different asymmetric conceptions; and the fourth, between alternative collective conceptions.

The disagreement between Talcott Parsons and C. Wright Mills is a
double disagreement. Its two aspects are contained in Parson's
statement that

> to Mills, power is not a facility for the performance of function in, and on
> behalf of, the society as a system, but is interpreted exclusively as a facility
> for getting what one group, the holders of power, wants by preventing
> another group, the 'outs,' from getting what it wants.[136]

The first disagreement centres on the very question of whether
power is or is not asymmetric—or, as Parsons (but not Mills) puts it,
'zero-sum'. Here Mills follows Weber and other asymmetric theorists of power, identifying it with control, dependence, and inequality;
'By the powerful', he writes, 'we mean, of course, those who are able
to realize their will, even if others resist it.'[137] For Parsons, by
contrast, this view is 'highly selective' and serves to 'elevate a
secondary and derived aspect of a total phenomenon into the central
place'.[138] Power is comparable to money: it becomes a facility for the
achievement of collective goals through the agreement of members of
a society to legitimize leadership positions whose incumbents further
the goals of the system. Thus the amount of power in the system can
be increased by analogy with credit creation in the economy. This
view of power and authority deflects attention from all cases where
power is exercised over and authority imposed upon others, and in
general from power differentials and conflicts of interest. It is not a
relation between individuals and groups, but a system property—
the capacity to use authoritative decisions to further agreed-upon,
collective goals.

This leads to the second disagreement, which is over whether
power is attributed to systems or to social actors. Parsons sees power
as a system resource—'a generalized facility or resource in the

---

[136] Parsons, 'The Distribution of Power in American Society', a review of C.
Wright Mills's *The Power Élite, World Politics* (Oct. 1957) repr. in *C. Wright Mills
and The Power Élite*, ed. G. W. Domhoff and H. B. Ballard (Boston: Beacon, 1968),
p. 82.

[137] C. Wright Mills, *The Power Élite* (New York and London: Oxford Univ. Press,
1956), p. 9.

[138] Parsons, 'The Distribution of Power in American Society', pp. 82 *et seq*. Cf. A.
Giddens, 'Power', on the writings of Talcott Parsons in his *Studies in Social and
Political Theory* (London: Hutchinson, 1977).

society'.[139] Authority is 'the institutionalization of the "rights" of leaders to expect support from the members of the collectivity.' It is, in other words, the set of rights enabling leaders to command support and hence the precondition for the system's power to be exercised. Thus authority is not a form of power (e.g., legitimate power), but rather a *basis* of power, indeed the *only* basis of power. There is therefore no such thing as 'illegitimate power'; power is by definition legitimate. Thus, 'the threat of coercive measure, or of compulsion, without legitimation or justification, should not properly be called the use of power at all . . .'[140]

By contrast, Mills attributes power to social actors. 'Power', he writes,

has to do with whatever decisions men make about the arrangements under which they live, and about the events which make up the history of their times . . . in so far as such decisions are made, the problem of who is involved in the making of them is the basic problem of power. In so far as they could be made but are not, the problem becomes who fails to make them.

Like other élite theorists, Mills sees power as exercised by individual or collective actors—who today 'have the power to manipulate and manage the consent of men.' Authority, in this view, is one of the forms of power—'power that is justified by the beliefs of the voluntarily obedient', alongside manipulation ('power that is wielded unknown to the powerless') and coercion.[141]

The debate within the Marxist tradition between Nicos Poulantzas and Ralph Miliband is in some ways parallel to that between Parsons and Mills. In this debate too, the disagreement is partly over whether power is attributable to agents or to the structures and systems within which they act. According to Poulantzas, Miliband had

difficulties . . . in comprehending social classes and the the State as *objective structures*, and their relations as an *objective system of regular connections*, a structure and a system whose agents, 'men', are in the words of Marx, 'bearers' of it—*Träger*. Miliband constantly gives the impression that for him social classes or 'groups' are in some way reducible to *inter-personal*

---

139 Parsons, 'The Distribution of Power in American Society', p. 83.

140 Id. 'Authority, Legitimation and Political Action', p. 181; 'On the Concept of Political Power', *Proceedings of the American Philosophical Society*, 107 (1963), p. 250.

141 Wright Mills, 'The Structure of Power in American Society', in *Power, Politics and People: The Collected Essays of C. Wright Mills*, ed. I. L. Horowitz (New York and London: Oxford Univ. Press, 1963), p. 23.

relations, that the State is reducible to inter-personal relations of the members of the diverse 'groups' that constitute the State apparatus, and finally that the relation between social classes and the State is itself reducible to inter-personal relations of 'individuals' composing social groups and 'individuals' composing the State apparatus.

This conception, Poulantzas continues,

> seems to me to derive from a *problematic of the subject* which has had constant repercussions in the history of Marxist thought. According to this problematic, the agents of a social formation, 'men', are not considered as the 'bearers' of objective instances (as they are for Marx), but as the genetic principle of the levels of the social whole. This is a problematic of *social actors*, of individuals as the origin of *social action*: sociological research thus leads finally, not to the study of the objective co-ordinates that determine the distribution of agents into social classes and the contradictions between these classes, but to the search for *finalist* explanations founded on the *motivations of conduct* of the individual actors.[142]

Miliband, in response to this, maintains that Poulantzas

> is here rather one-sided and that he goes much too far in dismissing the nature of the state élite as of altogether no account. For what his *exclusive* stress on 'objective relations' suggests is that what the state does is in every particular and at all times *wholly* determined by these 'objective relations': in other words, that the structural constraints of the system are so absolutely compelling as to turn those who run the state into the merest functionaries and executants of policies imposed upon them by 'the system'.

Poulantzas, writes Miliband, substitutes 'the notion of "objective structures" for the notion of a "ruling" class', and he falls into

> a 'hyperstructuralist' trap, which deprives 'agents' of any freedom of choice and manœuvre and turns them into the 'bearers' of objective forces which they are unable to affect. This perspective is but another form of determinism—which is alien to Marxism and in any case false, which is much more serious. Governments can and do press against the 'structural constraints' by which they are beset.[143]

Also at issue between Poulantzas and Miliband is whether all power is class power. Indeed, Poulantzas *defines* power as '*the capacity of a social class to realise its specific objective interests.*'[144]

---

[142] N. Poulantzas, 'The Problem of the Capitalist State', *New Left Review*, 58 (Nov.–Dec. 1969), p. 70.

[143] R. Miliband, 'The Capitalist State: Reply to Nicos Poulantzas', *New Left Review*, 59 (Jan.–Feb. 1970), p. 57; and *Marxism and Politics* (Oxford: Oxford Univ. Press, 1977), p. 73. Cf. S. Lukes, 'Power and Structure'.

[144] Poulantzas, *Political Power and Social Classes*, trans. T. O'Hagan (London: New Left Books and Sheed & Ward, 1973), p. 104.

Miliband, on the other hand, seeks to allow a (historically variable) place for (relatively autonomous) state power: he seeks to avoid any 'confusion between *class power* and *state power*, a distinction which it is important not to blur'.[145] Both writers, however, agree in seeing the 'legitimation' of authority as a form of power, though Poulantzas follows Althusser and Gramsci's third model of hegemony in speaking of this as occurring within the 'state ideological apparatuses', while Miliband argues that

there is absolutely no warrant for speaking of 'state ideological apparatuses' in regard to institutions which, in bourgeois democratic societies, are not part of the state; and much which is important about the life of these societies is lost in the obliteration of the distinction between ideological apparatuses which are mainly the product of 'civil society' and those which are the product and part of the state apparatus.[146]

The 'community power debate' within recent American political science is a debate between disputants who share a general conception of asymmetric power as control, or the securing of compliance, but who disagree about how it is to be identified and measured. More specifically, they agree in seeing power as exercised when A affects B in A's but against B's interests, but they disagree about how this idea is properly to be understood and applied in research—and this disagreement largely stems from differing conceptions of what are to count as interests and how they may be adversely affected, which stems from fundamental differences of philosophical and methodological positions and ultimately of world view.

Robert Dahl, Nelson Polsby, and their colleagues employ a 'one-dimensional' view of power which involves a focus on behaviour in the making of decisions on (key) issues over which there is an observable conflict of (subjective) interests, seen as express policy preferences revealed by political participation. Thus Polsby writes that

one can conceive of 'power'—'influence' and 'control' are serviceable synonyms—as the capacity of one actor to do something affecting another actor, which changes the probable pattern of specified future events. This can be envisaged most easily in a decision-making situation.

And he argues that identifying 'who prevails in decision-making' seems 'the best way to determine which individuals and groups have "more" power in social life, because direct conflict between actors

145 Miliband, *Marxism and Politics*, p. 54.   146 Ibid. 57.

presents a situation most closely approximating an experimental test of their capacities to affect outcomes.'[147] Thus Dahl's central method in *Who Governs?* was to

determine for each decision which participants had initiated alternatives that were finally adopted, had vetoed alternatives initiated by others, or had proposed alternatives that were turned down. Their actions were then tabulated as individual 'successes' or 'defeats'. The participants with the greatest proportion of success out of the total number of successes were then considered to be the most influential.[148]

Peter Bachrach and Morton Baratz criticize this view of power as restrictive and, by virtue of that fact, as giving a misleadingly sanguine pluralist picture of American politics. Power, they claim, has two faces. The first face is that examined by Dahl and his colleagues, according to which 'power is totally embodied and fully reflected in "concrete decisions" or in activity bearing upon their making.' But, they maintain, it is also exercised

when A devotes his energies to creating or reinforcing social and political values and institutional practices that limit the scope of the political process to public consideration of only those issues which are comparatively innocuous to A. To the extent that A succeeds in doing this, B is prevented, for all practical purposes, from bringing to the fore any issues that might in their resolution be seriously detrimental to A's set of preferences.

The second face of power exists 'to the extent that a person or group—consciously or unconsciously—creates or reinforces barriers to the public airing of policy conflicts' by 'non-decision making' —that is, decision-making that 'results in suppression or thwarting of a latent or manifest challenge to the values or interests of the decision-maker'. Such power, however, only shows up where there is conflict, overt or covert; in the absence of such conflict, 'the presumption must be that there is consensus on the prevailing allocation of values'.[149] In sum, the two-dimensional view of power involves a qualified critique of the behavioural focus of the one-dimensional (qualified because it still assumes that non-decision-making is a form of decision-making), and it allows for consideration of the ways in

---

[147] N. W. Polsby, *Community Power and Political Theory* (New Haven, Conn. and London: Yale Univ. Press, 1963), pp. 3–4.

[148] R. A. Dahl, *Who Governs?: Democracy and Power in an American City* (New Haven, Conn. and London: Yale Univ. Press, 1961), p. 336.

[149] P. Bachrach and M. S. Baratz, *Power and Poverty in Theory and Practice* (New York: Oxford Univ. Press, 1970), pp. 7, 8, 44, 49.

which decisions are prevented from being taken on potential issues over which there is an observable conflict of (subjective) interests, seen as embodied either in express policy preferences revealed by political participation, or in covert or deflected subpolitical grievances.

I have, in turn, criticized this two-dimensional view[150] as being both too behaviourist and too individualistic, and because of its insistence that for power to exist there must be observable conflict and the existence of grievances, albeit covert. A three-dimensional view of power can be elaborated which incorporates the first two but allows for consideration of the subtler and less visible ways in which potential issues are kept out of politics through the behaviour of groups and practices of institutions (which may not be analysable in terms of individuals' decision-making and may indeed be manifested by individuals' inaction). Moreover, such power may be exercised in the absence of observable conflict and grievances; is it not the supreme exercise of power to avert conflict and grievance by influencing, shaping, and determining the perceptions and preferences of others? Such a view requires the hypothesis of a contradiction between the interests of those exercising power and the real interests of those who silently acquiesce. Doubtless, such a hypothesis raises several acute difficulties of theory and research; but such difficulties are not solved by adopting the alternative, and methodologically easier, hypothesis that power of this kind cannot exist.

As for authority, proponents of the first view tend to see political authority as authority by convention in classical liberal-democratic terms: it is voluntarily given in the form of renewed consent at regular elections (which also enable the electorate to exercise 'indirect influence on the decisions of leaders').[151] Bachrach and Baratz, however, are equivocal on the topic of authority. They see it as one of the means of control, or securing compliance (along with the threat of sanctions, influence, force, and manipulation), where 'B complies because he recognises that [A's] command is reasonable in terms of his own values', because either its content or the procedure by which it is reached is legitimate and reasonable. Yet they seem unsure about whether it is a form of power, involving a 'possible conflict of values', or an 'agreement based upon reason'.[152] Consideration of the third

---

[150] Lukes, *Power: A Radical View* (London: Macmillan, and Atlantic Highlands, NJ: Humanities Press, 1974).   [151] Dahl, *Who Governs?* p. 101.
[152] Bachrach and Baratz, *Power and Poverty*, pp. 34, 37, 20.

dimension of power opens up the whole question of how and to what extent the internal acceptance of rules, of authoritative reasons and rules of recognition may be imposed by the superordinate upon the subordinate.

Finally we may refer to an interesting difference of view between two thinkers with much in common by way of intellectual background—Hannah Arendt, who is a postclassical political theorist and Jürgen Habermas, a neo-Marxist social philosopher. This dispute occurs within the collective or communal family of conceptions of power.

Arendt denies that 'Power, strength, force, authority, violence . . . are but words to indicate the means by which man rules over man.' She rejects the tradition of thinking that reduces 'public affairs to the business of domination' and appeals rather to 'another tradition and another vocabulary no less old and time honoured', common to the Athenians, the Romans, and the eighteenth-century revolutionaries, a tradition which employed 'a concept of power and law whose essence did not rely on the command–obedience relationship and which did not identify power and rule or law and command.' For Arendt, power

corresponds to the human ability not just to act but to act in concert. Power is never the property of the individual; it belongs to a group and remains in existence only so long as the group keeps together. When we say of somebody that he is 'in power' we actually refer to his being empowered by a certain number of people to act in their name.[153]

Authority, Arendt believes, 'has vanished from the modern world'; it 'grew out of the Roman experience of foundation and was understood in the light of Greek political philosophy', and it has 'nowhere been re-established', indeed, all modern revolutions since the French are failed attempts to re-establish it. It involved 'the religious trust in a sacred beginning' and 'the protection of tradition and therefore self-evident standards of behavior'. Its hallmark was 'unquestioning recognition by those who are asked to obey; neither coercion nor persuasion is needed'.[154]

[153] Arendt, *On Violence*, pp. 43, 44, 40, 44.
[154] Ead., 'What is Authority?', in Arendt, *Between Past and Future* (New York: Viking Press, 1968 edn.), pp. 91, 141; *On Violence*, p. 45. Arendt remarks that if authority is to be defined, 'it must be in contradistinction to both coercion by force and persuasion through arguments' ('What is Authority?' p. 93).

Habermas recognizes Arendt's conception of power as denoting 'not the instrumentalisation of *another's* will, but the formation of a *common* will directed to reaching agreement'—the 'power of agreement-oriented communication to produce consensus.' This is reminiscent of Habermas's own notion of 'consensus brought about in unconstrained communication', in which 'those involved are oriented to reaching agreement and not primarily to their respective individual successes'. But he differs from Arendt with respect to the way he grounds this 'communication concept of power' and the historical and political significance he attaches to it. For Arendt, such power derives from a view of a non-deformed 'public realm' based on classical political models, which in the modern world finds its expression in revolutionary attempts to establish political liberty (American town-hall meetings in 1776, the Parisian *sociétés populaires* between 1789 and 1793, sections of the Paris Commune in 1871, the Russian Soviets in 1905 and 1917, the *Rätedemokratie* in Germany in 1918) and its antithesis in totalitarian rule. Habermas sees this position as based on an anachronistic image of the Greek polis, 'inapplicable to modern conditions'. Arendt's view of politics excludes 'strategic action', the 'struggle for political power', and is unconnected to the economic and social environment in which it is embedded through the administrative system. For her, politics is identified with 'the praxis of those who talk together in order to act in common'. On the other hand, Habermas values in her thesis the idea that legitimate power is generated (as opposed to acquired, maintained, and employed) through 'common convictions in unconstrained communication'.[155]

For Habermas, political rule has rarely been the expression of such unconstrained consensus. Rather, systematically restricted communication and illusory ideologies have served to legitimate power, through 'convictions subjectively free from constraint, convictions which are however illusionary'.[156] This neo-Marxist twist to the old tale of power and authority comes as no surprise. For a complex set of reasons, Habermas holds that late capitalism faces a legitimation crisis as the state, whose class character becomes increasingly transparent, is increasingly unable to maintain its legitimacy. For him,

---

[155] Habermas, 'Hannah Arendt's Communications Concept of Power', *Social Research*, 44/1 (Spring 1977), pp. 4, 5, 6, 14, 17, 21, 18.
[156] Ibid. 22.

legitimate power, based on undistorted communication, represents a counterfactual ideal of emancipation at the basis of critical theory.[157] Like other contemporary conceptions of power and authority, this embodies a view of 'the natural necessities and opportunities of human life' and a 'conception of social cooperation' whose roots lie deep in the history of social and political theory.

[157] See Habermas, *Legitimation Crisis*, trans. T. McCarthy (Boston: Beacon Press, 1975; London: Heinemann, 1976).

7

Perspectives on Authority

What is authority? It is an old question. Indeed, Hannah Arendt in the first *Nomos* volume asked 'what *was* authority?' somewhat nostalgically, fearing that even the answer might be lost in the mists of antiquity. But the question goes on being asked and has recently received much renewed attention from political and legal philosophers.

The question is, on the face of it, at least two questions. It could be the analytical question: what are the elements of the concept of authority and how are they structured? What are the criteria by which we may recognize the possession, exercise, and acceptance of authority? How is it to be distinguished from other forms of influence over persons and from, say, persuading, threatening, advising, and requesting? Or it could be the normative question: what is legitimate authority? What is it that renders authority legitimate? What justifies the claims of authority as being worthy of acceptance? When should utterances be treated as authoritative?

Discussions of authority divide over the issue of how the analytical question relates to the normative question. Some hold that the questions are quite distinct: that we can elucidate the concept of authority and as a separate matter ask when, if ever, submission to it is justified. They may well go on to say that this latter question is not a timeless one; that what is justified in one context and from one point of view may not be so in and from another. Others hold that the questions cannot be divorced in this way. They hold that to do so is to advance a 'relativized' notion of authority, according to which 'we simply state what authority is had by whom from a certain point of view'[1] and that this 'severs the connection between authority and practical reason'.[2] For them the non-relativized notion is primary

This chapter was first published in 1987.

[1] J. Raz, *The Authority of Law* (Oxford: Oxford Univ. Press, 1979), p. 11.
[2] Ibid. Cf. Hannah Pitkin, *Wittgenstein and Justice* (Berkeley, Calif.: University of California Press, 1972), pp. 280 ff.

and is presupposed by the relativized notion. On this view of the matter, to analyse authority is to analyse legitimate or justified authority, to which different people in different times and places lay claim and submit, some rightly, some wrongly. It is on this view not a matter of meaning that a person can have authority, be an authority or in authority only if his authority is recognized by some people whose identity will vary with the nature of his authority (though in practice, especially in political contexts, it will be contingently true that such recognition will be a condition of his exercising his legitimate authority effectively). On this second approach, establishing the grounds on which an authoritative utterance should be recognized as such is prior to all empirical inquiry into beliefs and practices. On the first, it is not. Indeed, on the first view, what is authoritative will not, in any given case, be independent of a whole web of beliefs, some explicit and some implicit in practices. Of course, not anything can be a ground or reason for treating an utterance as authoritative (e.g., that it is loud—though that could be a sign that there is such a reason). But what counts as such a reason will be internal to a web of beliefs.

Both approaches, however, concur in the aim of enabling us to identify relations of authority and distinguish them from others. What I seek to suggest in this chapter is that such identification is an even more complex matter than is often supposed and always involves a process of interpretation. More particularly, I claim that every way of identifying authority is relative to one or more perspectives and is, indeed, inherently perspectival, and that there is no objective, in the sense of perspective-neutral, way of doing so. This feature of attributions of authority has, I think, been far too little attended to in the voluminous literature on the topic, including that compatible with its recognition.

Without analysing or exploring the notion of 'perspective' here,[3] I mean it to refer to a point of view, a more or less integrated set of ways of seeing and judging matters of fact and practical questions, not excluding basic moral and political questions, and incorporating beliefs about the possibilities and necessities of social life, and about how the self, its relation to society, and its manner of reasoning are to be conceived. In this domain, of course, the reality upon which

---

[3] See my 'Relativism in its Place', in M. Hollis and S. Lukes (eds), *Rationality and Relativism* (Oxford: Blackwell, 1982).

perspectives bear is itself in part constituted by contending perspectives. To speak thus of perspectives is not in itself to embrace any deep
form of relativism: some will be, for example, more perspicuous or
comprehensive or consistent than others. Typically, different perspectives—and at what points and how much they differ will in turn
be variously interpretable—are associated with different positions
within a social relation (such as an authority relation), with different
social and political roles (e.g., the judicial, the bureaucrat's, and the
citizen's perspectives) and with different activities (e.g., the actor's
and observer's perspectives). How to individuate perspectives is a
complex question into which I cannot go here. The question of
whether differences of belief and judgement are variations within
one perspective or demarcations between two cannot be answered in
the abstract and in general. The answer will depend on the reasons
for which perspectives are being discriminated, I do not of course
mean to suggest that any one person ever adopts only one perspective. We all engage in multiple relations, roles, and activities and
accordingly adopt and negotiate multiple perspectives.

For the purposes of what follows, I shall distinguish a number of
potentially different perspectives. First, with respect to the authority
relation itself, we can distinguish between the exerciser or holder of
authority and those who accept or are subject to it. I shall, in the
time-honoured philosophical fashion, call the first A and the second
B and thus speak of *perspective A* and *perspective B*. I shall call the
observer (who may or may not be internal to the authority relation or
to the society in which it occurs) C and his perspective *perspective C*.
Authority relations generally occur within a wider framework of
social norms and conventions, legal and customary. Some of these
are officially and definitely interpreted by judges, courts, and repres-
entatives of the state. I will call this perspective society's official
perspective or *perspective SO*. This is likely to diverge at various
points from prevalent, unofficial, and informal understandings of
such norms, rules, and conventions. I shall call such unofficial ways
of understanding *perspective SU*—and, on the plausible assumption
that these will be various and conflicting, $SU_1, SU_2 \ldots SU_n$. It is,
however, often suggested that there is, in some or most societies, an
underlying consensus that will be implicit in, though distinct from,
SO and $SU_1 \ldots SU_n$, which may be elicited by a sensitive interpretation or reconstruction of a society's beliefs and practices. This notion
of consensus has long played a role in contemporary sociology and

has recently surfaced in political philosophy. It is what Michael Walzer relies on in order to determine the criteria that demarcate his 'spheres of justice'.[4] And it is what John Rawls supposes will result from the confrontation of a society's unreconstructed beliefs with theoretical criticism through 'reflective equilibrium'. Let us call this third, consensual social perspective *perspective SC*. (We can see it as an amalgam of perspectives SO and SU interpreted from perspective C.) Finally, we may postulate a putative impersonal, 'objective' and 'archimedean' perspective from which all other perspectives may be assessed. Rawls calls it a standpoint that is 'objective and also expresses our autonomy', which 'enables us to be impartial, even between persons who are not contemporaries but who belong to many generations'. To 'see our place in society from the perspective of this position' is, he eloquently continues, 'to see it *sub specie aeternitatis:* it is to regard the human situation not only from all social but from all temporal points of view'. It is 'the perspective of eternity'—not 'a perspective from a certain place beyond the world, nor the point of view of a transcendent being; rather it is a certain form of thought and feeling that rational persons can adopt within the world'.[5] Thomas Nagel calls it 'a conception of the world which as far as possible is not the view from anywhere within it'.[6] Let us call this perspective *perspective O*. One central question this chapter seeks to address is whether there is indeed any such perspective.

I now turn to consider some attempts to analyse the nature of authority. All mark out a distinctive mode of securing compliance which combines in a peculiar way power over others and the exercise of reason. On the one hand, authority appears to be part of that network of control concepts that includes power, coercion, force, manipulation, persuasion, etc. As Hobbes said, 'command is a precept in which the cause of the obedience depends on the will of the commander' and 'the will stands for the reason'. Even authority over belief appears to involve an influence that bypasses rational argument. On the other hand, reason is plainly involved: authority offers a reason and operates through reasoning. Moreover, only rational agents are capable of claiming, recognizing and accepting authority. As Friedrich observed, it involves 'a very particular kind

[4] Walzer, *Spheres of Justice* (Oxford: Martin Robertson, 1983).
[5] Rawls, *A Theory of Justice* (Oxford: Clarendon Press, 1972), p. 587.
[6] Nagel, *Mortal Questions* (Cambridge: Cambridge Univ. Press, 1979), p. 208.

of relationship to reason', namely 'the potentiality of reasoned elaboration'.[7]

I shall first consider three accounts exemplifying the first, 'relativized' approach presented above, in order to illustrate the different perspectives that they exemplify. I shall then turn to a further account that illustrates the second approach in order to show that even an account that explicitly seeks to avoid perspective dependence fails and must fail to do so.

Consider first Max Weber's celebrated account of authority. Weber was, of course, concerned with *Herrschaft*, or domination, but he was interested specifically in 'the authoritarian power of command', as against 'domination by virtue of a constellation of interests (in particular by virtue of a position of monopoly'). Domination in Weber's preferred sense indicated the securing of compliance which occurs 'as if the ruled had made the content of the command the maxim of their conduct for its very own sake'.[8] He wrote, 'The merely external fact of the order being obeyed is not sufficient to signify domination in our sense; we cannot overlook the meaning of the fact that the command is accepted as a "valid" norm.'[9]

Of course, Weber was well aware that commands may be obeyed for a wide variety of reasons: 'the command may have achieved its effect upon the ruled either through empathy or through inspiration or through persuasion by rational argument or through some combination of these three principal types of influence of one person over another'.[10] Indeed,

In a concrete case the performance of a command may have been motivated by the ruled's own conviction of its propriety, or by his sense of duty, or by fear, or by 'dull' custom, or by a desire to obtain some benefit for himself.[11]

Yet it is a striking fact that Weber's sociology of domination never explores these possibilities by investigating the question 'When and why do men obey?' or looks at authority relations from below, that is, from perspective B. On the contrary, his classification of authority is exclusively from perspective A, in terms of prevailing rationales for

[7] C. J. Friedrich, 'Authority, Reason and Discretion', in id. (ed.), *Authority*. *NOMOS I*, The American Society of Political and Legal Philosophy (Cambridge, Mass.: Harvard Univ. Press, 1958), p. 35.

[8] Max Weber, *Economy and Society*, ed. G. Roth and C. Wittich, 2 vols. (New York: Bedminster, 1968), ii. pp. 943, 946.

[9] Ibid. ii. 946.   [10] Ibid.   [11] Ibid. ii. 946–7.

obedience—claims typically made by those in command. As Parkin observes, Weber never asks 'whether the legitimations put out by traditional, charismatic and legal-rational authorities differed in the degree to which they were actually endorsed by the masses'.[12] On the contrary, he proceeds throughout 'as though widespread endorsement of all three types of legitimation was typically found among all and sundry'. It is 'as if Weber simply assumed the correctness of Marx's dictum that the prevailing ideas in any society are the ideas of its ruling class'.[13] I suspect this may be because Weber, as a cynical 'realist' concerning power, and despite his talk of the 'voluntary' acceptance of maxims, basically saw prevailing principles of legitimation (especially democratic ones) as 'myths' injected into the masses by élites. At all events, the Weberian approach, while offering an illuminating classification of authority claims, succeeds in identifying authority relations by only taking account of perspective A. Authority on this view is the securing of compliance by command on the basis of claims, of the three indicated types, assumed to be accepted by the commanded.

Consider next the illuminating analysis of the authority relation offered by Richard Friedman, as consisting in two tiers: first, 'that special and distinctive kind of dependence on the will or judgment of another so well conveyed by the notion of a "surrender of private judgment;"' and second, 'the recognition and acceptance of certain criteria for designating who is to possess this kind of influence'.[14] This analysis is intended to cover both the cases of 'an authority' and 'in authority'.

In both cases, 'we have to see the notion of authority in connection with the idea of a very special sort of reason for action (or belief)'; one difference being that 'belief in authority calls for internal assent, whereas the notion of acting in conformity to the commands of authority allows for the dissociation of thought and action'.[15]

A claim to the former, Friedman suggests, rests on the ground of 'superior knowledge or insight, that makes belief, and not merely external conformity, the appropriate response to authority'.[16] It

---

[12] F. Parkin, *Max Weber* (London: Methuen, 1982), p. 78. [13] Ibid.
[14] R. B. Friedman, 'On the Concept of Authority in Political Philosophy', in R. Flathman (ed.), *Concepts in Social and Political Philosophy* (New York: Macmillan, 1973), pp. 131, 134.
[15] Ibid. 135. [16] Ibid. 143.

presupposes an inequality of knowledge, insight, or wisdom prior to the authority relation itself; and it presupposes the epistemological claim that such superior knowledge, insight or wisdom is in principle available. It presupposes, in short, 'a world of common beliefs and the recognition of inequality in the capacity of men to understand those beliefs'.[17]

By contrast, the relation of those 'in authority' to those who defer to them presupposes a world in which there is

a complex *recognition* of dissensus and equality at the substantive level over against which men are prepared to step up to the procedural level and abide by the decisions of the person designated as being 'in authority,' whether or not those decisions happen to coincide with their 'private' opinions.[18]

Indeed, authority serves to mark off the distinction between private and public in this sense. Such authority is a response to a 'predicament' in which 'a collection of individuals wish to engage in some common activity requiring a certain degree of coordinated action but they are unable to agree on what the substance of their common behavior should be.'[19] In general, according to Friedman, both forms of authority imply

some mutually recognized relationship giving the one the right to command or speak and the other the duty to obey. Authority thus involves a form of influence that can only be exercised from within a certain kind of normative arrangement accepted by both parties.[20]

Friedman's account is decidedly an improvement on Weber's. It hinges on the notion of mutual recognition: what is essential is that perspectives A and B agree in 'a certain kind of "recognition" that the person to whom one defers is entitled to this sort of submission'.[21] Legitimation claimed and the according of legitimacy coincide in a shared recognition of entitlement. That recognition may be based on a very wide range of possible 'marks' or credentials of authority —'office, social station, property, "great" power, pedigree, religious claims, "miracles" (Augustine), etc.'[22]

A number of problems are raised by this account. Less seriously, it seems obvious that many cases of 'an authority' over belief need not involve mutual recognition of that authority; such authorities can go unrecognized and they can be seen as authorities

[17] Friedman, 'On the Concept of Authority', p. 146.
[18] Ibid. 145–6.   [19] Ibid. 140.   [20] Ibid. 134.
[21] Ibid. 131.   [22] Ibid. 133.

unwittingly or posthumously. Similarly, persons 'in authority' may sometimes properly be said to have it even if those subject to it fail to endorse it, as parents and teachers know well. Second, Friedman's discussion of the 'marks' of authority does not successfully distinguish between *signs* and *grounds:* the crown and sceptre are the former, the regal office they betoken the latter. But two more serious problems arise. First, what are the criteria by which these 'marks' are recognized as marks of authority? Is it just up to the parties in an authority relationship to fix on anyone they wish to recognize as authoritative? And second, what is the nature of that recognition? Is it like a 'cue' triggering off 'blind obedience' and the 'surrender of judgement?' Or is a process of rational judgement involved?

These last two questions are addressed by the third account we will consider, namely that of Richard Flathman. He answers the first by placing the authority relation within a wider 'practice' of authority in which shared values and beliefs prevalent in a community play a constitutive part. And he answers the second by firmly resisting the notion of a 'surrender of private judgement', maintaining this notion to be 'at the very least, seriously misleading'.[23]

For Flathman, both 'in authority' and 'an authority' relations are 'grounded in shared values and beliefs to which we are referring as the authoritative':[24] the 'partly constitutive character of the values, beliefs, actions and so forth of subscribers . . . to a set of rules, institutions, etc.' is 'a central feature of our entire theory of authority'.[25] But how are these to be identified and just how do they bear on the authority relation? Sometimes, Flathman seems to be referring to perspective SO, as when he, rather oddly, assumes that 'the values and beliefs which make up Marxism–Leninism are now among the constitutive features' of the practice of authority in the Soviet Union.[26] Sometimes, he seems to be referring to SU, without any real sensitivity to the systematic divergences it embraces—as when, rather baldly, he remarks that 'if we are trying to determine whether Ivan had authority in sixteenth-century Russia we must ascertain the criteria that had standing among sixteenth-century Russians and we must determine whether sixteenth-century Russians thought those criteria were satisfied.'[27] Sometimes, as when

---

[23] Flathman, *The Practice of Political Authority* (Chicago: Univ. of Chicago Press, 1980), p. 124.

[24] Ibid. 26.   [25] Ibid. 231–2.   [26] Ibid. 87.   [27] Ibid. 228.

discussing the shared values and beliefs of modern liberal democracies, as allowing for disagreement and the practice of civil disobedience, he seems to be embracing a version of perspective SC.

But a further and deeper problem is raised by his rejection of the notion of the surrender of private judgement and his insistence that participants in the practice of authority are making 'judgments grounded in evidence and reason', that there is within the authoritative 'a basis both for grounded, reasoned judgments concerning it and for grounded reasoned disagreements concerning those judgments'[28] and his call for a 'critical justificatory theory of authority'.[29] Do such judgements transcend the confines of prevailing authoritative beliefs and values? Or, to make the same point conversely, does the 'authoritative' in part determine what counts as convincing evidence or a good reason? What kind of a constraint does 'evidence and reason' place upon the constitutive character of the 'authoritative?' Flathman rejects what he calls 'collectivistic subjectivism' but we need to know more about why he does so.

So I turn finally to an account of authority that fearlessly avoids such dangers and temptations by offering a straightforwardly rationalist 'critical justificatory theory of authority' on the assumption that this can be done independently of and prior to any 'relativized' way of conceiving it, while acknowledging that 'the relativized notion is useful because it reveals the views of people or societies concerning non-relativized authority'.[30] The account in question is that developed in a number of writings by Joseph Raz. I shall refer here to his 1979 book *The Authority of Law* and to his 1985 article 'Authority and Justification'[31] in which the relation between authority and reason and the justification of authority are systematically explored.

Raz, starting from the 'basic insight' that 'authority is ability to change reasons for action',[32] sees authority as 'a species of normative power' which changes such reasons by exclusion. Thus, orders are both first-order reasons (for acting) and 'exclusionary reasons' which 'exclude by kind and not by weight': their impact is 'not to

---

[28] Flathman, *Political Authority*, p. 234.   [29] Ibid. 232.
[30] Raz, *The Authority of Law*, p. 11.
[31] Id., 'The Justification of Authority', in *Philosophy and Public Affairs* 14 (Winter 1985), 2–29.
[32] Id., *The Authority of Law*, p. 16.   .

change the balance of reasons but to exclude action on the balance of reasons'.[33] Accepting authority involves 'giving up one's right to act on one's judgment on the balance of reasons';[34] the authority is legitimate if such exclusionary reasons are valid.

When, then, is authority legitimate? What renders its exclusionary reasons valid? Raz advances what he calls the 'dependence thesis', namely that '*All authoritative directives should be based, in the main, on reasons which already independently apply to the subjects of the directives and are relevant to their action in the circumstances covered by the directive.*'[35] The 'normal' and 'primary' way to show that one person should be acknowledged to have authority over another is given by what he calls the 'normal justification thesis': it is to show '*that the alleged subject is likely better to comply with reasons which apply to him (other than the alleged authoritative directives) if he accepts the directives of the alleged authority as authoritatively binding and tries to follow them, rather than by trying to follow the reasons which apply to him directly.*'[36] These reasons need not be confined to the furthering of his interests (as when a military officer orders soldiers to defend their country, against their personal interests). Other justifications for accepting authority—such as consent, or respect for the law, or identification with a community—are merely secondary. They are valid only if they accompany the primary reason. Typical of situations where the normal justification holds are those presenting co-ordination problems, including prisoner's dilemma type situations. Indeed, Raz argues, solving co-ordination problems is one of the important tasks of political and many other practical authorities. The key idea (especially in relation to politics) is what Raz calls 'the service conception of the function of authorities'—namely, that 'their role and primary normal function is to serve the governed', which they do when they 'help them act on reasons which bind them'.[37]

Raz's attempt is to 'explain the notion of legitimate authority

---

[33] Ibid. 22, 23.
[34] Ibid. 26. However, 'there is no reason for anyone to restrain their thoughts or their reflections on the reasons which apply to the case' ('The Justification of Authority', p. 10) and one may always challenge a putatively authoritative directive on jurisdictional grounds by questioning whether it has violated the conditions of its rightful power.
[35] Id., 'The Justification of Authority', p. 14.
[36] Ibid. 19.   [37] Ibid. 21.

through describing what one might call an ideal exercise of authority'. It is through their 'ideal functioning' that the practice of
authorities must be understood. This is given by how they publicly
claim that they attempt to function, which is 'the normal way to
justify their authority'.[38]

This is an unwarrantably rapid summary of Raz's complex
account, which is the most perspicuous analysis of the concept to
date and the most systematic attempt I know of to escape the
problems we have been investigating, by presenting an analysis of
authority relations that purports explicitly not to be an account of
'what authority is had by whom from a certain point of view'.[39] Does
it do so?

I doubt it. For Raz, 'the normal and primary way of justifying the
legitimacy of an authority is that it is more likely to act successfully
on the reasons which apply to its subjects';[40] accepting legitimate
authority offers the advantage of having found 'a more reliable and
successful guide to right reason'.[41] But how are we to ascertain what
the reasons that apply to authority's subjects are and in what
'success' in acting on them or guiding us to them consists?

There is a whole range of cases where the answers to these
questions seem obvious and uncontroversial. The traffic policeman,
the tax authorities, legislators, judges, military officers, parents can
all be seen as 'in the main', at least in certain areas, directing us to act
on reasons that independently apply to us, so that we may properly
see them as having the right to replace people's own judgement on
the merits of the case. Of course the legitimacy of such authorities is
(in perhaps ascending order of frequency) questioned, on particular
occasions, over whole ranges of cases, and (as with anarchists,
pacifists, and revolutionaries) in general. It may be questioned in
various ways. They may be held to have a false or misconceived idea
of the 'reasons which apply to [their] subjects'. Lawmakers and
judges may be denounced for being out of touch with the interests
and needs of those they purport or are claimed to protect and guide
(as they have been by blacks in the United States or opponents of
abortion). Military leaders may appeal to duties and commitments
that both soldiers and citizens reject (as in the United States during
the Vietnam War or Israel during the later stages of the invasion of

---

[38] Raz, 'The Justification of Authority', p. 27.   [39] *The Authority of Law*, p. 11.
[40] 'The Justification of Authority', p. 20.   [41] Ibid. 25.

Lebanon). Secondly, the legitimacy of authorities may be questioned on grounds of 'reliability' and 'success', the reasons applying to their subjects being taken as given. Corrupt policemen and incompetent military regimes (rarely) lose their legitimacy in this way. But either way, Raz would probably argue, questioning the legitimacy of particular authorities, even in general, in these ways does not show that they would not be legitimate if the conditions set by the normal justification thesis were to be met.

I fail to see how the reasons that apply to authority's subjects, on which authoritative directives should be based, are to be ascertained in a perspective-neutral manner. The objectives an authority is to further are not determinable a priori and are often matters of intense controversy. On the other hand, it is plausible to suggest that, once such objectives are agreed, the question of a given authority's 'reliability' and 'success' (like that of an investment consultant) could be seen as a matter of fact, yet even this is not obvious. What is being judged: the institution or its agents, and over what period of time? Raz's phrase 'in the main' leaves leeway here too for judgement and interpretive dispute.

The sorts of cases we have considered are plainly those on which this account of legitimate authority is centrally based and to which it is most obviously applicable. The most obviously applicable cases are those in which authority establishes or helps sustain conventions, seen as solutions to co-ordination problems, or enables people to escape prisoner's dilemma type situations. More generally, this account works best for all those cases where there is what we might call an extrinsic relation between authoritative directives and reasons they depend on and replace. Authority on this view is an invaluable device to achieve, more reliably and successfully, independently given and agreed objectives that would otherwise be less easy or impossible to attain. Even here, as we have seen, there is much room for interpretive dispute as to which objectives are relevant and what constitutes success.

But what of cases where the relation between authority and reason is intrinsic: where the objectives authority serves are internal to, that is shaped and sustained by, the authority relation itself. The examples that come most naturally to mind here are religious, though the point is far wider than that. The role of the priesthood is, in part, to lead men along the path of righteousness or truth, as it is interpreted by the priesthood—to show the way to destinations that people might not have conceived apart from it (that is, apart from the institution and tradition it embodies)—and may not even be characterizable without presupposing it (e.g., living according to the Torah). The fundamentalist preacher, say, and his congregation are in a relationship of self-reinforcing authority, in which the word of God (as he interprets its expression in the Bible) gives them reasons for actions concerning which he is, in turn, the authoritative guide.

Religious examples demonstrate this intrinsic relation with clarity. Here the 'primary normal function' of authority is not always best described as 'serving the governed'. Of course, religions often do have instrumental functions, promising (as magic typically does) to bring benefits in the here and now or (more probably) in the hereafter. But they also have soteriological functions and Durkheimian social functions, both of which involve *transforming* rather than serving their adherents—by leading them to salvation, imbuing them with faith, giving meaning to their lives, and so on. In such cases, the legitimacy of authority does not lie in its reliability and success in securing independently given objectives, as measured against some objective standard, since it itself defines the objectives and sets the standard. And this applies, beyond religious cases, to all cases of intrinsic authority, where Raz's picture of an exclusionary reason justifiably pre-empting the balance of reasons does not really fit. A better picture might be that of a dominant reason that reduces the significance of other reasons that would otherwise prevail, and removes the point of weighing them. Thus (to take disparate examples at random): charismatic leaders define their followers' goals, the legitimacy resting on 'the belief in and devotion to the extraordinary, which is valued because it goes beyond the normal human qualities' and 'transvalues everything';[42] the Party prescribes certain objectives as primary; psychoanalysts (on one view of what they do) transform their patients' self-understanding; women exhibit patriarchal attitudes. In all these cases, it seems that if authority is justified, it is justified from a point of view, namely that of the authority itself, which becomes that of the subject.

It may, of course, be replied that only extrinsic authority is legitimate: only if putative authorities guide their subjects extrinsically to 'right reasons' can their claims be justified. In this case, we are

---

[42] Weber, *From Max Weber: Essays in Sociology*, ed. and trans. H. H. Gerth and C. Wright Mills, (London: Routledge & Kegan Paul, 1948), pp. 296, 250.

owed a doctrine of 'right reason', indicating which *are* the 'reasons which bind them'. Moreover, it is not clear why, on principle, this reply should be given. Are there no cases of legitimate intrinsic authority? More generally, it may be suggested that the analysis proposed is, in principle, neutral between different perspective-dependent accounts within which different reasons, or sorts of reasons, can be judged to be 'right reasons'. This suggestion would bring Raz's analysis much closer to the position this paper seeks to advocate, since it leaves the answer to the question, When is authority legitimate? perspective-dependent. However, for the reason indicated in the previous paragraph, it is not clear that the analysis itself, with its 'service conception' of authority's function, successfully captures the nature of authority as understood in all contexts and cultures.

We are, it is clear, back to the problem with which we began. We are offered a test by which claims to authority that are imposed (à la Weber), mutually recognized (à la Friedman) or culturally given (à la Flathman) are to be judged genuine or spurious. Could such a test be perspective-neutral?

The very idea of such a test is central to our cultural tradition. Since the Enlightenment, we have believed that some such test should be available, distinguishing 'right' from spurious reasons, autonomy from heteronomy, self- from other-directedness, and providing a bedrock for practical judgement. This strand of our tradition is deeply hostile to priestly power, paternalism, and mystifying ideologies of all kinds. Basic to it is the image of an autonomous rational individual. Consider now the metaphor at the heart of Raz's account. 'Exclusionary reasons', excluding by kind rather than changing the balance of reasons, conjure up the old image of the scales of justice, and therewith an underlying and specific conception of the subject of authority. It suggests, in a word, a distinctly judicial conception of the individual, weighing and balancing, in an impartial spirit, the reasons that present themselves, in order to reach an independent judgement as to what to do or think 'all things considered'—but on occasion allowing 'binding' reasons to prevail. Yet this picture of the individual is not unique. Other pictures exist to which other styles of reasoning are central[43]—Talmudic, Confucian, Buddhist, etc.—

---

[43] See M. Carrithers, S. Collins, and S. Lukes (eds.), *The Category of the Person: Anthropology, Philosophy, History* (Cambridge: Cambridge Univ. Press, 1985).

whose relevance to the testing of authority claims merits investigation. Indeed, the thought suggests itself that Raz's aspiration to perspective-neutrality shapes his very notion of the subject, and that this aspiration and notion are no less perspective-dependent than any other.

Indeed, Raz freely admits that his argument is 'inescapably a normative argument', 'part of an attempt to make explicit elements of our common traditions', a 'partisan' account 'furthering the cause of certain strands in the common tradition by developing new or newly recast arguments in their favour'.[44] The critical justificatory theory of authority he develops is true to 'our' concept of authority and behind it to 'our' notion of the reasoning subject. It offers a test for legitimacy that is tailor-made for Friedman's 'second world', riven by conflicting interests and opinions but with a shared interest in the procedural resolution of co-ordination problems. It is, unquestionably, worth defending and propagating, in a world in which authoritarian and obscurantist notions of authority are rife and growing. But it is, while compelling, 'our' view, gaining its plausibility from the web of beliefs in which it is embedded. For this reason, I agree with Flathman's suggestion that 'caution is appropriate in positing—as for example Joseph Raz does—a "non-relativized" notion of authority that is a presupposition of the "relativized" notions we in fact find among this or that historical people.'[45]

[44] Raz, 'The Justification of Authority', p. 27.
[45] Flathman, *The Practice of Political Authority*, p. 77.

PART III

8

Can the Base be Distinguished from the Superstructure?

> In the social production of their life, men enter into definite relations that are indispensable and independent of their will, relations of production which correspond to a definite stage of development of their material productive forces. The sum total of these relations of production constitutes the economic structure of society, the real basis, on which rises a legal and political superstructure, and to which correspond definite forms of social consciousness.
>
> K. Marx, 'Preface to *A Contribution to the Critique of Political Economy*', in Marx and Engels, *Selected Works*, 2 vols. (Moscow, Foreign Languages Publishing House, 1962), i. 362–3 (trans. slightly amended).

I suppose that this must be the most well-known and argued-over pair of sentences in the entire Marxist canon. Ever since Engels tried to sort out some of the problems they raise, they have been returned to again and again, both by Marxists, orthodox, 'critical', and 'neo', and by critics and opponents of Marxism. Some have suggested that they, and the text from which they come (the Preface to *A Contribution to the Critique of Political Economy*), should be seen as over-simplified and even unimportant, when set against the great mass of Marx's and Engels's writings about political economy and history. But Marx clearly saw the 'general conclusion' he reports here as having 'continued to serve as the guiding thread' of his studies; and the thoughts distilled in these two sentences are as distinctive of Marxism as is the continuing dispute over what it is that they really mean.

They raise at least five issues: the theory of developmental stages,

This chapter was first published in 1983.
I am grateful to G. A. Cohen, David Miller, and Joseph Raz for their very helpful comments on an earlier draft.

the relation between structure and agency, that between material productive forces and social production relations, that between the base, or economic structure, and the legal and political superstructure, and that between the superstructure and its corresponding forms of consciousness. I shall here focus exclusively on the fourth of these issues (leaving largely aside the relations between the third and the fourth and between the fourth and the fifth) by asking the narrow but deep question: Can the economic structure, or base, be distinguished from the superstructure? This is a basic question, for unless it can, the explanations promised by historical materialism, at least as set out in the Preface, will fail. I shall consider the question by presenting the negative answer to it advanced by John Plamenatz and the positive answer advanced by G. A. Cohen.[1] Plamenatz's carefully stated doubts constituted a major foil for Cohen's recent attempt to make sense of Marx's historical materialism, in the most coherent and analytically refined defence it has yet received. It should therefore be peculiarly instructive to examine the grounds for Plamenatz's scepticism and see whether Cohen's ingenious arguments succeed in showing it to be misplaced.

Plamenatz makes two claims. One looks empirical, the other conceptual, and each is expressed in both a particular and a general form.

(1*a*) The first claim, in its particular form, is that the economic structure 'is to a considerable extent independent of production, that there are other things besides production making it what it is'; and, furthermore, 'the relations of production or property . . . in turn can profoundly affect production'. Thus,

If we identify relations of production with relations of property (as I think we must if they are to have any identity at all), it becomes easy to see that they are not determined by what is produced and how it is produced.

Moreover, the system of property, both by putting fetters on the development of productive forces and by creating opportunities, 'has

---

[1] Plamenatz's arguments are most fully set out in *Man and Society* (London: Longman, 1963), ii. pp. 274–92. Cohen challenges them in three places: 'On Some Criticisms of Historical Materialism, 1', *Proceedings of the Aristotelian Society*, suppl. vol. 44 (1970), pp. 121–42; 'Being, Consciousness and Roles: On the Foundations of Historical Materialism', in C. Abramsky and B. Williams (eds.), *Essays in Honour of E. H. Carr* (London: Macmillan, 1974); and *Karl Marx's Theory of History: A Defence* (Oxford: Clarendon Press, 1978), esp. chaps. 3 and 8.

a great influence on what is produced and how it is produced'. Since the so-called, but misdescribed, relations of production 'owe their character only in part to the form of production, may they not owe it equally to the other sides of social life? In what sense, then, are they the real foundation of these other sides?'[2]

(1*b*) This question leads us to the general form of Plamenatz's first claim, which concerns 'every attempt to distinguish, among the larger aspects of social life, between a fundamental causal factor and what is derivative from it'. 'No doubt', he writes,

if we take a small enough part of social life, we can easily show that it is derivative, in the sense that it is much more affected by the rest of social life, or even by some other part of it, than it affects it. If we take something like fashion in dress, we can show that it greatly depends on certain other things which it hardly influences. But if we take larger sides of social life, like religion or science or government, it is no longer plausible to treat any of them as fundamental or derivative in relation to the others.[3]

(2*a*) The second claim, in its particular form, is that the relations of production 'cannot be defined without using moral or normative concepts': 'Unfortunately, it is quite impossible to define these relations except in terms of the claims which men make upon one another and recognise—except in terms of admitted rights and obligations'.[4]

(2*b*) The general form of this second claim is that 'all properly social relations are moral and customary; they cannot be adequately defined unless we bring normative concepts into the definitions, unless we refer to rules of conduct which the persons who stand in those relations recognize and are required to conform to'. For,

Since claims and duties and mental attitudes are involved in all social relations, in every side of social life, no matter how primitive, since they are part of what we mean when we call a human activity social, we cannot take any side of social life and say that it determines, even *in the last resort*, whatever that may mean, men's moral and customary relations and their attitudes towards one another.[5]

How does Cohen rebut these claims and what alternative does he offer? In the first place, he largely *agrees* with Plamenatz as to the identity of the relations of production. For both writers, the relations of production are social relations and should be understood, in the context of historical materialism, to *include* what Plamenatz calls

---

[2] *Man and Society*, ii. pp. 275–83.
[3] Ibid. 283.   [4] Ibid. 283, 281.   [5] Ibid. 283–4, 284–5.

property relations and Cohen ownership relations (though Cohen, unlike Plamenatz, takes these not to be legal relationships but relations of *effective control*) and to *exclude* what Cohen calls purely material work relations and Plamenatz 'relations involved in production'[6] (though Plamenatz, unlike Cohen, also includes what Acton calls 'paratechnological' relations, which are needed to make production go smoothly[7]).

Against Plamenatz's first (general) claim, Cohen maintains that *whether* or not it is plausible to treat 'larger sides of social life' as fundamental or derivative in relation to others cannot be decided in advance of a clarification of what constitutes a 'side of social life' and of what it is for A to affect B more than B affects A, and of a careful study of the historical record, in the light of such clarifications. In particular, Cohen suggests that Plamenatz's observation about fashion, as obviously more influenced than influencing, though intuitively plausible, must rely on an implicit principle of interpretation which, when made explicit, might show whether or not a 'larger side of social life' may influence another more than it is influenced by it.[8]

Against Plamenatz's second (general) claim, Cohen argues that, on Plamenatz's view of 'determination', A determines B if variations in A explain variations in B. On this view of 'determination', Cohen writes,

it is conceptually in order to assert that the character of men's ideas and customs is determined by the stock of instruments of production available to them and/or by their level of economic development. Each of the latter can be described without referring to customs or ideas.

Indeed, Cohen argues, Plamenatz is wrong even in his general claim about sides of social life, for

it is not clear that a side of social life, as he conceives it, is incapable of determining the ideas associated with it, as he understands determination. The ideas associated with a side of social life may vary as and *because* the side as a whole varies, and this will meet his sense of 'determine'.[9]

---

[6] Plamenatz, *Man and Society*, p. 279. Cohen originally included these (in 'On Some Basic Criticisms . . .') but excludes them in *Karl Marx's Theory of History* (see p. 35 n.).

[7] See *Man and Society*, ii. p. 280 and H. B. Acton, *The Illusion of the Epoch* (London: Cohen and West, 1955). Acton's arguments on the general topic of this paper parallel those of Plamenatz, and Cohen's arguments are developed in response to both authors.

[8] Cohen, 'Being, Consciousness and Roles', p. 87.   [9] Ibid. 88.

But the key issue, so far as historical materialism is concerned, is raised by (2*a*): whether as Cohen claims, the economic structure 'may be so conceived that it is free of all such superstructural encumbrances'. In facing this issue, Cohen takes up the challenge by submitting 'a method of *conceiving* the economic structure which excludes from it the legal, moral, and political relationships of men'. He does this in response to what he calls 'the problem of legality': 'if the economic structure is constituted of *property* (or *ownership*) relations, how can it be distinct from the *legal* superstructures which it is supposed to explain?' His proffered solution is to propose '*rechtsfrei* descriptions of production relations' and then 'show how production relations, so described, may be said to explain property relations'.[10] I shall not here discuss Cohen's account of that explanation as functional explanation, but focus rather on his attempt to conceive the economic structure independently of the superstructure, that is, non-normatively.

That attempt consists in displaying ownership as a matter of enjoying rights, formulating for every ownership right a 'matching power' and then describing production relations in terms of such powers, which 'match' property relations. Thus the pertinent ownership rights (such as the rights to use or to withhold the means of production [or labour power], to prevent other persons using them, or to alienate them) are said to 'match' corresponding powers, where 'power' is defined as follows:

a man has power to φ if and only if he is able to φ, where 'able' is non-normative. 'Able' is used normatively when 'He is not able to φ' may be true even though he is φ-ing, a logical feature of legal and moral uses of 'able'. Where 'able' is non-normative, 'He is φ-ing' entails 'He is able to φ'.

The relationship of 'matching' is explicated as fully determined by replacing the word 'right' by the word 'power' in the phrase 'right to φ'. Cohen adds that the possession of powers does not entail possession of the rights they match, or vice versa: 'Only possession of a *legitimate* power entails possession of the right it matches, and only possession of an *effective* right entails possession of its matching power.'[11]

Rights, Cohen further maintains, not only match (non-normative)

10 Cohen, *Karl Marx's Theory of History*, pp. 235, 217–18, 225.
11 Ibid. 220, 219.

powers. On the (unargued) ground that 'a power is always a power to do something', he argues that some rights (e.g. my right that no one else use my land) are equivalent to the duties of others to forbear, and these will match others' lack of power, or inability. So, an adequate *rechtsfrei* account of the economic framework of production relations which allegedly 'matches' the legal framework must incorporate 'not only powers or abilities, but also inabilities or constraints'. But here again,

just as a power is distinct from the effective right ensuring it, so a constraint is distinct from the enforced duty imposing it. It is not trivial to say that the serf is constrained to work because he is legally obliged to.[12]

Cohen gives two illustrations of how this programme might be put to work: ideal-typical and descriptive. The first is a contrast between the ideal-typical proletarian (who owns his labour power) and the ideal-typical slave (who does not). Applying his method, Cohen concludes that the slave does not have the power to withhold his labour power, while the proletarian does have this power, but only with respect to a given capitalist, not the capitalist class as a whole. The second comes 'closer to reality' by considering the 'rights and powers of contemporary workers, in countries where bourgeois legality prevails'. Applying his method again, Cohen concludes that, with the development of workers' collective power, through unions, workers do now, though in a qualified sense, have the power to withhold their labour power, and indeed the further power individually to escape their proletarian situation: they are, therefore, 'not *de facto* "owned" by the capitalist class'. On the other hand, their power to overthrow capitalism and their power to build socialism are, in various ways, obscured from their consciousness, and limited by all kinds of costs and difficulties.[13]

If Cohen's programme were to be carried through, it would, he claims, enable one to *explain* property relations, that is show how 'the property relations change in the service of changes in production relations (which in turn reflect development of the productive forces)'. So, for example, following Mantoux, one can explain the collapse of the law of settlement in terms of, first, the law's violation, as production relations allowing mobility were formed illegally, and second, the scrapping of the law, thereby re-establishing conformity

[12] Cohen, *Karl Marx's Theory of History*, p. 237.   [13] Ibid. 222–3, 240–5.

between 'rights and powers, the *de jure* situation and the *de facto*, property relations and production relations'. Other examples are the eventual legal recognition of escaped serfs as freemen in cities, the repeal of the law restricting entry into the clothing industry (allowing 'a proletariat of textile workers to exist *de jure* as well as *de facto*'), the repeal of the Combination Acts and the development of early trade union legislation, the abolition of feudal tenure of land at the Restoration, the development of factory legislation, and the use of Roman law in capitalist society to facilitate the development of certain production relations.[14]

More generally, Cohen argues, property relations are thus

functionally explained by production relations: legal structures rise and fall according as they promote or frustrate forms of economy favoured by the productive forces. Property relations have the character they do because production relations require that they have it.

In human society might frequently requires right in order to operate or even to be constituted. Might without right may be impossible, inefficient, or unstable.

In general, production relations are given stability by their legal expression. Historical materialism asserts that that legal expression is to be explained by its function, which is to help sustain an economy of a particular kind: 'right *r* is enjoyed because it belongs to a structure of rights, which obtains *because* it secures a matching structure of powers'.[15]

I have characterized Cohen's programme of purging the base of normative elements, or seeking to identify 'a *rechtsfrei*, (*moralitäts-frei*, etc.) economic structure to explain law (morals, etc.)'. It is now time to ask: can it be carried through?

In the first place, Cohen's own account of his programme is insufficiently radical. For he speaks of the 'proletarian' and the 'slave', 'landowners' and 'capitalists' as having or lacking (non-normative) powers. But in speaking thus, he is not speaking non-normatively, since the actors in question are not identified in a non-normative fashion. A slave, for example, is a slave just because he lacks certain rights, just as a landowner by definition possesses certain rights. Statements attributing powers to occupants of roles such as these are plainly not *rechtsfrei*, at least where they have or

---

[14] Ibid. 226–9.   [15] Ibid. 231, 232.

lack these powers in virtue of their roles. So, to carry out Cohen's programme systematically, one must eliminate all reference to features of the actors and their roles that refer to or presuppose rights and, more generally, ownership relations. Unless this is done, one will not have excluded from the economic structure 'the legal, moral and political relationships of men'. The principle of a *rechtsfrei* conception of the economic structure must be applied rigorously.

In reply to this, it might be claimed, as Cohen does, that the economic structure consists in production relations which relate terms that do not belong to the structure itself (though they do belong to the economy). On this account, one could describe the structure as relating variables, just like the structure of a bridge or an argument: the economic structure is a form whose proper description makes no reference to the persons or productive forces related together by it, and indeed necessary for it to exist. But the relations in question hold by virtue of the rights and obligations attaching to the roles occupied by persons so related: as Cohen himself says, 'The structure may be seen not only as a set of relations but also as a set of roles.' Therefore, a proper description of the structure will not, as Cohen rightly says, make specific reference to the specific role-*occupants*, but it can scarcely avoid reference to their normatively defined roles. To this, of course, Cohen will reply that such roles *can* be identified non-normatively: as he puts it, 'economic roles in the required technical sense will be determined not by what persons are *de jure* entitled and obliged to do, but by what they are *de facto* able and constrained (= not able not) to do'.[16] We shall come to this claim shortly. Only if it can be sustained, will Cohen's programme have been carried out rigorously.

But, in the second place, we must ask: can it be carried out at all? Recall that the aim is to identify an economic structure of production relations, as a set of *de facto* powers, which will in turn explain the superstructure of law, morality, etc., as a set of rights and obligations. Let us, then, look more closely at this purged or purified 'matching' economic framework of 'powers or abilities' and 'inabilities or constraints'.

I propose here to offer three arguments. The first two attack Cohen's project indirectly; only the third meets it head on. The former, if accepted, put in question the idea that the economic

---

[16] Cohen, 'Being, Consciousness and Roles', p. 95.

structure, conceived as a set of 'powers and constraints', could be described in a single, determinate, objective and rationally incontestable manner. If this is doubted, then the 'hardness' of the economic structure (and thus of historical materialism itself) is no longer easy to believe in: how it is conceived will be relative to perspectives that are, in turn, not normatively neutral. The latter puts in question Cohen's claim that norms can be seen as bringing about and sustaining relations of production while remaining no part of their content.

First, then, what count as an agent's abilities and inabilities will be closely dependent upon how that agent is conceived (which only strengthens the first point made above). If the agent (whether individual or collective) is conceived in a sufficiently 'substantial' way, then that agent's abilities will appear to be very narrowly circumscribed; if conceived sufficiently abstractly, they may appear to be very wide indeed. Consider the question: did Bukharin have the power, or ability, to resist Stalin? If you incorporate into your conception of Bukharin enough about his history, his personality traits, his loyalties, commitments, beliefs, and attitudes, then your answer may very well be no. If, however, you conceive him as an abstract, choosing self, capable, within limits (which limits?), of changing course, modifying his traits, abandoning commitments and beliefs, then you may well answer yes. Or consider the question: did the British Labour Government in 1929 have the power, or ability, to avert (or at least better manage) the economic crisis? Here again, the answer depends upon how that Government is conceived—as irremediably constituted by given traditions of thought and action, or as capable of alternative strategies in a time of crisis. Or, to take Cohen's own example, different conceptions of contemporary British workers yield different answers to the question of what powers they have (to withold labour collectively, to escape individually, to overthrow capitalism, to build socialism) and how much of such powers they have. Moreover, if the agents in question are defined in terms of their *roles*, that is *eo ipso* to define their abilities and inabilities, assuming of course that they act in accordance with their roles. But in terms of *which* roles should they be defined, and how role-determined should they be taken to be?

Second, what counts as enabling or constraining is never a simple matter of fact but it is always relative to background assumptions and judgements, some of them normative. To attribute abilities to agents is to accept as possibly true a set of conditionals, most of them counterfactual, of the form 'under conditions C, agent A will do or be x', and to attribute an inability is to rule some such conditionals out. But a deep question is: what are to be included in the conditions specified in the antecedent? Until that is answered, attributions of abilities and inabilities remain indeterminate. But it cannot be answered in a definitive and rationally incontestable manner.

Consider Cohen's own example of the slave's alleged inability to withhold his labour power. Under certain interpretations of C, this is plainly false, even on pain of death, of some, even perhaps of most slaves (as the history of slave rebellions demonstrates). If, however, one includes in C the condition that the slave behaves 'reasonably' or 'normally' (that is, that he conforms to yet-to-be-specified norms of reasonableness), then Cohen's claim may well be true. Here I merely wish to draw attention to the fact that not merely is the latter interpretation not normatively neutral, but the choice between them is not so either. Accordingly, no Cohenite description of the economic structure of slavery could be normatively neutral. So, to sum up these two arguments, I have suggested that if it is sought to describe the base in terms of abilities and inabilities, powers and constraints, then (1) which description is appropriate will always be contestable and (2) this will be so partly on normative, that is moral and political, grounds.

Third, it is worth focusing directly on one type of enabling and constraining condition, namely *norms*.

In general, enabling and constraining conditions may be external or internal to agents. Thus some physical factors are plainly external and some psychological factors plainly internal. Within a certain range, however, whether they are external or internal will itself depend on how the agent is conceived, where the boundaries of the self or the collectivity in question are drawn.

Norms are distinctive in being both external and internal, and in a particular way. They confront individuals as externally given but they can only be generally effective in enabling and constraining them in so far as they are (in H. L. A. Hart's phrase) 'internally accepted'. Of course, I may be induced to comply with a custom or convention or moral principle or legal rule by the fear of the sanction that would be brought to bear in the case of my non-compliance, but no set of norms stably regulating the behaviour of adults could rely on this mechanism alone. For such regulation to be generally effective, there must exist a high degree of intersubjective acceptance of rules, and of the purposes the rules are taken to serve (though an individual need not believe, in any given case, that his compliance will lead to the fulfilment of that purpose). In short, a stable system of enablements and constraints, to be effective, requires that I and relevant others are generally motivated by certain kinds of shared (teleological) reasons for acting and not acting.[17] These give such enablements and constraints their distinctively normative character.

Now, it is essential to Cohen's programme that such enablements and constraints be identifiable in non-normative terms, that is in abstraction from what gives them their distinctively normative character. The programme, he claims, 'says what production relations are, not what maintains them'. He cites the case of an illegal squatter who secures his dominion over a tract of land by having retainers who use force illegally on his behalf, or by perpetrating a myth that anyone who disturbs his tenure of the land will be damned to eternal hell-fire. What that squatter has *in common with* a legal owner of similar land, whose tenure is protected by law, is that both have the *power to use their land*. This, so the argument runs, is the content of the production relation in question, in the one case sustained by force and myth, in the other by the law. So the relations embodying normative enablements and constraints are, on Cohen's argument, abstractable from the norms that may have brought them about and maintain them in being. Is this so?

Consider the basic economic relationship of contract. If any relation of production is central to the economic structure of capitalism, this must be it. Can it be described in the manner proposed?

Interestingly, Durkheim took Herbert Spencer to be asserting just this—that economic life consisted in 'the spontaneous accord of individual interests, an accord of which contracts are the natural expression', society being 'merely the stage where individuals exchanged the products of their labour, without any properly social influence coming to regulate this exchange'. To this Durkheim replied that 'in the play of these relations themselves . . . social influence makes itself felt. For not everything in the contract is contractual.' By this he meant that 'a contract is not sufficient unto itself, but is possible only thanks to a regulation of the contract which

[17] See G. H. von Wright, *Explanation and Understanding* (London: Routledge & Kegan Paul, 1971), pp. 145 ff.

is originally social'. Recall that Durkheim defined the social in terms
of externality, constraint, and generality (throughout society), plus
independence (of individual circumstances); and that he saw the law,
in particular, and norms, in general, as paradigmatically social
phenomena. Contract law 'determines legal consequences of our acts
that we have not determined . . . We co-operate because we wish to,
but our voluntary co-operation creates duties for us that we did not
desire.' Contract law is not 'simply a useful complement of individual agreements; it is their fundamental norm'.[18] Durkheim is here
making two points (which he did not distinguish from one another):
that contract law, together with a whole network of customary and
conventional norms, combine to define the social practice of contracting; and that other such laws and norms regulate contractual
behaviour, rendering certain actions possible and proscribing others
on pain of sanctions. In short, the relation of contract is, in this
double sense, essentially norm-governed. Does not this fundamental
objection apply to both Marx and Spencer—or at least to Cohen's
Marx and Durkheim's Spencer?

But, it may be asked, is there not a *rechtsfrei* relationship here,
abstractable from the norms that govern it, in either sense?

How would we go about describing it? Cohen's answer is: in terms
of the abilities and inabilities of the contracting partners. But abilities
and inabilities to do . . . what? The performance of contractual
obligations is normally described in a vocabulary (paying wages,
supplying services, buying and selling, honouring debts) which
already presupposes the institution of contract and its regulating
norms, as well as a whole network of supporting informal norms. In
this sense, the norms that define the practice of contracting enter into
the description of the activities involved in that practice. To this, it
may be replied that a thin 'behavioural' description of such activities
(e.g. handing over money of a certain value, performing certain
tasks, etc.) could suffice in the description of the abilities and
inabilities. But the trouble is here that such thin 'behavioural'
descriptions would underdetermine the appropriate thick, normatively loaded descriptions: only some payments of money by certain
persons in certain ways would count as 'payment of wages', only
certain kinds of task performance as the supplying of a contracted

---

[18] E. Durkheim, *The Division of Labour in Society* (London: The Free Press of
Glencoe and Collier–Macmillan, 1933), pp. 203, 211, 215, 214 (trans. amended).

service. Recall that Cohen's non-normative relations of production are intended to be 'matching'. But how could the 'thin' non-normative description of transactions and dependencies between agents succeed in identifying *just those* transactions and dependencies which the normative relations involve unless the normative description were already, implicitly or explicitly, presupposed?

Suppose, however, that we overlook this difficulty, arising from the first sense in which contracts are norm-governed. What about the second sense: that is, the sense in which laws and conventions supply agents with certain kinds of *reasons* for acting and not acting, thereby enabling people to do what they otherwise would not, and preventing them from doing what they otherwise would? Can one describe contractual relationships in terms of abilities and inabilities in a way that abstracts from the operation of such reasons?

An ability and an inability, as we have already seen, are explicable as sets of conditionals, most of them counterfactual. In a pure, non-normative relationship of power—say, of simple coercion—my ability to secure an outcome may be stated as a set of conditionals of the following type: 'If I order my slave to sweep the floor, making threat t, he will do so' or 'If I threaten workers with redundancy, they will come into line'. But what of normative power-relationships? Here a whole new range of counterfactual conditionals enters the story, of the following type: 'If I offer employment at the going rate for the job, the workers will accept the offer' or 'If I break the agreement thus made, they will come out on strike'. In these cases the enablements and constraints *consist in* internally accepted norms and would not exist if attitudes changed. The normative beliefs in question enter irreducibly into the description of the powers and constraints linking the contracting parties. In other words, the norms, both informal and formal (the pay norm and the legal obligation to pay it once agreed), *are* what enables and constrains the parties—enabling the employers to secure the work on the terms agreed, but not if the terms are broken, by giving the parties certain reasons for acting as they do.

Let us return to the illegal squatter and the legal landholder. I can sum up the two points just made concerning norm-governed economic relationships by observing that (1) both squatter and proprietor can, it is true, keep people off their land; (2) the proprietor, unlike the squatter, can in addition secure the respect of people for his title to the land (e.g. should he wish to bequeath it); and (3) he can do so only by virtue of the reason-giving prevalent legal norms governing ownership of property and informal norms governing what landholders may legitimately lay claim to. From all of which I conclude that one cannot identify the powers and constraints embodied in norm-governed economic relationships independently of the norms which, in both senses, govern them.

Is there any interpretation of Cohen's purportedly purified economic structure, allegedly purged of all normative, superstructural encumbrances, that escapes the foregoing objections?

So far as I can see, there are only two possibilities. On the one hand, Cohen's proposal may be a purely linguistic one—a proposed translation manual converting all statements about rights and obligations into statements couched in a purged vocabulary of 'matching' powers and constraints.

There are, however, two decisive objections to this interpretation. First, it will not serve Cohen's purpose, since the objectionable normative elements would all survive, albeit covertly, in the identified economic structure: the purging would be solely at the linguistic level. But second, this is plainly not Cohen's intention anyway. His aim, after all, is coherently to 'represent property relations as distinct from, and explained by, production relations'.[19] He believes that his proposed *rechtsfrei* characterizations refer to a set of relations distinct from and explanatory of those referred to by talk of rights and duties in the normal sense. Thus, he explains away Marx's own continued adherence to legal terminology when speaking of the relations of production by remarking that

there was no attractive alternative. Ordinary language lacks a developed apparatus for describing production relations in a *rechtsfrei* manner. It does have a rich conceptual system for describing property relations, strictly so called. Given the poverty of the vocabulary of power, and the structural analogies between powers and rights, it is convenient to use rights-denoting terms with a special sense, for the sake of describing powers.[20]

In short, Cohen clearly believes that his proposed *rechtsfrei* terms (and Marx's allegedly special use of *rechtsvoll* terms) identify relations distinct from, if structurally analogous to, those that rights-denoting terms normally identify.

[19] Cohen, *Karl Marx's Theory of History*, p. 219.
[20] Ibid. 224.

The only alternative possibility I can see is that Cohen's economic structure, composed of powers and constraints, is intended to *exclude* all those that are norm-governed. But to this interpretation too there are two decisive objections. The first is that this would result in a hopelessly impoverished, indeed scarcely coherent, conception of the economic structure. The second objection is that, in any case, it is doubtful that this *is* Cohen's Marx: that is, that Cohen's programme of identifying a non-normative economic structure is to be understood in this way. For, in answering the possible objection that he is merely expounding the so-called 'force theory', condemned by Engels, Cohen remarks, as we have seen, that

> our definition of production relations does not stipulate how the powers they unfold are obtained or sustained. The answer to that question does involve force, but also ideology and the law. The programme says what production relations are, not what maintains them.[21]

I have argued that these two are the only remaining interpretations of Cohen's general programme of purging the economic structure of superstructural encumbrances, that neither does the job; and that neither squares with Cohen's intentions. There is, however, a third and final possibility: to reduce the generality of the programme. That is, one could read it as an attempt to purge the economic structure only of specifically legal elements, narrowly defined, as distinct from those pertaining to custom, convention, and morality. (It is, after all, formulated in response to the so-called 'problem of legality'.) Interestingly enough, this interpretation fits rather well the historical cases that Cohen cites to illustrate how his programme enables one to explain changes in property relations—the free circulation of labour in violation of the law of settlement which was eventually scrapped, the admitting of those of low status to the clothing industry in violation of a law eventually repealed, the formation of illegal unions leading to their eventual legal recognition, and the process leading to the early factory legislation: 'the struggle led to fairly well recognized practices, and then the law broke its silence and gave the facts legal form'.[22] In all these cases, informal norm-governed practices (responding, it is true, to developing productive forces, which they in turn facilitate) eventually acquire legal form.

But this, less general, interpretation of Cohen's programme once

[21] Ibid. 223.   [22] Ibid. 229.

more encounters two decisive objections. It does not square with Cohen's general objective of finding 'a method of conceiving of the economic structure which excludes from it the legal, moral and political relationships of men'. And second, therefore, it does not succeed in distinguishing the base from the superstructure, in the manner required. At the most, it distinguishes an expanded (norm-governed) 'base' from a diminished (narrowly legal) 'superstructure'.

What, then, are we to conclude from this dispute between Plamenatz and Cohen with respect to the question with which I began?

First, that Cohen makes of Plamenatz some perfectly proper demands for clarification. Second, that he rightly points to the need to specify more clearly what kind of 'determining' is involved in historical materialism; and in his book he has contributed greatly to this task. But third, that he has failed to solve the (misleadingly) so-called 'problem of legality' or, more generally, to purge the economic structure of normative elements and thus to distinguish the base from the superstructure.

What follows from this last conclusion? Nothing directly about the explanatory power of Marxist ideas, to the extent that what we may now call this non-distinction is neither assumed nor implied by them. And indeed it is not obvious that even the 'technological' reading of historical materialism that Cohen favours, or Marxian-type class analysis, or, in general, a Marxist approach to the explanation of social processes, whether in primitive or early or modern societies, do require it. It is irrelevant to the distinctions between material and social factors, between class position and class consciousness, and between economic as against legal, political, and ideological factors (provided that these terms are taken to identify spheres of social life that are not required to be conceivable independently of one another). It is, moreover, a dead, static, architectural metaphor, whose potential for illumination was never very great and which has for too long cast nothing but shadows over Marxist theory and Marxist practice. Is it not now time to consign it to the scrap-heap?

9
Can a Marxist Believe in
Human Rights?

This question might seem absurd for either of two opposite reasons.

On the one hand, one might counter with the question: *Can anyone believe in human rights?* This question might be asked from a utilitarian perspective, in the spirit of Bentham's view of natural rights as 'simple nonsense' and of natural and imprescriptible rights as 'nonsense upon stilts.'[1] It was in this spirit, for instance, that Sir George Cornewall Lewis saw expressions such as 'original rights, natural rights, indefeasible rights, inalienable rights, imprescriptible rights, hereditary rights, indestructible rights, inherent rights, etc.', as having

taken their origin from the theory of the state of nature and the social compact; but they are frequently used by persons who have never heard of this absurd and mischievous doctrine, and would perhaps reject it if they knew it. All that these persons mean is, that in their opinion, the claims which they call *rights* ought, in sound policy, to be sanctioned by law. It is the duty of such persons to show that sound policy requires what *they* require; but as this would require a process of reasoning, and as reasoning is often both hard to invent and to understand, they prefer begging the question at issue by employing some of the high sounding phrases just mentioned.[2]

Many modern Anglo-Saxon political philosophers still see utilitarianism as the major alternative to rights-based moral and political theories, which are often defended by contrast with it.[3]

Alternatively, the counter-question might be asked from a nonutilitarian perspective. So, for example, Alasdair MacIntyre, in

This chapter was first published in 1982.

[1] Jeremy Bentham, 'Anarchical Fallacies', in *The Works of Jeremy Bentham*, ed. J. Bowring (Edinburgh, 1843), ii. p. 494.

[2] Cornewall Lewis, *On the Use and Abuse of Some Political Terms* (London: Clarendon Press, new edn., 1898), pp. 33–4.

[3] See H. L. A. Hart, 'Between Utility and Rights', in A. Ryan (ed.), *The Idea of Freedom: Essays in Honour of Sir Isaiah Berlin* (Oxford: Clarendon Press, 1979).

developing a 'social teleological', quasi-Aristotelian view, observes that it would be

a little odd that there should be such rights attaching to human beings simply *qua* human beings in light of the fact . . . that there is no expression in any ancient or medieval language correctly translated by our expression 'a right' until near the close of the middle ages: the concept lacks any means of expression in Hebrew, Greek, Latin or Arabic, classical or medieval, before about 1400, let alone in Old English, or in Japanese even as late as the mid-nineteenth century. From this it does not of course follow that there are no natural or human rights; it only follows that no one could have known that there were. And this at least raises certain questions. But we do not need to be distracted into answering them, for the truth is plain: there are no such rights, and belief in them is one with belief in witches and unicorns.[4]

'Natural or human rights', he holds, are 'fictions'—as is 'utility' (but not, it seems, the 'human *telos*' or 'the common good').

I do not propose here to try and answer this counter-question. I will merely observe that belief in human rights appears to be very widespread, as do actions motivated by such belief, not only among politicians, statesmen, and international lawyers, but among activists for civil and political rights at home and against oppression and repression abroad. Of course, such commitments are, in many cases, significantly selective and even hypocritical. But it seems unduly cynical to regard them as always wholly so. Here I simply wish to observe that they are particularly in evidence on the left and, within the left, among Marxists.

Which leads me directly to the second, diametrically opposite, reason for thinking my initial question absurd. For one might counter with the question: *Why shouldn't a Marxist believe in human rights? Plainly, many do, and do so sincerely, and act on their beliefs.* Consider, for example, the following observations of G. A. Cohen:

The language of natural (or moral) rights is the language of justice, and whoever takes justice seriously must accept that there are natural rights. Now Marxists do not often talk about justice, and when they do they tend to deny its relevance, or they say that the idea of justice is an illusion. But I think that justice occupies a central place in revolutionary Marxist belief. Its presence is betrayed by particular judgments Marxists make, and by the strength of feeling with which they make them. Revolutionary Marxist belief often misdescribes itself, out of lack of clear awareness of its own nature, and

---

[4] MacIntyre, *After Virtue: A Study in Moral Theory* (London: Duckworth, 1981), pp. 66–7.

Marxist disparagement of the idea of justice is a good example of that deficient self-understanding.[5]

Interestingly, Marxists in the contemporary world are not reluctant to use the language of 'human rights'—especially in struggles against reactionary regimes.

I do not doubt that Marxists across the world, especially since the Resistance to the Nazis, have been in the forefront of struggles against all kinds of tyranny and oppression, often in the name of human rights. Indeed, I would argue that the establishment and protection of basic civil and political rights often depends on the existence of a strong and well-organized labour movement, and that Marxist parties and groups have often played a central role in achieving this.

So the question is not whether those whose beliefs and affiliations are Marxist in fact believe in human rights. It is, rather, whether they can *consistently* do so. But the question thus formulated is still not adequate. For I am certain that many of those who are called, and call themselves, Marxists and who believe in human rights hold a consistent set of beliefs that do not contradict their belief in and actions for human rights.

The question should therefore be reformulated thus: can those whose beliefs and affiliations are Marxist believe in human rights and remain consistent with central doctrines essential to the Marxist canon—by which I mean the ideas of Marx, Engels, and their major followers, including Lenin and Trotsky, in the Marxist tradition? Putting the question this way of course inevitably raises the issue of how 'the Marxist tradition' is properly to be identified and interpreted, who are the 'true Marxists', and so on. Fortunately, it is my belief (grounds for which I will indicate below) that, in this area, there is a well-defined and unambiguous unity of view in the mainstream Marxist tradition which can be identified both at the level of explicit statement and implicit theory.

But the question still needs further refinement. What is it, after all, to believe in human rights? It is, I take it, to believe that there are such rights and to be prepared to act on that belief. Indeed, the sincere holding of such a belief is precisely tested by the putative believer being so prepared, when the occasion arises. Believing that there are

[5] Cohen, 'Freedom, Justice and Capitalism', *New Left Review* 126 (Mar.–Apr. 1981), p. 12.

human rights, it should be noted, involves a lesser commitment than believing that there are natural rights: the latter belief involves attributing to such rights epistemic properties and a metaphysical status about which a believer in human rights may remain neutral.

Here I shall follow Feinberg in defining 'human rights' as 'generically moral rights of a fundamentally important kind held equally by all human beings, unconditionally and unalterably.'[6] They are sometimes understood to be 'ideal rights', or rights that are not necessarily actually recognized but which ought to be so, that is, ought to be positive rights and would be so in a better or ideal legal system. Sometimes they are understood to be 'conscientious rights', that is, the claim is to recognize them as valid by reference to the principles of an enlightened conscience. Are they absolute?

To be absolute in the strongest sense, they would have to be absolutely exceptionless in all circumstances and thus never vulnerable to legitimate invasion: they must *always* trump other reasons for a policy or action, including rights of other kinds, and other rights of the same kind. But this is an impossibly strong requirement. It would rule out virtually all the rights specified in the UN *Universal Declaration of Human Rights* and, in particular, active negative rights (rights not to be interfered with) and positive rights (rights to be treated in certain ways). These latter—for instance, the so-called 'social and economic rights' and, in general, rights to be given the means of living a decent life, or even a life at all[7]—depend for their implementation on the availability of resources and, therefore, they cannot be absolute in this sense. Perhaps the only completely absolute rights are rights not to be degraded and exploited, or, more generally, the right to be treated with equal concern and respect. But what this last means is hard to specify in concrete terms, and one may suspect that its claim to absoluteness may derive from this very fact.

6 Joel Feinberg, *Social Philosophy* (Englewood Cliffs: Prentice-Hall, 1973), p. 85.
7 Such as the rights 'to work, to free choice of employment, to just and favourable conditions of work and to protection against unemployment', to 'just and favourable remuneration', to 'rest and leisure, including reasonable limitation of working hours and periodic holidays with pay', to 'a standard of living adequate for the health and well-being of himself and of his family, including food, clothing, housing, and medical care and necessary social services, and the right to security in the event of unemployment, sickness, disability, widowhood, old age or other lack of livelihood in circumstances beyond his control', to 'education' and indeed 'to choose the kind of education that shall be given to their children', and 'freely to participate in the cultural life of the community to enjoy the arts, and to share in scientific advancement and its benefits'.

It is therefore perhaps better to say that human rights are strongly prima-facie rights which, in general, are justified as defending people's vital interests and which, in general, outweigh all other considerations bearing on some policy or action, whether these concern goals and purposes or the protection of other, less central rights. They thus have a 'trumping' aspect:[8] to believe in them is to be committed to defending them, even (or rather especially) when one's goals or strategies are not to be served, and indeed may be disserved, by doing so.

To put this another way, talk of rights is a way of asserting the requirements of a relationship of justice, from the viewpoint of the persons benefiting from it: it involves adopting 'the viewpoint of the "other(s)" to whom something (including, *inter alia*, freedom of choice) is owed or due, and who would be wronged if denied that something.'[9] Talk of *human* rights is to do this, while emphasizing the fundamental and prima-facie overriding status of this viewpoint with respect to certain matters, specifically those central to the flourishing of human beings. Proof that such talk is serious is being prepared to abandon goals and policies and strategies, except in rare and extreme cases, when the claims such rights invoke conflict with their implementation.

To put this yet another way, rights might, following Robert Nozick, be seen as 'side constraints'—moral constraints upon goal-directed behaviour.[10] This way of viewing rights (rather than building the minimization of the violation of rights into one's goals, in a kind of calculating 'utilitarianism of rights') reflects the basic Kantian principle of treating persons as ends and not merely as means, of ruling out certain ways persons (or the Party or the State) may use others. It is not hard to see how these could exclude murder, physical aggression and injury, psychological manipulation and intimidation, the denial or distortion of information, preventing free association and dissent from the existing order, the use of terror, arbitrary arrest and detention, the deliberate punishment of the innocent, discrimination of the basis of ascribed characteristics, and the denial of access to the means of life, labour, and the cultural resources of a community. In citing Nozick, I do not, however, subscribe to his

---

[8] See Ronald Dworkin, *Taking Rights Seriously* (London: Duckworth, 1977).
[9] John Finnis, *Natural Law and Natural Rights* (Oxford: Clarendon Press, 1980), p. 205.
[10] Nozick, *Anarchy, State and Utopia* (Oxford: Blackwell, 1974), ch. 3.

so-called 'libertarian' account of what violation of rights thus under-stood involves, such as, for instance, taxing people, without their consent, to benefit others. I do, however, endorse his analysis of rights (and thus by implication human rights) as side constraints, as well as his view of their basis. They

> express the inviolability of other persons. But why may not one violate persons for the greater social good? Individually, we each sometimes choose to undergo some pain or sacrifice for a greater benefit or to avoid a greater harm: we go to the dentist to avoid worse suffering later; we do some unpleasant work for its results; some persons diet to improve their health or looks; some save money to support themselves when older. In each case, some cost is borne for the sake of the overall good. Why not, *similarly*, hold that some persons have to bear some costs that benefit other persons more, for the sake of the overall social good? But there is no *social entity* with a good that undergoes some sacrifice for its own good. There are only individual people, with their own individual lives. Using one of these people for the benefit of others, uses him and benefits the others. Nothing more. What happens is that something is done to him for the sake of the others. Talk of an overall social good covers this up. (Intentionally?). To use a person in this way does not sufficiently respect and take account of the fact that he is a separate person, that his is the only life he has. He does not get some overbalancing good from his sacrifice . . .[11]

So believing in human rights involves accepting side constraints upon the pursuit of one's goals for Kantian reasons. Nozick believes that they are absolute and timelessly applicable in all social contexts, but it seems much more plausible to see them as strongly prima facie (for the reason already suggested), and as applicable only in certain kinds of social setting (at least, where there is a minimum level of subsistence and framework of social order). I shall not here go further into the questions of (1) under which stringent conditions prima-facie rights might be overridden, (2) in which kinds of social setting they are relevantly applicable or (3) upon what characteristics of persons the constraints are based. All these are, of course, fundamental questions which must be answered in any adequate account of human rights.

So our initial question has now been specified as follows: Can one believe in human rights (in the manner defined above) and remain consistent with the canonical Marxist tradition? I propose to seek an answer to this question in two ways: first, by citing what the Marxist

---

[11] Nozick, *Anarchy, State and Utopia*, p. 32–3.

canon explicitly has to say on this topic; and second, by stating what I take to be the 'deep theory' underlying its explicit statements.

In the *German Ideology* Marx and Engels wrote: 'As far as *Recht* is concerned, we with many others have stressed the opposition of communism to *Recht*, both political and private, as also in its most general form as the rights of man.'[12] This is an accurate statement about all their writings, from 'On the Jewish Question' onwards.

In that work, Marx wrote of 'the so-called *rights of man* as 'simply the rights of a *member of civil society*, that is, of egoistic man, of man separated from other men and from the community'. Liberty 'as a right of man is not founded upon the relations between man and man, but rather upon the separation of man from man. It is the right of such separation. The right of the circumscribed individual, withdrawn into himself', its practical application being the right of private property. *This* right, the 'right of self-interest', Marx saw as forming 'the basis of civil society', leading 'every man to see in other men, not the *realisation*, but rather the *limitation* of his own liberty'. In general,

None of the supposed rights of man . . . go beyond the egoistic man, man as he is, as a member of civil society; that is, an individual separated from the community, withdrawn into himself, wholly preoccupied with his private interest and acting in accordance with his private caprice. Man is far from being considered, in the rights of man, as a species being; on the contrary, species-life itself—society—appears as a system which is external to the individual and as a limitation of his original independence. The only bond between men is natural necessity, need and private interest, the preservation of their property and their egoistic persons.

The *political community* is 'a mere means of preserving these so-called rights of man'. 'Human emancipation' contrasts with these rights of man (or human rights): it

will only be complete when the real, individual man has absorbed into himself the abstract citizen; when as an individual man, in his everyday life, in his work, and in his relationships, he has become a *species-being*; and when he has recognised and organised his own powers (*forces propres*) as *social* powers so that he no longer separates this social power from himself as *political* power.[13]

[12] K. Marx and F. Engels, *Collected Works* (London: Lawrence and Wishart, 1975), v. p. 209.
[13] *Karl Marx: Early Writings*, ed. T. B. Bottomore (London: C. Watts and Co., 1963), pp. 24–6, 31.

Marx and Engels always wrote disparagingly about the language of rights and justice. It is true that in 1864 Marx helped draft the *General Rules of the International Working Men's Association*, whose members were enjoined to acknowledge 'truth, justice and morality, as the basis of their conduct towards each other and towards all men, without regard to colour, creed or nationality', and the principle of *'no rights without duties, no duties without rights'*, while 'the struggle for emancipation of the working classes' is described as a struggle 'for equal rights and duties, and for the abolition of all class rule'.[14] Moreover, in his *Inaugural Address*, Marx urged workers to 'vindicate the simple laws of morals and justice, which ought to govern the relations of private individuals, as the rules paramount of the intercourse of nations'.[15] On the other hand, he explained these unfortunate phrases in a letter to Engels of 4 November 1864: 'I was obliged', he wrote, 'to insert two phrases about "duty" and "right" into the preamble, ditto, "truth, morality and justice," but these are placed in such a way that they can do no harm.'[16]

In *Capital*, Marx scorned Proudhon's appeal to an ideal of justice. What opinion, he asked,

should we have of a chemist, who, instead of studying the actual laws of the molecular changes in the composition and decomposition of matter, and on that foundation solving definite problems, claimed to regulate the composition and decomposition of matter by means of 'eternal ideas,' of 'naturalité' and 'affinité'? Do we really know any more about 'usury' when we say it contradicts 'justice éternelle', 'équité éternelle,' 'mutualité éternelle,' and other 'vérités éternelles' than the fathers of the church did when they said it was incompatible with 'grace éternelle,' 'foi éternelle' and 'le volonté éternelle de Dieu'?[17]

And in the *Critique of the Gotha Programme*, he once more made clear his rejection of this kind of moral vocabulary:

I have dealt more at length with . . . 'equal right' and 'fair distribution' . . . in order to show what a crime it is to attempt, on the one hand, to force on our Party again, as dogmas, ideas which in a certain period had some meaning but have now become obsolete verbal rubbish, while again perverting, on the

---

[14] *General Rules of the International Working Men's Association: Preamble* (1864), in Marx and Engels, *Selected Works*, 2 vols. (Moscow, Foreign Language Publishing House, 1962), i. pp. 386–9.
[15] *Inaugural Address of the Working Men's International Association*, ibid. 385.
[16] Marx and Engels, *Selected Correspondence* (Moscow: Foreign Languages Publishing House, n.d.), p. 182.   [17] Marx, *Capital* (Moscow: 1959), i. 84–5.

other, the realistic outlook, which it cost so much effort to instill into the Party but which has now taken root in it, by means of ideological nonsense about right [*Recht*] and other trash so common among the democrats and French socialists.[18]

As for the moral bases for human rights claims, whether they be 'conscientious rights' or 'ideal rights', he was no less uncompromising. Morality, like 'religion, metaphysics, all the rest of ideology and their corresponding forms of consciousness' had 'no history, no development, but men, altering their material production and their material intercourse alter—along with these—their real existence and their thinking and products of their thinking.'[19] Moreover, the working class has 'no ideals to realize, but to set free elements of the new society with which the old collapsing bourgeois society itself is pregnant.'[20]

Engels argued similarly. Justice, he remarked, attacking Proudhon, is 'but the ideologized, glorified expression of the existing economic relations, at times from their conservative, and at other times from their revolutionary side.' The 'idea of equality, both in its bourgeois and its proletarian form' was 'anything but an eternal truth'. As he wrote in *Anti-Dühring*:

We therefore reject every attempt to impose on us any moral dogma whatsoever as an eternal, ultimate and forever immutable ethical law on the pretext that the moral world, too, has its permanent principles which stand above history and the differences between nations. We maintain on the contrary that all moral theories have been hitherto the product, in the last analysis, of the economic conditions of society obtaining at the time. And as society has hitherto moved in class antagonisms, morality has always been class morality; it has either justified the domination and the interests of the ruling class, or, ever since the oppressed class became powerful enough, it has represented its indignation against this domination and the future interests of the oppressed.[21]

The subsequent mainline Marxist tradition is, on this topic, quite consistent, though emphases shift, as the revolutionary struggle intensifies. Thus Kautsky echoed Marx's and Engels' criticism of Proudhon and Lassalle, speaking with scorn of 'Ethical Socialism' as 'endeavours . . . in our ranks to modify the class antagonisms, and to

[18] Id., 'Critique of the Gotha Programme', *Selected Works*, i. p. 25.
[19] Marx and Engels, 'The German Ideology', *Collected Works*, v. p. 36–7 (trans. amended).
[20] Marx, 'The Civil War in France', *Selected Works*, i. p. 523.
[21] Engels, *Anti-Dühring* (Moscow, 1959), p. 131.

meet at least a section of the Bourgeoisie half way', the 'historical and social tendency' of the Kantian ethic being 'that of toning down, of reconciling the antagonisms, not of overcoming them through struggle'. For Kautsky, moral tenets 'arise from social needs', 'all morality is relative', and what is 'specifically human in morality, the moral codes is subject to continual change'.[22]

Lenin held that there is in Marxism 'not a grain of ethics from beginning to end'.[23] As he told the Komsomol Congress in 1920,

We say that our morality is entirely subordinated to the interests of the proletariat's class struggle . . . Morality is what serves to destroy the old exploiting society and to unite all the working people around the proletariat, which is building up a new, a communist society . . . To a Communist all morality lies in this united discipline and conscious mass struggle against the exploiters. We do not believe in an eternal morality, and we expose the falseness of all the fables about morality.[24]

As for Trotsky, his pamphlet *Their Morals and Ours* clearly shows his view that 'morality more than any other form of ideology has a class character'. As for 'norms obligatory upon all'—whose 'highest generalisation . . . is in the "categorical imperative" of Kant'—these are vacuous and appeal to them is 'a necessary element in the mechanics of class deception', since

in all decisive questions people feel their class membership considerably more profoundly and more directly than their membership in 'society.' The norms of 'obligatory' morality are in reality filled with class, that is, antagonistic content. The moral norm becomes the more categoric the less it is 'obligatory upon all.' The solidarity of workers, especially of strikers or barricade fighters, is incomparably more 'categoric' than human solidarity in general.

Indeed, Trotsky comes to the heart of the matter in stating that such norms 'become the less forceful the sharper the character assumed by the class struggle. The highest form of the class struggle is civil war which explodes into mid-air all moral ties between the hostile classes.'

What, then, of 'lying, violence and murder': are these 'incompatible with a "healthy socialist movement"'? Trotsky answers this question with another:

[22] Karl Kautsky, *Ethics and the Materialist Conception of History*, trans. J. B. Askew (Chicago Mass.: Charles H. Kerr & Co., n.d.), pp. 69, 178, 192, 184.
[23] V. I. Lenin, 'The Economic Content of Narodism and the Criticism of it in Mr. Struve's Book', *Collected Works* (Foreign Language Publishing House, Moscow: 1960–3), i. 421.   [24] Id., *Collected Works*, xxi. 291–4.

What, however, is our relation to revolution? Civil war is the most severe of all forms of war. It is unthinkable not only without violence against tertiary figures but, under contemporary technique, without killing old men, old women and children.

But, he goes on to ask, do such lying and violence in themselves warrant condemnation?

Of course, even as does the class society which generates them. A society without social contradictions will naturally be a society without lies and violence. However there is no way of building a bridge to that society save by revolutionary, that is, violent means. The revolution itself is a product of class society and of necessity bears its traits. From the point of view of 'eternal truths' revolution is of course 'anti-moral'. But this merely means that idealist morality is counter-revolutionary, that is, in the service of the exploiters.

But is not civil war a 'sad exception': can it not be held that 'in peaceful times a healthy socialist movement should manage without violence and lying'? But this, according to Trotsky, is 'a pathetic evasion. There is no impervious demarcation between "peaceful" class struggle and revolution. Every strike embodies in an un-expanded form all the elements of civil war.' Lying, violence, and murder are therefore 'an inseparable part of the class struggle even in its most elementary forms.' But '"Just the same", the moralist continues to insist, "does it mean that in the class struggle against capitalists all means are permissible: lying, frame-up, betrayal, murder, and so on?"' Trotsky's answer is clear-cut and specifically excludes the notion of moral side constraints. He sees the problem as one of revolutionary morality and thus as inseparable from 'revolu-tionary strategy and tactics':

Permissible and obligatory are those and only those means, we answer, which unite the revolutionary proletariat, fill their hearts with irreconcilable hostility to oppression, teach them contempt for official morality and its democratic echoers, imbue them with consciousness of their own historic mission, raise their courage and spirit of self-sacrifice in the struggle.[25]

I cited above a passage from the *German Ideology* in which Marx and Engels make clear their view of *Recht* and thus of the rights of man: 'As far as *Recht* is concerned, we with many others have

---

[25] L. Trotsky, J. Dewey, and G. Novack, *Their Morals and Ours: Marxist versus Liberal Views on Morality* (New York: Pathfinder Press, 4th edn., 1979), pp. 15, 16, 15–16, 27–8, 37.

stressed the opposition of communism to *Recht*, both political and private, as also in its most general form of the rights of man.' What are the deep reasons for communism's rejection of *Recht*?

'*Recht*', like '*droit*' and '*diritto*', is a term used by continental jurists for which there is no direct English translation. As Hart has observed, these expressions

seem to English jurists to hover uncertainly between law and morals, but they do in fact mark off an area of morality (the morality of law) which has special characteristics. It is occupied by the concepts of justice, fairness, rights and obligation (if this last is not used as it is by many moral philosophers as an obscuring general label to cover every action that we ought to do or forbear from doing).[26]

Gierke defined *Recht* as meaning: '(*a*) a system of law existing objectively as an external norm for persons, and (*b*) a system of rights enjoyed by those persons, as "Subjects" or owners of rights, under and by virtue of that norm.'[27] In short, *Recht* identifies that branch of morality concerned with determining when one person's freedom may be limited by another's and thus which actions should be made the subject of the positive laws of any actual legal system.

How did Marx, Engels, and their followers conceive of *Recht*? Marx wrote of juridical relations (*Rechtsverhältnisse*) that 'like forms of state [they] are to be grasped neither through themselves nor through the so-called universal development of the human spirit, but rather are rooted in the material conditions of life, whose totality Hegel comprehended under the term "civil society".'[28] And Engels wrote that 'social justice or injustice is decided by the science which deals with the material facts of production and exchange, the science of political economy.'[29] In short, the principles of *Recht* are not to be understood as objective norms, as a set of independent rational standards by which to assess social relations, but must themselves always

---

[26] H. L. A. Hart, 'Are There any Natural Rights?' *Philosophical Review* 64 (1955), repr. in Richard Flathman (ed.), *Concepts in Social and Political Philosophy* (New York: Macmillan, 1973), p. 442.

[27] Otto Gierke, *Natural Law and the Theory of Society, 1500–1800*, trans. Ernest Barker, 2 vols. (Boston: Cambridge Univ. Press, 1934; repr. Boston: Beacon (1 vol.), 1957), p. 39.

[28] Marx, 'Preface to a Contribution to the Critique of Political Economy', *Selected Works*, i. p. 362 (trans. amended).

[29] Marx and Engels, *Kleine Ökonomische Schriften* (Berlin: 1955), p. 412, cited in Allen Wood, 'The Marxist Critique of Justice', *Philosophy and Public Affairs* (Spring 1972), p. 15.

in turn be explained as arising from and controlling those relations.[30]

This suggests the first Marxist reason for opposing *Recht*, namely, that it is inherently ideological. It claims to offer 'objective' principles specifying what is 'just' and 'fair' and defining 'rights' and 'obligations'; it claims that these are universally valid and serve the interests of all members of society (and perhaps all members of any society); and it claims to be 'autonomous' of particular partisan or sectional interests. But from a Marxist point of view all these claims are spurious and illusory. They serve to conceal the real function of principles of *Recht*, which is to protect the social relations of the existing order, a function that is better fulfilled to the extent that the claims are widely accepted. Marxism, in short, purports to unmask the self-understanding of *Recht* by revealing its real functions and the bourgeois interests that lie behind it.

It does not, of course, follow from this that communists should all become 'immoralists' violating every bourgeois right and obligation. That would, in any case, be poor tactics. What does follow is that the principles of *Recht* should have for them no rationally compelling authority. And it follows from *this* that it makes no sense to criticize capitalism for failing to live up to such principles, for being unjust, violating the rights of workers, etc. (except as a tactical move).

But there is a further and deeper reason for communism's opposition to *Recht* which can be unearthed if we ask the question: to what problem are the principles of *Recht* a response? To this question jurists and philosophers give different answers, but these answers have in common a view of human life as inherently conflictual, and potentially catastrophically so, thus requiring a framework of authoritative rules, needing coercive enforcement, that can be rationally justified as serving the interests of all. *Recht* is a response to what one might call the 'conditions of morality', inherent in the human condition, and these may be more or less acute, just as the response will take different forms in different societies.

Consider David Hume's summary account of the conditions of morality: for Hume 'tis only from the selfishness and confin'd generosity of man, along with the scanty provision nature has made for his wants, that justice derives its origin'.[31] In his 1977 book on

---

[30] See ibid. and Wood, *Karl Marx* (London: Routledge & Kegan Paul, 1981), pt. III, 'Marxism and Morality'.

[31] D. Hume, *A Treatise of Human Nature* (1739) ed. L. A. Selby-Biggs (Oxford: Clarendon Press, 1951), p. 495, bk. III, pt. II, sect. II).

ethics, John Mackie, citing this statement of Hume's, alongside Protagoras and Hobbes, sought to identify what he calls a 'narrow sense of morality' (which looks very like *Recht*) as 'a system of a particular sort of constraints on conduct—ones whose central task is to protect the interests of persons other than the agent and which present themselves to an agent as checks on his natural inclinations or spontaneous tendencies to act.' Mackie argues, following Hume, that morality, in this narrow sense, thus defined, is needed to solve a basic problem inherent in the human predicament: that 'limited resources and limited sympathies together generate both competition leading to conflict, and an absence of what would be mutually beneficial co-operation.'[32] Or consider John Rawls's account of what I have called the conditions of morality and what he calls 'the circumstances of justice': these are 'the normal conditions under which human co-operation is both possible and necessary' and they 'obtain whenever mutually disinterested persons put forward conflicting claims to the division of social advantages under conditions of moderate scarcity.'[33]

Now it is a peculiar and distinctive feature of Marxism that it denies that the conditions of morality are inherent in human life. It certainly denies that limited altruism and resources are invariant features inherent in the human condition. On the contrary, it maintains that they are historically determined, specific to class societies, and imminently removable. Neither limited resources, nor limited sympathies, nor in general conflicts of interest and antagonistic social relations are fundamental to the human predicament. To assume that they are is itself an ideological illusion (propagated by *Recht*)—ideological in serving to perpetuate the existing class-bound social order. Marxism supposes that a unified society of abundance is not merely capable of being brought about but is on the historical agenda, and indeed that the working class is in principle motivated to bring it about and is capable of doing so.

Thus *Recht* is not merely inherently ideological, stabilizing class

---

[32] J. L. Mackie, *Ethics: Inventing Right and Wrong* (Harmondsworth: Penguin 1977), pp. 106, 111. See also id., 'Can there be a Right-based Moral Theory?' *Midwest Studies in Philosophy*, 3 *Studies in Ethical Theory*, 1978 (Univ. of Minnesota Press, Minneapolis, Minn.: 1980).

[33] Rawls, *A Theory of Justice* (Oxford: Clarendon Press, 1972), pp. 126, 128.

societies and concealing class interests, and falsely purporting to adjudicate competing claims, limit freedoms, and distribute costs and benefits in a universally fair, objective, and mutually advantageous manner. It also presupposes an account of the conditions that call it forth that Marxism denies. For Marxism holds that, broadly, all significant conflicts of interests are to be traced back to class divisions. So, for example, Marx and Engels could speak of communism as 'the *genuine* resolution of the conflict between man and nature and between man and man',[34] and speculate about the abolition of crime under communism, and suggest that 'social peace' might succeed 'social war';[35] and Trotsky, as we have seen, could proclaim that the future 'society without social contradictions will naturally be a society without lies and violence'. Certainly the Marxist canon has virtually nothing to say about any bases of conflict, whether social or psychological, other than class.

By furnishing principles for the regulation of conflicting claims and interests, *Recht* serves to promote class compromise and thereby delays the revolutionary change that will make possible a form of social life that has no need of *Recht*, because the conditions of morality or the circumstances of justice will no longer obtain. In this respect, I think that Marx's view of morality as *Recht* is exactly parallel to his view of religion, concerning which he wrote 'The abolition of religion as the illusory happiness of the people is a demand for their true happiness. The call to abandon illusions about their condition is the call to abandon a condition which requires illusions.'[36] Analogously, the call to abandon illusions about 'the rights of man' and 'justice' is the call to abandon the conditions of morality and the circumstances of justice.

Can a Marxist believe in human rights? We have seen that the test of such a belief arises in cases of conflict between such rights claims and the requirements of one's goals or strategy. So, is a Marxist prepared to protect and defend such rights in situations where they conflict with his or her goals—which, as I have just argued, include the eventual abolition of the very need for such rights?

[34] *Karl Marx: Early Writings*, p. 155 (trans. amended).
[35] See Paul Phillips, *Marx and Engels on Law and Laws* (Oxford: Blackwell, 1980), chap. 4.
[36] Marx, 'A Contribution to the Critique of Hegel's Philosophy of Right: Introduction', *Karl Marx, Early Writings*, p. 44.

Now, I do not doubt that very many Marxists have defended such rights honourably and heroically. But they often do so in situations where there is no conflict between the goals of their struggle and the rights they defend. Take the resistance to Fascism, or struggles against racism and colonialism, or the opposition of the left to Latin American dictatorships, or the consistent activities of Trotskyists against repression in the Soviet Union and Eastern Europe. But the real test of a belief in human rights comes when the goals of the struggle or strategy come into conflict with the defence of rights claims. Here, so far as I can see, the Marxist canon provides no reasons for protecting human rights. And indeed, it even gives reasons against doing so, if one follows Trotsky in holding (1) that no significant line can be drawn between peaceful class struggle and revolution, and (2) that there is no way of building a bridge to communist society save by revolutionary, that is violent, means. On these assumptions, the only side constraints to one's actions will be one's own (or the Party's) strategic and tactical judgements as to what means one's ends require.

From which I conclude that a Marxist cannot, in the sense indicated, believe in human rights. Those many non-hypocritical and non-self-deceiving Marxists who do so can only, therefore, be revisionists who have discarded or abandoned those central tenets of the Marxist canon which are incompatible with such a belief.

10
Marxism and Dirty Hands

Lenin asked the question: what is to be done? A second question, which Lenin did not ask is: what is not to be done? A third question arises when answering the first and second yields incompatible directives. How are we to understand and respond to such situations, in which, as Machiavelli put it, the Prince must learn, 'among so many who are not good', how 'to enter evil when necessity commands' for the good of the Republic? This is the classical problem of dirty hands. What, if anything, does Marxism have to say about it?

I

As it happens, some of the twentieth century's most compelling representations of this problem—or, rather, of the conflict between Marxist and non-Marxist approaches to it—come from two Marxist playwrights: Brecht and Sartre. Brecht addressed it in his remarkable play *Die Massnahme (The Measures Taken)*, written in 1929–30, which has been accurately described as 'an exact and horrifying anticipation of the great confession trials of the Stalinist era'.[1] In this play, 'Four Agitators' decide to shoot a soft-hearted 'Young Comrade' who has flouted Party discipline, in order to relieve suffering because, as he puts it, 'misery cannot wait'. The 'Young Comrade's' action had placed the 'Four Agitators' and the revolution in danger. The 'Four Agitators' explain:

> And so we decided: we now
> Had to cut off a member of our own body.
> *It is a terrible thing to kill.*
> We would not only kill others, but ourselves as well,
> If the need arose.

This chapter was first published in 1986.

[1] Martin Esslin, *Brecht: A Choice of Evils* (London: Eyre Methuen, 3rd rev. edn., 1980), p. 144.

> For violence is the only means whereby this deadly
> World may be changed, as
> Every living being knows.
> And yet, we said
> We are not permitted to kill. At one with the
> Inflexible will to change the world, we formulated
> The measures taken.

To which the 'Control Chorus' responds:

> It was not easy to do what was right.
> It was not you who sentenced him, but
> Reality.

For 'what is needed to change the world' are

> Anger and tenacity, knowledge and indignation
> Swift action, utmost deliberation
> Cold endurance, unending perseverance
> Comprehension of the individual and comprehension of the whole:
> Taught only by reality can
> Reality be changed.[2]

Elsewhere in the play, the Control Chorus expresses its view even more clearly:

> With whom would the just man not sit
> To help justice?
> What medicine is too bitter
> For the man who's dying?
> What violence should you not suffer to
> Annihilate violence?
> If at last you could change the world, what
> Could make you too good to do so?
> Who are you?
> Sink in filth
> Embrace the butcher but
> Change the world: it needs it![3]

Eight years later, Brecht was to write in a less ruthless vein, seeking some understanding for the present perpetrators of necessary evils from their future beneficiaries:

> You who will emerge from the flood
> In which we have gone under
> Remember

---

[2] B. Brecht, *The Measures Taken and Other Lehrstucke*, trans. Stefan Brecht (London: Eyre Methuen, 1977), pp. 32–4.
[3] Ibid. 25.

When you speak of our failings
The dark time too
Which you have escaped.

For we went, changing countries oftener than our shoes
Through the wars of the classes, despairing
When there was injustice only, and no rebellion.

And yet we know:
Hatred, even of meanness
Contorts the features.
Anger, even against injustice
Makes the voice hoarse. Oh, we
Who wanted to prepare the ground for friendliness
Could not ourselves be friendly.

But you, when the time comes at last
And man is a helper to man
Think of us
With forbearance.[4]

Sartre confronted the problem most directly in his plays *Les Mains sales* (1948) and *Le Diable et le bon dieu* (1951). In the latter play, Sartre has the violent revolutionary peasant leader say to the pacifist Tolstoyan, Goetz: 'In a single day of virtue you have created more deaths than in thirty-five years of malice' and Goetz reflects: 'On the Earth at present Good and Evil are inseparable'.[5] And in *Les Mains sales*, Sartre's 'Young Comrade', Hugo, argues thus with the Party secretary, Hoederer:

HUGO. I've never lied to our comrades. I . . . What use would it be to fight for the liberation of mankind if you despised them enough to stuff their heads with lies?

HOEDERER. I lie when I must and I despise no one. I didn't invent the idea of lying; it was born of a society divided into classes and each of us inherited it at our birth. We shan't abolish lies by refusing to lie ourselves; we must use every weapon that comes to hand to suppress class differences.

HUGO. Not all methods are good.

HOEDERER. All methods are good when they are effective.

HUGO. Then what right have you to condemn the Regent's policy? He declared war on the USSR because it was the best way of safeguarding our national independence.

HOEDERER. Do you imagine I *condemn* him? I've no time to waste. He did

---

[4] Brecht, 'To Those Born Later', in *Bertholt Brecht Poems 1913–1956*, ed. and trans. J. Willett, *et al.* (London: Methuen, 1976), pp. 319–20.
[5] J.-P. Sartre, *Le Diable et le bon dieu* (Paris: Livre de Poche, 1961), p. 224.

what any poor fool of his caste would have done in his place. We're not fighting men or a policy, but against the class which produced that policy and those men.

HUGO. And the best method you can find to carry on this fight is to offer to share the power with them?

HOEDERER. Exactly. Today, it is the best method [*Pause*]. How attached to your purity you are my boy! How frightened you are of soiling your hands! All right, stay pure! Who does it help, and why did you come to us? Purity is an ideal for a fakir or a monk. You intellectuals, you bourgeois anarchists, you use it as an excuse for doing nothing. Do nothing, stay put, keep your elbows to your sides, wear kid gloves. My hands are filthy. I've dipped them up to the elbows in blood and slime. So what? Do you think you can govern and keep your spirit white?[6]

This, most dramatically put, is the problem of dirty hands. It has an interesting structure that is worth analysing. Sometimes, the problem is unhelpfully posed in the form of the question: 'Does the end justify the means?' There are several things seriously wrong with this question. To begin with, it is doubly ambiguous. In the first place, 'the end' could mean the 'end-in-view' at the time of action, or the end likely to be achieved by it, or the end in fact achieved. And, second, the formula of the end justifying the means could mean either that given certain ends (which?), in whichever of these three senses, any means could be justified; or it could mean that, when it comes to justifying means, the nature of the end, in whichever of the three senses indicated, makes a difference (but what difference?). But the question is misleading for a deeper reason, too. It assumes that, in justifying 'means', there is an overall metric, a unified scheme of evaluation within which the values of means and ends alike are commensurable: that they can be impartially assessed or *weighed* (and, on the most ruthless interpretation of the formula, the costs of means will always be *outweighed* by the positive value of certain ends).

Yet this assumption of commensurability is precisely what the problem of dirty hands puts in question. For the problem arises when what is, from one point of view, the overall good is attainable only by the committing of what, from another point of view, are wrongful acts. On the one hand, we endorse and pursue the attainable good; on the other, we condemn and regret the uncancelled wrongs

---

6 Sartre, *Les Mains sales*, trans. Kitty Black, as *Crime Passionel* (London: Methuen, 1961), pp. 94–5.

committed in its pursuit. Machiavelli captured this dual structure perfectly when he said that in such cases, 'while the act accuses, the result excuses'. The point is that both the accusation and the excuse stand. As Michael Walzer has observed, commenting on Machiavelli's argument:

> His political judgments are indeed consequentialist in character, but not his moral judgments. We know whether cruelty is used well or badly by its effects over time. But that it is bad to use cruelty we know in some other way. The deceitful and cruel politician is excused (if he succeeds) only in the sense that the rest of us come to agree that the results were 'worth it' or, more likely, that we simply forget his crimes when we praise his success.[7]

The problem of dirty hands is, of course, a completely general and familiar one, arising in all spheres of life. It arises whenever, while doing the best thing in the circumstances, we know that we have done wrong. It tends, however, to be peculiarly stark in political cases where the good attained tends to be general and the wrongs committed specific. The Defence of the Realm, the Cause of the Revolution, the Glory of the Republic may have been furthered, but particular people have been betrayed, lied to, or done in.

The issue is how to put together the points of view from which the former is endorsed and the latter condemned. Is there after all an overall, unified consequentialist theory within which each can be fitted, yielding a determinate solution, all things considered, to the question of what is to be done? Or is a Kantian, deontological, rights-based position the only defensible one, in which moral principles set firm constraints by which all action—including political action—is to be finally judged? Or are we rather caught 'between utility and rights', committed on the one hand to the maximizing consequentialist picture and, on the other, to a narrow view of morality to which the notion of rights, justice, and the protection of basic liberties and interests of individuals is central? If so, the problem of dirty hands is the *locus classicus* of such a conflict. Indeed, we shall see that only if some such conflict is presupposed, is the problem of dirty hands a problem.

---

[7] Michael Walzer, 'Political Action: The Problem of Dirty Hands', *Philosophy and Public Affairs*, 2 (Winter 1973), p. 175.

II

There are, I believe, four main ways of responding to this problem that are worth indicating briefly. The first three, in different ways, seek to dissolve or defuse the problem; only the fourth faces it directly.

First, there is what I shall call the *ideological response*. I here use 'ideological' in a quasi-Marxist sense to indicate a view that makes claims to objectivity, comprehensiveness, and universality of application, while being one-sided, abstract, and distortive of the reality it purports to represent, and all to the advantage of some social interests against others. On this view, there is essentially no problem of dirty hands, since, provided that overall good is attained, *dirty hands are really clean*. The problem is dissolved or thought away by theoretical fiat. This response can take a *consequentialist* form, of which the most familiar version is utilitarianism, or it can take what I shall call an *Orwellian* form, for reasons that will appear shortly.

The consequentialist form simply asserts that actions and policies are to be judged solely by whether they contribute to the best available outcome overall, all things considered. In any given case, there is only one correct answer to the question: what is it right to do? If the appropriate calculations show what is the right thing to do in the circumstances, then that is the right thing to do. Of course, a utilitarian, for example, may well go on to give a utilitarian explanation of and justification for ordinary moral rules (by which 'the right thing to do' might be judged wrong): he may account for the principles of justice and the rights and obligations by which we ordinarily live and, further, for the sense of obligation that we attach to these and the guilt we feel when we violate them. But if, in any given case, the right answer to the question, what is it right to do? requires us to override the constraints of ordinary morality, then in that case, to do so could not be wrong.

The consequentialist or utilitarian merely says that dirty hands, in this case, are clean. The Orwellian goes further: he redescribes the means in the light of the end pursued. Here, the means are purified or sanctified; the dirty hands are washed clean by the nobility or the correctness of the cause. Actions that might appear to be (in Machiavelli's phrase) contrary to 'those things by which men are considered good' are ideologically redefined. You do not kill heretics; you maintain and protect the faith. You do not torture or wrongfully arrest or imprison people; you maintain law and order or eliminate the class enemy. You do not repress freedom of speech; you eliminate harmful opinions, and prevent obscenity and the spread of corruption. You do not intervene in other countries' affairs; you liberate freedom-loving peoples. You do not invade a country; you offer friendly assistance against counter-revolutionary subversion.

Second, there is what I shall call the *moralistic response*. This is a high-minded view of politics, according to which *politicians should always have clean hands*. It advances a view of political life as, in principle, no less subject to ethical principles than other spheres of social life, either as things actually are or as they could be. This response thus takes two forms: the *liberal* and the *Utopian*.

The liberal form of the moralistic response relies on a deontological theory that is in turn justified by reference to the will of God or the Moral Law or some notion of personal integrity or respect for persons. It applies to politics, as to the rest of life, a moral theory that is, at least in its moralistic form, consequence-insensitive. As with the utilitarian, there are determinate answers to problems of practical judgement which, in this case, stem from a Theory of the Right (or rights); if the theory is rigorously followed, it will enable its practitioners to keep their spirits white.

The Utopian form looks forward to a coming transformation of political life that will overcome the ethical irrationalities of the present world. Thenceforward, political life will be purified, and the problem of dirty hands will disappear—not through the imposition or the manipulation or the engineering of consensus, but through enlightenment and insight. This Utopian vision can often take a chiliastic form well described by Max Weber:

In the world of realities, as a rule, we encounter the ever-renewed experience that the adherent of an ethic of ultimate ends suddenly turns into a chiliastic prophet. Those, for example, who have just preached 'love against violence' now call for the use of force for the *last* violent deed, which would then lead to a state of affairs in which all violence is annihilated.[8]

There is (to anticipate) a strong strain of this in Marxism and no better exemplar of it than Trotsky, who held that 'a society without

---

[8] Weber, 'Politics as a Vocation', in *From Max Weber: Essays in Sociology*, ed. and trans. H. H. Gerth and C. Wright Mills (London: Routledge & Kegan Paul, 1948), p. 122.

social contradictions will naturally be a society without lies and violence. However, there is no way of building a bridge to that society save by revolutionary, that is violent means.'[9] As he wrote in 1920,

the road to socialism lies through a period of the highest possible intensification of the principle of the state . . . Just as a lamp, before going out, shoots up a brilliant flame, so the state, before disappearing, assumes the form of the dictatorship of the proletariat, i.e. . . . the most ruthless form of state, which embraces the lives of the citizens authoritatively in every direction.[10]

Third, there is what we may call the *cynical response*. This is low-rather than high-minded, and it usually relies upon a sharp dichotomy between public (or political) and everyday (or private) life. On this view, *everyone in politics has dirty hands*: politics is a sink of corruption, self-interest, and ambition. This response tends to exist at the level of popular attitude rather than developed theory, and it can often represent a rational, if politically dangerous, response to prevalent political practice. It is a view traditionally, but wholly falsely, attributed to Machiavelli and labelled 'Machiavellian'. Machiavelli, on the contrary, firmly advocated the fourth response.

This is what I shall (tendentiously) call the *political response*, which alone recognizes the problem of dirty hands as a problem with which politicians, citizens, and, under modern conditions, the institutions of a democratic system must come to terms. It involves seeing what, in their quite different ways, both Machiavelli and Max Weber saw: that there is in political life no impartial arbiter, no neutral standpoint from which 'correct' practical conclusions can be derived. It involves recognizing the consequences for the character of politicians and the virtues they typically develop of the fact that, by virtue of their role, they must regularly confront this problem on behalf of the rest of us, in routine and small forms as well as heroic and tragic ones.[11] It involves establishing and maintaining institutions and social conditions which sustain the necessary tension within the dualistic structure to which I have referred. It is vital to keep alive the sense, among politicians and citizens alike, that

    9 Trotsky, *Their Morals and Ours* (New York: Pathfinder Press, 4th edn., 1969), p. 27.
    10 Id., *Terrorism and Communism* (Ann Arbor, Mich.: Univ. of Michigan Press, 1961), p. 177.
    11 See Bernard Williams, 'Politics and Moral Character', in his *Moral Luck* (Cambridge: Cambridge Univ. Press, 1981).

deception, betrayal, and worse, when they are committed for the public good, violate morally important principles and commit un-cancelled wrongs. And it is important to call those who violate such principles to explain and excuse. In short, there must be public watchfulness, journalistic scrutiny, a tradition of and effective mechanisms for public accountability. For all this a free press, an independent judiciary, and a competitive party system appear to be minimum preconditions.

III

How, then, does Marxism respond to the problem? To begin with, I need hardly allude to the complex and rich variety of strands within the Marxist tradition. That tradition is, of course, a contested terrain, in which the solemn orthodoxies of the Second and Third Internationals have faced many and various forms of heterodoxy and revisionism, from Bernstein and the Austro-Marxists to the Frank-furt and the Budapest Schools. I see orthodox, Russified Marxism as only one line of (arrested) development within the Marxist tradition, one which happens to have had momentous world-historical effects in practice, while others have undoubtedly been far truer to the letter and the spirit of Marx's thought. Nevertheless, I strongly disagree with my friend Bertell Ollman who, responding to Professor Walicki's fine piece on Marx and Freedom in the *New York Review of Books*, proclaimed that:

Most Western Marxists have come to understand that there is little to learn about socialism (understood as a form of society that can be built in our countries) from the experience of the 'socialist' world. Unfortunately, and with a few outstanding exceptions, these same distorting experiences have meant that there is little to learn about Marxist theory (especially as it applies to the unfolding potential of capitalism, its/our possible future) in the works which have come out of these countries, whether communist or anti-communist.[12]

On the contrary, the 'distorting experience' of 'actually existing socialism' exhibits repeated failures of Marxist theory and ideology, both within and outside the 'socialist' world, to provide a basis for

---

[12] Bertell Ollman, letter to *New York Review of Books*, 31/4 (15 Mar. 1981), p. 48.

resisting measures taken in its name, despite some critical counter-
currents in the last few decades. Are there features of the original
theory that have disabled its inheritors from offering such resistance?
I myself think that there are. I believe that Marxism has from its
beginning exhibited a certain approach to moral questions that has
disabled it from offering moral resistance to measures taken in its
name; in particular, despite its rich view of freedom and compelling
vision of human liberation, it has been unable to offer an adequate
account of justice, rights, and the means-ends problem and, thus, an
adequate response to injustice, the violation of rights, and the resort
to impermissible means in the present. I believe that this disability
was transmitted from the original theory to its main descendants. I
also believe that it has characterized Marxist ideology far and wide.
The experience of the Eastern bloc and the rich literature that has
come out of it, and that of other socialist countries as well, is
centrally important in the exploration of these issues, which should
be of even greater concern to socialists than to their opponents.

My principal claim is that there is a central core or structure of
moral thinking fashioned by Marx and Engels that is partly constitutive of the bibliocentric tradition that is Marxism, by which even the
heterodox have been deeply imprinted. I shall briefly seek to analyse
that structure, in order to delineate Marxism's response to the
problem of dirty hands.

That structure can be best understood if we draw a distinction
between what I shall call the morality of *Recht* and the morality of
emancipation. The first comprises what Herbert Hart has called 'an
area of morality (the morality of law) which has special characteristics . . . occupied by the concepts of justice, fairness, rights and
obligation'.[13] The second denotes a setting free from the prehistory
of human bondage, which culminated in wage-slavery and exploitation, and thus it refers to that ideal of transparent social unity and
individual self-realization in which 'the contradiction between the
interest of the separate individual or the individual family and the
common interest of all individuals who have intercourse with one
another has been abolished.'[14] It is the morality of *Recht* that
Marxism condemns as ideological and anachronistic, and the moral-

---

[13] H. L. A. Hart, 'Are There any Natural Rights?' *Philosophical Review* 64 (1955),
pp. 177–8.
[14] Marx and Engels, *Collected Works* (London: Lawrence and Wishart, 1975), v.
p. 46.

ity of emancipation that it adopts as its own. Indeed, human emancipation in part consists precisely in emancipation from *Recht* and the conditions that call it into being.

How did Marx and Engels and their followers conceive of *Recht*? Marx wrote of relations governed by *Recht (Rechtverhältnisse)* that,

like forms of state, [they] are to be grasped neither from themselves nor from the so-called general development of the human mind, but rather have their roots in the material conditions of life, the sum total of which Hegel . . . combines under the name 'civil society' whose anatomy is to be sought in political economy.[15]

For Hegel, 'civil society' meant 'the war of each against all' to be found in the capitalist market-place: it denoted the competitive, egoistic relations of emergent bourgeois society in which individuals pursued their respective particular interests, treating one another as means to their respective ends and exercising what Hegel called 'subjective freedom'. Hegel saw certain rights and principles as governing such relations (e.g., private property rights and the principles of contractual justice), and he saw the state as the sphere of citizenship, of 'objective freedom', institutionalizing internally accepted norms of ethical life and providing the framework within which the mutually destructive forces of civil society could be contained. In this way, a rational synthesis of subjective and objective freedom is attained in the modern bourgeois state.

For Marx, on the contrary, both the rights and the principles governing the relations of civil society, and the state itself, were rooted in and a means of stabilizing the production relations and thus the class relations of a given social order. The principles of *Recht* were to be understood only in this perspective. As Engels wrote, 'social justice or injustice is decided by the science which deals with the actual facts of production and exchange, the science of political economy'.[16] In short, the principles of *Recht* are to be understood neither (through themselves) as a set of objective norms, a set of independent rational standards by which to assess social relations, nor, following Hegel, as a rational way of ordering such relations which finally unites subjective with objective freedom. Rather, the

---

[15] Marx, Preface to *A Contribution to Political Economy*, in Marx and Engels, *Selected Works* (Moscow: Foreign Languages Publishing House, 1962), i. 362.
[16] Cited in Allen Wood, 'The Marxian Critique of Justice', *Philosophy and Public Affairs*, 1/3 (Spring 1972), 15.

principles of *Recht* must always be explained as arising, like the social relations they govern and stabilize, out of given material conditions.

This suggests the first Marxist reason for opposing *Recht*, namely, that it is inherently ideological. It claims to offer 'objective' principles specifying what is 'just' and 'fair' and defining 'rights' and 'obligations'; it claims that these are universally valid and serve the interests of all the members of society (and perhaps all members of any society); and it claims to be independent of particular partisan or sectional interests. But from a Marxist point of view, all these claims are spurious and illusory. They serve to conceal the real function of principles of *Recht*, which is to protect the social relations of the existing order, a function that is better fulfilled to the extent that the claims are widely accepted as 'objectively' valid. Marxism, in short, purports to unmask the self-understanding of *Recht* by revealing its real functions and the bourgeois interests that lurk in ambush behind it.

It does not, of course, follow from this that all communists should become immoralists, violating every bourgeois right and obligation in sight. That would, in any case, be poor tactics. What does follow is that the principles of *Recht* should have, for the communist, no rationally compelling force. And it follows from this that it makes no sense to criticize capitalism for failing to live up to such principles —for being unjust, violating the rights of workers, etc. (except as a tactical move).

But there is a further and deeper reason for communism's opposition to *Recht*, which can be unearthed if we ask the question, To what problem are the principles of *Recht* a response? To this question jurists and philosophers give different answers, but these answers have in common a view of human life as inherently conflictual, and potentially catastrophically so, thus requiring a framework of authoritative rules, sometimes needing coercive enforcement, that can be rationally justified as serving the interests of all. *Recht* is a response to what one might call the 'conditions of *Recht*', inherent in the human condition, and these may be more or less acute, just as the response will take different forms in different societies.

Consider David Hume's summary account of the conditions of *Recht*; for Hume, ''tis only from the selfishness and confin'd generosity of men, along with the scanty provision nature has made for his wants, that justice derives its origin.'[17] In his 1977 book on ethics, John Mackie, citing this statement of Hume's alongside Protagoras and Hobbes, sought to identify what he calls a 'narrow sense of morality' (which looks very much like *Recht*) as a 'system of a particular sort of constraints on conduct—ones whose central task is to protect the interests of persons other than the agent and which present themselves to an agent as checks on his natural inclinations or spontaneous tendencies to act.' Mackie argues, following Hume, that morality—in the narrow sense thus defined—is needed to solve a basic problem in the human predicament, that 'limited resources and limited sympathies together generate both competition leading to conflict, and an absence of what would be mutually beneficial co-operation.'[18] Or consider Kant's celebrated discussion of man's 'unsocial sociality' and of the problem to which the *Rechtstaat* is the solution:

Given a multitude of rational beings who, in a body, require general laws for their own preservation, but each of whom, as an individual, is secretly inclined to exempt himself from this restraint: how are we to order their affairs and establish for them a constitution such that, although their private dispositions may be really antagonistic, they may yet so act as a check upon one another, that, in their public relations, the effect is the same as if they had no such evil sentiments.[19]

Or consider, finally John Rawls's account of what I have called the conditions of *Recht* and what he calls the 'circumstances of justice': these are 'the normal conditions under which human co-operation is both possible and necessary', and they 'obtain whatever mutually disinterested persons put forward conflicting claims to the division of social advantages under conditions of moderate scarcity'.[20] These are 'elementary facts about persons and their place in nature' and, for justice to obtain, 'human freedom is to be regulated by principles chosen in the light of these natural restrictions'.[21]

These various suggestions combine to identify three jointly sufficient conditions for the existence of justice and rights. (Whether in

[17] Hume, *A Treatise of Human Nature* (1739), ed. L. A. Selby-Bigge (Oxford: Clarendon Press, 1951), p. 495.

[18] J. L. Mackie, *Ethics: Inventing Right and Wrong* (Harmondsworth: Penguin, 1977), pp. 106, 111.

[19] I. Kant, *Perpetual Peace. A Philosophical Essay*, ed. and trans. M. Campbell Smith (New York: Garland, 1972), p. 154.

[20] Rawls, *A Theory of Justice* (Oxford: Clarendon Press, 1972), pp. 126, 128.

[21] Ibid. 257.

their imagined absence there would be a need for principles of justice and the recognition of rights is a question largely unaddressed within Marxism.) Clearly scarcity, or limits to desired goods, and egoism, or at least the absence of total and unconditional altruism, generate conflicting claims, and thus the need to adjudicate which claims are valid and, of these, which have priority. More deeply (and this is what Rawls's account implicitly adds to Hume's and Kant's), it is the conflict of interests, resulting from different individuals' (and groups') different and conflicting conceptions of the good that define those interests, which renders such adjudication, and the protections rights afford, necessary. Hume mistakenly thought that if you increase 'to a sufficient degree the benevolence of men, or the bounty of nature . . . you render justice useless, by supplying its place with much nobler virtues, and more favourable blessings.'[22] But even under conditions of co-operative abundance and altruism, there will—if conceptions of the good conflict—be a need for the fair allocation of benefits and burdens, for the assigning of duties and the protection of rights: but we should then need them in the face of the benevolence rather than the selfishness of others. Altruists, sincerely and conscientiously pursuing their respective conceptions of the good, could certainly cause injustice and violate rights. For every conception of the good favours certain social relationships and forms of life, and certain ways of defining individuals' interests—or, more precisely, certain ways of conceiving and ranking the various interests, deriving from their roles and functions, that individuals have. It also disfavours other conceptions. In a world in which no such conception is fully realized and universally accepted, even the non-egoistic adherents of one threaten the adherents of others: hence the need for justice and rights.

But what if divergent conceptions of the good, and of interests, were to converge within a single moral and political consensus? Here, a fourth condition comes into view: the lack of perfect information and understanding. For even under co-operative abundance, total altruism, and the unification of interests within a common conception of the good, people may get it wrong. They may fail to act as they should towards others, because they do not know how to or because they make mistakes, with resulting misallocations of burdens and benefits, and damage to individuals' interests. We may,

[22] Hume, *A Treatise of Human Nature*, pp. 494–5.

therefore, say that if these four conditions obtain, a necessity exists for finding principles of justice for distributing social advantages and disadvantages, and principles specifying rights and duties to protect us from one another's depredations and abuses, whether these be selfish or benevolent, intended or unintended.

Now, it is a peculiar and distinctive feature of Marxism that it denies that these conditions of *Recht* are inherent in human life. *Recht*, Marx and Engels wrote, 'arises from the material relations of people and the resulting antagonism of people against one another.'[23] Both could, and would, be overcome. Marxism specifically denies that scarcity, egoism, and social and moral antagonisms are invariant features inherent in the human condition, and it looks forward to a 'transparent' form of social unity, in which social life will be under the rational control of all. In short, it envisages the removal of the basic causes of significant conflicts of interest in society. As Marx and Engels wrote in *The Holy Family*: 'If enlightened self-interest is the principle of all morality, man's private interests must be made to coincide with the interest of humanity . . . If man is shaped by environment, his environment must be made human.'[24]

Marxism maintains that the conditions of *Recht* are historically determined, specific to class-societies, and imminently removable. None of limits to desired goods, limited sympathies, antagonistic social relations, and corresponding moral ideologies, or the opaqueness or reified character of social relations is essential to the human predicament. To assume that they are is itself an ideological illusion (propagated by *Recht*)—ideological in serving to perpetuate the existing class-bound social order. Marxism supposes that a transparent and unified society of abundance—a society in which the very distinctions between egoism and altruism, the public sphere of politics and the private sphere of civil society, and 'the division of the human being into a *public man* and a *private man*'[25] have been overcome—is not merely capable of being brought about, but is on the historical agenda and, indeed, that the working class is in principle motivated to bring it about and is capable of doing so.

Thus, *Recht* is not merely inherently ideological, stabilizing class societies and concealing class interests, and falsely purporting to

---

[23] Marx and Engels, *Collected Works*, v. 318.
[24] Ibid. iv. 131 (trans. amended).   [25] Ibid. iii. 155.

adjudicate competing claims, limit freedoms, and distribute costs and benefits in a universally fair, objective, and mutually advantageous manner. It also presupposes an account of the conditions that call it forth, an account that Marxism denies. For Marxists hold that, broadly, all significant conflicts are to be traced back to class divisions. So, for example, Marx and Engels could speak of communism as 'the *genuine* resolution of the conflict between man and nature and between man and man',[26] speculate about the abolition of crime under communism, and suggest that 'social peace' might succeed 'social war'; and Trotsky, as we have seen, could proclaim that the future 'society without social contradictions will naturally be a society without lies and violence.'[27] Certainly, the Marxist canon has virtually nothing to say about any bases of conflict, whether social or psychological, other than class. It is virtually innocent (and totally so at the level of theory) of any serious consideration of all the interpersonal and intrapersonal sources of conflict and frustration that cannot, or can no longer, plausibly be traced, even remotely, to class divisions.

By furnishing principles for the regulation of conflicting claims and interests, *Recht* serves to promote class compromise and thereby delay the revolutionary change that will make possible a form of social life that has no need of *Recht* because the conditions of *Recht* or the circumstances of justice will no longer obtain. In this respect, I think that Marx's view of morality as *Recht* is exactly parallel to his view of religion, concerning which he wrote: 'To abolish religion as the *illusory* happiness of the people is to demand their *real* happiness. The demand to give up illusion about the existing state of affairs is the *demand to give up a state of affairs which needs illusions*'.[28] Analogously, the demand to give up illusions about the 'rights of man' and 'justice' is the demand to give up the conditions of *Recht* and the circumstances of justice. Once emancipation from such conditions or circumstances arrives on the historical agenda, the morality of emancipation dictates the bringing into being of a world in which the morality of *Recht* is unnecessary. In that world, the conditions that made such a morality necessary will, as Engels put it, have been not only overcome but forgotten in practical life. This is the meaning of Lukács's accurate statement that the 'ultimate object-

---

26 Marx and Engels, *Collected Works*, iii. 296.
27 Trotsky, *Their Morals and Ours*, p. 27.
28 Marx and Engels, *Collected Works*, iii. 176.

ive of communism is the construction of a society in which freedom of morality will take the place of the constraints of *Recht* in the regulation of all behaviour.'[29]

In such a society, principles of justice, and more generally of *Recht*, are assumed to have withered away: they have, as Engels said, been forgotten in practical life. By what principles or standards, then, is this society to be judged superior? What kind of morality is the 'really human morality' that it embodies? How are its claims to be validated? By an appeal to intuition? Much of Marx's and Marxist writings could be seen in that light: frequent appeal is made to the reader's sense of indignation and sympathy, and also his sense of what is 'worthy of human nature'. Yet it is an elementary Marxist thought that moral intuitions will be prime candidates for class-related bias. There seems to be no good Marxist reason to suppose such intuitions to be universally shared, even by fully reflective agents, let alone to appeal to them in practical reasoning. Is the indicated morality deontological, then, perhaps Kantian? There is, as the neo-Kantians saw, much to support this view in the canonical texts—as, for example, in Marx's condemnation of capitalist exchange relations as social relations in which each becomes a means of the other and, more generally, in his frequent talk of the slavery, degradation, and indignity inherent in capitalist relations. Or is it at root utilitarian? There is much support for this as well in what Marx and later Marxists have said. Communism will not only be more efficient and productive, it will abolish misery, unhappiness, and frustration. As Lenin said, working people's lives will be eased and their welfare maximized. Or is it, rather, perfectionist, committed to an Aristotelian realization of distinctively human potentialities and excellences? Much evidence can be cited to support this interpretation, for example, Marx's claim that it is every person's 'vocation designation, task' to 'achieve all-round development of all his abilities'.[30]

Marx was no moral philosopher, and he did not discuss the differences between these different kinds of morality. I suspect that if he had done so, he would have responded that under communism they all come to one anyway: that communism will at one and the

---

[29] G. Lukács, *Political Writings: 1919–29*, ed. Rodney Livingstone (London: New Left Books, 1972), p. 48.
[30] Marx and Engels, *Collected Works*, v. 292.

same time embody what (Marx held) is intuitively, essentially 'human', respect, human worth, or dignity, and maximize both welfare and self-development. Certainly, there is within the Marxist tradition no discussion of the possibility of conflicts between these various ideals. Rather than pursuing these recondite questions any further, I shall here simply assert that, if we are concerned with the question, 'What constitutes emancipation—what makes the realm of freedom really (rather than formally) free?' it is the teleological, Aristotelian, perfectionist Marx we must follow. For the freedom that capitalism denies and communism promises is systematically couched in the language of 'species powers', potentiality, and self-actualization.

In the self-transforming and self-realizing process of emancipation, one factor is crucial: free time. As Marx wrote in the *Grundrisse*, 'free time—which is both idle time and time for higher activity—had *naturally* transformed its possessor into a different subject.'[31] And Marx also stressed this in what is perhaps his best-known text on the subject:

In fact, the realm of freedom actually begins only where labour which is determined by necessity and mundane considerations ceases; thus in the very nature of things, it lies beyond the sphere of actual material production . . . Freedom in this field can only consist in socialized man, the associated producers rationally regulating their interchange with nature, bringing it under their common control, instead of being ruled by it as by the blind forces of Nature; and achieving this with the least expenditure of energy and under conditions most favorable to, and worthy of, their human nature. But it nonetheless still remains a realm of necessity. Beyond it begins the development of human energy which is an end in itself, the true realm of freedom, which, however, can blossom forth only with this realm of necessity as its basis. The shortening of the working day is its basic prerequisite.[32]

There is, as Heller notes, a somewhat different possibility sketched out in the *Grundrisse*, where, in a visionary anticipation of automation, Marx writes of a future in which:

Labor no longer appears so much to be included within the production process: rather the human being comes to relate more as watchman and regulator to the production process itself . . . [the worker] steps to the side of

---

[31] Marx, *Grundrisse*, trans. Martin Nicholaus (Harmondsworth: Penguin Books in assoc. with *New Left Review*, 1973), p. 712.

[32] Marx, *Capital*, iii. ed. and trans. F. Engels (Moscow: Foreign Languages Publishing House, 1962), pp. 799–800.

the production process instead of being its chief actor. In this transformation, it is neither the direct human labor he himself performs, nor the time during which he works, but rather the appropriation of his own general productive power, his presence as a social body—it is, in a word, the development of the social individual which appears as the great foundation-stone of production and of wealth. . . . As soon as labor in the direct form has ceased to be the great well-spring of wealth, labor time ceases and must cease to be its measure, and hence exchange value must cease to be the measure of use value.[33]

But note that in this vision too, it is the time for free development that is crucial; but here that development takes place in the form of scientific understanding and technical control, enjoyed for their own sake as a 'vital need' within the production process itself. For, in general, Marx held that

free time, *disposable time*, is wealth itself, partly for the enjoyment of the project, partly for the free activity which—unlike labor—is not dominated by *the pressure of an extraneous purpose which must be fulfilled*, and the fulfillment of which *is regarded as a natural necessity or a social duty*, according to one's inclinations.[34]

And here we come to what is, I believe, the heart of the matter. It is emancipation from the pressure of 'extraneous purposes', from 'what is regarded as a natural necessity or a moral duty', that is the key to Marx's conception of 'real' freedom, and thus the meaning of emancipation. This is perhaps why Marx and Engels rejected Max Stirner's view that 'in communist society there can be a question of "duties" and interests', holding these to be 'two complementary aspects of an antithesis which exists only in bourgeois society'.[35] This, I believe, is why they thought that:

Communism differs from all previous movements in that it overturns the basis of all earlier relations of production and intercourse, and for the first time treats all naturally evolved premises as the creations of hitherto existing men, strips them of their natural character and subjugates them to the power of the united individuals . . . The reality which communism creates is precisely the true basis for rendering it impossible that anything should exist independently of individuals, insofar as reality is nevertheless only a product of the preceding intercourse of individuals.[36]

[33] *Grundrisse*, p. 705.
[34] Marx, *Theories of Surplus Value*, iii (Moscow: Foreign Languages Publishing House, 1962), p. 257.
[35] Marx and Engels, *Collected Works*, v. 213.
[36] Ibid. 81.

But if this is a correct interpretation, then a host of questions crowds in upon us. What makes a purpose count as extraneous? Not (unless Marx is saddled with a purely subjective, phenomenological notion of alienation) whatever the agent counts as such. But what, then, are individuals' authentic, non-extraneous purposes? Marx imagines a world in which the question does not even arise, because its answer is both not in doubt and correctly understood, both obvious and true (a world, therefore, free of moral scepticism). And are there not natural necessities which human activity (including labour) must fulfil as a prerequisite of social co-operation in general and (as both Weber and Durkheim thought) of a complex modern social order in particular? And as for social *duties* (this takes us back to the withering away of *Recht*), is their disappearance conceivable, even in a world inconceivably more abundant and co-operative than our own—either in the sense that the required tasks now conceived as duties would disappear or that they would no longer be seen as duties? And many further and wider questions arise, which we cannot explore here.

I hope, however, to have said enough to display what I have called the core moral structure of Marxism. This is, in brief, a form of consequentialism that is long-range and perfectionist. It therefore comes as no surprise that Marxism has throughout its history been deeply and unremittingly anti-deontological: hence the systematic hostilities among the orthodox to Kant and Kantianism. Mainline Marxism has always required an exclusive commitment to the attainment of emancipation. 'He who fights for Communism', wrote Brecht, 'has of all virtues only one: that he fights for Communism'.[37] The purportedly 'eternal', 'universal', and 'abstract' principles adduced by deontological theories are, from a Marxist viewpoint, both without foundation and, if applied, irrelevant to and obstructive of the consequences Marxism requires action to promote.

IV

My conclusion is that, in its response to the problem of dirty hands in politics, Marxism combines, in a distinctive way, ideology and Utopia. It is ideological, first, in the purely consequentialist form. It

[37] Brecht, *The Measures Taken*, p. 13.

one-sidedly rules out or ignores, in the assessment of human action and character, all that it holds to be irrelevant to the project of human emancipation. In particular, Marxism ignores the interests of persons in the here and now and immediate future, both victims (intended and unintended) and agents, in so far as these have no bearing on that project. It is like utilitarianism in offering an explanation for the constraints of ordinary morality (though it offers a different explanation), but unlike it in offering little scope for justifying them: on the contrary, it holds that such constraints are likely to be class deceptions lying in ambush to trap the unwary. Moreover, the justification for such constraints that a utilitarian can offer will incorporate in its calculations benefits to agents in the here and now and the foreseeable future. For the Marxist, such benefits are, in themselves, irrelevant. The long-term character of Marxist consequentialism, its focus on future benefits to future persons, makes it markedly less sensitive than even utilitarianism to the moral requirement of respecting the basic interests and liberties of persons in the present and immediate future.

All this explains why Marxism has throughout its history been at best ambivalent about the domain and the language of *Recht*. Moral vocabulary of this kind gets in the way of a clear-headed pursuit of the emancipatory project. Marx was wont to call it 'obsolete verbal rubbish' and 'ideological nonsense': the conceptions of *Recht* are, Marx and Engels thought, conceptions which people 'ought to get out of their heads'.[38] Removing those conceptions, and the vocabulary within which they are couched, would enable one to see present injustices and violations of rights not as such but, rather, as either obstacles or means to future emancipation. In this way, the ground for the Orwellian response is prepared: the language of morals is to be revised to purge it of *Recht*-like features.

But Marxism is also Utopian, as we have seen, though in a very special way. It is a kind of anti-Utopian utopianism, with a built-in inhibition against specifying the nature of the Utopia to whose realization it is committed. Its anti-utopianism, for which there are several reasons, has consistently inhibited Marxists from spelling out what the morality of emancipation implies for the future constitution and organization of society. It has repeatedly presumed to foresee the

---

[38] Marx, *Critique of the Gotha Programme*, in Marx and Engels, *Selected Works* (Moscow: Foreign Languages Publishing House, 1962), p. 25; and id., *Complete Works*, v. 362.

future, in which that emancipation is somehow guaranteed, while foreswearing the clarification of the long-term consequences by which alternative courses of action can be judged. In short, it has offered the unsubstantiated promise of a world 'without lies and violence', thereby rendering their acceptance in this world easier than it might have been.

I believe that the structure of thinking that I have sought to sketch here is to be found throughout the Marxist tradition. It is to be found among the Bolsheviks and among their major Marxist critics, Luxemburg and Kautsky. It is, above all, to be found, in splendidly lucid and forthright expression, in the writings of Trotsky, who would doubtless have regarded this chapter as yet another instance of 'Kantian-priestly and vegetarian-Quaker prattle'.[39]

[39] Trotsky, *Terrorism and Communism*, p. 82.

PART IV

11
Of Gods and Demons: Habermas and Practical Reason

'Practical questions', according to Habermas, 'admit of truth':[1] 'just (*richtige*) norms must be capable of being grounded in a similar way to true statements'.[2] Truth, on his view, means 'warranted assertibility': this is shown when participants enter into a discourse and 'a consensus can be realized under conditions that identify it as a justified consensus'.[3] If, he writes,

philosophical ethics and political theory are supposed to disclose the moral core of the general consciousness and to *reconstruct* it as a normative concept of the moral, then they must specify criteria and provide reasons: they must, that is, produce theoretical knowledge.[4]

Thus for Habermas judgements about moral and political questions can be rationally grounded and differences about such questions can be rationally resolved.

His position thereby contrasts with those of noncognitivists, moral

---

This chapter was first published in 1982. Prof. Habermas has replied to some of the arguments advanced here, in the concluding chapter to *Jürgen Habermas: Critical Debates* (London: Macmillan, 1982).

[1] Habermas, *Legitimation Crisis*, trans. T. McCarthy (Boston: Beacon Press, 1975; London: Heinemann, 1976).

[2] Id., 'Wahrheitstheorien', in *Wirklichkeit und Reflexion: Walter Schulz zum 60. Geburtstag*, ed. H. Fahrenbach (Pfullingen: Neske, 1973), p. 226. 'I suspect', he adds, 'that the justification of the validity claims contained in the recommendation of norms of action and of evaluation can be just as discursively tested as the justification of the validity claims implied in assertions. Of course, the grounding of just (*richtigen*) commands and evaluations differs in the structure of argumentation from the grounding of true statements. The logical conditions under which a rationally motivated consensus can be attained differ as between practical and theoretical discourse' (ibid., 226–7). Habermas uses the term '*richtig*' in such a way as to imply that there is a truth of the matter as to whether norms, commands, or evaluations are *richtig* or not.

[3] Ibid. 239–40.

[4] Habermas, *Communication and the Evolution of Society*, trans. T. McCarthy (Boston: Beacon Press, and London: Heinemann, 1979, pp. 202–3.

sceptics, subjectivists, relativists, and pluralists of various kinds, and it relies upon a conception of rationality that is sufficiently comprehensive to allow rational solution to such perennial and inherently controversial questions as: Which rules, laws, distributive arrangements, etc., are just? Is the state's claim to legitimacy valid or empty? What is the scope of legitimate authority? And so on.[5] Thus he seeks to 'vindicate the power of discursively attained, rational consensus against the Weberian pluralism of value systems, gods and demons', speaking disdainfully of the 'empiricist and/or decisionist barriers, which immunize the so-called pluralism of values against the efforts of practical reason'.[6] Habermas's rationalism has, moreover, a distinctively Hegelian dimension. He postulates the possibility of society reaching a stage of transparent self-reflection, among parties who are 'free and equal' and whose discourse has reached a stage where 'the level of justification has become reflective', in the sense that mythological, cosmological, religious and ontological modes of thought have been superseded and 'rational will-formation' can be achieved, free of dogmas and 'ultimate grounds', through ideal mutual self-understanding.[7]

Within the Marxist tradition, Habermas's position is a distinctive one. By and large, Marxists have been dismissive, even contemptuous, of morality, for reasons examined in Part III of this volume, and relatively uninterested in the problem of justifying norms and normative judgements. Among those who considered the question, Engels, Kautsky, and Trotsky saw no need for such justification, though speaking of a 'really human morality which stands above

---

[5] Habermas, *Communication and the Evolution of Society*, p. 200. On this point see R. J. Bernstein, *The Restructuring of Social and Political Theory* (New York: Harcourt Brace Jovanovich, 1976).

[6] Habermas, *Legitimation Crisis*, p. 107. The passage by Max Weber, to which Habermas refers, is the following: 'What man will take upon himself the attempt to "refute scientifically" the ethic of the Sermon on the Mount? For instance, the sentence "resist no evil", or the image of turning the other cheek? And yet it is clear, in mundane perspective, that this is an ethic of undignified conduct; one has to choose between the religious dignity which this ethic confers and the dignity of manly conduct which preaches something quite different; "resist evil—lest you be co-responsible for an overpowering evil". According to our ultimate standpoint, the one is the Devil and the other the God, and the individual has to decide which is God for him and which is the Devil. And so it goes throughout all the orders of life' (*From Max Weber: Essays in Sociology*, ed. and trans. H. H. Gerth and C. Wright Mills (London: Routledge & Kegan Paul, 1948), p. 148). For a no less eloquent statement of the same viewpoint see Leszek Kolakowski's 'Ethics without a Moral Code', *Triquarterly* 22 (1971), esp. pp. 172–4.   [7] Habermas, *Communication*, pp. 186, 185, 184.

class antagonisms and above any recollections of them',[8] of an unfolding 'general human morality',[9] and of the 'liberating morality of the proletariat'.[10] It was the neo-Kantian Marxists and the Austro-Marxists who explicitly raised the question of such justification, heretically distinguishing between facts and values and offering transcendental arguments purporting to justify the struggle for socialism in terms of universal values. It was, however, Lukács who developed the position that arguably accords most closely with Marx's own view on this subject: that from the privileged standpoint of the proletariat, engaged in the revolutionary transformation of the world, the subject and object of history are united, as the process of history becomes identical with the free development of consciousness and, accordingly, moral judgement becomes identical with the self-understanding of the universal class as it destroys the old world to create a new one. On this view the norms and institutions thereby created require no further justification: they are constitutive of the various ascending 'stages' of 'truly human' society.[11]

Habermas makes none of these moves, proposing instead, as an inheritor of the tradition of critical theory, to develop a mode of theorising that is grounded, in Max Horkheimer's phrase, by an interest in the future, and in particular by 'the idea of a reasonable organization of society that will meet the needs of the whole community' as a goal of human activity which is 'immanent in human work, but . . . not correctly grasped by individuals or by the common mind'.[12] However, unlike his predecessors in this tradition, Habermas makes a serious attempt to give content and grounding to the key notion of emancipation, seeing it as immanent not in work but in communication. His central idea is that

the *design* of an ideal speech situation is necessarily implied in the structure of potential speech, since all speech, even intentional deception, is oriented toward the idea of truth. This idea can be analyzed with regard to a consensus achieved in unrestrained and universal discourse. Insofar as we master the means for the construction of the ideal speech situation, we can

---

[8] F. Engels, *Anti-Dühring* (Moscow: Foreign Languages Publishing House, 1959).

[9] Karl Kautsky, *Ethics and the Materialist Conception of History*, trans. J. B. Askew (Chicago, Mass.: Charles H. Kerr & Co., n.d.), p. 160.

[10] L. Trotsky, *Their Morals and Ours*, 4th edn. (New York: Pathfinder Press, 1969), p. 37.

[11] For this interpretation of Lukács and Marx, see Leszek Kolakowski, *Main Currents of Marxism*, 3 vols. (Oxford: Clarendon Press, 1978).

[12] Horkheimer, *Critical Theory* (New York: Seabury Press, 1973), p. 213.

conceive the ideas of truth, freedom and justice, which interprenetrate each other—although of course only as ideas.[13]

His whole theory of universal pragmatics is devoted to establishing these claims and I cannot directly consider them here.[14] I shall concentrate rather on Habermas's claim to have established a vantage-point from which the social world can be critically analysed and from which one can identify ideological deception and normative power—forms of domination whose legitimacy is imposed and which rely on 'contingent and forced consensus', on 'preventing questions that radicalize the value-universalism of bourgeois society from even arising'.[15]

Let us, then, look more closely at Habermas's recent attempt to specify that critical standpoint. A social theory critical of ideology can, he writes,

identify the normative power built into the institutional system of a society only if it starts from the *model of the suppression of generalizable interests* and compares normative structures existing at a given time with the hypothetical state of a system of norms formed, *ceteris paribus*, discursively. Such a counterfactually projected reconstruction . . . can be guided by the question (justified, in my opinion, by considerations from universal pragmatics): how would the members of a social system, at a given stage in the development of productive forces, have collectively and bindingly interpreted their needs (and which norms would they have accepted as justified) if they could and would have decided on organization of social intercourse through discursive will-formation, with adequate knowledge of the limiting conditions and functional imperatives of their society?[16]

Such ideal discourse would be solely concerned with discussing the 'bracketed validity claims' (to intelligibility, truth, rightness, and sincerity) of participants' speech-acts and its sole goal would be to test them, so that

no force except that of the better argument is exercised, and that, as a result, all motives except that of the cooperative search for truth are excluded. If under these conditions a consensus about the recommendation to accept a norm arises argumentatively, that is, on the basis of hypothetically pro-

---

[13] Habermas, 'Toward a Theory of Communicative Competence', *Inquiry*, 13 (1970), p. 372.
[14] They are admirably treated in John B. Thompson's essay in J. R. Thompson and D. Held (eds.), *Jürgen Habermas: Critical Debates* (London: Macmillan, 1982).
[15] Habermas, *Communication*, pp. 188, 198.
[16] Id., *Legitimation Crisis*, p. 113.

posed, alternative justifications, then this consensus expresses a 'rational will'. Since all those affected have, in principle, at least the chance to participate in the practical deliberation, the 'rationality' of the discursively formed will consists in the fact that the reciprocal behavioral expectations raised to normative status afford validity to a *common* interest ascertained *without deception*. The interest is common because the constraint-free consensus permits only what *all* can want; it is free of deception because even the interpretations of needs in which *each individual* must be able to recognize what he wants become the object of discursive will-formation. The discursively formed will may be called 'rational' because the formal properties of discourse and of the deliberative situation sufficiently guarantee that a consensus can arise only through appropriately interpreted, *generalizable* interests, by which I mean needs *that can be communicatively shared*. The limits of a decisionistic treatment of practical questions are overcome as soon as argumentation is expected to test the generaliz*ability* of interests, instead of being resigned to an impenetrable pluralism of apparently ultimate value orientations (or belief-acts or attitudes).[17]

In what follows I shall examine this attempt to establish a vantage-point that purports to yield a rational basis for critical theory in order to see whether it succeeds in providing a determinate notion of emancipation (from ideology, imposed legitimacy, forced consensus, etc.) and whether it fulfils its promise of eliminating a 'decisionistic' treatment of practical questions and avoiding 'an impenetrable pluralism of apparently ultimate value orientations'.

There is, to begin with, much to be said for the practical implications of Habermas's general approach. He maintains, correctly, that any serious social analysis—and certainly a Marxist or critical theorist—must address the question: are social norms which claim legitimacy genuinely accepted by those who follow and internalize them, or do they merely stabilize relations of power? His central insight is that, in asking this (exceedingly complex) question, one must reason counterfactually and engage in a complicated thought-experiment—albeit guided by general theoretical considerations and relevant empirical evidence—in order to determine whether forms of power, manipulation, mystification, etc., are at work, shaping and deflecting the beliefs and preferences of actors in such a way as to preclude them from thinking and acting as they would otherwise autonomously do. In order to determine this, Habermas argues, we need to postulate undistorted communication among all affected by the norms in

---

[17] Ibid. 107–8.

question, in which they articulate their needs and in which they both form and discover their interests and the norms that they can rationally accept as binding. Thus he writes that

only communicative ethics guarantees the generality of admissible norms and the autonomy of acting subjects, solely through the discursive redeemability of the validity claims with which norms appear. That is, generality is guaranteed in that the only norms that may claim generality are those on which everyone affected agrees (or would agree) without constraint if they enter into (or were to enter into) a process of discursive will-formation.[18]

Habermas here reveals his firm commitment to the view (fundamentally at odds with any Leninist or Lukácsian assumption of privileged access in the imputation of interests) that people are the sole judges of their own interests, which are formed and discovered through dialogue on the part of all concerned—a political commitment to opening up public, democratic processes which Habermas has elsewhere described as 'the conversation of citizens'.[19] Contrary to the assumptions of technocrats, he has portrayed 'the depoliticization of the mass of the population and the decline of the public realm as a political institution' as 'components of a system of domination that tends to exclude practical questions from public discussion': the 'enlightenment of political will', he argues, 'can become effective only within the communication of citizens'.[20] His general approach leads him, therefore, to see democracy, not as any particular institutional form, but as a 'self-controlled learning process', in which the problem is to find 'arrangements which can ground the presumption that the basic institutions of society and the basic political institutions would meet with the unforced agreement of all those involved, if they could participate, as free and equal, in discursive will-formation'.[21]

But, aside from these admirable political implications of his approach, it remains to examine exactly *how* he proposes to establish a determinate rational basis for social criticism, an 'Archimedean point', as John Rawls might say, 'for assessing the social system' that 'is not at the mercy, so to speak, of existing wants and interests'.[22] How does Habermas propose to specify which norms and claims to

---

[18] Habermas, *Legitimation Crisis*, p. 89.
[19] Id., *Towards a Rational Society: Student Protest, Science and Politics*, trans. J. J. Shapiro (Boston: Beacon Press, 1970; London: Heinemann, 1971).
[20] Ibid.   [21] Id., *Communication*, p. 186.
[22] Rawls, *A Theory of Justice* (Oxford: Clarendon Press, 1972), p. 261.

legitimacy are capable of securing the rational consent of social actors—actors to a greater or lesser extent caught up in structures of 'normative power', 'illegitimate domination' that 'meets with consent', and 'contingent and forced consensus'?[23]

Habermas offers as his answer the 'model of the suppression of generalisable interests'—a hypothesis or 'counterfactually projected reconstruction' specifying of all the actors in question which of their interests are 'generalisable', how they would interpret their needs, and which norms they would accept as justified under conditions of unconstrained communication. It is true that Habermas observes that the 'social scientist can only hypothetically project this ascription of interests; indeed a direct confirmation of this hypothesis would be possible only in the form of a practical discourse among the very individuals or groups involved'. It can, he maintains, be indirectly confirmed (it would perhaps be better to say supported) through 'empirical indicators of suppressed interests'. Following Claus Offe (who likewise seeks a 'critical standard' for identifying structures that perpetuate 'suppressed, that is latent, claims and needs'), Habermas mentions specifically (1) the existence of an observed discrepancy between legal norms and actual legal practices; (2) codified rules which systematically exclude claims from the political agenda (claims which thus express suppressed interests); (3) the existence of a discrepancy between claims that are made and the level at which they are politically allowed satisfaction; and (4) comparative evidence, drawn from different political systems, which indicates, *ceteris paribus*, which possibilities are actualized when putatively repressive structures are absent or removed.[24] But before we can know whether the hypothesis of suppressed generalizable interests is either directly confirmed or indirectly well supported, we must first know what the hypothesis *is*. The prior issue is to establish whether such a hypothesis can be intelligibly advanced and what precisely it amounts to.

Two deep and connected difficulties are raised by Habermas's proposal. First, just how counterfactual is the hypothesis in question? Just how much of the real past and present are we to alter in the proposed thought-experiment? More particularly, to what extent, if

[23] Habermas, *Legitimation Crisis*, p. 111; Id., *Communication*, pp. 202, 188.
[24] Id., *Legitimation Crisis*, p. 114.

at all, is the identity of the agents preserved across the transition between the actual and the imagined possible world?

There appear to be three possible answers to this last question, to each of which Habermas seems to be drawn, each of which is unsatisfactory, and none of which suits his purposes. The first is that the *actual* agents are to be imagined in conditions of undistorted communication (thus he speaks of the 'interests that would have to find expression among those involved if they [*sic*] were to enter into practical discourse').[25] The second is that *typical* or *representative* actors are to be imagined in such conditions (thus he speaks of 'representatively simulated discourse' between groups with conflicting interests and also describes the discoursing partners as 'the members of a social system, at a given stage in the development of productive forces').[26] The third is that ideally rational, theoretically defined agents are to be imagined in such conditions (thus he speaks of the 'ideal speech situation', the participants in which must presumably be ideally constituted, having reached a level of cognitive and moral development that will enable rational consensus to be reached). The first answer suggests a counterfactual of the form 'Under (counterfactual) conditions C, the real-life actors A_1 would agree on X.' The second suggests a counterfactual of the form 'Under conditions C, typical actors A_2 (defined by, say, their membership in conflict groups or their incumbency of roles) would agree on X.' The third suggests a counterfactual of the form 'Under conditions C, ideally rational actors A_3 (defined by a theory of rationality) would agree on X.'

The problem with the first answer is that no reason is given for supposing that the actual agents would, under the conditions supposed (that is, where there is 'a symmetrical distribution of chances to select and employ speech acts and an equal opportunity to assume dialogue roles'),[27] reach the required rational consensus. Indeed, there is surely every reason to suppose that *they* would not, since *they* would continue to exhibit all kinds of traits conducive to 'distorted communication'—prejudices, limitations of vision and imagination, deference to authority, fears, vanities, self-doubts, and so on. Doubtless many of these traits will be the outcome of relations of domination and exploitation within the family and the larger society, but

25 Habermas, *Legitimation Crisis*, p. 114.   26 Ibid. 117, 113.
27 T. McCarthy, *The Critical Theory of Jürgen Habermas* (London: Hutchinson, 1978), p. 306.

they will be sufficiently integral to, and internalized within, the personalities of actual people to make it implausible to suppose their eradication without those people becoming different people. Real participants in ideal communication would hold fast to their conceptions of their needs and interests and the norms they accept, to the extent that these conceptions are integral to their very identity.

The problem with the second answer is that the agents in question are constructs of a social theory which specifies relevant conflict groups or roles and their associated needs and interests, and the norms that regulate them. But, in that case, the counterfactual hypothesis will be a direct entailment of the theory and will do no more than spell out what, for the postulated conflict groups and role incumbents, are, according to the theory, negotiable or shared interests, true of self-interpreted needs and generally acceptable norms. In other words, this solution does no more than employ the counterfactual to spell out the implications of a theory accepted on other grounds, and its plausibility as a rational foundation for critical theorizing is no stronger than those grounds themselves.

The problem with the third answer is a familiar one to students of Kant and Rawls. If we are asked to imagine what ideally rational agents would do under the posited conditions, the whole argument turns on the nature of those agents and the constraints set by the conditions. If these together are such that the appropriate answers are necessarily reached, then the counterfactual hypothesis emerges as vindicated but only because it has been so formulated that it must do so. Ideally rational people in an ideal speech situation cannot but reach a rational consensus.

None of these answers suits Habermas's purposes, since his aim is to identify suppressed interests, 'contingent and forced consensus', and illegitimate domination, which requires him to specify and render plausible the counterfactual hypothesis that the individuals and groups in question would, under specified alternative conditions, acknowledge *their* true interests, *their* real and unforced consensus, and the claims to legitimacy *they* genuinely accept. John Stuart Mill reasoned thus when comparing the higher and lower pleasures, deferring to the judgement of the person who had experienced both: Habermas offers a version of this argument transposed to a collective and communicative level. And Habermas is quite right to observe that Marx reasons in this way, making the crucial, further assumption that 'the consciousness of justified and, at the same time, suppressed interests' is a 'sufficient motive for conflict' to realize those interests.[28] The problem for Habermas is that none of his suggested answers to the question posed gives a plausible rendering of the counterfactual hypothesis required.

A further possible answer might be suggested: that under the imagined conditions of ideal communication, actual actors would be so transformed as to become capable of the requisite rational consensus. But this proposal encounters two severe objections. First, there is every reason to suppose that this would not be so, if socialization processes and relations of economic and political power remain unchanged: to suppose the contrary could be described as a rationalist illusion, typical of the eighteenth century, inconceivable to a Marxist. And second, even if it were so, the greater the change from the actual agents to the ideally rational agents, capable of reaching the requisite consensus, the less relevant would be the deliberations of the latter to the purpose at hand—which is to establish how the actual participants would think and feel, were alleged structures of domination to be overthrown.

This first difficulty I have been considering can be summed up in the question: *Who* are the participants in the unconstrained discourse that is held to offer the possibility of rational consensus? The second difficulty, to which I now turn, can be summed up in the question: *What* are they supposed to agree about?

In the first place, they are to interpret their needs 'collectively and bindingly' and in such a way that 'each individual must be able to recognize what he wants' and this becomes 'the object of discursive will-formation'. This seems to amount to a strong insistence on the self-ascription of desires and needs by autonomous agents and their acceptance of responsibility for the consequences of such self-ascriptions. Moreover, Habermas stresses the public and discursive nature of such self-ascriptions.[29] Second, in the light of such public, discursively reached self-ascriptions of desires and needs, they count certain norms as 'justified' and 'legitimate' if they fulfil 'commonly accepted needs'.[30] Another way that Habermas expresses this is to

---

[28] Habermas, *Legitimation Crisis*, p. 114.
[29] This is one of many interesting points of convergence with Rawls, who also stresses the importance of publicity: see Habermas, *A Theory of Justice*, pp. 177 ff.
[30] Id., 'Wahrheitstheorien', p. 245.

say that the norms must 'express' and 'regulate' 'generalizable interests'. By 'generalizable interests' he says he means '*needs that can be communicatively shared*'. Thus rationally justified norms are those which 'express' and 'regulate' 'generalizable interests', that is needs that are publicly self-ascribed by autonomous and responsible participants in unconstrained discourse.

As yet this is a cloudy formula, and it is worth pressing on to see if clarification issues in a determinate solution. How, then, are we to recognize norms which express and regulate 'generalizable interests'? Habermas addresses this question. How, he asks, is it possible to separate by argument generalizable interests from 'those that are and remain particular'? His answer is that 'the only principle in which practical reason expresses itself' is 'the principle of universalization'.[31] He speaks of this principle as a 'bridge principle' comparable with the principle of induction:

Induction serves as a bridge principle for justifying the logically discontinuous passage from a finite number of singular statements (data) to a universal statement (hypothesis). Universalization serves as a bridge principle for justifying the passage to a norm from descriptive indications (concerning the consequences and side effects of the application of norms for the fulfilment of commonly accepted needs).[32]

The rationally justified norms to be agreed are, then, universalized. But what does this mean? There is a good case for distinguishing three forms or stages of universalization.[33] At the first stage, the principle of universalization simply dictates that the rules or norms guiding and controlling human conduct make no essential reference to proper names or indexical terms: that is to say, purely numerical differences are treated as irrelevant, so that what is right (or wrong) for you or your group is right (or wrong) for me and my group, unless there are morally relevant differences between us or our situation (with no restriction as to what can count as a morally relevant difference). At the second stage, the principle dictates that the rules or norms must be subject to a further test, namely putting oneself in the other person's or group's place. This test will allow through only those norms or rules which the actors are prepared to go on applying, no matter how they might change in respect of their mental and

---

[31] Id., *Legitimation Crisis*, p. 108.
[32] Id., 'Wahrheitstheorien', p. 245.
[33] In what follows, I am indebted to the discussion of this question in J. L. Mackie, *Ethics: Inventing Right and Wrong* (Harmondsworth: Penguin, 1977), chap. 4.

physical qualities, resources and social status; on this test, 'differences can be fairly regarded as relevant if they look relevant from whichever side you consider them'.[34] At the third stage, a further, more stringent test is applied, namely that account is taken of rival and alternative desires, tastes, preferences, ideals, and values. Now one must simultaneously take account of conflicting points of view, and seek maxims that will be acceptable from all viewpoints. This test will allow through only those norms and rules which give equal weight, in some sense, to all interests, those interests being determined by rival preferences, values, and ideals.

The test at the first stage allows in all kinds of rules that are clearly partisan and unfair (e.g. all blacks should have an inferior education). Similarly the test at the second stage allows in universal rules that favour some preferences, values, and ideals as against others (e.g. a puritan code of conduct). We might perhaps assume, therefore, that Habermas is thinking of the third stage of universalization.

But the problem with the third stage of universalization is that the test is so severe that it is not clear that any rules or norms will pass, and it is certainly very far from guaranteed that unconstrained discourse between the parties will yield action-guiding principles of this sort. There would appear to be two possible approaches to this problem. One is the highly ambitious strategy of seeking to derive, through reflection on features inherent in the human condition and general facts about society, a determinate set of principles that will pass the test. This is John Rawls's approach. The 'circumstances of justice', which are 'the normal conditions under which human cooperation is both possible and necessary', obtain wherever 'mutually disinterested persons put forward conflicting claims to the division of social advantages under conditions of moderate scarcity'. Knowing this, and accepting that 'individuals not only have different plans of life but there exists a diversity of religious and philosophical belief, and of political and social doctrines', the parties in Rawls's 'original position', operating behind a veil of ignorance (about their own natural assets, future positions, and plans of life), have the task of unanimously settling on 'principles of justice that are genuinely neutral as between alternative plans of life'.[35] These principles, for

---

[34] Ibid. 91–2.

[35] Rawls, *A Theory of Justice*, pp. 226–30. Rawls even claims that 'to see our place in society from the perspective of this position is to see it *sub specie aeternitatis*: it is to regard the human situation not only from all social but also from all temporal points

Rawls, 'not only specify the terms of cooperation between persons but they define a pact of reconciliation between diverse religious and moral beliefs, and the forms of culture to which they belong':[36] they are 'principles of accommodation between different moralities',[37] intended to secure 'social cooperation among equals for mutual advantage'.[38] Two crucial and telling objections that have been made against this approach, in the Rawlsian form, are, first, that his principles are not uniquely derivable from his hypothesized choice situation, and, second, that the 'original position' and its abstract, theoretically defined inhabitants have been so artificially constructed as to yield a predetermined solution, which has therefore no independently compelling qualification for the title '*the* principles of justice'.

A less ambitious approach to applying the test at this third stage of universalization is that of Mackie, who argues that the test is too severe: given radically divergent preferences and values and the obstinate moral disagreements arising therefrom, 'we must lower our sights a little, and look not for principles which can be wholeheartedly endorsed from every point of view, but for ones which represent an acceptable compromise between the different actual points of view'.[39] On this view of morality as compromise, there will no longer be any reason to suppose that a definitive or uniquely determinable set of rules or maxims can be arrived at through general rational argument: rather, there will be contingently different principles and rules, depending on the actual circumstances, divergences and possibilities of agreement. These must be 'invented' and 're-invented' anew in the recurrent quest for mutual accommodation.

Neither of these approaches to universalization would seem to suit Habermas's purposes. Rawls's quest for an Archimedean point

of view' (ibid. 587). Ronald Dworkin, similarly, has argued that the constitutive political morality of liberalism rests on the idea that 'government must be neutral on what might be called the question of the good life', that 'political decisions must be, as far as is possible, independent of any particular conception of the good life, or of what gives value to life' ('Liberalism', in *Public and Private Morality*, ed. S. Hampshire (Cambridge: Cambridge Univ. Press, 1978), p. 127).

[36] Rawls, *A Theory of Justice*, p. 221.
[37] Id., 'Fairness to Goodness', *Philosophical Review* 84 (1975), p. 539.
[38] Id., *A Theory of Justice*, p. 14.
[39] Mackie, *Ethics*, p. 93.

eludes him, for the reasons suggested and others,[40] while Mackie's position does not yield a uniquely rationally justified outcome, only contingent compromises. But in any case, Habermas appears to reject a basic assumption shared by both these approaches, namely that morality is a means of solving the problem posed by the conflicts generated by limited resources and limited sympathies, with a view to securing mutually beneficial co-operation. To the contrary, he explicitly distinguishes 'norms that may claim generality' from 'compromise',[41] which he describes as a case of 'normative power' involving a 'normed adjustment between particular interests' that 'takes place under conditions of a balance of power between the parties involved'. Although such compromise may be 'indirectly justifiable' through discourse, it is plainly seen as distinct from and contrasting with the case of 'interests that permit of a rational will': a compromise can be justified only where 'a balance of power among the parties involved and the non-generalizability of the negotiated interests exist'.[42]

Nor indeed is it surprising that Habermas should take this line, since the entire Marxist tradition is committed to denying that morality is a response to an inherent limitation of resources and sympathies in the human condition—a view classically expressed by Hume when he wrote that 'It is only from the selfishness and confined generosity of man, along with the scanty provision nature has made for his wants, that justice derives its origin'.[43] On the contrary, Marx and subsequent Marxists see both limitations as historically contingent and socially generated and look forward to overcoming both in a unified society of abundance.

What, then, if all this is so, does Habermas understand by the principle of universalization as expressed in the formula 'generalizability of interests'? In truth, I find it difficult to say. A clue may lie

[40] For an argument in support of this claim, see the present author's *Essays in Social Theory* (London: Macmillan, and New York: Columbia Univ. Press, 1977), chap. 10.

[41] Habermas, *Legitimation Crisis*, p. 89.

[42] Ibid. 112.

[43] D. Hume, *A Treatise of Human Nature* (1739), ed. L. A. Selby-Bigge (Oxford: Clarendon Press, 1951), p. 495, bk. iii, pt. ii, sect. ii. For an interesting discussion of 'morality as compromise', see Arthur Kuflic, 'Morality and Compromise', in J. R. Pennock and J. W. Chapman (eds.), *Compromise in Ethics, Law and Politics, Nomos XXI*. This being the *Yearbook of the American Society for Political and Legal Philosophy* (New York: New York Univ. Press, 1979).

in his attack on the Rawlsian notion of 'primary goods' as supposedly 'neutral means for attaining an indefinite multiplicity of concrete ends selected according to values'. He argues that this picture is misleading, that the Rawlsian primary goods are not compatible with all forms of life that could be chosen, but involve 'clearly circumscribed "opportunity structures"' and imply a particular underlying form of life, of private commodity production and exchange relations, and familial, occupational, and civil privatism. In the light of this critique, he argues for the possibility that

the 'pursuit of happiness' might one day mean something different—for example, not accumulating material objects of which one disposes privately, but bringing about social relations in which mutuality predominates and satisfaction does not mean the triumph of one over the repressed needs of the other.[44]

The idea seems to be that there will be an endogenous change of preferences on the part of social actors (induced by ideal discourse?) such that preferences, tastes, values, ideals, plans of life, etc. will to some large degree (to what degree?) be unified and no longer conflict. On this interpretation, the principle of universalization would require that norms and rules pass the test that they should embody common aims, regulate shared activities and lead to common and shared satisfactions ('needs that can be communicatively shared'). But why should one suppose such a moral change to be either possible, necessary, or desirable? It is true that *Legitimation Crisis* is, in part, addressed to showing such a change to be on the historical agenda in late capitalist societies and there are, of course, good arguments in favour of a more unified, less conflictual, privatized and consumerist form of life than is predominant in contemporary capitalist societies; but I cannot find in Habermas's writings any argument for the thesis that such a form of life (which is, in any case, barely even sketched, except in the most abstract possible manner) is either an appropriate interpretation of the principles of universalization or uniquely capable of rational justification.

I turn now to the question of whether Habermas has justified his claim that his approach overcomes 'the limits of a decisionistic treatment of practical questions as soon as argumentation is expected to test the generaliz*ability* of interests'.[45] I cannot see that it

---

[44] Habermas, *Communication*, pp. 188–9.
[45] Id., *Legitimation Crisis*, p. 108.

does so. For the principle of universalization, at all the three stages I have discussed, requires, at each stage, a *decision* whether or not to let one's actions and choices be guided only by maxims and norms which pass the test in question. As Mackie has remarked, 'the universalisability of moral judgements . . . does not impose any rational constraint on choices of action or defensible patterns of behaviour'.[46] At every stage it is not merely logically possible but in fact quite common for people to opt out of, or not opt into, these ways of reasoning. And this argument applies, with equal force, to Habermas's own (putative) version of the universalization principle.

I conclude from all this that (1) these arguments do not succeed in establishing a determinate, uniquely rational basis for critical theory; (2) they do not dispense with the role of decision in moral and political thinking; and (3) they do not therefore disprove the thesis of value pluralism.

Habermas has, however, advanced a further set of considerations which are intended to provide an 'empirical' and a 'systematic' basis for the objectivity and universality of standards of rationality as he conceives them. These considerations are intended to provide further grounding for his positive claim to establish a determinate rational basis for critical theory and thereby his rejection of 'decisionism' and Weber's 'rationally irresoluble pluralism of competing value systems and beliefs'.[47] I refer to his application of Piaget's and Kohlberg's cognitive developmental psychology.

I cannot here discuss in detail Habermas's intriguing attempt to use these ideas to try to reconstruct historical materialism by incorporating within it a theory of the development of normative structures. I shall refer only to the gist of his argument, in so far as it concerns the question at issue here. His basic thought is that, since cognitive developmental psychology is 'well corroborated and . . . has reconstructed ontogenetic stages of moral consciousness', it should be possible to reconstruct these stages logically, that is, 'by concepts of a systematically ordered sequence of norm systems and behavioral controls', and at the highest stage to identify a corresponding 'universal morality, which can be traced back to fun-

---

46 Mackie, *Ethics*, p. 99.
47 Habermas, *Legitimation Crisis*, p. 100.

damental norms of rational speech'.[48] With extraordinary boldness, he traces homologies between ego development on the one hand, and 'the social evolution of moral and legal representations', of 'world views', and 'the historical constitution of collective identities' on the other.[49] Just as the ego develops from the symbiotic, through the egocentric and the sociocentric-objectivistic to the universalistic stages of development, and from pre-conventional through conventional to post-conventional patterns of problem-solving,[50] so, Habermas argues, it should be possible to develop a 'communication theory' that would analyse 'the symbolic structures that underlie law and morality, an intersubjectively constituted world, and the identities of persons and collectivities', that would show normative structures to have their own 'internal history' which has a 'direction of development' that can be characterized by such concepts as 'universalization and individualization, decentration, autonomization, and becoming reflective'.[51] In short, the 'stages of law and morality, of ego demarcations and world views, of individual and collective identity formations' can be seen as stages in progress towards increasing rationality, measured by 'the expansion of the domain of consensual action together with the re-establishment of undistorted communication'.[52] Such progress can be seen as a sequence of developmental stages of moral consciousness, corresponding to stages of development in interaction competence. At the final, post-conventional stage, 'systems of norms lose their quasi-natural validity; they require justification from universalistic points of view'.[53]

Do these considerations help to render the 'universalistic' perspective of the highest stage, and the principles and judgements it delivers, determinate, uniquely rational and objective, and do they

---

[48] Id., *Zur Rekonstruktion des Historischen Materialismus* (Frankfurt: Suhrkamp, 1976), p. 205 ('History and Evolution', trans. D. J. Parent, *Telos* 39 (Spring 1979), 8); id., *Legitimation Crisis*, p. 95.

[49] Id., *Communication*, pp. 99, 102, 110.

[50] Kohlberg's six stages of moral consciousness are: (1) punishment-obedience orientation, involving maximization of pleasure through obedience; (2) instrumental hedonism, involving maximization of pleasure through exchange of equivalents; (3) 'good-boy/nice-girl' orientation, involving concrete morality of gratifying interactions; (4) law-and-order orientation, involving concrete morality of a customary system of norms; (5) social-contractual legalism, involving civil liberties and public welfare; and (6) ethical-principles orientation, involving moral freedom.

[51] Habermas, *Communication*, pp. 116–17.

[52] Ibid. 120.   [53] Ibid. 156.

bypass the need for a decision to adopt it? It is notable that Kohlberg has himself argued a similar case to that of Habermas. He has claimed to 'have successfully defined the ethically optimal end-point of moral development', that 'there is a sense in which we can characterize moral differences between groups and individuals [which are themselves to be understood as differences in stage or developmental status] as being more or less adequate morally'.[54] For Kohlberg, the later stages of development are 'cognitively and ethically higher or more adequate', the final sixth stage being 'a more universalistic, moral orientation, which defines moral obligations in terms of what alternatively may be conceived as (a) the principle of justice, (b) the principle of role-taking, or (c) the principle of respect for personality', this stage being 'the most adequate exemplification of the moral'.[55] In this sense, Kohlberg argues for the 'superiority of Stage 6 judgements of duties and rights (or of justice) over other systems of judgements of duties and rights'.[56] Habermas, similarly, argues for both an empirical and a systematic 'superiority' of universal morality.[57]

But Kohlberg in fact established only that there are recurrent sequences of stages of preferred modes of moral reasoning employed by growing children in different contexts and cultures.[58] The claim that this repeated sequence is a development towards greater adequacy only makes sense if one applies specific criteria of adequacy, criteria that are themselves disputable and indeed disputed among moral thinkers, philosophical and otherwise. In Kohlberg's theory such criteria are already built into his 'scientific' theory. The claimed superiority of the later stages over the earlier and the last stage over the rest is necessitated neither by the observed data, nor by the fact that the later modes of reasoning may logically presuppose earlier modes, nor by the fact that they may imply cognitive superiority or require more elaborate conceptual thinking. There is no inherent compulsion in Kohlberg's claim that Stage 6 reasoning is ethically

---

[54] L. Kohlberg, 'From Is to Ought: How to Commit the Naturalistic Fallacy and Get Away with it in the Study of Moral Development', in *Cognitive Development and Epistemology*, ed. T. Mischel (New York: Academic Press, 1971), pp. 153, 176.

[55] Ibid. 208, 218.

[56] Ibid. 214–15.

[57] Habermas, *Legitimation Crisis*, p. 95.

[58] See the critique of Kohlberg by William Alston in *Cognitive Development and Epistemology*. Also see P. R. Dasen, 'Cross-cultural Piagetian Research: A Summary', *Cross Cultural Psychology* 3 (1972), pp. 23–40.

optimal: as Alston has observed, 'many moral philosophers who are surely at least as conceptually sophisticated as Kohlberg's Stage 6 subjects take positions in moral philosophy that reflect Stages 4 or 5'.[59] It is a claim that many can and will dispute, and it cannot be established by stipulatively defining 'moral' so that Stage 6 becomes 'the most adequate exemplification of the moral'. And the same arguments apply, *pari passu*, to Habermas's claim, *contra* Kohlberg, that there is an ultimate Stage 7 at which 'the principle of justification of norms is no longer the monologically applicable principle of generalizability but the communally followed *procedure* of redeeming normative validity claims discursively'.[60]

Indeed, these arguments can only be strengthened by considering the very disagreement between Kohlberg (and by implication Rawls[61]) on the one hand, and Habermas on the other, as to the nature of the highest stage. Kohlberg has argued that the highest stage of moral development implies the notion of justice as 'reversibility', a kind of 'ideal role-taking' which involves 'differentiating the self's perspective from the other's and co-ordinating the two so that the perspective from the other's view influences one's own perspective in a reciprocal fashion'.[62] This amounts to a moral decision procedure, which Kohlberg calls 'moral musical chairs', that is, 'going round the circle of perspectives involved in a moral dilemma to test one's claims of right or duty until only the equilibrated or reversible claims survive'.[63] (Kohlberg further claims that his decision procedure yields the same solutions as Rawls's idea of decision in the 'original position'.) By contrast, as we have seen, Habermas maintains that Kohlberg's approach is 'monological' and fails to attain 'the level of a universal ethic of speech' where self-

---

[59] Alston, in *Cognitive Development and Epistemology*, p. 275.

[60] Habermas, *Communication*, p. 90.

[61] Rawls claims support from the ideas of Piaget and Kohlberg, in seeking to indicate 'the major steps whereby a person would acquire an understanding of an attachment to the principles of justice as he grows up in this particular form of a well-ordered society' (*A Theory of Justice*, p. 461; see sects. 69–72). On the other hand, *contra* Kohlberg, Rawls is clear that the claimed superiority of his theory of justice 'is a philosophical question and cannot, I believe, be established by the psychological theory of development alone' (ibid. 462). Kohlberg, reciprocally, sees Rawls's theory as consonant with his own.

[62] Kohlberg, 'Justice as Reversibility', in *Philosophy, Politics and Society*, 5th ser., ed. P. Laslett and J. Fishkin (Oxford: Blackwell, 1979), p. 266.

[63] Ibid. 262.

ascriptions of interests become 'the object of practical discourse'.[64] If my interpretation of Habermas's understanding of universalization, set out above, is correct, he assumes that such practical discourse will lead to an endogenous change of preferences and perspectives on the part of the communicators such that shared needs and 'consensual action'[65] will predominate. Yet how can one rationally resolve this difference between two such rational men? How can one conclude which is rationally and morally superior—Kohlberg's Stage 6 or Habermas's Stage 7, and the norms and judgements they respectively generate—other than by *deciding* between them? Of course, one might at this point maintain that the very distinction between 'decision' and 'rational argument' is misleading here. After all, would not any such decision be based on *reasons*: do we not decide on the basis of *rational grounds*? But neither Habermas nor Kohlberg (nor Rawls) has shown that there is a neutral or objective standpoint from which the reasons grounding alternative decisions can themselves be assessed as more or less rational.

So I conclude that this line of argument also fails to establish the critical vantage-point that Habermas seeks and that we have not yet escaped the Weberian gods and demons.

64 Habermas, *Communication*, p. 90.
65 Habermas, *Communication*, p. 110.

12

C. B. Macpherson and the Real and Ideal Worlds of Democracy

Brough Macpherson's democratic theory strikes a distinctive note. Resolutely Anglo-Saxon in its range of reference and its crisp, clear, analytic style, it unites a Marxist-inspired critique of 'capitalist market society with its class-division'[1] and of the underlying market assumptions of the justifying theory of liberal democracy with the constructive 'liberal' aim of 'retrieving' from that theory the 'notion of a democratic society as one that provides equally for the self-development of all the members of a political community'.[2] His motivating animus is against possessive individualism—'this perverse, artificial, and temporary concept of man', inherited from 'classical liberal individualism', as 'essentially a consumer of utilities, an infinite desirer and infinite appropriator' whose over-riding motivation is 'to maximise the flow of satisfactions, or utilities, to himself from society'.[3] His positive commitment, by contrast, is to a 'co-operative and creative individualism' which rescues 'the humanist side of Mill's liberalism (the side based on his idea of man as essentially an exerter and developer of his human capacities) from the possessive individualist side (based on the Benthamite concept of man as essentially consumer and appropriator)'.[4] Thus he places himself among 'those who accept and would promote the normative values that were read into the liberal-democratic society and state by

This chapter was first published in 1979.

[1] Macpherson, *The Life and Times of Liberal Democracy* (Oxford: Clarendon Press, 1977), p. 21.

[2] Id., 'The False Roots of Western Democracy', in Fred R. Dallmayr (ed.), *From Contract to Community: Political Theory at the Crossroads* (New York and Basel: Marcel Dekker, 1978), p. 26.

[3] Id., *Democratic Theory: Essays in Retrieval* (Oxford: Clarendon Press, 1973), 20, 63, 24; id., *Life and Times*, p. 43.

[4] Id., 'Individualist Socialism? A Reply to Levine and MacIntyre', *Canadian Journal of Philosophy*, 6/2 (June 1976), p. 198.

John Stuart Mill and the nineteenth- and twentieth-century idealist theorists, but who reject the present liberal-democratic society and state as having failed to live up to those values, or as being incapable of realising them'.[5]

Macpherson's project, therefore, has four main components. First, to identify the origins of market assumptions in the political theories of the seventeenth century and to trace their history from Locke through the classical economists to Bentham and James Mill and thence down to the present. Second, to trace the distinctive features of liberal democracy in 'the real world of democracy', in contradistinction to the communist and the populist or 'under-developed' variants. The 'life and times of liberal democracy' is portrayed as the historical amalgamation of possessive market ideas and ethical humanist claims that, in the nineteenth-century economy of scarcity, were, rightly, seen as necessarily linked together: the only way to free all individuals 'to use and develop their human capacities fully' was 'through the productivity of free-enterprise capitalism'.[6] The third component, therefore, is an argument to show that actual or prospective technological developments make possible a post-scarcity form of liberal democracy in which there is 'a possibility of our discarding the market concept of the essence of man, and replacing it by a morally preferable concept, in a way that was not possible when previous generations of liberal-democratic thinkers, from John Stuart Mill on, attempted it'.[7] Hence, the fourth component of Macpherson's project: to inquire into 'a possible future model of liberal democracy' which is based on 'the equal right to self-development',[8] being a model of 'participatory democracy', combining 'a pyramidal council structure with a competitive party system',[9] involving 'a stronger sense of community than now prevails'[10] and new and expanded conceptions of liberty,[11] property,[12] and human rights.[13]

This project is subject to various criticisms. Two are worth singling out, both of which deny the feasibility of a democratic theory's discarding one side of liberalism while building on the other.

[5] Macpherson, 'Do We Need a Theory of the Stage?' *Archives européennes de sociologie/European Journal of Sociology*, 18/2 (1977), p. 224.

[6] Id., *Life and Times*, pp. 21–2.

[7] Id., *Democratic Theory*, p. 37.

[8] Id., *Life and Times*, pp. 21–2.   [9] Ibid. 112.   [10] Ibid. 100.

[11] See id., *Democratic Theory*, chap. 5.

[12] See ibid. chap. 6.   [13] See ibid. chap. 13, sect. 5.

From a Marxist perspective, its attempt to preserve continuity with liberalism (or one side of it) and 'bourgeois political practice' may be judged to be 'reformist'. On this view, there is no 'possibility of "retrieving" the old order, while doing away with its defining characteristic: a market in labour and goods': what is required is a 'shift of terrain . . . a shift in politics, a changed political practice, a changing of sides in the class struggle'. Macpherson's position is social democratic, a form of left-wing liberalism, an effort to 'reform or manage' capitalism, mitigating its worst features while obscuring its essential traits, and resting 'its faith on the development of productive capacities and the progressive and continuous evolution of political forms'.[14]

From an oddly parallel liberal standpoint, Macpherson's project of breaking with liberalism's market assumptions while retrieving its ethical core may be judged to be unrealistic, on the argument either that the former are ineliminable, applying to all advanced or all non-stagnant, growth-oriented societies, or that the former are inseparable from the latter or that there is, indeed, no conflict between them, since 'self-development' is compatible with, indeed may essentially require, market incentives and competitive striving. Thus many contemporary liberal thinkers, among them John Rawls and Robert Nozick, argue (in different ways) for *both* a market system based on incentives and a Humboldtian/Millian vision of the maximal development of human individuality.[15] At issue here, between Macpherson and such thinkers, may be an account of what constitutes human fulfilment, or of the conditions under which it may be approximated, or both.

Neither of these criticisms of Macpherson's project seems compelling to me. On the contrary, I take it to be a project that is of the greatest interest and importance, above all at a time when the advanced capitalist states are undergoing a cumulative 'legitimation crisis',[16] and the issues of the limits of the state's intervention in the economy, of the costs of growth and of market morality, and of

---

[14] Andrew Levine, 'The Political Theory of Social Democracy', *Canadian Journal of Philosophy*, 6/2 (June 1976), esp. pp. 191–3.

[15] See Rawls, *A Theory of Justice* (Oxford: Clarendon Press, 1972), pp. 523–5; Nozick, *Anarchy, State and Utopia* (Oxford: Blackwell, 1974), pt. III.

[16] See Habermas, *Legitimation Crisis*, trans. T. McCarthy (Boston: Beacon Press; London: Heinemann Educational, 1976); James O'Connor, *The Fiscal Crisis of the State* (New York: St Martin's Press, 1973), and the writings of Claus Offe.

forms of widening democratic participation are on the agenda of public debate.[17] Indeed, it is especially relevant to the Mediterranean liberal democracies where 'Eurocommunism' has raised in a new form the whole issue of continuity with liberal democracy in the transition to socialism.[18]

So while endorsing Macpherson's project, I shall rather address a number of problems arising out of his execution of it. I shall say nothing about its first component. Here his achievement has been the most considerable and the most effective, especially his brilliant interpretation of the seventeenth-century roots of market theory. Of course, all kinds of questions can be, and have been, raised with respect to his controversial interpretations of Hobbes, Locke, the Levellers, Bentham, the Mills, and so on, but I shall not be concerned with such questions here.

As for the second component, his view of the 'real world of democracy' does raise a number of problems, chief among them the following. His account is in terms of the 'justifying theories' of liberal, communist, and third-world democracy, seen as ideological contenders on the world stage—'three concepts of democracy actively at work in the world today', none of which can realistically be claimed to be 'the only true democracy' and each of which is claimed by its adherents to be superior.[19] But he does not attempt, in relation to the latter two kinds, any analysis of the relation between theory and practice, concept and reality. Thus liberal democracy gets

[17] See Michael Best and William Connolly, *The Politicized Economy* (Lexington, Mas.: D. C. Heath, 1976).

[18] To which one might add today (1990) that the post-Communist societies of Eastern Europe face, or will face, issues to which Macpherson's project is relevant, as they (re)introduce the market while simultaneously seeking to (re-)establish liberal democracy.

[19] Macpherson, *The Real World of Democracy* (New York and Oxford: Oxford Univ. Press, 1966), pp. 58, 35, 36–7. Macpherson does not come clean as to how much of a moral/political relativist he is. Are these concepts incommensurable, such that there are no common standards to which they appeal; or are they competitors in the same race? He suggests the latter when he describes them as sharing 'the same ultimate moral end'—'to provide the conditions for the full and free development of the essential human capacities of all the members of society'—but differing 'as to what conditions are needed, and as to how they must move to achieve those conditions' (p. 37). But this argument would be undercut if the contending concepts of democracy involved different accounts of what *constitutes* 'the full and free development of the essential human capacities'. Macpherson appears to believe that there is one and only one correct account, but he offers no argument to support this belief.

bad marks for failing to live up to its values, being tied to 'an inherently unequal market economy',[20] but the other two are not marked at all, but treated rather as alternative concepts 'prevailing' elsewhere,[21] as though theory adequately described reality. Not only does this approach ignore the extent to which societies of these kinds fail by their own standards (and the structural reasons for this) but it also precludes consideration of the extent to which there are shared common standards by which all three systems may be judged.

It is, perhaps, for this reason that Macpherson can say of communist states that they could plausibly claim to be democratic in the 'broader sense' that contains 'an ideal of human equality' which 'could only be fully realised in a society where no class was able to dominate or live at the expense of others', since although there is an 'absence or severe restriction of civil and political liberties', there is, according to the 'socialist model' [sic], no 'transfer of powers from some men to others for the benefit of the others'.[22] And perhaps it is for the same reason that he can characterize 'newly independent underdeveloped countries' (in the mid-1960s) as examples of a single type, whose democratic doctrine invokes 'the will of an undifferentiated people as the only legitimate source of political power' and in which 'there are few or no exploitative class divisions once the foreign rule has been ended', since, with a few exceptions (such as the Congo and Vietnam) 'the independence movement has expelled the foreigners decisively enough that the class analysis is inapplicable'.[23]

These judgements are, to say the very least, not very persuasive and accordingly they have the effect of weakening an analysis that purports to be of 'the real world'. According to that analysis, 'societies that have rejected the capitalist system' (the communist and newly independent underdeveloped countries) have the (inherent) 'moral advantage' of not diminishing 'any man's satisfaction by a compulsive transfer of part of his powers to others for the benefit of others' and the (temporary) 'moral disadvantage' of not providing the same civil and political liberties—which, however, they 'have every reason to introduce . . . as soon as they can afford them'[24]

[20] Id., 'The False Roots', p. 19.

[21] e.g., id., *Real World*, pp. 35–6.

[22] Ibid. 22; id., *Democratic Theory*, pp. 14–15.

[23] Id., *Real World*, pp. 23, 29, 31, 32. Macpherson here appears to deny the reality of 'neo-colonialism', 'dependency', 'unequal development', the role of 'national bourgeoisies', etc., on which there is by now a vast literature.

[24] Ibid. 66.

(their non-introduction presumably being explained by low productivity). Such a balance-sheet could only begin to be convincing after a full description of the actual moral record of the societies in question, an attempt to explain their failures (indicating to what extent these are structural and inherent), and a clear statement of the standards against which they are being judged.

On the other hand, Macpherson does give us a highly suggestive sketch of this kind with respect to liberal democracy, from which he concludes that it has a poor record when measured against its own ethical and humanist ideals by virtue of its class division and in particular of 'scarcity and the extractive market situation that have made people behave atomistically'.[25] To the extent to which these features are removed, he argues, a non-market and egalitarian form of liberal democracy becomes possible.

This raises the central problem of the third component of Macpherson's project: what socialists traditionally call 'the problem of the transition'. This is, of course, not just Macpherson's problem. But his formulations raise a number of specific problems to which I shall merely allude here. Does 'the prospective conquest of scarcity',[26] which is the precondition for the transition, imply a no-growth society? If so, is it realistic in the context of the contemporary international economy, and, if it is, does not ideal democracy then become the privilege of the affluent in a highly unequal world? What, in the transition, is the role of class-based politics and class struggle? Which social or political forces are progressive and democratic, in Macpherson's sense of moving towards the abandonment of the (capitalist?) market?

More generally, what, in the transition, is the relation between a change in consciousness and political action? In 1965, Macpherson argued, with respect to communist societies, that

[p]eople who have been debased by their society cannot be morally regenerated except by the society being reformed, and this requires political power ... there is no use relying on the free votes of everybody to bring about a fully human society. If it is not done by a vanguard it will not be done at all.[27]

25 Macpherson, 'Individualist Socialism?' p. 199.
26 Id., *Democratic Theory*, pp. 22–3.
27 Id., *Real World*, pp. 19–20.

In 1977, with respect to liberal democracies, he wrote of a kind of dialectic between changes in consciousness and increasing democratic participation—finding the possible 'loopholes' in the 'vicious circle' which links consumer consciousness, social inequality, and low participation (such weak points including the increasing awareness of the costs of economic growth, and of the costs of political apathy, in local communities and at the work-place, and increasing doubts about the ability of corporate capitalism to meet consumer expectations while reproducing inequality).[28] A crucial question, to which we need an answer, is why the 1965 answer should not apply to liberal democracies (especially since Macpherson holds that in them individuals are 'culturally conditioned to think of themselves as infinite consumers'[29] and are thus, presumably, 'debased by their society') or, for that matter, why the 1977 answer, or some version of it, should not apply to non-liberal democracies. Needless to say, such questions are of the greatest contemporary moment, and it is a virtue of Macpherson's work that it raises them in an acute form.

It is with Macpherson's attempt at the fourth component of his grand project—to develop a 'non-market theory' of liberal democracy—that the remainder of this chapter will be concerned. To anticipate, my argument will be that this attempt is successful in separating out the developmental from the possessive elements of liberal individualism but that it fails in so far as it does not carry the argument through to the criticism of that very individualism itself.

It is probable, Macpherson argues, that 'the continuance of Western societies combining individual liberties and democratic rights depends on those societies providing their members with an equal right to realise their essence as exerters, enjoyers and developers of their individual human capacities'.[30] Thus his theory of ideal democracy invokes an 'ontological' view of man's 'essence', and, in particular, the supersession of one such view by another:[31] 'the postulate of man as essentially consumer and appropriator' must be superseded by the 'concept of man as essentially an exerter and enjoyer of his own powers'.[32] Or, in another formulation, it must be realized that 'man's essence is not maximisation of his utilities but

---

[28] See Id., *Life and Times*, p. 106.
[29] Id., *Democratic Theory*, p. 62.
[30] Ibid. 36.   [31] Ibid. chap. II.   [32] Ibid. 37, 32.

maximisation of his human powers'.[33] How, then, does Macpherson conceive of these powers and how are they to be maximized?

In earlier formulations, he writes of the 'ethical' concept of a man's powers as signifying 'a potential for realising some human end' and necessarily including 'not only his natural capacities (his energy and skill) but also his *ability* to exert them'.[34] In a later, and clearer, formulation, he speaks rather of the 'developmental concept of power' (in the singular) as signifying 'a man's ability to use and develop his capacities'.[35] The amount of a man's power 'always depends on his access to the means of exerting his actual capacities' and is to be 'measured in terms of the *absence of impediments* to his using his human capacities'. In short, 'a man's power, defined as the quantity of his ability to use and develop his human capacities, is measured by the quantity of external impediments to that ability'. The amount of a man's abilities, he writes, 'depends on present external impediments'; the amount of his capacities 'on innate endowment and past external impediments'.[36]

Thus 'ability' is seen as the absence of 'external' impediments (and might, therefore, more naturally be called 'opportunity'; we will, however, stick to Macpherson's usage). 'Capacities', by contrast, appear to signify an 'inner' potential, which may or may not be externally blocked. This distinction between 'external' and 'internal' is problematic: how it is drawn depends on how the 'individual' is conceptualized, where the boundaries of the agent's self are taken to lie, what he may be taken, and take himself, to have internalized.[37] For example, are moral or legal obligations, or the requirements of loyalty, say, to an individual or a group or an institution, or the cultural imperatives of the 'success ethic' to be counted as 'external' or 'internal'? It is true that, in one lonely paragraph, Macpherson acknowledges that 'society' is not 'only an impeding agent' but also 'a positive agent in the development of capacities', a 'medium' and a 'necessary condition' of their development.[38] But this acknowledgment does not extend to his seeing social relations as in part constitutive of the identity of the individual, which is, accordingly, transformed as those relations change. It is just because, on the

---

[33] Macpherson, *Democratic Theory*, p. 32.
[34] Ibid. 9.   [35] Ibid. 42.   [36] Ibid. 40, 58, 71, 52.
[37] See the essay 'Power and Structure' in my *Essays in Social Theory* (London: Macmillan, and New York: Columbia Univ. Press, 1977), and also Joel Feinberg, *Social Philosophy* (Englewood Cliffs, NJ: Prentice-Hall, 1973), chap. 1, esp. pp. 12–13.   [38] Id., *Democratic Theory*, p. 57.

contrary, he sees the individual ('man') abstractly as an atom whose nature ('capacities') is independent of the relations in which he is involved, that he can suppose his capacities and his ability to be separately identifiable (indeed measurable) and independently generated. If, however, the nature and identity of the individual is, even partly, determined by his social relations, then these will also play a role in determining both his potentialities and the impediments to their realization.

We have seen that Macpherson, in explication of his central concept of 'developmental power', whose maximization is to be the touchstone of a future liberal democratic system, uses three inter-related notions: *ability*, *impediments*, and *capacities*. Let us look at them more closely.

Let us begin with 'capacities'. These are described variously as 'natural', 'human', and—most often—'essentially human'. At one point, they are classified as 'rational, moral, aesthetic, emotional, and productive in the broadest sense'.[39] Somewhat more specifically, he writes that they may 'be taken to include the capacity for rational understanding, for moral judgment and action, for aesthetic creation or contemplation, for the emotional activities of friendship and love, and, sometimes, for religious experience', and also 'for transforming what is given by Nature' (in a sense broader than 'the capacity for materially productive labour'), 'for wonder or curiosity', 'for laughter', and 'for controlled physical/mental/aesthetic activity, as expressed for instance in making music and in playing games of skill'.[40]

While acknowledging that the essentially human capacities 'might be variously listed', and that 'such a list could be extended and rearranged in many ways', and whether they are 'attributed to divine creation, or to some evolutionary development of more complex organisms', he takes their existence to be a 'basic postulate' which is both 'empirical', 'verifiable in a broad way by observation', and 'a value postulate, in the sense that rights and obligations can be derived from it without any additional value premise, since the very structure of our thought and language puts an evaluative content into our descriptive statements about "man"'.[41] That postulate is, as we have seen, the 'view of man's essence not as a consumer of utilities but as a doer, a creator, an enjoyer of his human attributes'[42]—such attributes consisting in the capacities listed above.

---

[39] Ibid. 61–2.   [40] Ibid. 4, 54.   [41] Ibid. 53–4.   [42] Ibid. 4.

Various perplexing problems arise here. Take, in the first place, the capacities listed. To suppose that, as characterized, they are sufficiently determinate for their degree of realization, and thus their maximization, to be specified is to beg a set of crucial questions. For people widely disagree about what *constitutes* 'rational understanding', 'moral judgment and action', 'aesthetic creation and contemplation', true 'religious experience', and so on. (Thus liberals and Marxists disagree with one another, and among themselves, about how rationally to explain their social world; utilitarians, contractarians, intuitionists, and perfectionists give conflicting accounts of morality; proponents of high and low culture disagree about the nature of art; adherents of different religions notoriously disagree about the nature of religion, etc.) To label human capacities by reference to their achievement is either to leave their nature indeterminate or to suppose such contested questions resolved in one way rather than another, which, to say the least, requires argument, and is question-begging, since alternative answers may be tied to alternative theories of human nature. Furthermore, history, especially recent history, gives some chilling lessons concerning the dangers to a liberal society, let alone liberal democracy, of a society's supposing such questions to be authoritatively resolved.

In the second place, one may ask, why *this* list? What, for example, of the human capacities for consumption and acquisition, for emulation and competition, for status-ranking, for domination and subjection, for the infliction and the acceptance of suffering, or indeed for malevolence, cunning, degradation, destructiveness, and brutality of all conceivable kinds? What principles govern the selection of Macpherson's (admittedly vaguely specified) list? Is his argument not really a way of endorsing certain forms of life by dignifying them, without warrant, as uniquely realizing 'essentially human capacities'?

This question cannot be resolved, as Macpherson suggests, empirically ('by observation') since the capacities I have mentioned, and doubtless many others, are indubitably characteristic of humans, even 'essential' to them—and not obviously less in evidence than those on Macpherson's list. Moreover, they are often held to justify forms of social and political life that he would reject, and some of which he would abhor. Nor will it resolve the question to appeal to 'the very structure of our thought and language', since 'we' differ about human nature and what is essential to it, and some—from

Plato and St Augustine to de Maistre, Nietzsche, and Dostoevsky's Grand Inquisitor, not to mention Locke and Bentham—have asserted very different basic postulates and drawn very different social and political conclusions. Furthermore they have, in general, assumed that the social and political problem is not to maximize human capacities but rather to minimize the harmful consequences of their exercise.

This difficulty, of establishing a determinate set of 'essentially human capacities' as the basis for a justificatory theory of democracy, is only rendered more acute by a further assumption Macpherson makes, which he admits to be 'at first sight . . . a staggering one': namely, the 'postulate of the non-opposition of essentially human capacities'.[43] The case for a democratic society, he argues, fails without this assumption. A 'fully democratic society is only possible when both genuine and contrived scarcity have been overcome'; then 'the essential human capacities may all be used and developed without hindering the use and development of all the rest'.[44] But surely this assumption is pretty staggering at second and third sight too. For why should we suppose that there ever could be a society in which 'rational, moral, aesthetic, emotional and productive' activities and relations would not be subject to regulation, limitation, and mutual adjustment, in the light of principles of justice, rendered necessary by conflicting claims and interests? To reply, as Macpherson might, that such regulation and limitation could never constitute a diminution of human capacities, if it were just—according, perhaps, to rules 'that can be rationally demonstrated to be necessary to society, and so to [man's] humanity'[45]—is, once more, to beg the question. For such a reply would, once more, build a particular moral vision into the notion of 'essentially human capacities'.

What we have so far shown is that Macpherson's 'essentially human capacities', with respect both to their content and their selection, presuppose, rather than ground, a particular moral theory. In the absence of any transcendental or quasi-transcendental argument to the contrary (à la Kant or Rawls or Habermas) such a conclusion is inescapable. And indeed, of course, Macpherson appeals to such a moral theory—which, he claims, derives from 'Western humanist and Christian traditions that go back to the

---

[43] Macpherson, *Democratic Theory*, p. 55. [44] Ibid. 55, 54.
[45] Ibid. 56.

Greeks and to medieval natural law' and which he invokes by
speaking of 'the *equal* right of every man to make the best of
himself'.[46] This is basically a form of individual moral perfectionism.
For Macpherson's argument to stick, such a theory must play the role
of specifying ideal possibilities whose realization is blocked by actual
social and political arrangements and to whose realization social and
political action is to be directed. But, unfortunately, Macpherson
says very little about how such possibilities *are* to be specified—what
constitutes human excellence and, most importantly, what forms of
social life or what sorts of social, cultural, and institutional activities
and relationships would enable it to flourish, indeed *constitute* its
flourishing. In the absence of such specification, we simply have the
promise of an abstract, anti-utilitarian, individualistic moral perfectionism, formulated in the language of man's essentially human
capacities.

To all this, Macpherson might reply that one must start at the
other end: we 'must start', he writes, 'from the hindrances' or
'impediments' to the realization of such counterfactual, ideal
possibilities.[47] Thus his analysis 'concentrates on the hindrances in
modern market societies . . . because this is what requires most
analysis if we are to find a way through from a liberal market society
to a fully democratic society'. A 'social and political theory can only
be concerned with impediments that are socially variable', as
opposed to 'physical impediments which cannot be altered by any
action of society'; moreover, he focuses on *external* rather than
'internalised' impediments on the arguments, first, that the latter
were external before they were internalized, and, second, that they
are 'analytically more manageable'; besides, they interact with internal ones, each reciprocally reinforcing the other, but, conversely, a
rational analysis of external impediments may contribute 'to the
breakthrough of consciousness, and so to a cumulative reciprocal
reduction of both kinds of impediment, and a cumulative realisation
of democracy'.[48] Accordingly, the following impediments are 'de-
duced from the human condition': 'lack of adequate means of life',
'lack of access to the means of labour', and 'lack of protection against
invasion by others'.[49]

The great virtue of this position is that, under the first two

---

[46] Macpherson, *Democratic Theory*, pp. 32, 21.   [47] Ibid. 57.
[48] Ibid. 57, 59, 76.   [49] Ibid. 59 and 60 *ff.*

headings, it considers constraints or restrictions on liberty which most liberal theorists systematically ignore, and in particular the restrictions upon choice implicit in the manipulation of demand and in the consequences of material inequality, especially of the ownership of property. However, once one leaves the more obvious forms of deprivation (e.g., poverty or unemployment), the specification of 'impediments' becomes more problematic. Macpherson's key idea is that non-ownership of—or the lack of free access to—'materials to work on or work with' (land and, more particularly, capital) constitutes such an impediment, diminishing non-owners' powers since they have to 'pay for the access with a transfer of part of their powers'.[50]

This argument will only really carry conviction when supplemented by a specification of the precluded possibilities that non-ownership impedes (which would, I believe, show that non-ownership is not the only way of denying access to the means of labour). Only then can a satisfactory argument be mounted against those who claim that the market and private property are not impediments to but rather conditions of the liberation of human possibilities. What is missing, in other words, is a detailed demonstration of what desirable and possible forms of relationship and activity are blocked by the central institutions of capitalism. In its place we have an abstract argument, purporting to show that, because these institutions involve 'a continuous transfer of power' between 'non-owners and owners of the means of labour',[51] they impede the maximization of (abstract) individuals' (unspecified) powers.

This, however, points to a deeper difficulty still. The 'maximization of powers' is the maximization of individuals' 'ability' to use and develop their human capacities, as measured by the impediments to their doing so. It therefore amounts, formally speaking, to a set of counterfactuals which specify what individuals could attain but for specified present preventing causes. But how are these counterfactuals to be specified?[52] How distant is the possible world we must imagine from the actual world? (Of course, the more distant it is, the greater the scope and complexity of the impediments or preventing

[50] Ibid. 64.   [51] Ibid. 65.
[52] On this problem, see the recent brilliant book by Jon Elster, *Logic and Society: Contradictions and Possible Worlds* (Chichester and New York: Wiley, 1978), and my 'Power and Structure'.

causes.) In other words, how much of the actual world are we to take as given in setting up the counterfactuals? Or, in yet other words, what do we hold constant in comparing the actual with the possible? In particular, do we hold the very individuals, the maximization of whose abilities (power) is in question, to be constant, or themselves subject to transformation, and, if so, to what extent? *Which* individuals' powers are to be maximized: present, actual individuals or future, 'morally regenerated' ones?

Sometimes, Macpherson speaks of the counterfactual 'standard by which the theory must judge the democratic quality of any society' as 'the presently attainable maximum (i.e., the maximum level of abilities to use and develop human capacities given the presently possible human command over external Nature)' and of those capacities as being 'actual capacities'.[53] Elsewhere, however, he stresses that it is not enough 'to claim only to maximize the use of each man's present capacities': to maximize men's powers is 'to maximize the future development, as well as the present use, of each man's capacities', including 'those whose capacities had been stunted by external impediments'.[54] Such fully developed capacities can be conceived as a quantity, being 'the *amount* of [a man's] combined and co-ordinated mental, physical and psychic equipment, whether as it actually exists at a given time or as it might exist at some later time or under certain different conditions.'[55] But the whole problem lies here. For what *are* these different conditions? Do they include the 'regeneration' of the individuals concerned, their reshaping or 're-education', and, if so, to what degree? How is the line to be drawn between developing an individual's capacities and changing that individual?

What I hope to have shown is that Macpherson's account of human powers raises the following crucial and difficult questions. First, the 'essentially human capacities' rely for their specification upon an abstract, individualist ethical perfectionism, not yet spelled out. Second, the impediments to their use and development remain indeterminate, as long as those capacities and the forms of social life

---

[53] Macpherson, *Democratic Theory*, pp. 58, 40.

[54] Ibid. 57.

[55] Ibid. 56. Thus, he even writes that 'the full development of human capacities, as envisioned in the liberal-democratic concept of man—at least in its more optimistic version—is infinitely great. No inherent limit is seen to the extent to which men's human capacities may be enlarged' (p. 62).

which both enable and constitute their realization remain unspecified. And third, the ability to realize them, whose maximization is the criterion of liberal democracy, is therefore indeterminate for these reasons, and for the further decisive reason that the (abstract) individuals, whose powers are to be maximized, are likewise indeterminate.

The great merit of Macpherson's liberal democratic theory is that it brings back into prominence the critical developmental perspective of the ethical and humanist side of liberalism and that it brings, from Marxist theory, a sharp awareness of the structural and institutional obstacles, within capitalism, to human emancipation. It has nothing to say about the nature of such obstacles in non-capitalist societies and it is (understandably) indecisive concerning the possible mode of transition from a capitalist to a post-capitalist form of liberal democracy.

However, it remains at an inappropriate level of abstraction and thereby bears the stamp of the liberal individualism it so acutely criticizes. Individuals and their powers and capacities are conceived in abstraction from the social relations and forms of community which, on the one hand, impede and, on the other, facilitate and constitute their further development. By reasoning exclusively in terms of man and the individual, Macpherson retains too much of the abstract humanism for which Marx criticized Feuerbach.[56] Social relations structure human activities and potentialities, which cannot be conceived independently of them, and this applies both to actual and to possible societies. Any fully developed democratic theory must get into the detailed business of comparing the actual and possible structures of living which are implicit in contemporary political struggle and debate. In short, for Macpherson's great project of retrieving liberal-democratic theory from the possessive individualism of the liberal tradition to be carried through to its conclusion, his penetrating critique of its possessiveness must be completed by an abandonment of its individualism.

---

[56] As Marx wrote in his sixth thesis on Feuerbach, 'the essence of *man* is no abstraction inherent in each separate individual. In its reality it is the *ensemble* of social relations'.

13

Alasdair MacIntyre: The Sociologist versus the Philosopher

I. In a New Dark Age?

When values conflict, what is to be done? According to Max Weber, 'the ultimately possible attitudes towards life are irreconcilable and hence their struggle can never be brought to a final conclusion'. Reason is helpless here. Compare the Sermon on the Mount with the ethic of manly conduct. Or take MacIntyre's examples of conflicting prevalent views about whether modern wars can be just, whether abortion should be permitted, whether justice requires more or less government regulation and redistribution, and whether it favours claims based on acquisition and entitlement or claims based on need. 'According to our ultimate standpoint', Weber wrote, 'the one is the devil and the other the God, and the individual has to decide which is God for him, and which is the devil. And so it goes throughout all the orders of life'.

This answer, and the whole world view from which it stems, is anathema to the author of this exhilarating and richly rewarding book.[1] In rejecting Weber, and behind him Nietzsche, he mounts a full-scale argument against a whole range of linked contemporary doctrines. In particular, he attacks emotivism (the view that all value judgements are just expressions of preference) which he sees as 'embodied in our culture', and its corollary that there are no objective and impersonal moral standards, as well as the conception of an irreducible plurality of incommensurable values, and the modern liberal view that government and law should be neutral between rival conceptions of the good life. He criticizes the conception of rationality as attaching only to means (ends being individually chosen and

This chapter was first published as two book reviews, one in 1981, the other in 1988.

[1] Alasdair MacIntyre, *After Virtue: A Study in Moral Theory* (London: Duckworth, 1981).

without rational grounding), a view exemplified by social scientists' spurious claims to expertise and the practices of bureaucracies; and also the modern individualist conception of the self, 'abstract and ghostly', distinct from its 'social embodiments', roles and contexts, making choices without criteria, and the associated philosophical concept of the autonomous moral subject in which individuals are primary and society secondary, and 'the identification of individual interests as prior to, and independent of, the construction of any moral or social bonds between them'.

What, then, is the nature of the argument, where does it lead, and is it convincing?

It is at once philosophical and sociological, for MacIntyre holds that no 'adequate philosophical analysis in this area could escape being also a sociological hypothesis, and *vice versa*', since 'we have not yet fully understood the claims of any moral philosophy until we have spelled out what its social embodiment would be'. It is also historical, exploiting classical scholarship and literary criticism through a series of sketches (of Homeric Greece, of Athenian Society and the plays of Sophocles, of medieval conflicts, of Benjamin Franklin and Jane Austen) that tell an overall story of a great moral transformation—a transformation in the meaning of moral concepts and their place in social life: these 'were originally at home in larger totalities of theory and practice in which they enjoyed a role and function supplied by contexts of which they have now been deprived'. In particular, virtue-concepts have 'become as marginal to the moral philosopher as they are to the morality of the society which he inhabits' and 'modern moral utterance and practice can only be understood as a series of fragmented survivals from an older past'.

In the earlier stages of the story—in Homeric Greece, Athens, and medieval Europe

evaluative and especially moral theory and practice embody genuine objective and impersonal standards which provide rational justification for particular policies, actions and judgements and which themselves in turn are susceptible of rational justification.

Both the *polis* and the medieval kingdom are conceived as 'communities in which men in company pursue the human good and not merely as—what the modern liberal state takes itself to be—providing the arena in which each individual seeks his or her own private good'. In such pre-modern societies,

> the individual is identified and constituted in and through certain of his or her roles, those roles which bind the individual to the communities in and through which alone specifically human goods are to be attained; I confront the world as a member of this family, this household, this clan, this tribe, this city, this nation, this kingdom. There is no 'I' apart from these.

In such contexts, the virtues have a central place: they are a crucial component (or as MacIntyre says, *internal* to) the goods men seek—sustaining the relationships necessary to their achievement, the individual's pursuit of the good as a whole life's project or quest, and the historical traditions that such relationships and pursuits embody. MacIntyre draws distinctions between the unreflective and role-centred virtues of Homeric and other heroic societies, the more complex Athenian view, allowing for (limited) questioning and tragic conflicts of good with good, the Aristotelian stress on the unity of the virtues and on a specifically human *telos*, or end, and the medieval, Christian stress on the fact of evil and the quest for ultimate redemption in a community of reconciliation (Aquinas seeking to unite the last two). He notices (if too briefly) their different catalogues and conceptions of the virtues. But from all this he derives a 'partial account of a core conception of the virtues'— incorporating truthfulness, justice, and courage—which are basic to any common pursuit of the good, 'in the light of which we have to characterise ourselves and others, whatever our private moral stand-point or our society's particular moral codes may be'.

The later stages of MacIntyre's story trace the gradual disintegration of these virtue-centred moralities, whose quintessential exponent was Aristotle. They were repudiated, with the rise of science and the rejection of teleology, between the fifteenth and seventeenth centuries, thereby leading to the Enlightenment project of discovering rational secular foundations for morality. But, says MacIntyre, that project—in the hands of Smith, Hume, Diderot, and, above all, Kant—had to fail, because 'moral judgements are linguistic survivals from the practices of classical theism which have lost the context provided by these practices'. Both the proper ends of man and the laws of God disappear from the scene. The meaning of moral and other evaluative expression changes. Now what are called statements of 'fact' cannot entail what are taken to be 'evaluative' or 'moral' conclusions and moral controversies become unsettlable.

The breakdown of this Enlightenment project, MacIntyre claims, 'provided the historical background against which the predicaments of our own culture can become intelligible'. Once the modern world has repudiated the moral traditions of whch Aristotle's thought was the intellectual core, all subsequent attempts by moral philosophers to provide some alternative rational secular account of the nature and status of morality have failed, and must do so, as Nietzsche saw. Our moral language and practice are in 'grave disorder' arising from

the prevailing cultural power of an idiom in which ill-assorted conceptual fragments from various parts of our past are deployed together in private and public debates which are notable chiefly for the unsettlable character of the controversies thus carried on and the apparent arbitrariness of each of the contending parties.

The modern moral culture of liberal individualism (whose central flaws MacIntyre rather implausibly sees Marxism as reproducing) offers no solution to this disorder. It relies on 'pseudo-concepts' and 'moral fictions', such as 'utility' and 'natural or human rights': belief in them, he says, 'is one with belief in witches and unicorns'. It has little place for 'any conception of society as a community united in a shared vision of the good for man (as prior to and independent of any summing of individual interests) and a *consequent* shared practice of the virtues'. It can issue in no agreement upon any catalogue of these or indeed upon their fundamental importance. Modern politics is 'civil war carried on by other means' and government 'a set of institutional arrangements for imposing a bureaucratised unity on a society which lacks genuine moral consensus'. From an Aristotelian point of view (which is of course MacIntyre's),

a modern liberal society can appear only as a collection of citizens of nowhere who have banded together for their mutual protection . . . They have abandoned the moral unity of Aristotelianism, whether in its ancient or medieval forms.

This, then, is where the argument has led: to an embracing of Aristotle as against Nietzsche and Weber. 'The Weberian view of the world', he writes, 'cannot be rationally sustained; it disguises and conceals rather than illuminates and it depends for its power on its success at disguise and concealment.' Only by adopting a modified Aristotelian view, MacIntyre argues—a 'socially teleological account' which, however, does not rely on Aristotle's metaphysical biology and allows for tragic conflicts of good with good—can we adequately understand where we have got to and how we got there. We will then see the universalism and individualism of modern culture as 'a degeneration, a grave cultural loss', as the modern self 'in acquiring sovereignty in its own realm lost its traditional boundaries provided by a social identity and a view of human life as ordered to a given end'. We will see that all political traditions in our culture, including Marxism, are exhausted and that we are 'in a state so disastrous that there are no large remedies'. What, then, is to be done? On his last page, MacIntyre answers: engage in 'the construction of local forms of community within which civility and the intellectual and moral life can be sustained through the new dark ages which are already upon us.'

Is this argument convincing? Is its account of the Great Transformation as a 'scheme of moral decline', its critique of the central culture of liberal and bureaucratic individualism, its defence of 'the lost morality of the past', and its catalogue of core virtues and human goods rationally compelling?

To ask this question is to reveal a deep inconsistency at its heart. For MacIntyre the sociologist of morals, the 'lost morality of the past', rooted in 'local particularity and community', claiming 'objectivity and authority', licensing the derivation of moral conclusions from factual claims, presupposing a fully social self, is genuinely *lost*: as he says, the possibility of the rational justification it provided 'is no longer available'. Conversely, the universalizing and individualist morality of the present, with its value pluralism, fact-value distinction and autonomous choosing self is, for us, inescapable. How then can MacIntyre the philosopher *appeal* to the 'genuine objective and impersonal standards' embodied in the former, to its denial of the fact-value distinction and its social view of the self to back his critique of the modern ethos? For according to that ethos, these are claims internal to one moral view that have no rationally compelling power.

Not only is the argument inconsistent; it is also circular. How can he justify *choosing* Aristotle against Nietzsche other than by criteria furnished by Aristotle and unmasked by Nietzsche? What justifies his account and catalogue of the virtues if not evaluations deriving from a lost teleological morality of virtue? Why are 'utility' and 'rights' moral fictions but not the human *telos* and the 'common good'? In short, his argument assumes the truth of his conclusions.

He promises in a future volume to provide a systematic account of rationality, which might rebut these charges. In advance of that, one can only say that this argument for an objective and impersonal ethics—like all the others he finds wanting—also fails to carry conviction. It is, however, fresh, original, and full of incidental insights, though it gets fast and loose when the going gets rough; and it includes a striking discussion of the limited role of generalizations in the social sciences that makes a real and important contribution to the philosophy of social science. This is unquestionably one of the most lively, interesting, and provocative books in social theory to have appeared for at least a decade. If it does not displace Weber's answer, it sheds floods of light on the question.

II. The Way Out, or Back?

After Virtue proclaimed, not without satisfaction, that 'we still, in spite of the efforts of three centuries of moral philosophy and one of sociology, lack any coherent rationally defensible statement of a liberal individualist point of view'. It also offered a promise: that 'the Aristotelian position can be restated in a way that restores rationality and intelligibility to our own moral and social attitudes and commitments.' To redeem that promise, MacIntyre made another: to write a book that would offer an accont of what it is to be rational that would both support his restatement of Aristotelianism and justify that support. This is that book.[2]

The trouble with the argument of *After Virtue* was that it was caught in a dilemma. On the one hand, MacIntyre the sociologist of morals offered a compelling account of the fragmented moral world of modernity, riven by unsettlable moral conflicts, speaking an impoverished moral vocabulary, inhabited by rootless and homeless individuals, capable of distancing themselves from their various roles and of making moral choices and decisions on the basis of their 'preferences' and 'values'. On the other hand, MacIntyre the moral philosopher purported to recommend a return to a world we have lost, located in an idealized Greek past, in which there was moral

---

[2] *Whose Justice? Which Rationality?* (London: Duckworth, 1988).

unity, a rich and thick vocabulary of role-centred virtues, where the individual was fully constituted by his place in the social order, where the agonies of moral choice and decision, and indeed moral uncertainty, were unknown because practical rationality came naturally to everyone aware of the requirements of his station and its duties.

But if the sociologist were right, the philosopher could make no such case: 'we' cannot become, in the relevant respects, 'pre-modern'. As Bernard Williams has put it, there is no route back from reflection.

Does *Whose Justice? Which Rationality?* show the way out, or back? Far from it. Indeed, it only sharpens the dilemma by offering an account of rationality, as tradition-bound, which itself only serves to reinforce the inaccessibility to post-Enlightenment thought of the very case MacIntyre seeks to make. The thinkers of the Enlightnment and their successors, he writes, 'proved unable to agree as to what precisely those principles were which would be found undeniable by all rational persons.' Consequently, 'the legacy of the Enlightenment has been the provision of an ideal of rational justification which it has proved impossible to attain.'

MacIntyre's solution to this typically modern problem is to extol the virtues of pre-modern societies in which 'there was and is a common stock of beliefs whose expression in language was and is treated as the utterance of evident truth', of the polis as the 'locus of rationality because it embodied the idea of the "good" and the "best" and enabled systematic forms of activity to be "unambiguously ordered" and individuals to "occupy and move between well-defined roles'. In such a world, as Aristotle showed, 'the apparent and tragic conflict of right with right' arises from the inadequacies of reason, not from the character of moral reality.

The case is made no more persuasive by the fact that MacIntyre loads the dice throughout. He is consistently charitable towards Plato, Aristotle, Augustine, Aquinas, and Hutcheson but unrelentingly hostile, above all, to Hume and to modern liberalism generally. Thus Aristotle's justification of slavery and his exclusion of women from citizenship are (plausibly) claimed to be excisable from his thought while leaving his central argument intact; yet Hume is described as 'articulating the principles of the dominant English social and cultural order', an order itself deeply inhospitable to philosophy. Of modern liberalism he has much of interest and depth to say, not least about its conception of 'the individual', but it is uniformly negative, or at least intended to be so.

Liberalism, too, is a tradition; though, unlike the congregations of evangelical fundamentalists, it does not recognize that it too is a 'community of pre-rational faith', whose 'parish magazine' is the *New York Times*. This is read by the 'affluent and self-congratulatory liberal establishment', whose clergy are the lawyers, and is insensitive to the cultural depth of traditions. Hence

the confident teaching of texts from past and alien cultures in translation not only to students who do not know the original languages but by teachers who do not know them either; the conducting of negotiations, commercial, political and military, by those who suppose that not knowing each other's languages cannot debar them from understanding each other adequately; and the willingness to allow internationalised versions of such languages as English, Spanish and Chinese to displace both the languages of minority cultures and those variants of themselves which are local, dialectical languages in use.

Most seriously, MacIntyre's very account of rationality, which after all is the book's central theme, is (and makes a virtue of being) question-begging. The book consists of an 'outline narrative history of three traditions of inquiry into what practical rationality is and what justice is, and in addition an acknowledgement of a need for the writing of a fourth history, that of liberalism.' Liberalism, in his account, turns out to be just another tradition which 'does not provide a neutral independent ground from which a verdict may be passed upon the rival claims of conflicting traditions'. But, as he acknowledges, if this is so, it does not follow that there is no such neutral ground. Nor indeed does it follow that, in political and moral argument, we should not aim for such neutrality and for such perspective-independent bases for agreement as can be found, across cultures and traditions.

MacIntyre boldly asserts that there is a 'deep incompatibility' between 'the standpoint of any rational tradition of inquiry', such as he defends, and the dominant modes of contemporary discussion, academic and non-academic, committed to 'the fiction of shared, even if unformulable, universal standards of rationality'. His case, in a nutshell, is that 'progress in rationality is achieved only from a point of view'.

Moreover, 'one's rationality should not be merely supported by but partly constituted by one's membership in and integration into a social institution of some one particular type.' So to be rational is to see the moral world from the right institutional standpoint, and to 'engage in the formulation, elaboration, rational justification and criticism of accounts of practical rationality and justice ... from within some one particular tradition in conversation, cooperation and conflict with those who inhabit the same tradition.'

If any of MacIntyre's readers are persuaded by his arguments, this will, by his own account, be because they are co-inhabitants of his Aristotelian–Augustinian–Thomistic tradition. (They may be old-timers or, like MacIntyre himself, relatively recent immigrants from other quite different traditions.) They will be convinced because, sharing the same history and speaking the same language, they 'have every reason at least so far to hold that the rationality of their tradition has been confirmed in its encounters with other traditions'. The rest of us, *New York Times* or *New Statesman and Society* in hand, may well feel rather left out in the cold.

14
Václav Havel: on 'The Power of the Powerless'

On Freedom and Power is a remarkable collection of essays which has for some time deserved translation and a wider readership for two sorts of reasons. On the one hand, these essays are important historical documents. They are evidence of great interest to the historian and observer of contemporary communism in Czechoslovakia and within the Soviet bloc as a whole. More importantly, they are valuable texts in their own right. They are essays of interpretation, argument, and analysis that shed light not only upon the nature of contemporary communism but, more widely, on some basic political questions that arise in the West no less than in the East. Moreover, they address these questions in a fresh and challenging way.

I

As historical documents, they are to be seen as the product and expression of the Czechoslovak experience of 'real socialism' at a moment when the opposition to it crystallized and coalesced in a peculiarly dramatic way. They represent the first flowering of theoretical reflection on the part of a wide variety of intellectuals in the period between the founding of the Charter in 1977 and the subsequent persecution of its signatories and supporters.

One of the first instances of such reflection was Václav Benda's essay, 'The Parallel Polis' (written in May 1978 and circulated in *samizdat* in Czechoslovakia).[1] This argued powerfully for the

This chapter first appeared in 1985 as the Introduction to Havel's *The Power of the Powerless: Citizens against the State in Central Eastern Europe* (London: Hutchinson, 1985). Most of the quotations in the text are from the essays in that book in which Havel's is the title essay.

[1] Published in English in *Palach Press Bulletin* (London: Palach Press, 1979).

growth of a whole range of 'parallel' cultural, educational, economic, even political structures. Benda sought in this way to transform an 'abstract moral attitude' into a unifying factor and source of
dynamism, which would thus have a field of activity and a positive
goal: the creation of a 'parallel society'. Benda had in mind the
cultural underground, especially rock music (decisive in the very
beginnings of the Charter itself), and graphic art, alternative theat-
rical performances, unofficial publishing, unofficial education, both
for children and adults, parallel information services, the 'creation of
conditions for political discussion and the formulation of political
opinions', a parallel 'foreign policy', and co-operation with parallel
movements inside the eastern bloc. Benda's essay led to much
discussion, some of it continued in these essays.

No less important was Václav Havel's 'The Power of the Powerless'. Like his plays (notably *The Garden Party*, *The Memorandum*,
The Increased Difficulty of Concentration, and *The Interview*), this
gives a striking and penetrating portrayal of the distinctive
bureaucratic structure of domination in eastern Europe today and its
complex roots in, and impact on, the relationships of ordinary life.
Havel's essay made a great impression and formed the centrepiece to
a collection of eighteen essays published in 1979 in *samizdat*.

The 1979 collection, originally entitled *On Freedom and Power*,
was intended as a joint Czechoslovak-Polish venture, the beginnings
of a projected collaboration across frontiers. This project met with
harassment and persecution in Czechoslovakia and, with the rise of
Solidarity in Poland, it assumed different forms. The Poles were from
the start much impressed by what Havel and the other were saying.
For instance, the Warsaw Solidarity leader, Zbygniew Bujak, commented in 1981 that Havel's essay 'gave us theoretical backing, a
theoretical basis for our actions. He enabled us to believe in their
effectiveness. Until I read his text I was full of doubts.'[2] Paradoxic-
ally, at that time (1978–80) there was significantly greater space for
a parallel *polis* and developing the power of the powerless in Poland
than there ever was in Czechoslovakia. Unofficial publishing, for
example, had reached immense proportions and the 'Flying University' was significantly more extensive and organized than the under-
ground 'Patočka University' in Czechoslovakia. More important still
was the growth of independent, 'parallel' unions in the Baltic ports

[2] *Krytyka* 8 (Warsaw, 1981), and repr. in *Aneks* (London, 1982), p. 35.

and the links between intellectuals and workers, notably through the 'Workers' Defence Committee' (*KOR*). One central reason for this difference was, of course, the protective existence, and sometimes assistance, of the Catholic Church in Poland. The Poles, in a sense, saw the Czechoslovaks as helping to develop the theory for their emerging practice—and the debate was continued by Adam Michnik and others in Poland. Most of the essays in *On Freedom and Power* were published in Polish *samizdat* periodicals soon after they were written and they were widely discussed and commented upon. Such comments and responses appeared as individual articles in Polish *samizdat* magazines, not, as originally intended, in a second volume of *On Freedom and Power*. A more active and mutual collaboration was temporarily postponed with arrests and trials in Czechoslovakia and the eruption of Solidarity in Poland in late 1980. Nevertheless, the Czechoslovak-Polish discussion continued and developed out of this early and formative discussion.

On Freedom and Power, and the discussions flowing from it, can be seen as one Czechoslovak link in the chain of indigenous oppositional movements that reaches back to East Germany in 1953, Poland and Hungary in 1956, and Yugoslavia and Czechoslovakia itself in the mid-1960s, and forward to events in Poland. And indeed these essays look both backwards and forwards. The ghosts of 'reform communism', 'Dubčekism', 'socialism with a human face' (and, behind them, of all the earlier 'revisionist' attempts to 'humanize' east European Marxism) stalk some of these pages. These essays also appeal, variously, to Czech national traditions, notably its suppressed literary heritage and the ethical teachings of Jan Patočka, to non-Marxist social democracy, to Catholicism, Woytilla-style, to lay protestantism, and to a kind of transplanted Trotskyism. They all, however, share a commitment to the rule of law and the restoration of civic virtue, the official commitment to, and betrayal of which they all unite in exposing. This was and remains the meaning of Charter 77, of which all the authors are signatories.

They also look forward, though with less agreement and less certainty, to innovative forms of opposition, alternative ways of acting and living, new ways of turning moral gestures into political activity. The overwhelming problem was how to convert the tiny minority of Chartists into a significant social and political force, how to make connections with the concerns and interests of the silent, or rather *silenced*, majority. It was clear from an early stage that the programme of the Charter could not achieve this. As Kusý puts it succinctly, the claim that the Charter could make it possible for people to live in truth and justice and for decency and legality to prevail within the existing framework was unconvincing:

If we understand this defence as an exclusively moral appeal, it is utopian; if we take it to be a tactical confrontation with the powers that be, it is Švejkian;[3] if we see it as a political program, it is inconsistent, half-hearted and toothless.

This problem raised by Kusý runs like a thread through all these essays and subsequent Charter discussions. In Poland, for fifteen extraordinary months, this problem at least seemed to be solved.

One may even venture the thought that this collection may turn out to have been one of the last remnants of recognizably socialist dissent in the Soviet bloc. None of these essays is explicitly unfriendly to the socialist idea or socialist principles. None advocates a return to capitalism or even liberal democracy; and none is touched by the various forms of free market ideology that have since become dominant in the Anglo-Saxon West. Most engage in the 'immanent critique' of so-called 'real socialism' for failing to live up to its principles, which none explicitly rejects. With the exception of Uhl, and in a different way Hájek, these authors have no particular attachment to the *Marxian* socialist tradition, but they do not reject it either (though Havel suggests that there was in its origins a 'genetic disposition to the monstrous alienation characteristic of its subsequent development'); some explicitly adhere to democratic, non-Marxist socialist traditions. The socialist tradition, in one form or another, still haunts these essays.

Events in Poland have already marked a decisive move away from this position. I vividly recall talking to Jacek Kuroń in Warsaw in 1980 (six months before Solidarity) and asking him whether he thought contemporary Poland or western capitalist democracies were nearer to socialism. His response was instructive. We could not, he said, discuss my question any longer in such terms. 'What we have here', he said, gesturing around him '*is* socialism. We must use other

---

[3] The term Švejkian refers here and throughout to the ironic and naïve, but earnest adoption of official regulations and commands, as if they were always appropriate and genuine guides to action. The term derives from the main character of Jaroslav Hašek's humorous and satiric novel, *The Good Soldier Švejk*. Švejk was an infantry man who, in the Austro-Hungarian army during the First World War, exploited his apparent stupidity to survive military life.

vocabulary and talk, for example, of democratizing the state apparatus. The language and indeed the very conceptual structure of socialism was, for Kuroń then, hopelessly compromised.[4] And it is noteworthy that Solidarity, the largest popular revolution (albeit initially 'self-limiting' and eventually aborted) against communist rule ever to have erupted was a remarkable amalgam of the ethical teachings of Catholicism, of Polish nationalism, of liberal democratic values and of a basic egalitarianism. But this last feature was not dominant and it had no particular links with socialism, even with a human face.

There are many reasons why the Czechoslovaks did not and could not follow the Poles. But in one respect at least they are all at one. The aspirations of 'socialism with a human face' à la Dubček (now called reform communism) now seem hopelessly antiquated, above all in Czechoslovakia. There is a felt need for a new framework that is at once morally, intellectually, and politically compelling. Hence the appeal of Christianity, especially Catholicism (increasingly popular and increasingly repressed), nationalism, and the various varieties of contemporary conservatism, some highly reactionary (the very word 'progressive' is contaminated). Some voices in Charter circles may still speak the language of democratic socialism. Yet it seems possible that one of the long-term achievements of 'real socialism' in the Soviet bloc may turn out to be the extinction there of the entire socialist tradition as a theoretical system worthy of serious consideration, let alone allegiance, wherever it is practised. (It has not exactly helped the prospects of socialism in the West either.) *On*

---

[4] According to the Czechoslavak writer Milan Šimečka, 'existing socialism' has turned 'a movement totally geared to the future into a self-satisfied present. It has thus stolen from socialism any future it might have had. There can be no other way of understanding the term; indeed that is how it is officially interpreted. What it says is that socialism as a model for a just and ever-changing order of society has ceased to exist: socialism is neither more nor less than the system we have in the Soviet Union and the countries of eastern Europe. Miroslav Kusý has accurately described this as an 'ostensive' definition, typical of a time of ideological desperation. When asked to define socialism, they point their finger and say: this is socialism. The finger is never quite sure whether it should also point in the direction of Yugoslavia, China, or even Albania. But what it does say quite clearly is that only the actually existing systems of socialism can be taken seriously—everything else, above all Eurocommunism, is poppycock designed to deceive public opinion. Democratic socialism is just such poppycock, and the worst of all was the ludicrous and short-lived socialism with a human face in Czechoslovakia' (Milan Šimečka, *The Restoration of Order: The Normalization of Czechoslovakia* (London: 1984)).

Freedom and Power helps explain and partially resist that ironic and tragic development.

II

The essays *On Freedom and Power* are not, however, merely symptomatic. They attempt to explain and interpret the Czechoslovak and more generally the east European system and the nature of, and prospects for, opposition within it. As such, they greatly repay attention and reflection.

Taken together, they constitute a wide spectrum of approaches to the analysis of contemporary state socialism, ranging, one might say, from the Catholic right to the Trotskyist left. One *might* say this —but anyone familiar with central and eastern Europe knows how treacherous the left–right continuum can be. Where do the Stalinists lie, with their own commitment to economic levelling? Was the Prague Spring on the *right*? Is the Charter a *middle-of-the-road* document? Seeing the absurdity of such questions is the first essential step to grasping east and central European realities.

The centrepiece of this collection is Havel's 'The Power of the Powerless'. It is a remarkable synthesis of socio-political analysis and literary imagination, of theoretical abstraction, and phenomeno-logical description, which moves easily and illuminatingly from speculations about modernity and the nature of 'our system' to the famous greengrocer who puts the sign 'Workers of the World, Unite!' among his onions and carrots. Why does he do this? Havel's brilliant exploratory answer to this question reaches further into the bases of east European communism than many an academic study or political scientist's treatise. He pinpoints what is 'radically new' in such systems, as distinct from both classical dictatorships and open societies, in a way that is both fresh and suggestive, and which avoids both sentimental moralism and tendentious political terminology. The 'post-totalitarian' system is a distinctive world, instantly recog-nizable as capturing the lived experience of east Europeans in a way that academic models fail to do.

Havel's sharp insights into its dynamics and structure are echoed in the other essays here, and notably developed in Kusý's. Havel observes, in particular, that the greengrocer declares his loyalty (and he can do no other if his declaration is to be accepted) in the only way the regime is capable of hearing: that is, by accepting the prescribed *ritual*, by accepting appearances as reality, by accepting the given rules of the game. In doing so, however, he has himself become a player in the game, thus making it possible for the game to go on, for it to exist in the first place.

Kusý's remarkable essay can be read as an extended development of this rich theme. He writes that Havel

has exposed very graphically the deeper significance of the greengrocer's behaviour, which has nothing to do with the proletariat, nor with vegetables, but rather with the formal manifestation of the greengrocer's socialist consciousness, which for him is related directly to his livelihood. The greengrocer who refused to display the assigned slogan, or who replaced it with a more relevant one, such as 'Workers of the World, Eat Vegetables!' or 'Vegetarians of the World Unite!' might stand a chance of increasing his turnover, were he not prevented from doing so by immediate dismissal for loss of confidence according to Section 53, paragraphs 1 and 2 of the Labour Code. Real socialism does not rely on spontaneous manifestations of socialist consciousness by the citizen, but rather extracts such manifestations by tight monitoring and heavy legal sanctions.

Kusý shows brilliantly how the system successfully ties people's (in this case, the greengrocer's) interests to the formal acceptance of this 'as if' ideology—to a 'silent agreement' between the powerful and the powerless. In this way, they both survive. The role of the Charter, however, is precisely that of ruining 'this whole game of "as if"' by 'consistently calling things by their proper names'. How playing such a role could be liberating, rather than self-defeating, is the large question raised by Kusý, and indeed all the essays in this collection. There are various divergences among the authors represented here. For Havel, the system is 'post-totalitarian'; for others it is still 'totalitarian'; for Uhl it is bureaucratic centralism (from an economic point of view) and bureaucratic dictatorship (from a political point of view)—a view that Havel directly contests. There is also a clear contrast between Benda's Catholic-based 'radical conservatism', with its vision of a 'return to the sources' of life and politics, involving 'commitment to a playful and sacred concern for the affairs of the *polis*' and Uhl's talk of 'embryonic revolutionary consciousness' and his vision of an international 'anti-bureaucratic revolution' that would involve 'the expansion of direct democracy to the detriment of representative democracy' and lead to 'a society-wide system of self-management'. Some, such as Zvěřina and Černý, stress the spiritual and cultural dimensions respectively; others, such as Hájek and Ruml, are more directly political, both linking the domestic scene to the international context, the former concerned with points of influence and receptivity within official circles, the latter with the silenced majority and its possible responses to 'dissidents'. Battěk represents a strongly anti-communist form of independent, internationally minded socialism; Hejdánek a kind of rights-based democratic liberalism, prepared to recognize the 'fundamentally democratic nature of socialism', Christian, and Marxist influences, and the need to separate civil society and the state and democratize both.

There are also, however, notable continuities. All agree that the age of ideological socialist commitment and enthusiasm is long past, and that the present system rests upon what Vohryzek calls 'a total vacuum of civil will, a *perpetuum silentium*, passivity and quiescence': 'quiet disagreement is one of the pillars' of what Vohryzek persists in seeing as 'totalitarian power'. All see this vacuum or silence as the central problem of interpretation and the overwhelming obstacle to be overcome. What is the meaning of that silence? Or rather, what is the political meaning of all the various activities of everyday life—the greengrocer's slogan, the general retreat into privacy and withdrawal from public concerns, the turn to consumer values (stressed by a number of our authors), graft, corruption, and skiving on a mass scale, pushing up the value of labour, the telling of jokes—on which the entire system depends? To what extent, and when, can they be seen as forms of *resistance* rather than quiescence?

Of course, the system is also a massive system of control and coercion. Behind it—the obvious sometimes needs to be restated—stands the Red Army, without which the system would not survive for a moment. Central to such control, as Vohryzek argues, is the officially proclaimed 'right to work' which, ironically enough, is invoked in threatening and punishing dissenting intellectuals and professionals and their children with *manual labour*. Fulfilling, identity-conferring work becomes a privilege within this system; manual work (especially of the unproductive variety) a punishment.

Yet, as Vohryzek also notes, the silence is one of 'silent disagreement'. This profoundly important point indicates another common theme of these essays: that the term 'dissident' is misleading in suggesting that those who speak out are a small and isolated minority *who think differently from the rest.* The point, rather, is that they are few and isolated just because they speak aloud, and reflect upon, what everyone thinks.

III

The interest of *On Freedom and Power*, seen as a collection of explanatory and interpretative texts, reaches, however, beyond the confines of central and eastern Europe and the analysis of contemporary communist systems. There is rich material here for reflection upon the mechanics of power, the nature and effects of ideology, the meaning of a public sphere, the point and justification of civil disobedience, and the links between morality and politics. Such classical questions are addressed, Czechoslovak-style, in the form of *feuilletons*, 'published' originally in *samizdat*, and combine hard thinking with literary flair, and both with a pressing sense of immediacy and sometimes danger. There is, as a matter of fact, little idle small-talk (although there is much rich humour) among Czechoslovak intellectuals. There is also scant reason and little opportunity for scholasticism, erudition, and idle flights of fancy for their own sakes. The essays in *On Freedom and Power* are, in my view, examples of applied political theory at its best: reflections upon fundamental moral and political questions that link (in C. Wright Mills's phrase) public issues and private troubles, and thereby reach to the heart of things.

Students of power can derive much from Havel's essay and students of ideology much from Kusý's; and students of both much from reading them together. I know of few subtler and more thought-provoking discussions of the way in which power becomes impersonal and anonymous, a feature of the system in which individuals are caught up, such that they become 'agents of its automatism . . . petty instruments of social autototality'. Also worthy of particular note is Havel's distinction between 'the post-totalitarian system' and 'classical dictatorships', in which the line of conflict between rulers and ruled can still be drawn according to social class. In the post-totalitarian system,

this line runs *de facto* through each person, for everyone in his or her own way is both a victim and a supporter of the system. What we understand by the system is not, therefore, a social order imposed by one group upon another, but rather something which permeates the entire society and is a factor in shaping it . . .

As for ideology, Havel treats it as 'an increasingly important component of power, a pillar providing it with both excusatory legitimacy and an inner coherence'. By giving individuals 'the illusion of an identity, of dignity and of morality while making it easier for them to *part* with them', enabling them 'to deceive their conscience and conceal their true position and their inglorious *modus vivendi*, both from the world and from themselves', it creates a 'bridge of excuses between the system and the individual' spanning 'the abyss between the aims of the system and the aims of life'. As I have suggested above, Kusý's essay is a fascinating further exploration of this theme. His concept of the ideology of 'as if' (echoing Vaihinger's *Philosophy of 'As If '*) is a neat and subtle variation upon a familiar Orwellian theme:

> those who preach it behave *as if* the ideological kingdom of real socialism existed in 'what we have here now', *as if* they had, in all earnestness, convinced the nation of its existence; the nation behaves *as if* it believed it, *as if* it were convinced that it lived in accordance with this ideologically real socialism.

This, too, is a rich idea worthy of further development and applications to other ideological systems. To what extent, for example, does it capture the present 'revival' of Islam? To what extent, in our own society, are 'belief' and 'commitment' to various causes sustained in such inglorious ways?

All the essays bear eloquent witness to the manifold consequences of the lack of a public sphere, an arena in which collective concerns and interests may be articulated and public policy debated and formulated openly. Equally, they all exemplify—as do the lives of their authors—the case for resistance through the reasoned and principled gesture in defiance of unjust laws, directed at the conscience of one's fellow-citizens—in other words, civil disobedience. Yet such resistance requires there to be a minimal public sphere to make its point and achieve its results. Draft resistance in the United States during the Vietnam War, Gandhi's campaigns against the British in India, and various law-breaking activities of western peace movements precisely rely upon the possibility that rulers will respond to such appeals to the *public* conscience. What many east Europeans have often held (and not always unjustly) against certain sections of the western peace movement is that they, and others in the west, have sometimes failed to understand that just this possibility is absent in the East. Ironically, it is precisely those laws that have extinguished public life in Czechoslovakia that render the typical activities of Chartists—such as unofficial publishing, lectures, and seminars, the circulation of banned books and manuscripts, under-ground cultural activities—illegal. Indeed, pursuit of the very activities banned in the East is a necessary condition for the occasional effectiveness of civil disobedience in the West.

What could render it more effective in the East? One answer is: far greater responsiveness and support from the west. For, as recent Polish events have demonstrated, even if a direct, indeed revolution-ary confrontation with the ruling powers must fail in such systems, they may be amenable to well-judged western pressure, especially in the context of economic adversity. The moral is, perhaps, that the 'parallel *polis*' should be seen as not merely a potentiality within central and eastern Europe, but in the form of international solid-arity outside it. This moral was suggested in Benda's original essay. It is implicit in various recent developments, notably the regular visits by western philosophers and others to Prague seminars, and the opening up of a dialogue between the Charter and sections of the western peace movement.[5]

Finally, the essays are all, in different ways, reflections upon the links between morality and politics. All see a line between morality and politics, though they draw it in different places. All distrust mere *moralizing* and the falsely reassuring thought that taking a moral stand is enough, under present conditions, to make such a stand

---

[5] See *Voices From Prague: Czechoslovakia, Human Rights and the Peace Movement*, ed. Jan Kavan and Zdena Tomin (London: European Nuclear Disarmament and Palach Press, 1983). Also relevant here is a recent Charter document which states: 'We consider the emergence of the independent peace movement in the West to be a major watershed . . . for our strivings to obtain more democratic and freer conditions in our part of Europe', while insisting that 'peace and democracy are indivisible, that it is naïve to consider building peace on the ruins of civil liberties and democratic rights' (Charter Document no. 14/84: *Open Letter to the Third Conference on European Nuclear Disarmament*, trans. (London: Palach Press, 1984). On his release from prison, Havel gave an interview in which he said: 'I consider these young, long-haired people who keep demonstrating for peace in various western cities and whom I saw almost daily when I was in jail, where we were forced to watch the TV news, to be my brothers and sisters: they aren't indifferent to the fate of the world and they voluntarily take upon themselves a responsibility outside the sphere of their own personal well-being, and that—though in more difficult circumstances—is exactly what we are doing' (*Voices from Prague*, p. 42).

political. All are critical of the narrow conception of, and the vastly extended scope of, official political life in contemporary Czecho-slovakia. What are the political conditions for a morally healthy society? When they do not obtain, what forms of political action are morally appropriate and which are to be ruled out? In a system where political life is universally seen as involving deceit, manipulation, and opportunism, as an 'as if' game in which all the participants have 'dirty hands', how can a sense of morality in public life be re-discovered? These are fundamental and urgent questions and the experience of central and eastern Europe poses them in a peculiarly acute form.

15
Václav Havel: The Meaning of Life at the Ramparts

'Only by looking "outward"', the Czech playwright Václav Havel wrote to his wife Olga from prison,

by caring for things that, in terms of pure survival, he needn't bother with at all, by constantly asking himself all sorts of questions, and by throwing himself over and over again into the tumult of the world, with the intention of making his voice count—only thus does one really become a person . . .

Havel wrote this in prison, his third prison sentence: nine months (reduced on appeal by one month) for 'incitement to criminal activity'—or, to be precise, for encouraging people to lay wreaths of flowers in Wenceslas Square at the site of Jan Palach's suicide. He was first gaoled for his central part in founding Charter 77 and for writing a letter to Dr Husak. The second time, from 1979 to 1983—the period the letters come from—it was for presuming to join a committee to 'defend the unjustly prosecuted'.

His voice speaks through his plays, but only to theatre audiences abroad (including Poland). In his own country since the end of the 1960s his plays have been privately circulated and read, and performed only in private apartments. One of Czechoslovakia's finest living dramatists is thus (like others of his generation, such as Ivan Klíma, Milan Uhde and František Pavlíček) cut off from the artistic discipline he sees as having 'the greatest potential to be a social phenomenon in the true sense', from 'common participation in a particular adventure of the mind, the imagination and the sense of humour, and a common experience of truth or a flash of insight into the "life of truth"', from producers, actors, and audiences.

The plays are personal in a number of ways. Intense, concentrated,

This chapter was first published in March 1989. It was originally a review of Havel's *Letters to Olga: June 1979–September 1982*, trans. Paul Wilson (London: Faber, 1988).

yet playful and blackly funny, they project a distinctive vision of a world Tom Stoppard has described well: 'an absurd society raised only a notch or two above the normal world of state bureaucracy; the absurdities pushed to absurdity compounded by absurdity and yet saved from mere nonsense by their internal logic.' Yet they are also about the pressures of the impersonal on personal character, about personal disintegration and the struggle for personal integrity: 'all my plays', Havel writes to Olga, 'circle around the theme of the breakdown of identity and continuity'.

The theme, moreover, is always explored from the inside: 'in all my writings', he recently said, 'my starting-point has always been what I know, my own experience of this world I live in, my experience of myself'. This is most evident in the trilogy of 'Vanek' plays (*Audience*, *Private View*, and *Protest*), whose 'hero', a polite, soft-spoken intellectual who says 'No', is a thorn in the flesh both to the authorities and to the once-critical intellectuals who have made their peace with them, yet is speechless before the voiceless brewmaster who asks 'Who's gonna help me? Who can give a shit? I'm just the manure that makes your fancy principles grow.'

It is evident, too, in *Largo Desolato* (completed in 1984) and *Temptation* (1985). In the first, a philosopher, disintegrating under official pressure to renounce his work and thus himself, while moralizing 'friends' urge him to go on fighting, is condemned in the end not to be arrested or imprisoned. In the second, Havel's 'Faust play' (whose progress he periodically reports on to Olga), the Faust figure is a scientist dabbling in black magic who is tempted by an old tramp with rotting feet into doing deals, losing his soul by trying to save his skin.

Havel's personal experience is, of course, no ordinary one. Ludvík Vaculík mischievously suggests that Havel has cornered for himself the two 'extreme advantages' of being born rich (his grandfather was an architect—the Lucerna Palace in Wenceslas Square is by him—and one of the few self-made millionaires in the First Republic) and having the character-strengthening experience of prison. To Olga, Havel recalls the effects of his privileged background and his fatness as a child: 'instinctual mistrust of a classmate from a rich family found in my chubbiness a marvellous opportunity for unwitting "social revenge"'. In consequence, he always felt 'a little outside the given order, or on its margins', and that

I'm always running along (like that well-fed piglet) a short distance behind my marching classmates, trying to catch up and take my place with the others as a fully fledged and equal member of that moving body, and that I am powerless to do otherwise.

'I have', he adds, 'understandably, a heightened sense of order (wasn't that, too, characteristic of Kafka?)'. And elsewhere in the letters he notes that he has always had 'an amplified tendency to see the absurd dimensions of the world', yet absurdity is after all 'inseparable from the experience of meaning; it is, in a manner of speaking, its "obverse"'. It is 'the experience that something that has, should or could have aspired to meaning—that is, something intrinsically human—does not do so at all or else has lost it': 'the moon is not absurd. What is absurd is the junkyard man has left on it.'

The reference to Kafka is significant. In Kafka he recognizes 'an intensely personal and existential understanding of experience that borders on spiritual kinship . . .'. For Havel, what mattered was 'the quite trivial and "pre-theoretical" certainty' that Kafka 'was "right" and that what he writes is "exactly how it is"'. 'I have always been intensely aware', he tells Olga,

of matters like the alienation of man from the world, the dehumanisation and incomprehensibility of 'the order of things', the emptiness and unintentional cruelty of social mechanisms and their tendency to become ends in themselves, how things get out of control, fall apart, or, on the contrary, evolve to the point of absurdity, how human existence tends to get lost in the mechanised contexts of life, how easily absurdity becomes legitimate, the apparent nature of the 'real' and the ludicrousness of the 'important' etc. This experience of the world (at many points so akin to Kafka's) would obviously show up in my writing no matter what I wrote.

It is just this personal, existential evocation of experience that gives life, and indeed argumentative power, to Havel's political and cultural essays. In 'The Power of the Powerless', for instance, the image of a greengrocer who puts in his window, among the carrots and onions, a sign saying 'Workers of the World, Unite!' is the focus of an extraordinarily rich and suggestive analysis of the interior life of state socialism in Eastern Europe—its seductions and entrapments, its subterfuges and alibis, its 'as if' ideology of make-believe, its blurring of distinctions between superiors and subordinates, between 'them' and 'us', so that all are drawn into the same plot. The greengrocer, in short, declares his loyalty (and he can do no other if his declaration is to be accepted) in the only way the regime is capable of hearing; that is, by accepting the prescribed *ritual*, by accepting appearances as reality, by accepting the given rules of the game. In doing so, however, he has himself become a player in the game, thus making it possible for the game to go on, for it to exist in the first place.

As an account of the dynamics of impersonal power, of the workings of ideology and of the potential of the powerless, this essay is unrivalled in the academic 'theoretical' literature. Not that it is un- or pre-theoretical. It is, rather, a reflective reconstruction of lived experience. The same can be said for many of his other essays, such as the remarkable 'Politics and Conscience', written for an honorary doctorate at Toulouse University. (When news came of such a doctorate in Canada while he was in prison, he wrote to Olga, 'it helps me live here; I see it—among other things—as an indication that what I'm doing is understood'.) That essay—a meditation on the 'irrational momentum of anonymous, impersonal and inhuman power—the power of ideologies, systems, *apparat*, bureaucracy, artificial languages and political slogans—starts from and keeps returning to a compelling image from his boyhood, of a walk to school blighted by brown smoke billowing from some hurriedly built factory and scattering across the sky.

In *Letters to Olga*, the playwright and essayist is forced into a new form of expression by the censorship imposed by a fanatical prison commandant, a professed admirer of Hitler, who saw his rule over Havel and his co-prisoners as a welcome return to the good old Stalinist days. The constraints were tight: one letter a week to his wife, and only about 'family' and 'personal' matters (though nothing about prison conditions, which happened to be the most personal matter at the time), no humour, no corrections or crossings out, and (at various times) no reference to the 'order of being' ('The only order you can write about is the prison order'), no philosophy ('You can only write about yourself'), no more numbering your moods (when Havel started to explore some sixteen of these), no foreign words, no exclamation marks, and so on. Letters failed to get through and those that arrived move back and forth between the immediacy of prison life, his anxieties about Olga and friends outside, his frustrations over the lack of news, and contemplative passages, interspersed with powerful introspection, and, as the letters proceed, a taking-on of ever larger themes. The last cycle of letters is a sustained series of speculative and sometimes lyrical meditations, largely inspired by the French philosopher, Emmanuel Levinas.

It is an extraordinary book, a coherent series of reflections on all the central themes of Havel's life and work. Here, as Heinrich Böll remarked in a review of the *Letters*, 'the author of spiritually absurd and "humorous" dramas . . . reveals the brooding seriousness on which his work is founded'. A word of caution, though. As we have seen, humour was forbidden (there must be a play in that!) and Havel has himself acknowledged that some of the more abstruse philosophical vocabulary was a code to elude the rather non-philosophical censor: for example, instead of writing 'the regime', he would refer to the 'social collective manifestation of the not-I'.

At one point Havel remarks,

I'm no philosopher and it is not my ambition to construct a conceptually fixed system; anyone who tries to understand it that way will soon discover that I am perpetually contradicting myself, that I leave many things unexplained or explain them differently each time, etc.

It is an intriguing disclaimer, of which the Czech philosopher Ladislav Hejdánek has aptly said that if they do not expound philosophy, these letters certainly raise weighty philosophical issues. They do far more, for they are fresh and powerful reflections of an exceptionally active and acute mind on the nature of responsibility and its links with personal identity, on the necessity of a non-relative basis for moral judgements (which he calls the 'absolute horizon'), on the rational truth in religion, on the origins of fanaticism, on the nature of the theatre, on the reasons why human beings do good deeds, even when they do not gain from doing so and feel guilt at failing to do so, on what answer one can give to the question 'what is the meaning of life?' and on the desperate importance of caring about the question, and on many other such matters. Small wonder that these texts circulated among his friends, and more widely, as soon as they were received. As one of them recalls, 'not even while incarcerated behind prison walls did Havel allow his friends and acquaintances to rest'.

Havel has made his voice count. It speaks in a moral vocabulary, with great precision and vividness. It is secular in tone ('I am a child of the age of conceptual, rather than mystical thought'), though respectful and cautious in matters of religion ('I admit to an affinity for Christian sentiment and I am glad it's recognisable; nevertheless, one must be extremely cautious in such matters and weigh one's words well'; 'God . . . behaves too much like a person for me').

What it says is not, however, always comfortable or even palatable. To his fellow citizens he offers an overtly moral challenge to lead a 'life-in-truth', and to those that have left he offers the thought that the totalitarian systems of Eastern Europe are 'a convex mirror of all modern civilisation and a harsh, perhaps final call for a global recasting of that civilisation's self-understanding' and the suggestion that 'what is called 'dissent' in the Soviet bloc is a specific modern experience, the experience of life at the very ramparts of dehumanised power'. To the left, and to the peace movement in the West (whose brother if not comrade he has always been), he offers in 'An Anatomy of Reticence' an exceptionally subtle account of the deep reasons behind East Europeans' scepticism and reserve, and the difference between the anti-political politics of the dissidents and what he sees as the Utopian politics of his interlocutors. To western intellectuals seduced by the current fashions of postmodernist scepticism and nihilism about 'metanarratives' and 'foundations', he offers an unfashionable belief that the question of what life actually means is capable of an answer—and that both question and answer are to be found in personal experience.

The first, or rather the most frequent occasion for posing this all-important question only arises, I believe, when one first suffers or experiences, existentially, the 'gap', the abyss that separates the pleasures in life from one another. That, at least, is how I feel it. I have thrown myself enthusiastically into all kinds of things, from serving good dinners to working for a 'supra-personal' cause, yet these joyful activities were always restricted to particular temporal compartments of my life relating to a particular event or constellation of events, and thus I have always experienced them as mere 'islands of meaningfulness' floating in an ocean of nothingness.

Posing the question means,

among other things, asking whether those 'islands' are really so isolated, so randomly adrift on the ocean as they appear in moments of despair, or are they in fact merely the visible peaks of some coherent undersea mountain range?

Havel's final message is not to propose answers, least of all a definitive one, but that we should find ways of 'living with the question'.

'The tragedy of modern man', he writes to Olga, 'is not that he knows less and less about the meaning of his own life, but that it bothers him less and less'. *That* is Havel's distinctive voice. It will not easily be silenced.

PART V

16
The Future of British Socialism?

I

In 1932 R. H. Tawney published an article in which he reflected upon the events of the previous year: the collapse of the Labour Government and the massive electoral defeat of the Labour Party in which it lost 235 seats, with 30.8 per cent of the poll and 52 seats as against the National Government's 67.2 per cent and 554 seats. Tawney called his article 'The Choice Before the Labour Party'. The Party, he declared, needed 'a little cold realism' now it had 'an interval in which to meditate its errors'. His verdict on the late Government was 'pernicious anaemia producing general futility'.[1]

In 1984 we can look back on an electoral defeat that is, if less dramatic, more catastrophic.[2] Now, if ever, there is a need for 'cold realism' and meditation upon past errors. The verdict this time can only be suicidal self-absorption producing general non-credibility.

Indeed, the question must now be asked: *is* there a choice before the Labour Party? If there is, what, if any, are the party's prospects? And what, if any, are the prospects for socialism in Britain over the next decades? And what are the links between these? Despite the massive changes in the social and economic landscape, and even in the Labour Party, it is still worth going back to Tawney's essay as a reference point in seeking to address these questions. I do so because I agree with Anthony Wright that it is 'possible that it is Tawney rather than Trotsky who has more to contribute' to contemporary arguments within the Labour Party.[3]

This chapter was first published in 1984. I wish to thank A. H. Halsey and Gordon Marshall for discussions helpful to its writing.

[1] Tawney, 'The Choice before the Labour Party', *Political Quarterly* 3 (1932), pp. 323–45.

[2] See D. Massey, 'The Contours of Victory . . . Dimensions of Defeat', *Marxism Today* (July 1983), pp. 16–19 and E. Hobsbawm, 'Labour's Lost Millions', *Marxism Today* (Oct. 1983), pp. 7–13; and B. Pimlott (ed.), *Fabian Essays in Socialist Thought* (London: Heinemann, 1984), chap. 1.

[3] Wright (ed.), *British Socialism: Socialist Thought from the 1880s to the 1960s* (London: Longman, 1983), p. 13.

It might, of course, seem widely optimistic to propose Tawney's 1932 essay as a reference point for discussion, since it might conjure up the prospect of a future Labour majority on the scale of 1945 (presumably without the benefit of another World War).[4] In current circumstances, on the left, it would seem that a pessimist is a well-informed optimist. If a pessimist is someone without illusions in a tough world, then we had better all be pessimists. Thus, for example, we had better reject the notion that all the Labour Party needs is a period of further bleeding to cure it of its surfeit of crypto-Social Democrats and thereby turn it 'into a socialist party free from the constrictions hitherto imposed upon it by its leaders';[5] or that it is basically healthy and only needs a period of time to recuperate under its bright, new leadership; or that, though its condition is probably terminal, the 'future of the left lies in the consolidation of a new strength outside Parliament', in 'the support and encouragement of factory occupations, peace campaigns, black struggles and women's resistance'.[6] Being pessimists, however, does not mean that we should be fatalists.

Consider, first, Tawney's very title: 'The Choice before the Labour Party'. There are various ways of looking at the Labour Party of 1929–31. One view is that it was just *unable* to rise to the demands of the time—for example, because of its 'commitment to a Utopian socialism which incapacitated it from effectively working the parliamentary system and prevented it from coming to terms with economic reality',[7] or, alternatively, because it was enmeshed in 'labourism'. Another view is that there was no such *opportunity*: the Labour Party 'could not . . . reorganise economic life through state intervention' because of deficient understanding, lack of theory, the physical incapacity of the state, and the opposition of 'the bureaucracy, the Bank of England, the banks, the great financial institutions, most of industry' and 'the dead weight of conventional

[4] See I. Crewe, 'How to Link up and Pick up Vital Seats', *Guardian* (23 Mar. 1984).

[5] R. Miliband, 'Socialist Advance in Britain', in id. and J. Saville (eds.), *The Socialist Register 1983* (London: Merlin Press, 1983), p. 116. Miliband holds that 'whether the activists can . . . achieve the conquest of the Labour Party is more open than I had believed' (p. 117).

[6] D. Coates, 'The Labour Party and the Future of the Left', ibid. 100.

[7] R. Skidelsky, *Politicians and the Slump: The Labour Government of 1929–1931* (London: Macmillan, 1967), p. xii.

wisdom'.[8] Tawney, by contrast, took the view, as did many socialists at the time,[9] that there were lessons to be learned from 1931, choices to be faced and alternative paths to be pursued—though it is true that as the 1930s progressed, the Labour Party had made no significant break with the past.[10] An analogous range of views exists today. On one view, the Labour Party could never be a vehicle for socialism: 'cart-horses', Ralph Miliband once wrote, 'should not be expected to win the Derby'.[11] On another view, increasingly advanced on the right, at different levels of sophistication, the socialist project is, for a variety of reasons, inherently unrealizable or only realizable at an unacceptable cost. Certainly, anyone disposed to dispute both views must offer a detailed defence of his own against some powerful current counter-arguments.

For Tawney, the choice was clear-cut. The Labour Party could either be 'a political agent, pressing in Parliament the claims of different groups of wage-earners' or 'an instrument for the establishment of a socialist commonwealth, which alone, on its own principles, would meet those claims effectively, but would not meet them at once'. But 'it cannot be both at the same time in the same measure'. If it continued to be the first, with programmes that were more 'miscellanies' than programmes, offering 'the greatest possible number of carrots to the greatest possible number of donkeys', then it would continue to lack a 'stable standard of political values, such as would teach it to discriminate between the relative urgencies of different objectives'. Lacking such a standard, it 'lacks also the ability to subordinate the claims of this section of the movement or that to the progress of the whole, and to throw its whole weight against the central positions'. In short, it lacked 'any ordered conception of its task'.[12]

Labour's fundamental weakness, according to Tawney, was 'its lack of a creed'. The Labour Party was 'hesitant in action, because

---

[8] R. McKibbin, 'The Economic Policy of the Second Labour Government 1929–1931', *Past and Present* 68 (1975), pp. 121–3.

[9] See R. Eatwell and A. Wright, 'Labour and the Lessons of 1931', *History* 63 (1978), pp. 38–53.

[10] Ibid. 51; but see also Ben Pimlott, *Labour and the Left in the 1930s* (Cambridge: 1977, and Elizabeth Durbin's essay in *Fabian Essays*, chap. 4, for the view that in the field of policy-making, the Labour Party was in fact changing in important ways.

[11] Miliband, 'The Labour Government and Beyond', *The Socialist Register 1966*, p. 23.

[12] Tawney, 'The Choice before the Labour Party', pp. 335, 329, 338, 329.

divided in mind. It does not achieve what it could, because it does not know what it wants'. Being

without clear convictions as to its own meaning and purpose, it is deprived of the dynamic which only convictions supply. If it neither acts with decision nor inspires others so to act, the principal reason is that it is itself undecided.

This weakness was fundamental:

If it continues uncorrected, there neither is, nor ought to be, a future for the Labour Party. A political creed, it need hardly be said, is neither a system of transcendental doctrine nor a code of rigid formulae. It is a common conception of the ends of political action, and of the means of achieving them, based on a common view of the life proper to human beings, and of the steps required at any moment more nearly to attain it.[13]

Why did Tawney believe that such an energizing creed was a possibility that could be *chosen*? Because he did not believe that the interests of its actual and potential electorate were independent, given facts to which the Party must simply respond. On the contrary, he held that until

the void in the mind of the Labour Party is filled—till interests are hammered by principles into a serviceable tool, which is what interests should be, and a steady will for a new social order takes the place of mild yearnings to make somewhat more comfortable terms with the social order of today—mere repairs to the engines will produce little but disillusionment.

For,

the dynamic of any living movement is to be found, not merely in interests, but in principles, which unite men whose personal interests may be poles asunder, and that if principles are to exercise their appeal, they must be frankly stated.

It was, of course, objected that, by taking such a course, the Labour Party would alienate many of its supporters:

It may, for the time being; New Models are not made by being all things to all men. But it will keep those worth keeping. And those retained will gather others, of a kind who will not turn back in the day of battle.[14]

This raised the question of attitude or (a word he liked) 'spirit', which Tawney's essay both exemplifies and describes. 'If there is the right spirit in the movement', he wrote, 'there will not be any

---

13 Tawney, 'The Choice before the Labour Party', p. 327.
14 Ibid. 327–8, 336, 335.

question of the next Labour Government repeating the policy of office at all costs which was followed by the last.' The Labour Party, he wrote, must put essentials before sectional claims, and it must create 'a body of men and women who, whether trade unionists or intellectuals, put socialism first, and whose creed carries conviction, because they live in accordance with it'. When socialists come to power, they must do so, not 'as diffident agents of policies not their own, but as socialists'; they must 'have created behind them, before they assume office, a strong body of opinion, which "knows what it fights for, and loves what it knows"'. The Party must 'create in advance a temper and mentality of a kind to carry it through, not one crisis, but a series of crises'. Instead, it has

drugged itself with the illusion that, by adding one to one, it would achieve the millennium, without the painful necessity of clarifying its mind, disciplining its appetites, and training for a tough wrestle with established powers and property. It touched lightly on its objectives, or veiled them in the radiant ambiguity of the word socialism, which each hearer could interpret to his taste. So it ended by forgetting the reason for its existence. It has now to rediscover it.[15]

What, then, was the objective of a socialist party? The answer, Tawney said, was 'simplicity itself':

The fundamental question, as always, is: who is to be master? Is the reality behind the decorous drapery of political democracy to continue to be the economic power wielded by a few thousand—or, if that be preferred, a few hundred thousand—bankers, industrialists and land-owners? Or shall a serious effort be made—as serious, for example, as was made, for other purposes, during the war—to create organs through which the nation can control, in co-operation with other nations, its own economic destinies; plan its business as it deems most conducive to the general well-being; override, for the sake of economic efficiency, the obstruction of vested interests; and distribute the product of its labours in accordance with some generally recognised principles of justice? Capitalist parties presumably accept the first alternative. A socialist party chooses the second. The nature of its business is determined by its choice.

That business was

not the passage of a series of reforms in the interests of different sections of the working classes. It is to abolish all advantages and disabilities which have their source, not in differences of personal quality, but in disparities of wealth, opportunity, social position and economic power. It is, in short—it

[15] Ibid. 343, 340, 331, 335–6, 332.

is absurd that at this time of day the statement should be necessary— a classless society.[16]

Those who accept this objective, Tawney observed, may do so for more than one reason:

because they think it more conducive to economic efficiency than a capitalism which no longer, as in its prime, delivers the goods; or merely because they have an eccentric prejudice in treating men as men; or, since the reasons are not necessarily inconsistent, for both reasons at once. In either case, they are socialists, though on matters of technique and procedure they may be uninstructed socialists. Those who do not accept it are not socialists, though they may be as wise as Solon and as virtuous as Aristides. Socialism, thus defined, will be unpleasant, of course, to some persons professing it. Who promised them pleasure?

A future socialist government must 'apply to the affairs of its own country the principles which, it believes, should govern those of the world', aiming to extend the area of economic life controlled by some rational conception of the common good, not by a scramble, whether of persons, classes, or nations, for individual power and profit.[17]

In sum, Tawney's essay carries three lessons that are strikingly and urgently relevant to the present day.

The first is *anti-fatalism*. Of course, choices cannot be willed or conjured into existence whatever the objective circumstances. Nevertheless, Tawney's anti-fatalism provides a valuable antidote to a certain kind of electoral determinism that has prevailed in Labour Party debates ever since the 1950s, when the Revisionists embraced the *embourgoisement* thesis, and especially since the post-mortems on the 1959 election. It was then widely held that Labour's traditional working-class base was threatened by affluence.[18] Today, the opposite case is advanced: because of de-industrialization and the current recession, the proletariat is disappearing, as traditional proletarian occupations decline. Or it is argued, as by Eric Hobsbawm, that increasing sectionalism and public sector employment in the working class has halted the 'forward march of labour'.[19] Or labour support is said to be doomed by long-term social demographic trends.[20] Common to all such arguments is the assumption

---

[16] Tawney, 'The Choice before the Labour Party', pp. 332–3.

[17] Ibid. 333, 344–5.

[18] For example, see M. Abrams and R. Rose, *Must Labour Lose?* (Harmondsworth: Penguin, 1960).

[19] Hobsbawm, *The Forward March of Labour Halted*, ed. M. Jacques and F. Mulhern (London: Verso in assoc. with *Marxism Today*, 1981).

[20] See Crewe, *Guardian* (23 Mar. 1984).

that 'interests' on which the Labour Party essentially relies are fatally withering away. But, as Gareth Stedman Jones has well said, 'the "objective" realities of class discerned by social surveys and sociological analysis do not have any unambiguous bearing upon the fate of class-oriented political parties'.[21] And indeed, as Tawney shrewdly observed, the Labour Party is 'less of a class party than any other British party'.[22] It has, indeed, always relied upon substantial sectors of the middle classes for support to achieve majority governments.

Fatalism, however, extends far beyond the perennial analyses of Labour's prospects; it appears to have bitten deep into the electorate itself. The evidence from studies of public opinion and voting studies seems to suggest that Britain's apparently intractable economic problems have led to quiet disillusionment: people increasingly assume that widespread inequalities are unalterable and the economy beyond human control.[23] With such sentiments Thatcherism is peculiarly at home, and it has sought to nurture and breed them, while attempting to root out the very idea that social progress can be achieved through the rational exercise of political will. In this it has been outstandingly successful, propagating a fatalistic creed (the Hayekian canon banishes the very notion of social justice, seeking to replace a sense of injustice by the recognition of necessity, in the form of ill luck). In the face of such triumphant fatalism, the only option is, as Tawney proposed, 'to seize every opportunity of forcing a battle on fundamental questions'.[24] The only potentially effective means of resisting, and eventually rolling back, the present tide is to develop and propagate an alternative analysis of the present that reaches to fundamentals, and a vision of an alternative future to a 'society of go-getters' that is both appealing and feasible. That is the only way, if there is one, to stir and mobilize the deep and partly submerged counter-currents of our social and cultural life.

The second lesson concerns what we may call the *spirit of socialism*. For such a battle, there needs to be 'a body of conviction as

---

[21] Stedman Jones, 'Why is the Labour Party in a Mess?' in his *Languages of Class* (Cambridge: Cambridge Univ. Press, 1983), p. 242.

[22] Tawney, 'The Choice before the Labour Party', p. 333.

[23] See H. Newby, C. Vogler, D. Rose, and G. Marshall, 'From Class Structure to Class Action: British Working-Class Politics in the 1980s'. I have greatly benefited from reading this excellent analysis, on which much in the next section of this chapter draws. For further evidence on fatalism see J. Alt, *The Politics of Economic Decline* (Cambridge: Cambridge Univ. Press, 1979).

[24] Tawney, 'The Choice before the Labour Party', p. 337.

resolute and informed as the opposition in front of it'—a set of attitudes free of class hatred and aware that 'both duty and prudence require that necessary changes be effected without a breakdown' and that 'the possibility of effecting them is conditioned by international, as much as by domestic, factors'.[25]

What Tawney illustrates is something that has been all too rare in the history of the Labour movement and has never been more needed than today: 'moralism' with 'a hard cutting edge' that makes 'connections between moral valuations and social institutions with direct consequences for political practice'.[26] These consequences lie at different levels. One example, and it is not a trivial one, concerns personal life-style. If Labour leaders 'accept titles and other such toys, without a clear duty to the movement to do so', they 'widen the rift between its principles and practice', for 'livery and an independent mind go ill together'[27] and, in any case, 'how can followers be Ironsides if leaders are flunkies?'[28]

More generally, an 'ordered conception of its task' would enable the Party to cut a path through the jungle of conflicting sectional claims and, in particular, abandon its disastrous, self-defeating support for 'free collective bargaining'. It would encourage it to grasp the nettle of an effective incomes policy, instead of avoiding it, as in the last election campaign. Such support and avoidance can buy political allies and achieve famous victories (as over the Heath Government). But they have proved to be pyrrhic (as the Callaghan Government discovered) and they demonstrate beyond any question the Party's lack of any 'stable standard of political values' and 'ordered conception of its task'. For a real and effective incomes policy (such as the left *used* to advocate) is the only alternative to unemployment as a means of controlling inflation.[29] Achieving such control has long been a major preoccupation of the population at large. If a will and a way cannot be found to commit the unions to an effective incomes policy, within the Labour Party (the Social Democrats have a will, but no way), then not only will the prevailing fatalism about the inevitability of large-scale unemployment prove amply justified, but the Labour Party will finally show itself to be unserious about the pursuit of the socialist objective.

[25] Tawney, 'The Choice before the Labour Party', p. 336.
[26] Wright, *British Socialism*, p. 13.
[27] Tawney, 'The Choice before the Labour Party', pp. 334, 341.
[28] Ibid. 342.
[29] See W. Beckerman, 'A New Realism', *New Statesman* (2 Dec. 1983).

Which leads us, thirdly, to Tawney's account of the *socialist objective* itself. His statement of this is an admirably clear, coherent, and compelling statement of essentials which still captures much of what distinguishes a socialist from a liberal perspective (and socialists from Social Democrats anxious to purloin the mantle of Tawney's name and legacy). As Wright observes,[30] Tawney's 'discussion of equality in terms of equal worth and social solidarity has different foundations from a liberal approach concerned with identifying the criteria of "fairness" and social justice'. It centres upon the notion of social unity based upon common ends and shared values—what Anne Phillips calls the 'social' in socialism—and is indeed fully vulnerable to her admirable critique (in its 'eccentric prejudice in treating men as men'[31]). It is true that it lacks a critical sense of the varied forms of solidarity and the conflicts between these. Nor does Tawney grapple with the relations between solidarity, pluralism, and individuality. These are urgent tasks for socialist political theory. But his account does register a clear sense of what socialist solidarity is not—the 'scramble . . . for individual power and profit' and the 'tyranny of money'[32]—and it forms, I believe, as good a starting-point as any for building a socialist (as against a liberal or social-democratic) theory of justice.

Of course, it needs reformulating and rethinking in the light both of new, or newly visible, forms of oppression, injustice, and unfreedom, and of new social movements with new vocabularies and concerns. It must also grapple, as Peter Kellner argues,[33] with the problem of reconciling the community's good with that of preserving, indeed expanding, the role of voluntary transactions within it: exactly *when* should market forces operate and how should they be constrained and guided? In essentials, however, it still offers broad guidelines for reshaping Labour's 'common conception of its task', after the deforming and dispiriting years, under Wilson and Callaghan, of pragmatic capitulation ('They threw themselves into the role of the Obsequious Apprentice, or Prudence Rewarded, as though bent on proving that, so far from being different from other governments, His Majesty's Labour Government could rival the most respectable of them in cautious conventionality.[34]) It embodies

---

[30] In Pimlott, *Fabian Essays in Socialist Thought*, p. 88.
[31] Ibid. 230.　　　[32] Tawney, 'The Choice before the Labour Party', p. 345.
[33] In Pimlott, *Fabian Essays in Socialist Thought*, p. 151.
[34] Tawney, 'The Choice before the Labour Party', pp. 324–5.

a vision which is neither 'distributionist' nor 'productionist', but both together ('It is not a question, of course, either of merely improving the distribution of wealth, or merely increasing its production, but of doing both together.[35]) It is neither what is currently called 'libertarian', nor 'collectivist', in the manner of the Webbs, nor cautiously social-democratic, but begins to inject a distinctively socialist content into basic values central to (some of) our traditions, such as liberty, democracy, equal opportunity, justice and, indeed, solidarity. Kellner is right: it *is*

a measure of the Tories' ideological ascendancy that they have so successfully clothed the pursuit of privilege in the rhetoric of democracy—and a measure of Labour's retreat that our opposition in the name of fairness and decency should be so widely construed as an assault on liberty.[36]

If we are to move 'beyond the fragments', one prerequisite is a coherent scheme of socialist principles, to order priorities and unify adherents—'a body of conviction as resolute and informed as the opposition in front of it'. It was needed in the 1930s and it is needed today.

II

Yet the world of today is one that has been radically transformed since Tawney wrote, and the scale and dimensions of this transformation must be understood and faced.

Tawney could plausibly analyse his world in time-honoured and well-tried categories. Thus he could write of the 'economic power' of 'bankers, industrialists and land-owners', of overcoming the 'vested interests' they imposed in the way of a socialist distribution, and that

class-privilege takes more than one form. It is both economic and social. It rests on functionless property, on the control of key positions in finance and industry, on educational inequalities, on the mere precariousness of proletarian existence, which prevents its victims looking before and after.[37]

But this is a world we have lost, just as the Labour Party Tawney addressed was the Labour Party of yesterday. Economic power,

[35] Tawney, 'The Choice before the Labour Party', p. 333. Cf. Neil Kinnock's characterization of 'democratic socialism' as a '*productionist* philosophy': 'My Socialism', *New Statesman*' (7 Oct. 1983).
[36] In Pimlott, *Fabian Essays in Socialist Thought*, p. 147.
[37] Tawney, 'The Choice before the Labour Party', p. 334.

vested interests, class privilege and class oppression seemed (whether to Marxists or Fabians) clearly identifiable, as did the agency that would bring them to an end (whether it be revolutionary workers or rational professionals). It was a world in which Britain still played an independent world role and its social structure rested upon the central geological fault of the distinction between manual and mental labour. In this world, the organized working class had 'the consciousness of an estate with definite interests to defend and advance within the existing polity', through the trade union movement, while the consciousness of the professional classes was 'the ethic of service, of intelligence and expertise, in pursuit of humanitarian ends, of a civilizing mission both at home and abroad'. Trade unionism was 'the vehicle of the poor and the underprivileged', while 'the self-esteem of the old professional middle class'—experts, teachers, scientists, doctors, civil servants, preachers—'stemmed from their sense of difference from the working class and of helping the labour movement from an unassailed privileged position'.[38] The Labour Party expressed and represented this alliance which culminated triumphantly in 1945. Tawney, from one point of view, may be seen as its finest and most articulate exponent. But since the 1950s, the parties to this alliance have largely fragmented, and their unifying forms of class consciousness largely dissolved; while the Labour Party has ceased to function as its natural embodiment (uniting workers of 'hand and brain') combining the largely defensive interests of the working class with the evangelical, Christian-based conscience of the middle classes, under the acknowledged leadership of the latter.

Furthermore, it is unhelpful to speak of resuming 'the forward march of labour which began to falter thirty years ago'[39]—as though the problem were to continue a (once magnificent) journey across territory which, though it may have been substantially transformed by various new developments, is still recognizable by the old familiar landmarks. It is not enough to take note of the 'changes in British capitalism' (the rise of mass production and the concentration of production units, the growth of monopoly capitalism and the public sector, the political determination of the capitalist market and the massive rise in workers' living standards) and the 'changes within the

---

[38] Stedman Jones, 'Why is the Labour Party in a Mess?' pp. 247, 248.
[39] Hobsbawm, *The Forward March of Labour Halted*, p. 18.

working class' (the influx of women workers and immigrants, and the growth of divisive sectional struggles) in order to explain why 'common working-class interests' have failed to prevail and why the movement 'in the right general direction' seems 'to have got stuck', and to conclude that we are today

in a period of world crisis for capitalism, and, more specifically, of the crisis—one might almost say the breakdown—of the British capitalist society, at a moment when the working class and its movement should be in a clear position to provide a clear alternative and to lead British peoples towards it.[40]

Rather than resuming the 'forward march', the problem is now one of drawing up new maps, of regrouping the army and recruiting new forces. (Indeed the very metaphor of a 'forward march' will have to be abandoned. It never really fitted anyway, and it derives, as Raymond Williams has noted, 'from an antiquated kind of military campaign based on the poor bloody infantry'.[41])

For the truth is that the class structure has radically changed over the last decades, becoming both more complex and more obscure; that in consequence the parties to the old Labour alliance have fragmented in various cross-cutting, ambiguous, and contradictory ways; and that the complementary forms of class consciousness on which that alliance depended (the defence of unambiguous and shared collective interests allied with a middle class humanitarian conscience) have all but dissolved.

There have been massive changes in the nature of both capital and labour.[42] This has occurred within the context of an increasingly international economy, now dominated by international corporations, in which they have been restructuring the international division of labour, directing capital intensive production, research, and development to areas of high labour productivity and the best markets and labour intensive production to the Third World: as a result, Britain's economic decline, unemployment in skilled and semi-skilled occupations, and de-industrialization have been accelerated. The changes in capital have been in the direction of ever more complex forms of ownership and control, rendering them ever more

[40] Hobsbawm, *The Forward March of Labour Halted*, pp. 13, 17, 18.
[41] Raymond Williams, ibid.
[42] See Newby, *et al.*, 'From Class Structure to Class Action', and the refs. cited therein.

difficult to perceive and make sense of. It is no longer a question of Tawney's few thousand or few hundred thousand 'bankers, industrialists and land-owners' but of pension funds, multinational corporations, cartels, 'spheres of interest', and so on. Economic power and vested interests have become less and less representable: capitalism now lacks not so much a human face as a human form. As for the changes in labour, these have resulted from sectoral shifts in the economy between industries and from the restructuring and reorganization of labour within them.[43] Here the most notable effects have been the massive growth and diversification in the service sector, de-skilling and white-collar proletarianization and the increasing feminization of work. Furthermore, the de-industrialization and shedding of labour in the current recession has accentuated the division between those in work and the unemployed and underemployed. It is no longer a question of 'the mere precariousness of proletarian existence' but increasingly the precariousness of existing outside the proletariat—outside work and the organized working class.

Among all these developments, a number are particularly worth stressing. First, economic power has become more anonymous and invisible. Second, the contours of the occupational structure have become more difficult to discern. Third, the traditional image of the proletarian—as 'male, manual and muscular' (in David Lockwood's happy phrase)—is becoming increasingly inapplicable to the industrial scene. Fourth, the very distinction between manual and non-manual labour is less and less relevant. Indeed, fifth, labour or work itself, and the sphere of production, seems to be becoming less central to the identity and consciousness of workers, while consumption, especially with respect to housing and transport, has become more central to the definition of their basic interests.[44] A new dividing-line, between home owners and others, now cuts across older, fading class divisions, fragmenting the working class by dividing those with a stake in the financial and property markets from those dependent on

[43] See E. O. Wright and J. Singlemann, 'Proletarianization in Advanced Capitalist Societies; An Empirical Investigation into the Debate between Marxist and Post-Industrial Theorists over the Transformation of the Labour Process', Mimeo., Dept. of Sociology, Univ. of Wisconsin, 1978, cited in Newby, *et al.*, 'From Class Structure to Class Action'.

[44] See J. Westergaard, 'Class of "84"', *New Socialist* (Jan./Feb. 1984), 30–6 and Newby, *et al.*, 'From Class Structure to Class Action'.

state provision, and significantly affecting voting patterns, to the progressive disadvantage of the Labour Party, given its current policies. Consumption patterns increasingly shape and reflect how people view their interests, their reference groups, the welfare state, and the Labour Party. Sixth, those in employment, including the professional classes, have turned more and more to sectional distributional conflicts, exploiting their differential market situations and organizational resources to the full—a trend only increased under inflationary conditions, albeit tempered by recession. Seventh, the poor and the underprivileged are now to be found more and more outside the organized working class and the trade union bargaining process—among the unemployed, the unwaged, coloured immigrants, and one-parent families.

Finally, there appears to have been a reactive growth (encouraged by the combination of recession and inflation) of instrumental, pecuniary, egoistic, in short capitalist values and attitudes, and a disintegration of various moral frameworks within which these had a subordinate place and faced various countervailing forms of commitment, loyalty, and discipline—whether based on unionism, locality, or class. In part, these frameworks have been withering away as the industrial, urban, and social structure changes; in part, more recently, they are being stripped away in a systematic, ruthless and manipulative political onslaught on the organizations of the working class and the institutions of local government. In part too, this has occurred because of the successes of the welfare state and of Labour in power. For when Tawney wrote, the 'mere precariousness of proletarian existence' gave the ties of solidarity and community a clear instrumental point: the work-place, the union, the neighbourhood, the extended family, the Labour Party were vital means of defending, and advancing, shared interests in a hostile and uncertain world. Universal welfare provision, however inadequate and maladministered, has removed that context, further weakening the bonds of communal solidarity. In short, the moral background to the cash nexus may be fading away,[45] leaving us morally unencumbered in what Tawney, in his forthright way, called an 'acquisitive society'.

---

[45] See Westergaard, 'The Rediscovery of the Cash Nexus' in R. Miliband and J. Saville (eds.), *The Socialist Register 1970*.

III

If this is the world we live in, how, then, are the lessons of Tawney to be applied to it? Is it possible today to be anti-fatalist? Is it feasible to live by and to spread the spirit of socialism? How should the socialist objective be framed and pursued?

Certainly, the socialist project confronts some formidable obstacles in present-day Britain. Facing them with 'cold realism' carries several implications.

First, our social analysis must endeavour to grasp these hard realities, unencumbered by wishful and anachronistic notions of class and class structure. It must take seriously the consumption-related interests of people whose loyalties have already been alienated by the Labour Party's historically laudable single-minded commitment to state provision. It must accordingly begin to distinguish between capitalism and the market principle, and between different types of markets.[46] It must also address other forms of domination and powerlessness, injustice and unfreedom than the exploitative wage relation and particularly those rightly associated in the public mind with socialism and the Labour Party, such as the relation between welfare bureaucracies and their clients.

Second, there must be a renewal of the socialist educational tradition, in which Tawney, and the Fabians generally, played such a central part. There must be a massive effort to make the increasingly opaque and complex processes and relations to which I have alluded more widely intelligible to those caught up within them. This is partly a matter of fiercely campaigning against the cumulative and growing inequalities within the formal education system (in the 1990s there is likely to be a smaller proportion of working-class children than in the 1970s[47]) and resisting at every point the current drive to sharpen these. Within the curriculum the battle against orthodoxy and establishment-mindedness must be waged with new vigour: where are the radical and critical history books for primary

[46] On this intriguing question see e.g. C. E. Lindblom, *Politics and Markets* (New York: Basic Books, 1977); A. Clayre (ed.), *The Political Economy of Co-operation and Participation: A Third Sector* (Oxford: Oxford Univ. Press, 1980); and A. Nove, *The Economics of Feasible Socialism* (London: Allen & Unwin, 1983).

[47] As Gareth Williams suggests in the *Times Higher Education Supplement* (30 Mar. 1984); see also *Democratic Trends and Future University Candidates* (London: Royal Society, 1984).

schoolchildren? And the systematic, though selective, onslaught on social science, and sociology in particular, by the present Government and friendly opinion leaders, must be taken especially seriously. Here is a major area in which the old Fabian tradition of research—of measurement and publicity—must be continued and renewed. It is also a question of returning to the innovative educational traditions of the past outside the formal system. But it is no longer mainly in miners' lodges, the WEA, and Ruskin College that such renewal will be found, but in the use of the media—both at national level (television, a labour national newspaper) and at local level, through the creative participatory use of new technology, above all videos, whose democratic possibilities can only now be glimpsed. Socialist education must awaken after its long, comfortable sleep.

Third, we must finally cast off the belief, shared by both the Fabian and the Marxist components of the British socialist tradition, that, whatever its setbacks, capitalist development somehow naturally culminates in socialism. This is not just a question of rejecting an antique, falsely reassuring evolutionary optimism, the Whig history of the left. In part, as I have suggested, the very pursuit of socialist objectives has made them less widely appealing and less easily attainable. It is also a matter of taking anti-fatalism seriously, looking hard to see how and where capitalism can be *socialised*—by diffusing the ownership and control of capital, both personal and industrial, and to discover what forms the 'organs through which the nation can control, in co-operation with other nations, its own economic destinies' can take in the contemporary world of internationally imposed inequalities. The dominating and growing role of multinationals makes this task all the more urgent and difficult, and all the more scandalous the Labour Party's relative traditional disinterest in the socialist parties and movements beyond our shores, and especially on the European continent.

Fourth, we should welcome, rather than regret, the passing of 'consensus politics'. This was a form of politics within which socialist advance was never going to prove possible. Now there has been a clearing of the decks, and we should see this as an opportunity to rediscover and redefine a 'common conception of the ends of political action, and of the means of achieving them, based on a common view of the life proper to human beings, and of the steps required at any moment more nearly to attain it'.

Fifth, among these steps must be the immensely difficult business of forging alliances between potential constituencies, building outwards from the Labour Party's shrunken base and upon various forms of solidarity, including those based on local and urban communities, regionalism, ethnicity, and social movements. In this process, particular attention should be paid to the rejuvenation of local democracy—a central Fabian concern, since the Webbs, much neglected by the Labour Party in recent times. For it is at the local and regional level that powerlessness and inequality are most resented and have grown most dramatically. Unemployment and deprivation, poor public services, the 'Thatchervilles' of inner cities, inadequate housing and transport, high crime rates, unsatisfactory policing—on such issues successful campaigning can be mounted, as part of the necessary task of seeking interests that may be 'harnessed by principles into a servicible tool' to build a new social order.

Finally, we need to rethink and restate those principles in a way that will evoke a response from people who are justifiably sceptical of the socialist record (while in countless unacknowledged ways its beneficiaries) and of the Labour Party's claims to their allegiance, but for whom the available alternatives offer bleak prospects indeed. And we must do so with the driving purpose of recovering and mobilizing a latent anti-fatalistic consensus of sentiment and belief: a sense of outrage and of justice, and a belief in the centrality of welfare rights to citizenship and of political will to social progress. This was the battle the Fabians fought. For a time it seemed to have been won. It has not. Now we must take it up all over again, with no certainty of victory.

17
The Morality of Sanctions*

One should not rule out the thought that it could be illuminating to examine politicians' moral views, and even their implicit views about what morality is. It could be illuminating in two ways. First, such an examination may be essential to explaining how they act (though it need not involve accepting either their views or indeed their views about how their views relate to their actions). Second, it may help in clarifying the issues upon which they decide (though it may be not so much their views as the critical examination of them that does so). I suspect that Mrs Thatcher's opposition to sanctions against South Africa is such a case, in both respects.

I write this as she continues to resist the mounting international campaign for sanctions. On this issue she leads and President Reagan follows. He speaks of 'many in Congress and some in Europe . . . clamoring for sweeping sanctions against South Africa' and commends Mrs Thatcher for having 'denounced punitive sanctions as "immoral" and "wholly repugnant"': 'we believe', he says, 'Mrs Thatcher is right.' She also believes she is right. Indeed, the widespread and passionate opposition appears only to strengthen her in this conviction: as she has remarked, 'If I were the odd one out and I were right, it wouldn't matter, would it?': 'If you're alone,' she says, 'you only operate really by persuading. Your only way of persuading is by argument.'

What, then, *are* her arguments? As presented in a recent *Guardian* interview with Hugo Young,[1] these fall into three broad, though interrelated, categories, which we may call the tactical, the strategic, and the moral, though it is clearly the last to which, publicly at least, she gives most passionate voice.

The tactical argument holds sanctions to be ineffective, first, in producing the desired economic impact in South Africa and, second,

---

* This chapter was first published in 1987.
1 'Why Sanctions are Ineffective and Immoral', *Guardian* (9 July 1986).

in thereby producing the desired political impact: 'South Africa has colossal internal resources. A colossal coastline. And whatever sanctions were put on, materials would get in and get out. There is no way you can blockade the whole South African coastline. No way.' It is true, she concedes, that the banks, in pressing for the repayment of the South African debt last year, had some effect—an economic effect that, presumably, in turn affected political policies and attitudes. Yet these latter (unspecified) effects, she believes, came mainly from the influence of people inside South Africa fighting apartheid —meaning by this industry and 'some of the political parties'.

More generally, her view is that externally imposed economic pressure, even if economically effective, is politically counter-productive: 'I don't believe that punitive economic sanctions will bring about internal change' because 'even the moderates, black and white, would respond badly if they saw the West just hitting out at their country.' Indeed she claims universality for this argument: 'There is no case in history that I know of where punitive, general economic sanctions have been effective to bring about internal change.'

The strategic argument concerns the wider and longer-term effects of sanctions, in particular as these affect the interests of the West. She sees them as plainly damaging, jeopardizing supplies of raw materials and enhancing the Soviet threat:

Platinum comes in quantity from only two places, South Africa and the Soviet Union. Are people who say there's a moral question suggesting that the world supply of platinum should be put in charge of the Soviet Union? And there are other things. Your chemical chrome, your vanadium, and, of course, gold and diamonds. They would have a fantastic effect on the economy of the Soviet Union. To me it is absolutely absurd that people should be prepared to put increasing power into the hands of the Soviet Union on the grounds that they disapprove of apartheid in South Africa.

But it is the moral case for sanctions which, in her interviewer's words, constitutes 'the central thrust of the prime ministerial argument, that part of it which elicited her most withering scorn':

I must tell you I find nothing *moral* about people who come to see me, worried about unemployment in this country, or about people who come to say we must do more to help Africa—particularly black Africans. I find nothing *moral* about them, sitting in comfortable circumstances, with good salaries, inflation-proof pensions, good jobs, saying that we, as a matter of *morality*, will put x hundred thousand black people out of work, knowing that this could lead to starvation, poverty, and unemployment, and even greater violence.

What, Young asked, about the black leaders? But Mrs Thatcher was thumping the table: 'That to me is *immoral*. I find it repugnant . . . And you'll really tell me that you'll move people around as if they're pawns on a checkerboard, and say that's *moral*? To me it's *immoral*.' But what of the opinion represented by black leaders such as Tutu, Mandela, the ANC, the UDF, who advocate sanctions?

I totally reject it. Because I find it very difficult to know how they can turn round and say 'Put our people into acute difficulty. They've got good jobs. They're looking after their children. But pursue a policy which can lead to children being hungry.' I find it very difficult indeed.

Indeed,

I find it astonishing, utterly astonishing, that on the one hand we're doing everything to help Ethiopia, everything to relieve poverty and starvation, everything to get the right seeds, the right husbandry. And at the same time we're suggesting that you turn people who are in work, out of work. And add to the problems you've already got. When people call that moral, I just *gasp*.

The effects of sanctions would, moreover, be harmful, not only in South Africa but more widely:

Supposing you start with fruit and vegetables. That would be 90,000 people, blacks and their families, out of work. *Moral?* Poof! No social security. *Moral?* Up would go the prices here. Some of it would be sold out of the coastline, through third countries, re-marked, and perhaps come in at a higher price. And the retaliation we could have to things we export to South Africa! What is *moral* about that?

There seem to be several arguments here. First, there are two arguments *ad hominem*, which seek to undermine the case for sanctions by attacking its advocates. They are held to be in no position to argue their case, because of their own distance or immunity from their effects. They stand accused of, in effect, advocating the suffering of *others*, whom they thereby treat like 'pawns on a checkerboard'. Presumably, then, only the potential sufferers from sanctions have the right to make this case. Call this the *Discredit the Non-victim Argument*.

The second *ad hominem* argument accuses sanctions advocates of inconsistency. They are, it seems, for both relieving starvation and poverty and increasing them. They contradict in South Africa what they advocate in Ethiopia. Call this the *Discredit the Inconsistent Argument*. More, of course, needs to be said before an inconsistency can be shown to exist here. But note that, even if valid, neither of these first two *ad hominem* moral arguments bears on the argument for and against sanctions. The most either could show, if valid, is that those advocating sanctions are to be criticized for doing so.

Apart from these, there are two further arguments which can be discerned in Mrs Thatcher's responses to her interviewer which address the case for sanctions directly. These are inconsistent with one another; and in the light of this, it is not clear which of the two she wishes us to believe.

The first suggests that the mere fact that extensive suffering will result from sanctions is enough to condemn them—not, it should be noted, *greater* suffering than would flow from alternative policies (including inaction). What this argument proposes is that *any* suffering—or perhaps any extensive suffering constitutes a knockdown case against sanctions (or any other policy) causing it. Such suffering, as an economist might say, is given infinite negative value; no trade-off or calculations of the overall outcome are allowable. Call this the *No Extensive Suffering Argument*.

Finally, there is the argument that the sufferings sanctions occasion will, on the best estimation of likely overall effects, outweigh any good to be attained by them. The net effect of sanctions will, in other words, be negative, all things considered: they will do more harm than good. In so far as this is her argument, we need to have some idea of a time-scale, within which the judgement is being made, what the costs and benefits being compared are, and how future benefits are to be discounted against present costs, and vice versa. Clearly, the force of this entirely consequentialist argument depends on the conclusions of the tactical and strategic arguments turning out to be either unfavourable or only weakly favourable to the case for sanctions. Call this the *No Net Suffering Argument*.

The first two moral arguments are agent-relative: it is immoral for certain views to be advanced by certain people (those immune from their consequences, and those holding views held to contradict them). The second two are consequentialist, albeit incompatible (the first holding certain kinds of consequence to be absolutely inadmissible; the second claiming, on empirical grounds, that, all things considered, the consequential balance-sheet will be negative).

How powerful is this battery of arguments? About the tactical argument there is, of course, much to be said for and against sanctions—partly because of the sheer complexity of the situation, partly because of the multiplicity of different kinds of sanction, partly because of the inductive difficulties of deciding what is relevant in previous experience of sanctions, and partly because of the sheer unpredictability and contingencies of the fast-moving South African situation. But for this very reason it is plain that Mrs Thatcher's certainty about the economic and political *ineffectiveness* of sanctions is itself unwarranted. Her universal claim—that there is 'no case in history' where 'punitive, general economic sanctions have been effective to bring about internal change'—is either false or misleading. According to the Washington-based Institute for International Economics, one third of 103 episodes of economic sanctions can be counted a success (some applied by South Africa itself). If, however, 'punitive' and 'general' are given a strong interpretation, the claim is diversionary, since her argument is against any economic sanctions, taken severally, not all together, and in a 'punitive' manner (whatever this means).

There certainly are economic sanctions that could be *economically* effective. It is true that most are leaky, messy, erratic, and imperfect. It is true that South Africa has vast resources and that there would be massive evasion. Its $7 billion manufactured imports could be shipped from anywhere, and the resulting price rises would be tolerable; the oil would get in; and there would be perverse effects. The rising costs of imports would be protectionist in effect, encouraging import substitution (as with Sasol and Armscor) and the growth of a domestic (albeit uncompetitive) manufacturing industry; while forcing South Africa to default on its international debt would free resources by saving capital and interest repayments. It may have been true up to now that 'sanctions against South Africa are only rhetorically endorsed by front-line states, most of whom are secretly participating in ending the economic isolation of the apartheid state'.[2] Nevertheless, as Mrs Thatcher admits, last year's withdrawal of private loans to South Africa halved the value of the rand. A general freeze on new investment would undercut the dynamic of modernization in an economy heavily dependent on imported tech-

---

[2] Heribert Adam and Kogila Moodley, *South Africa without Apartheid: Dismantling Racial Discrimination* (Berkeley, Calif.: Univ. of California Press, 1986), p. 120.

nology; even a partial trade embargo would have some effect (the Rhodesian analogy is imperfect here); but, above all, the readily available weapon of forcing down the gold price would have a decisive and non-evadeable effect on South Africa's terms of trade. Indeed, even announcing an intention to hold the gold price steady could have this effect.[3]

But what about the political effects of these economic effects? Much here is, by nature of the case, imponderable. Certainly, no one should underestimate Afrikaner counter-suggestibility, especially under the present leader. In 1977, P. W. Botha declared the following to an interviewer:

The Afrikaner is a very interesting species. He doesn't always tell you what he has in mind, because he has learned through the ages to be careful—he's been sold down the river on many occasions. Basically we are a very friendly people, a deeply Christian people and we would like to see others live in peace because we know ourselves what it is to be persecuted. I personally know what my family had to pay in the history of South Africa for our survival. But one thing you must accept from me: if they force us to hit back, we'll use everything we have at our disposal. Carter is awakening again a feeling that we had hoped would remain slumbering; that if they don't want to accept that we are also reasonable and civilised people with a right to self-determination and if, for their own selfish reasons, they want to spit on us and destroy us from outside, then we'll fight back. Because we are also a proud people.[4]

Nevertheless, the relevant question is rather: what are the likely consequences of *not* imposing sanctions. On this point the Commonwealth Eminent Persons pronounced themselves

convinced that the South African Government is concerned about the adoption of effective economic measures against it. If it comes to the conclusion that it would almost remain protected from such measures, the process of change in South Africa is unlikely to increase in momentum and the descent into violence would be accelerated. In these circumstances, the cost in lives may have to be counted in millions.

If the black leadership 'comes to believe that the world community will never exercise sufficient effective pressure through other measures in support of their cause, they will have only one option remaining: that of ever-increasing violence'.[5] In short, the tactical

[3] See *The Economist* (19 July 1986), pp. 11–12.

[4] Anna Starcke, *Survival: Taped Interviews with South Africa's Élite* (Cape Town: Tafelberg, 1986), p. 61.

[5] Eminent Persons Group, *Mission to South Africa* (Harmondsworth: Penguin, 1986), p. 140.

argument against sanctions is not persuasive and least of all to those nearest the action, and it has no universal basis. To propose, as an alternative, internal pressure from industry and some of the political parties is either wishful or deceptive unrealism.

As for the strategic argument against sanctions, it is less plausible still. An interruption of platinum would at worst delay the introduction of anti-pollution car exhausts; and South Africa's share of chrome would not be crippling. As for gold, it is no longer essential to the world's monetary system, with the major industrial countries committed to its demonetization anyway. The international diamond cartel too could easily be broken by concerted governmental action.

As for the Soviet threat in South Africa, this is much overplayed by both Mrs Thatcher and President Botha—as ex-Prime Minister Edward Heath has been pointing out. The US Administration itself admits this. Its Deputy Assistant Secretary for African Affairs observed recently that 'Southern Africa is practically speaking well outside the zone of primary interest, indeed of its secondary interest. We believe that Moscow is aware of this fact and, in reality, spends little time thinking about the area'.[6]

What, then, of the *moral* arguments that so concern the Prime Minister? I see no force whatever in the *Discredit the Non-Victim Argument*. First, because it would prohibit most people from taking moral stands on many issues; second, because it is the responsibility of politicians to take a stand on just such issues as this; third, because Mrs Thatcher certainly does not apply this principle elsewhere; and fourth because, in any case, there is compelling evidence that potential victims of sanctions widely endorse them anyway.[7]

As for the *Discredit the Inconsistent Argument*, it misfires because the inconsistency in question is entirely of Mrs Thatcher's making. It is generated by imputing to sanctions advocates the *goal* of increasing poverty, starvation, and unemployment. The sad truth is that there is no humane and costless way to combat the sufferings of apartheid: the question at issue is how to minimize the costs without compromising the goal. The Prime Minister's new-found concern for the poor and starving of Africa and for the unemployed is no doubt

6 Cited in Adam and Moodley, *South Africa without Apartheid*, p. 120.
7 *Black Attitudes to Disinvestment: The Real Story*, An overview of the survey conducted in Sept. 1985 by Mark Orkin of the Community Agency for Social Inquiry in association with the Institute for Black Research, Johannesburg, 1985.

very touching, but those who share it are not being *inconsistent* in supporting policies which will, if effective, have as by-products, poverty, starvation, and unemployment, above all if the only alternatives—the by-products of *not* pursuing them—are continued extensive suffering of this and other kinds—including 'ever-increasing violence'.

What of the *No Extensive Suffering Argument?* It is hard to see how this could be seriously meant by Mrs Thatcher or any practising politician, whose trade, after all, essentially involves accepting responsibility for just such outcomes. The argument implies a view of morality that has no obvious place in her world, in which just wars are undertaken, counterrevolutionary movements supported, and even economic sanctions imposed (against communist states). It suggests a kind of moral purism or absolutism akin to pacifism. A principled refusal to engage in certain consequential calculations, to dirty one's hands by doing harm that would do credit to a Christian idealist or a dedicated Ghandian, ill suits the Iron Lady, Victor of inflation and the Falklands.

What, finally, of the *No Net Suffering Argument?* It precisely involves the weighing of consequences and assessment of risks, and, furthermore, some judgement about what counts for more and what for less (the relief of suffering, the promotion of welfare, the according of dignity?). One thing, however, is clear: there is no moral certainty in the offing.

Moreover, one must ask: with what are the net results of various forms of economic sanctions to be compared? The right answer is: with the likely net effects of not applying them (within some given time period). Avoiding or at least minimizing suffering is, of course, a properly moral aim, but it only tells against sanctions if there is a no-sanctions alternative causing less. Is it really plausible to suggest that allowing internal developments to unfold without external pressure (other than endlessly seeking to encourage dialogue à la Geoffrey Howe) looks more promising on balance—in the face of Afrikaner intransigence and deteriorating violence in the townships where the prospect looms of future 'killing fields' of Young Comrades, Cambodia-style, taking over the leadership of black revolt? Tragically, the possibility of a clean or a cleaner route to the dismantling of apartheid may be long past; and it may be that the human costs of *every* option can only mount as time passes.

What does this summary examination of Mrs Thatcher's morality (and her view of morality) with respect to sanctions illuminate? First, it is a striking and momentous instance of her so-called conviction politics, passionately claiming a moral certainty that purports to derive from arguments (we have looked at six) that do not survive dispassionate scrutiny. A moral passion, exuding certainty, claiming no other basis than reason. In fact, her position on sanctions is not so much moral as moral*istic*, substituting preaching and invective for argument and analysis, obscuring the issues of which it claims such clarity of vision. Second, it seems that, of all these arguments, only the last is worth taking seriously, but even this could only carry conviction under circumstances that are, tragically, by now all too implausible.

18
The Principles of 1989: Reflections on the Political Morality of the Recent Revolutions

In January 1990, as I write this, it is probably still too early to achieve an adequate understanding of the significance of last year's moment-ous events in China, the Soviet Union, and Eastern Europe. It is, however, already clear that the basic tenets of kremlinology stand in need of revision, as, almost daily, transformations occur that academic orthodoxy had declared systemically impossible. The theory of revolutionary change needs drastic attention, in the face of the democratic revolutions of Eastern Europe, which occurred with-out war between states or within them (apart from Romania) or fanaticism or vanguards, in a self-limiting manner and for goals that were limited and procedural rather than global and visionary. And, in general, the social scientists studying communist regimes should perhaps reflect on their collective failure to foresee even the possibil-ity of most of what occurred. Perhaps that failure has something to do with their virtually total neglect of the moral dimension of political life. For it is a striking fact that morally motivated actions and reactions, and *demoralization*, played a central role in all these events, from the Polish Round Table through the demonstrations and massacre in Tiananmen Square to the fall of Ceausescu.

One way of interpreting the significance of these events, now prevalent among journalistic and political commentators, is to see them simply as the collapse of one political ideology and the triumph of its rival. Thus, for *Newsweek* (1 Jan. 1990), '1989 was the year the communist god finally failed'. Others would extend the failure to the

This chapter was first published in Spring 1990. In writing it, I was much influenced by the ideas advanced by Maurice Glasman in an inspiring and impressive paper, 'The Rawlsian Revolutions in Eastern Europe', recently delivered to my seminar at the European University Institute, Florence. I hope he will develop them further.

socialist project as a whole, others to the very idea of the Left itself. Conversely, according to the *New York Herald Tribune* (15 Jan. 1990), 'the revolutions of 1989' were 'dominated by the ideals of pluralistic democracy and civil rights, a region-wide triumph for Western liberalism'. Others, who take such liberalism to be indissoluble from a more or less unbridled capitalism, see the revolutions as marking the definitive failure of a century-long mega-experiment in social, economic, and political progress and a return to the market-based system it was intended to transform and supersede.

There is doubtless much to be said for these interpretations. Certainly, there is no shortage of voices in Eastern Europe, and indeed in the Soviet Union, that will speak with enthusiasm in favour of them, and more particularly for their more stringent and strident versions. Nevertheless, in what follows here, I propose to take a different, and less ideological, tack, by asking two connected questions about political morality. First, what were the distinctive features of the prevailing political morality of communist regimes that was so massively rejected? And second, in the name of what? What distinguished the alternative political morality to which the revolutionary movements of 1989 in turn appealed?

By 'political morality' I mean a set of principles, that can be characterized at a fairly high level of abstraction, that underlie different, particular political positions that may be taken up by those who share them at any given time, or across time. They are, as Ronald Dworkin says, 'constitutive': 'political positions that are valued for their own sake', such that 'every failure fully to secure that position, or any decline in the degree to which it is secured, is *pro tanto* a loss in the value of the overall political arrangement'. Derivative positions, by contrast, are 'valued as strategies or means of achieving the constitutive positions'.[1] Thus different derivative views on policies—about taxation, say, or education, or, more generally, about the nature and scope of state intervention in the economy—may appeal to, or be justifiable by, the same set of constitutive principles; and likewise clusters of such derivative views will replace one another over time, as, say, New Deal liberalism replaced Old Deal liberalism (the example is Dworkin's). Of course, constitutive political positions may conflict with one another, for

---

[1] Dworkin, *A Matter of Principle* (Cambridge, Mass.: Harvard Univ. Press, 1985), pp. 184, 408, 184.

political moralities will almost inevitably embody conflicting values. But by a 'political morality' I here intend to mean the underlying structure within which and by virtue of which political value judgements are made and justified by those who share it, and which sets limits to the *kinds* of judgements that can be made.

I

What, by 1989, was the political morality of Official Communism? This may seem an odd question to those who are impressed by the corruption and cynicism of the élites ruling these regimes. Certainly 1989 was not lacking in lurid evidence of the former, notably from China, East Germany, Romania, and Bulgaria. Nor do I wish to imply that these regimes enjoyed a moral legitimacy among their populations—though this is a complex question, and there have clearly been variations across the communist world in this respect: compare the German Democratic Republic with Poland or Czechoslovakia, or indeed Czechoslovakia before and after 1968. It is, further, true, as Leszek Kolakowski has said, that in Poland at least by the mid-1980s, 'Marxism both as an ideology and as a philosophy' had 'become completely irrelevant . . . Even the rulers [had] largely abandoned this notion and even its phrases'.[2] What is, however, indisputable, is that Marxism, of however deformed or debased a sort, dominated, indeed monopolized the public sphere of these societies for decades (seven in the case of the Soviet Union) and provided the sole framework and discourse within which the governing élites could seek to justify their policies to their subjects, to themselves, and to the outside world. It is, therefore, worth trying to identify the constitutive features of that framework and discourse.

Marxism has always been a peculiarly bibliocentric creed. There were times of faith when the massive ideological apparatuses achieved success in inspiring hearts and shaping minds within the Party and far beyond. In the subsequent times of demoralization, the propaganda machine remained intact, its wheels went on turning, and the flow of words in work-places and offices, schools and universities, newspapers, radio, and television continued unabated, but now as 'noise' blocking out alternative forms of thought and

---

[2] Cited in V. Tismaneanu, *The Crisis of Marxist Ideology in Eastern Europe: The Poverty of Utopia* (London and New York: Routledge, 1988), p. 115.

expression.[3] But the words always related, directly or indirectly, to texts, and ultimately to the founding texts of the Marxist canon. And this was not just a question of the time-honoured practice of quotations from the Founding Fathers but went deeper and wider. The old books and pamphlets set their mark on vocabulary and syntax, on conceptual apparatus, polemical style, and forms of argumentation, indeed even furnished the criteria of what was to count as a valid argument.

This helps to explain the remarkable coherence and continuity of Marxism as a political morality across the entire continuum that ranges from its historically significant incarnations as a political ideology propagated by political élites to the most refined and intellectually sophisticated theories favoured by intellectuals, orthodox or 'critical'. For different reasons the same corpus of texts served as meat and drink to both. My claim is that, considered as a text-based structure of thought, the political morality of Marxism is more or less firmly imprinted on all the significant varieties of Marxism, official and deviant, vulgar and refined, deformed and revised.

What are the essentials of that structure? What distinguishes Marxism as a political morality is that it is a morality of emancipation. It promises communism as universal freedom from the peculiar modern slavery of capitalism through revolutionary struggle. The promise is (usually) long-term: the prospect of a world of abundance, co-operation, and social rationality—the free association of producers whose communal relations have overcome egoism, in full collective control of both the natural and social worlds which have become transparent to them. The world from which they are to be emancipated is one of scarcity, private property, the dull compulsion, anarchy and irrationality of market relations, exploitation, class domination, human degradation, reification, and alienation. The access to the promised realm of freedom is through struggle: hence the consistent appeal throughout the Marxist tradition of the metaphors of war, of strategy and alliances, of forward marches and glorious victories, and its ingrained suspicion of compromise. In short, as a political morality, Marxism is future-oriented: it is, indeed, a perfectionist form of long-range consequentialism.[4] The

---

[3] Tismaneanu's book, cited above, is a good recent study of all this.

[4] For an explanation of this claim, see my *Marxism and Morality* (Oxford: OUP, 1985), Conclusion and Chapter 10 of this volume.

practical question, 'What is to be done?'—how to act? what policy to pursue?—is always to be answered only by calculating what course is likely to bring nearer the long-term goal, the leap into the realm of freedom. The anxiety generated by that question is, however, traditionally diminished by two further assumptions: that capitalism is doomed, and has nowhere to go but its death; and that history is on the side of the working-class struggle, that long-term objective processes are at work that favour, and perhaps eventually guarantee, the leap into freedom.

There is, of course, as the history of Marxism superabundantly shows, enormous scope for dispute about all the elements in this picture: about how exactly to characterize socialism and/or communism, and in particular how economic planning and political decision-making are to proceed and relate to one another (on which the canon is studiedly unforthcoming); about what are the essential evils of capitalism, and which has explanatory priority, and through what kind of crisis they will issue in death; and about the famous problem of the 'transition'—how warlike, and what kind of war? how parliamentary? how reformist? All these sources of indeterminacy become all the more confusing, of course, as the two anxiety-diminishing assumptions lose their power to persuade.

But, even in the present confusion, it is clear that Marxism has always held, as a constitutive triad of positions: (1) that capitalism belongs to the realm of necessity; (2) that communism signifies the promised realm of a higher kind of social freedom; and (3) that emancipation into the latter from the former is a discontinuous change, a qualitative transformation of economy, polity, and culture. In this respect, Ernst Fischer was right to say that for Marxism,

Only the future is interesting, the fullness of what is possible, not the straitjacket of what has already been, with its attempt to impose on us the illusion that, because things were thus and not otherwise, they belong to the realm of necessity.[5]

From the perspective of Marxism, in short, certain necessary facts are, rather, historically contingent: falsely to suppose them to be necessary facts is to cling to an ideological fiction blocking human progress. Four such 'facts' strike me as of central importance. I shall call them the facts of scarcity, particularity, pluralism, and limited rationality.

[5] Cited in Tismaneanu, *The Crisis of Marxist Ideology*, p. 216.

By 'scarcity' I mean limits to desired goods. It may take at least the following four forms: (1) insufficiency of production inputs (e.g. raw materials) relative to production requirements; (2) insufficiency of produced goods relative to consumption requirements; (3) limits upon the joint realizability of different goals, resulting from external conditions (e.g. limitations of space or time); and (4) limits upon the joint realizability of different goals, resulting from the intrinsic nature of those goals (e.g. 'positional goods'—we cannot all enjoy high status or the solitude of a neighbourhood park). Marxism, in promising abundance, considers only scarcity (1) and (2), which it promises to overcome through the mastery of nature and through a superior form of economic and social organization, combined with appropriate changes in preferences brought about by higher, communal relations. It has nothing to say about (3) or (4), nor does it address contemporary ecological concerns about the eliminability, or costs of seeking to eliminate, (1).

By 'particularity' I mean that we are not all Kantians, or utilitarians: that human beings have their separate lives to live and are properly motivated by a whole range of distinct interests, from the purely personal through a whole gamut of more or less local or partial or particular concerns, to the most abstract and universal. In deciding how to act, we rightly give weight, at different times, to demands or claims that have different sources, but include our commitments and loyalties to relationships and activities that are special and exclusive. Marxism as a political morality belongs with those monistic moralities which require of individuals that they adopt a single privileged standpoint that abstracts from this motivational complexity and range, in its particular case requiring of individuals that they act solely in the postulated universal interests of future generations—or that they adopt the social identity and thus standpoint of the imminently victorious class, which, together with its standpoint, will wither away into the universal standpoint indicated. Without that extravagant assumption, Marxism has always had the greatest difficulty in linking its monistic motivational requirement with the likely motivations of actual people.

By 'pluralism' I mean the coexistence of different views about what is of central importance and value in human life, of what John Rawls has called divergent 'conceptions of the good', where the differences or divergences are not simply alternative way of spelling out a set of common principles that the adherents of each could recognize as shared in common among them. Alternative moralities, religions, world views, value-standpoints are in this way 'pluralistic', implying alternative conceptual structures, priorities of value, and forms of life when these are unassimilable to one another without destroying what is constitutive of each. Marxism does not address the possibility of pluralism, thus understood, in a general form, nor, therefore, the question of how to respond to it, for it simply assumes, in the manner of the Enlightenment, that Humanity is progressing, along however dialectical a path, towards moral convergence. That is why it has always typically treated actual instances of pluralist divergence—particular forms of religion or nationalism or indeed secular moralities such as utilitarianism—as deviations, if sometimes as useful short-cuts (as Lenin saw nationalism), along that path.

Finally, by 'limited rationality' I mean limits upon the capacity of human beings in real time to solve certain problems, theoretical and practical, or to do so without creating others that undermine their solution. These limits may be of various kinds—of access to or ability to process information, of theoretical knowledge or the means to apply it; and they may result from human incapacities, or from the nature of the object—from social complexity, say, or from ineliminable risk or uncertainty. To such contemporary concerns Marxism answers, once more with the voice of the Enlightenment, this time with a Hegelian, teleological accent: mankind only sets itself such problems as it can solve. The future is not only radiant but transparent: the social and natural worlds are alike in being in principle amenable to full prediction and control.

Marxism denies that these facts are necessary, but in doing so what does it deny? Not merely that they are present in all actual societies that have reached a certain level of economic development and social complexity. Not merely that, on the best estimates, they will be so present in all empirically feasible societies. (Marxism, after all, proposes a discontinuous leap into the realm of freedom, which our best estimates could not therefore predict, since they are based on present knowledge, which therefore draws the bounds of feasibility in the wrong place.) To say that these facts are necessary is to say that we cannot conceive of developed and complex societies that do not exhibit them—or could only do so at an unacceptable cost, by abandoning too much of all the rest of what we know and believe. They are facts at the very centre, rather than the periphery, of our cognitive universe. To imagine them, as Ernst Fischer says, otherwise, is, for us, literally to imagine Utopia.

I have argued that Marxism as a political morality takes scarcity, particularity, pluralism and limited rationality to be false necessities, as historically overcomeable (and in its confidently optimistic phase imminently so). What, then, follows from taking them to be real necessities? The most general answer to this question is, I suggest, the recognition of the need for principles of justice for the regulation of social life. For, taken together, these 'necessary facts' can be seen as constituting what Rawls calls the 'circumstances of justice'. They are conditions that *must*, in the appropriate sense, face the citizens of every conceivable society of a certain complexity and level of development. Within any such society (I here leave aside the question of inter-societal relations), they imply the inevitability of various kinds of conflict of interest that are, given these facts, structurally determined: a distributive struggle, involving conflicting claims upon limited resources of various kinds; conflicts facing both individuals and decision-making bodies at all levels of society, standing in the overlap of multiple intersecting circles of interest—individual, familial, local, regional, national, international, ethnic, religious, occupational, recreational, commercial, political, and so on—having to draw (different) lines between what is public and what private, and allocate priorities; cultural conflicts between different ways of life expressing divergent value-standpoints that cannot be flattened into 'shared understandings' or 'common meanings'; and policy conflicts over problems for which the 'correct' solution is neither on offer nor in the offing. To acknowledge all this is to accept that such a society can only have a chance of being both stable and democratically legitimate if its citizens are able, *as citizens*, to step back from all these conflicting interests and acknowledge as binding upon them a set of principles for the distribution of benefits and burdens, and for the assigning of rights to protect interests and corresponding obligations.

My argument has been that Marxism, official and unofficial, is constitutively inhospitable to this conclusion, essentially because it views all these conflicts as the pathologies of prehistory, and in particular as stemming from the anarchic production relations and class conflicts of capitalism. And it believes this in part just because it takes the facts of scarcity, particularity, pluralism, and limited rationality to be contingent, not necessary.

As supporting evidence, I would cite the consistent polemics that have characterized the Marxist canon, from Marx's *On the Jewish Question* onwards, against all talk of morality and in particular against the vocabulary of 'justice' and 'rights'—or, to be more precise, against the idea of believing in such notions, rather than adopting and propagating them, where appropriate, in the course of the struggle. So, in the *Critique of the Gotha Programme*, Marx writes of the notions of 'equal right' and 'fair distribution' as 'ideological nonsense', as 'ideas which in a certain period had some meaning but have now become obsolete verbal rubbish'.[6] In 1864, he apologized to Engels in the following terms; 'I was obliged', he wrote, 'to insert two phrases about "duty" and "right" into the Preamble to the Rules [of the International Working Men's Association], ditto "truth, morality and justice" but these are placed in such a way that they can do no harm'.[7] 'Justice', Engels once observed, is 'but the ideologized, glorified expression of the existing economic relations, now from their conservative, and at other times from their revolutionary angle'.[8] But it was Lenin who put the whole matter most clearly, to a Komsomol Congress in 1920:

We say that our morality is entirely subordinated to the interests of the proletariat's class struggle . . . Morality is what serves to destroy the old exploiting society and to unite all the working people around the proletariat, which is building up a new, a communist society . . . To a communist all morality lies in this united discipline and conscious mass struggle against the exploiters. We do not believe in an eternal morality, and we expose the falseness of all the fables about morality.[9]

But, surely, it will be said, Marxism has a powerful moral message. In particular, is socialism not about justice? And have Marxists not an honourable place in countless struggles against injustice and the violations of rights. President Havel himself recently, and eloquently, observed:

There was a time when . . . for whole generations of the downtrodden and oppressed, the word socialism was a mesmerising synonym for a just world,

---

⁶ K. Marx, *Critique of the Gotha Programme*, in Marx and Engels, *Selected Works*, 2 vols. (Moscow: Foreign Languages Publishing House, 1962), ii. p. 25.

⁷ Marx and Engels, *Selected Correspondence* (Moscow: Foreign Languages Publishing House, n.d.), p. 182.

⁸ Engels, *The Housing Question*, in Marx and Engels, *Selected Works*, i. pp. 624–5.

⁹ V. I. Lenin, *Collected Works* (Moscow: Foreign Languages Publishing House, 1960–3), xxxi. pp. 291–4.

a time when for the ideal expressed in that word, people were capable of sacrificing years and years of their lives, and their very lives even.[10]

But this objection misses the point. Of course Marxism has offered victims of injustice and oppression and those who sympathize with them an inspiring vision of a future free of both. The objection misses the inspirational core of that vision. What inspires those who grasp what Marxism promises is not the prospect of a complex, conflictual, pluralistic world regulated by principles of justice and the protections of rights, but rather the overcoming of complexity, conflict, and pluralism, of the very conditions that require such principles and protections—the prospect of a world in which justice and rights, together with class conflict and the oppression of the state, will have withered away. Communists have promised an end to injustice and oppression. What they promise, however, is not justice and rights, but, rather, emancipation from the enslaving conditions that make them necessary.

II

I turn, finally, to the second question I asked at the outset of this essay: to what and because of what political morality did the revolutionary movements of 1989—those that succeeded and those that did not, or have not yet—appeal? A properly academic answer to this question would doubtless distinguish among the different kind of evidence required properly to answer it, each of which would be given its proper weight—the writings of intellectuals, the speeches of leaders, the slogans and graffiti, the responses of the crowds, the oral evidence of different kinds of participants, the impressions of journalists, and so on, and among the different, though increasingly interdependent movements, and even among the different stages of these ever faster-moving events. Nevertheless, even without the benefit of these indispensable discriminations, which future scholarship will not fail to furnish, it already seems clear, at this short distance from them, that the revolutionary movements of 1989 were at one on at least the following decisive points.

First, they were citizens' movements and actively invoked the idea

[10] V. Havel, 'Words on Words', *New York Review of Books*, 36/21–2 (18 Jan. 1990), p. 6.

of citizenship. In virtually every case, they were appeals by and to citizens, that implied the stepping back from more particular and immediate commitments, loyalties, and interests. Hence the rhetoric of 'round tables' and 'forums', one of which was, indeed, civic and the other new in, among others, just this respect. The students of Tiananmen Square were seeking to transcend their generational and occupational identity and speak in the name of the 'people'; and indeed from mid-May, the demonstration expanded to over a million people, and included workers, Party bureaucrats, professionals, and even units of the military. One of the slogans shouted in demonstrations in East Germany, which, it seems, were similarly inclusive in composition, was 'We are the people!' The point is, perhaps, most dramatically made by the insignificance of ethnic and religious factors in the Timişoara uprising. It originated with the protests of Hungarian Protestants, but these, emphatically, were not what it was *about*. Only in the Caucasus and in Yugoslavia, especially Serbia, does this commitment to a pluralism-encompassing citizenship seem to be seriously in jeopardy.

Second, these were movements that appealed to a sense of distributive justice and fairness. For they were protests against the arbitrary allocation of advantage and opportunity, against the failed command economy that was itself a major source of scarcity as well as injustice, and in general against a system governed by no rationally defensible distributive principle, in which, from the ordinary citizen's point of view,

'they' can do everything they want—take away his passport, have him fired from his job, order him to move, send him to collect signatures against the Pershings, bar him from higher education, take away his driver's licence, build a factory producing mostly acid fumes right under his windows, pollute his milk with chemicals to a degree beyond belief, arrest him simply because he attended a rock concert, raise prices arbitrarily, anytime and for any reason, turn down all his humble petitions without cause, prescribe what he must read before all else, what he must demonstrate for, what he must sign, how many square feet his apartment may have, whom he may meet and whom he must avoid.[11]

There was, of course, no unified agreement about what distributive principles *would* be just, only that they should prevail; though all, including the gracefully departing élites, were further united in the

---

[11] Id., 'An Anatomy of Reticence', *Crosscurrents: A Yearbook of Central European Culture* (Ann Arbor, Mich.: Univ. of Michigan Press, No. 5, 1986), p. 5.

view that they could only do so if markets—including capital and labour markets—play a key role in both to the transition to and functioning of the future economy. The burning question for the future is, of course, just what kind and degree of public intervention in markets justice will require. One real possibility is that, in full recoil from real socialism, the post-revolutionary élites will embrace the full package of the counter-ideology of free-market liberalism, which, like Marxism but on different grounds, also rejects the very notion of 'social justice'.[12] Such an outcome, occurring under conditions of economic decline and crisis, and at the periphery of the world capitalist system, would indeed be a novel, late-twentieth-century version of the revolution betrayed.

Third, they were defensive movements, aiming at revolution in the name of procedural justice, the rule of law, the protection of individuals' basic constitutional rights and liberties—the Principles of 1789, as distinct from the positive social and economic rights added to them in the Universal Declaration of 1948. In part, they were directed at abuses and corruption by individuals (Ceausescu, Honecker, Zhivkov) and by a whole political class, as in China. These were certainly important in mobilizing people over grievances that took visible and outrageous forms. But at root the issue was the rejection of an entire institutional system that worked through command restrained only through bargaining and whose official rationale lay entirely in the future it promised rather than in its responsiveness to present, actual individuals' interests. Moreover, there was one particular individual right that was of especial significance in 1989: the right to free travel across frontiers. It was the mass effective exercise of this right and its subsequent recognition by the state that unleashed the East German events and thus all that followed from them. The right to leave one's country is, as Locke intimated, a right of peculiar significance, for only where it is effective can the according of consent to a regime or a system be a genuine choice. Clearly, Egon Krenz, in granting it, hoped thereby to establish the legitimacy of the German Democratic Republic; at the time of writing, that hope looks indeed forlorn.

Fourth, they were pluralist movements that demanded an end to the monopoly of power, to the *Nomenklatura*, to the euphemistically described 'leading role' of the Party, to 'ghost parties' in false

[12] For discussion of these grounds, see Chap. 4, above.

'alliances' playing proportional roles based on frozen statistics from the past, to the suppression of local, regional, and national issues, and of the real history (as in the Baltics) of how nations were incorporated into the Soviet Empire, and to the denial of expression, and institutional embodiment, to cultural, notably ethnic and religious, identities. In part, they embodied the expression of this pluralism or diversity, but, more significantly, they also expressed, often very clearly, a vivid sense, unavailable to the ruling structures, of the value of it.

Finally, they were sceptical movements—utterly sceptical not only of the content of what socialism had promised, both materially and morally, but of the very cognitive pretensions of the ruling parties who had in any case lost their way and abandoned any serious claim to knowledge-based, let alone science-based, authority. This is, in part, obviously a result of the massive economic failure of the prevailing system, as well as justified doubts about all the various attempts to reform it from within, from the Hungarian economic reforms onwards. But it also, perhaps, exhibits a deeper and more universal trend: a new sense, arising out of green concerns, of the complexity and uncertainty of the interaction between Man and Nature, and in consequence an awareness of the ecological consequences of the old Promethean Marxist vision of ending human exploitation through the exploitation of nature.

These were, in short, revolutions, some attempted, some successful, against *hubris*—the hubris of individual leaders, political élites, and indeed of an entire political class. They were also revolutions against the hubris of an arbitrary and oppressive system, economic, social, and political, whose claims to legitimacy were no longer, for the most part, even proclaimed by its rulers. But, above all, they were revolutions against the hubris of a political morality that for decades sustained that system and its leaders. In this sense, they were revolutions of fallen expectations, revolutions in the name of freedom—but of freedom as the recognition of necessity.

INDEX OF NAMES

SUBJECT INDEX

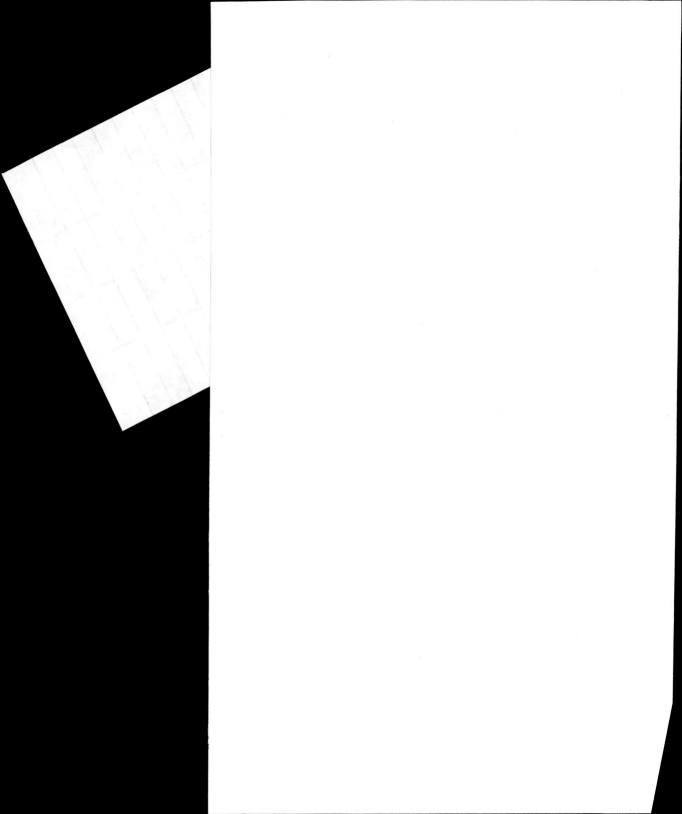

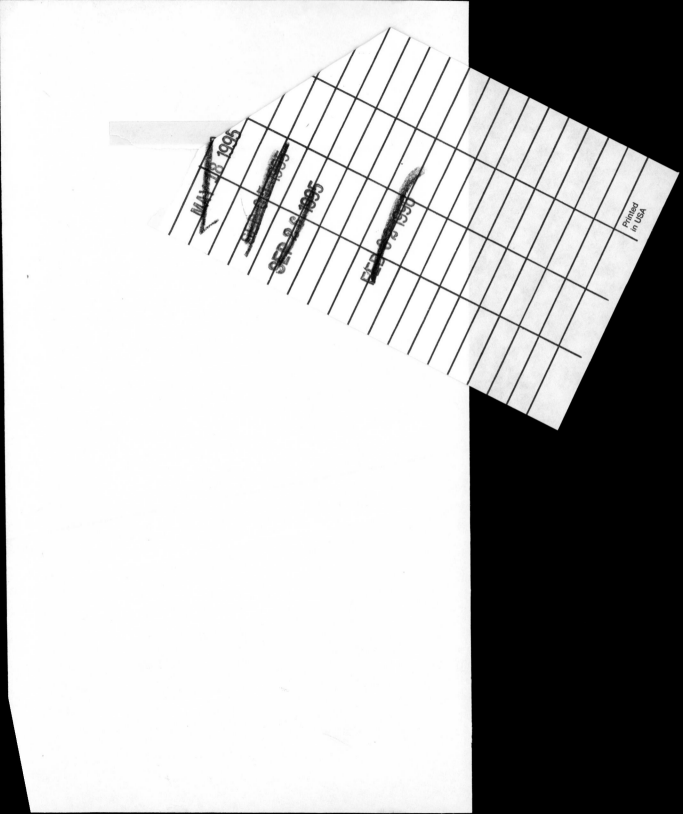